Third Workshop on New Frontiers in Summarization (NewSum 2021)

Punta Cana, Dominican Republic and Online
10 November 2021

ISBN: 978-1-7138-9178-9

Printed from e-media with permission by:

Curran Associates, Inc.
57 Morehouse Lane
Red Hook, NY 12571

Some format issues inherent in the e-media version may also appear in this print version.

Printed with permission by Curran Associates, Inc. (2024)

Association for Computational Linguistics
209 N. Eighth Street
Stroudsburg, Pennsylvania 18360

Phone: 1-570-476-8006
Fax: 1-570-476-0860

acl@aclweb.org

Additional copies of this publication are available from:

Curran Associates, Inc.
57 Morehouse Lane
Red Hook, NY 12571 USA
Phone: 845-758-0400
Fax: 845-758-2633
Email: curran@proceedings.com
Web: www.proceedings.com

EMNLP 2021

The Third Workshop on New Frontiers in Summarization (NewSum 2021)

Workshop Proceedings

November 10, 2021

Message from the Workshop Chairs

Developing intelligent systems which can produce concise, fluent, and accurate summaries has been a long-standing goal in natural language processing. The aim of this workshop is to provide a research forum for cross-fertilization of ideas towards this goal. We seek to bring together researchers from a diverse range of fields (e.g., summarization, language generation, cognitive and psycholinguistics) for discussions on key issues related to automatic summarization. This includes discussion on novel paradigms/frameworks, multilingual and cross-lingual setups, shared tasks of interest, information integration and presentation, new evaluation protocols, applied research and applications, and possible future research foci. The workshop aims to pave the way towards building a cohesive research community, accelerating knowledge diffusion, developing new tools, datasets, and resources that are in line with the needs of academia, industry, and government. This is the third edition of the workshop, following our previous workshops at EMNLP 2017 and EMNLP 2019. The workshop received 18 long paper submissions, of which 9 were accepted, and 14 short paper submissions, of which 7 were accepted. This resulted in an overall acceptance rate of 50%. We are pleased to have three invited speakers at this year's workshop: Asli Celikyilmaz (Facebook AI Research), Sebastian Gehrmann (Google Research), and Shashi Narayan (Google Research). Together, they cover a broad spectrum of work in summarization and adjacent areas. We would like to thank our invited speakers, as well as our programme committee members and workshop participants.

Giuseppe Carenini, Jackie Chi Kit Cheung, Yue Dong, Fei Liu, Lu Wang

Organizing Committee

Giuseppe Carenini (University of British Columbia, Canada)
Jackie Chi Kit Cheung (McGill University, Canada)
Yue Dong (McGill University & MILA, Canada)
Fei Liu (University of Central Florida, USA)
Lu Wang (University of Michigan, USA)

Invited Speakers

Shashi Narayan (Google)
Asli Celikyilmaz (Facebook AI Research)
Sebastian Gehrmann (Google)

Technical Committee

Enamul Hoque (York University)
Jiacheng Xu (The University of Texas at Austin)
Rui Zhang (Penn State University)
Hou Pong Chan (University of Macau)
Yuntian Deng (Harvard University)
Kristjan Arumae (Amazon)
Xiaojun Wan (Peking University)
Chris Kedzie (Rasa Technologies Inc.)
Naoaki Okazaki (Tokyo Institute of Technology)
Manabu Okumura (Tokyo Institute of Technology)
Yang Liu (Microsoft)
Tadashi Nomoto (National Institute of Japanese Literature)
Linzi Xing (University of British Columbia)
Ari Rappoport (Hebrew University)
Felice Dell'Orletta (Istituto di Linguistica Computazionale "A. Zampolli" (CNR), Pisa, Italy)
Margot Mieskes (University of Applied Sciences Darmstadt, Germany)
Rodrigo Souza Wilkens (University of Essex)
Maxime Peyrard (EPFL)
Benoit Favre (Aix-Marseille University LIS/CNRS)
Tobias Falke (Amazon)
Thiago Alexandre Salgueiro Pardo (University of São Paulo)
Jessica Ouyang (University of Texas at Dallas)
Wencan Luo (Google)
Florian Boudin (Université de Nantes - France)
Juan-Manuel Torres-Moreno (LIA Avignon Université)
Michael Elhadad (Ben Gurion University)
Esaú Villatoro Tello (Universidad Autónoma Metropolitana Unidad Cuajimalpa, México)
Yuning Mao (University of Illinois at Urbana-Champaign)
Wen Xiao (University of British Columbia)
Xinyu Hua (Northeastern University)
Patrick Huber (University of British Columbia)
Abram Handler (University of Colorado)
Wojciech Kryściński (Salesforce Research)

Alexander Fabbri (Yale University)
Greg Durrett (UT Austin)
Yang Gao (Royal Holloway, University of London, UK)
Ramakanth Pasunuru (UNC Chapel Hill)
Ido Dagan (Bar-Ilan University)

Table of Contents

Conference Program

9:00–10:30 Morning Session I

9:00–9:10 *Open remarks*
NewSum Organizers

9:10–10:00 *Keynote I*
Sashi Narayan (Google)

10:00–10:10 *Sentence-level Planning for Especially Abstractive Summarization*
Andreas Marfurt and James Henderson

10:10–10:20 *Template-aware Attention Model for Earnings Call Report Generation*
Yangchen Huang, Prashant K. Dhingra and Seyed Danial Mohseni Taheri

10:20–10:25 *Knowledge and Keywords Augmented Abstractive Sentence Summarization*
Shuo Guan

10:25–10:30 *Rewards with Negative Examples for Reinforced Topic-Focused Abstractive Summarization*
Khalil Mrini, Can Liu and Markus Dreyer

10:30–11:00 *Coffee break I*

11:00–12:00 Morning session II

11:00–11:50 *Keynote II*
Sebastian Gehrmann (Google)

11:50–12:00 *A Novel Wikipedia based Dataset for Monolingual and Cross-Lingual Summarization*
Mehwish Fatima and Michael Strube

12:00–13:00 *Lunch break*

13:00–14:30 Afternoon session I

13:00–13:50 *Keynote III*
Asli Celikyilmaz (Facebook AI Research)

13:50–13:55 *Evaluation of Summarization Systems across Gender, Age, and Race*
Anna Jørgensen and Anders Søgaard

13:55–14:00 *Evaluation of Abstractive Summarisation Models with Machine Translation in Deliberative Processes*
Miguel Arana-Catania, Rob Procter, Yulan He and Maria Liakata

14:00–14:10 *Capturing Speaker Incorrectness: Speaker-Focused Post-Correction for Abstractive Dialogue Summarization*
Dongyub Lee, Jungwoo Lim, Taesun Whang, chanhee lee, Seungwoo Cho, Mingun Park and Heuiseok Lim

14:10–14:20 *Measuring Similarity of Opinion-bearing Sentences*
Wenyi Tay, Xiuzhen Zhang, Stephen Wan and Sarvnaz Karimi

14:20–14:30 *EASE: Extractive-Abstractive Summarization End-to-End using the Information Bottleneck Principle*
Haoran Li, Arash Einolghozati, Srinivasan Iyer, Bhargavi Paranjape, Yashar Mehdad, Sonal Gupta and Marjan Ghazvininejad

14:30–15:00 *Coffee break*

15:00–16:15 Afternoon session II

15:00–15:10 *Context or No Context? A preliminary exploration of human-in-the-loop approach for Incremental Temporal Summarization in meetings*
Nicole Beckage, Shachi H Kumar, Saurav Sahay and Ramesh Manuvinakurike

15:10–15:20 *Are We Summarizing the Right Way? A Survey of Dialogue Summarization Data Sets*
Don Tuggener, Margot Mieskes, Jan Deriu and Mark Cieliebak

15:20–15:30 *Modeling Endorsement for Multi-Document Abstractive Summarization*
Logan Lebanoff, Bingqing Wang, Zhe Feng and Fei Liu

November 10 (continued)

15:30–15:35 *SUBSUME: A Dataset for Subjective Summary Extraction from Wikipedia Documents*
Nishant Yadav, Matteo Brucato, Anna Fariha, Oscar Youngquist, Julian Killingback, Alexandra Meliou and Peter Haas

15:35–16:15 ***EMNLP finding papers - Summarization***

16:15–16:45 ***Coffee break***

16:45–18:00 **Afternoon session III**

16:45–16:55 *TLDR9+: A Large Scale Resource for Extreme Summarization of Social Media Posts*
Sajad Sotudeh, Hanieh Deilamsalehy, Franck Dernoncourt and Nazli Goharian

16:55–17:00 *A New Dataset and Efficient Baselines for Document-level Text Simplification in German*
Annette Rios, Nicolas Spring, Tannon Kew, Marek Kostrzewa, Andreas Säuberli, Mathias Müller and Sarah Ebling

17:00–18:00 ***Mentoring Program***

Sentence-level Planning for Especially Abstractive Summarization

Andreas Marfurt
Idiap Research Institute, Switzerland
EPFL, Switzerland
andreas.marfurt@idiap.ch

James Henderson
Idiap Research Institute, Switzerland
james.henderson@idiap.ch

Abstract

Abstractive summarization models heavily rely on copy mechanisms, such as the pointer network or attention, to achieve good performance, measured by textual overlap with reference summaries. As a result, the generated summaries stay close to the formulations in the source document. We propose the *sentence planner* model to generate more abstractive summaries. It includes a hierarchical decoder that first generates a representation for the next summary sentence, and then conditions the word generator on this representation. Our generated summaries are more abstractive and at the same time achieve high ROUGE scores when compared to human reference summaries. We verify the effectiveness of our design decisions with extensive evaluations.

1 Introduction

Abstractive summarization has improved drastically in recent years due to more efficient decoder architectures, like the Transformer (Vaswani et al., 2017), and language model pretraining, such as BERT (Devlin et al., 2019). As a result of these advances, current state-of-the-art models reach the performance of extractive systems, and even surpass them on some datasets (Liu and Lapata, 2019; Lewis et al., 2019; Zhang et al., 2020).

Part of this success, however, is due to the development of stronger copy mechanisms such as the pointer-generator network (See et al., 2017) or attention to the source document (Rush et al., 2015). The so-generated summaries copy long sequences from the input document, strung together with filler words. While this achieves better results in the predominant evaluation metric ROUGE (Lin, 2004), it comes at the cost of the summaries' abstractiveness and coherence, two qualities that we expect from human-written summaries.

In this paper, we aim to generate more abstractive summaries without sacrificing ROUGE and coherence. We achieve this by including a planning step at the sentence level before generating the summary word by word. The idea is to plan an outline for the next summary sentence first at a higher level to give the model more capacity for abstraction. As a result, the model has to rely less on copying the input, and thereby generates more abstractive summaries. Our model, the *sentence planner*, is an encoder-decoder architecture. The encoder is initialized from pretrained BERT weights. The decoder is hierarchical, and consists of a sentence generator that plans an outline for the summary at the sentence level, and a word generator that is conditioned on this outline when generating the summary's words. Both generators attend to the source document in order to condition their predictions on the input. The sentence planner is trained end-to-end to predict the words of the target summary, with an additional guidance loss that encourages the sentence generator to produce the encoder's embedding for the target next sentence. This is the first work to propose a hierarchical Transformer decoder that generates a summary from latent sentence representations.[1]

We extensively evaluate our model on a recently published highly abstractive dataset and an established but more extractive corpus. We show that the sentence planner generates more abstractive summaries while improving the ROUGE scores of a state-of-the-art model without a hierarchical decoder. We use gradient attribution to quantify the impact of the sentence generator on the model's prediction as well as how much information from the document it captures. Moreover, we verify the effectiveness of our model components with an ablation study, and show that simply increasing the baseline's decoder parameters does not bring it up

[1]Our code is available at https://github.com/idiap/sentence-planner.

Proceedings of the Third Workshop on New Frontiers in Summarization, pages 1–14
November 10, 2021.

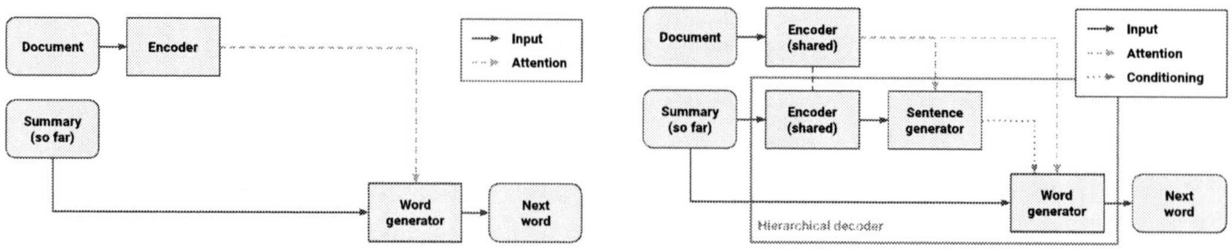

(a) BERTSUMEXTABS (b) Sentence planner

Figure 1: (a) BERTSUMEXTABS model. An encoder encodes the document, and a word generator generates the next word given previous words, while paying attention to the document. (b) Sentence planner model. A shared encoder separately encodes the document and each sentence of the summary generated so far. The sentence generator takes the summary sentence embeddings and predicts the next sentence embedding, which the word generator is then conditioned on. Both generators integrate document information through attention.

to par with the hierarchical decoder. Our automatic evaluations are confirmed in a human evaluation study, where the sentence planner improves upon its strong baseline in each of six quality categories.

Our contributions are twofold: (a) We are the first to propose a hierarchical Transformer decoder that generates summaries from a latent sentence-level plan, and (b) we perform an extensive evaluation of our model on two summarization datasets and show that it produces more abstractive summaries while retaining high ROUGE scores, two objectives that are in opposition.

2 The Hierarchical Decoder

Our approach builds on the BERTSUMEXTABS model (Liu and Lapata, 2019). Their model consists of an encoder initialized with an extractive summarization model, which in turn was initialized with a BERT model, and a randomly initialized Transformer decoder.[2] We keep the encoder the same. We replace the decoder with a hierarchical version by introducing a sentence generator that develops a high-level plan for the summary, and a word generator that is conditioned on this plan. A model diagram is shown in Figure 1. Section 2.1 describes how the sentence generator develops the outline for the summary, and Section 2.2 shows how the word generator makes use of it.

2.1 Sentence Generator

The sentence generator is a two-layer Transformer decoder. It receives as inputs the sentence representations of completed summary sentences, and generates a sentence representation for the next summary sentence.

Inputs. The inputs to the sentence generator are a sequence of representations of already completed summary sentences. These are computed by the same encoder that computes representations for the document tokens. For each individual previous summary sentence, the encoder computes its contextualized token embeddings. We use the contextual embedding of the end-of-sentence token as a representation for the sentence.[3] When generating the first summary sentence, there are no completed sentences, so we use a single zero vector as input to the sentence generator.

During training with teacher forcing, we use the previous portion of the reference summary as input to the encoder. Since the entire summary is known in advance, we can compute all inputs to the sentence generator in parallel.

Self-attention. The sentence generator's self-attention operates at the sentence level, which means the sequence length n for our Transformer decoder is very small (between 2 and 4 on average, see Section 4). As a result, the self-attention computation, which is quadratic in the sequence length, becomes extremely cheap. As in regular Transformer decoders, a causal mask prevents attention to future sentences.

Cross-attention. In the cross-attention, the sentence generator pays attention to the encoded document. Through this connection, the sentence generator is able to compare the already generated

[2] Even stronger results have recently been achieved when pretraining an entire sequence-to-sequence model on a task closer to summarization (BART (Lewis et al., 2019), PEGASUS (Zhang et al., 2020)). In this paper, we restrict ourselves to encoder initializations with the BERT model and do not consider other pretraining approaches, since these techniques are orthogonal to our contribution.

[3] We found that this performed better than alternative encodings of the summary, as discussed in Appendix A.

Dataset	Examples	Mean doc length		Mean summary length		Novel bigrams	Corefs
		words	sentences	words	sentences		
CNN/DailyMail	312085	685.12	30.71	52.00	3.88	54.33%	0.105
Curation Corpus	39911	504.26	18.27	82.63	3.46	69.22%	0.441

Table 1: Dataset statistics.

summary to the document and identify missing information that should appear in the next sentence.

Output. The output of the sentence generator is a representation r_{sent} for the next summary sentence. Section 2.2 describes how we condition the word generator on this sentence representation.

Guidance loss. We provide the sentence generator with an additional loss term for guidance. Since during training, we know the ground truth next summary sentence and can compute its encoding r_{gold}, we penalize the (element-wise) mean squared error between the gold and the predicted next sentence representation.

$$\mathcal{L}_{\text{MSE}} = \frac{1}{d} \sum_{i=1}^{d} ||r_{\text{gold}}^{(i)} - r_{\text{sent}}^{(i)}||_2^2 \tag{1}$$

where d is the representations' dimension. This loss term is added to the regular cross-entropy loss with a scaling hyperparameter λ, although we found $\lambda = 1$ to work well in practice.

We do not backpropagate the guidance loss's gradients from the sentence generator into the encoder to avoid a collapse to a trivial solution. Otherwise, the encoder might output the same representation for every sentence so that the sentence generator can perfectly predict it.

2.2 Word Generator

Our word generator is also a Transformer decoder. The regular Transformer decoder consists of layers l with self-attention, cross-attention and feed-forward sublayers. They are defined as follows:

$$s^l = \text{LN}(h^{l-1} + \text{SelfAtt}(h^{l-1})) \tag{2}$$

$$c^l = \text{LN}(s^l + \text{CrossAtt}(s^l, r_{\text{enc}})) \tag{3}$$

$$h^l = \text{LN}(c^l + \text{FFN}(c^l)) \tag{4}$$

where LN is layer normalization (Ba et al., 2016), SelfAtt stands for self-attention, CrossAtt is the cross-attention to the encoder outputs r_{enc}, and FFN is the feed-forward sublayer consisting of two fully-connected layers with an intermediate non-linearity.

In our word generator, we condition on the sentence representation by replacing Eq. 3 with

$$c^l = \text{LN}(s^l + \text{CrossAtt}(s^l, r_{\text{enc}}) + r'_{\text{sent}}) \tag{5}$$

where r'_{sent} is the sentence representation obtained from the sentence generator, passed through a fully-connected and a dropout layer. We do not differentiate between layers and add the same sentence representation in every layer and to every token.

We experimented with various ways to use attention in the word generator to integrate the sentence representation. However, the conditioning method presented above substantially outperforms the attention-based integrations of the sentence representation. We further discuss this topic in Appendix A.

At the end of a sentence, the word generator either outputs a special sentence separator symbol, prompting the sentence generator to generate the next sentence representation, or an end-of-summary symbol, stopping generation.

3 Experimental Setup

We now describe the datasets (§ 3.1) and metrics (§ 3.2) that we use to evaluate our model, and give implementation details (§ 3.3) to replicate our experiments. Dataset statistics are shown in Table 1.

3.1 Datasets

CNN/DailyMail. The CNN/DailyMail corpus was initially introduced as a question answering dataset in Hermann et al. (2015) and adapted for summarization by Nallapati et al. (2016), and has been widely used. The corpus's summaries are a concatenation of bullet points describing the highlights of the news article. They are therefore designed to be concise, but do not necessarily form a fluent summary. Extractive approaches perform well on CNN/DailyMail (Liu and Lapata, 2019).

Curation Corpus. The Curation Corpus (Curation, 2020) is a recently introduced dataset of professionally written summaries of news articles. The corpus is an order of magnitude smaller than

CNN/DailyMail, and its articles and summaries have fewer but longer sentences (see Table 1). We see this dataset as better representing the summarization task, since the summaries were written for this purpose specifically. Additionally, Curation Corpus's summaries span multiple sentences, in contrast to a dataset such as XSum (Narayan et al., 2018), which is a prerequisite for our approach. As a consequence, the majority of our experiments are conducted on Curation Corpus (see Section 4). We describe our preprocessing in Appendix B.

3.2 Metrics

ROUGE. The standard metric to automatically evaluate summarization systems is the ROUGE F1 score (Lin, 2004). It measures textual overlap between the generated candidate and the reference summaries. The length of text spans for computing the overlap can be arbitrary, but it is common to report unigram and bigram overlap (ROUGE-1, ROUGE-2), as well as the longest common subsequence (ROUGE-L).

Novel bigrams. The fraction of novel bigrams in the generated summary with respect to the source document measures its abstractiveness. More abstractive methods generally attain lower ROUGE scores. To see why, consider the case where the reference summary and the model copy from the document. The generated summary is guaranteed to get an exact match and high ROUGE. In the opposite case, where both the reference summary and the model generate novel text, there is a good chance that the choice of words is not exactly the same, resulting in low ROUGE.

Corefs. Inspired by Iida and Tokunaga (2012), we evaluate discourse coherence with a coreference resolution model. We count the number of coreference links across sentence boundaries as a proxy for the coherence of a summary, i.e. whether the sentences build upon information in the preceeding ones. Since summaries with more sentences could be favored by this count, we normalize by the number of sentences. To extract coreferences from the generated summaries, we use the neuralcoref[4] implementation. Table 1 shows the mean number of coreference links across sentence boundaries for the datasets' reference summaries. We clearly see that the summaries in the Curation Corpus are written in a much more coherent style than the ones from CNN/DailyMail. Specifically, the bullet point style summaries in CNN/DailyMail do not foster summaries whose sentences build on each other. However, this is a quality we would expect from human summaries, which is yet another reason to focus our analysis on the Curation Corpus.

3.3 Implementation Details

We use the code from BERTSUMEXTABS[5] for our experiments. For the decoder, they have their own Transformer implementation while we employ the popular huggingface library (Wolf et al., 2019). In our experiments, we control for the possible discrepancy between these two implementations by reporting BERTSUMEXTABS's performance with a huggingface Transformer as well.

We use the hyperparameters from BERTSUMEXTABS where not specified otherwise. For our implementation, a grid search found a learning rate of 0.001 for the BERT-initialized encoder and 0.02 for the randomly initialized Transformer(s) to work best. We use a fixed batch size of 3 with gradient accumulation over 5 batches. The hyperparameters for our implementation of BERTSUMEXTABS and our model are exactly the same, and we only tune the hyperparameters of the sentence generator with a grid search.

Our sentence generator is a 2-layer Transformer with 12 heads, a hidden size of 768, an intermediate dimension of 3072 for the feed-forward sublayer, and dropout of 0.1 for attention outputs. We do not apply dropout to the outputs of linear layers.

Curation Corpus. All our models are trained for 40,000 training steps, with a learning rate warmup of 2,500 steps. We did not see an improvement from initializing the encoder with a pretrained extractive model, and therefore initialize from BERT weights. We average the results from 5 runs, and also report the standard deviation in Appendix C.

CNN/DailyMail. Our models are trained for 200,000 training steps, with 20,000 warmup steps for the pretrained encoder, and 10,000 warmup steps for the randomly initialized Transformer(s), following Liu and Lapata (2019). We also use their model checkpoint of BERTSUMEXT to initialize the encoder in all our models.

[4] https://github.com/huggingface/neuralcoref

[5] https://github.com/nlpyang/PreSumm

Model	ROUGE			Sentences		Novel Bigrams	Corefs
	R-1	R-2	R-L	Number	Length		
Gold summaries	-	-	-	*3.46*	*28.0*	*69.22%*	*0.441*
BSEA (Liu and Lapata, 2019)	42.95	17.67	37.46	2.73	27.3	36.77%	0.267
BSEA (our implementation)	43.37	17.92	37.73	2.76	28.5	37.29%	0.283
Sentence planner	**44.40**	**18.31**	**38.69**	3.15	28.2	**39.29%**	**0.289**

Table 2: Results on Curation Corpus. Mean over 5 runs. Best result in bold.

Model	IG	Conductance
BSEA	-	-
+ Sentence generator	25.1%	32.3%
+ $\mathcal{L}_{\text{MSE}}$ (= Sentence planner)	36.6%	29.1%

Table 3: Attribution study. IG: Attribution of the model predictions to r_{sent} vs. to cross-attention. Conductance: Attribution of the predictions to the article via r_{sent} vs. via cross-attention.

4 Results

We now turn to evaluation of our method. First, we show the results on Curation Corpus (§ 4.1). With attribution techniques (§ 4.2) and an ablation study (§ 4.3) we uncover how the model uses the sentence generator component. Increasing the number of parameters of BERTSUMEXTABS (BSEA) does not provide the same improvements as our approach (§ 4.4). On the CNN/DailyMail dataset, our model generates more abstractive summaries while retaining high ROUGE scores (§ 4.5). Finally, a human evaluation validates the results from our automatic metrics (§ 4.6).

4.1 Results on Curation Corpus

Table 2 shows the results of our evaluation on the Curation Corpus. The sentence planner substantially improves ROUGE scores compared to BERTSUMEXTABS. The relative difference is between 2.2% and 2.5% for the different ROUGE variants. A noticeable difference also exists between the ROUGE scores of the two base model implementations, which is why we continue reporting the scores for both in the following.

The sentence planner's summaries are more abstractive than those of BERTSUMEXTABS, as indicated by the number of novel bigrams. However, there is still a large gap to the reference summaries displayed on the first line. The sentence planner generates substantially more sentences than BERTSUMEXTABS on average, moving it closer to the gold summaries. The mean number of words within those sentences stays close to the reference statistic. [6]

The mean number of coreferences across sentence boundaries, normalized by the number of sentences, is similar for all models, with the best score achieved by the sentence planner. This number is lower than for the reference summaries but substantially higher than for references and generated summaries from the CNN/DailyMail corpus (see Section 4.5).

4.2 Attribution to Sentence Representation

A natural question to ask is whether the sentence representation r_{sent} is actually used by the word generator. We therefore compare the attribution of the model predictions to r_{sent} with the attribution to the output of the cross-attention. We use the Integrated Gradients (IG) algorithm (Sundararajan et al., 2017) with respect to these intermediate representations. We choose the zero vector as a baseline r_0, but taking the mean of r_{sent} over the test examples as a baseline provides similar results. We then integrate along the path from r_0 to r_{sent}

$$(r_{\text{sent}} - r_0) \int_{\eta=0}^{1} \frac{\partial F(x, r_0 + \eta(r_{\text{sent}} - r_0))}{\partial r_{\text{sent}}} \quad (6)$$

for a given input x. In practice, we discretize the integral and sum over 50 integration steps with linearly spaced η values. The case for the attribution to the cross-attention output is analogous. We report the relative attribution to r_{sent} in Table 3. The result is averaged over the first 100 examples in our

[6]The mean number of sentences and (to a lesser extent) their average length can be influenced by a length penalty hyperparameter α, which is set between 0.6 and 1 (Liu and Lapata, 2019). BERTSUMEXTABS with no penalty ($\alpha = 1$) produces the same number of sentences and words as the sentence planner with the largest penalty ($\alpha = 0.6$), but a large gap in ROUGE-(1/2/L) remains: (0.7/0.6/0.6). Consistent with Sun et al. (2019), we find that ROUGE scores increase with length and α, but we also find that novel bigrams decrease. In order to not favor one side of the trade-off over the other, we stick with the setting of $\alpha = 0.95$ from Liu and Lapata (2019) for both models.

Model	ROUGE		
	R-1	R-2	R-L
BSEA (our implementation)	43.37 (0.37)	17.92 (0.17)	37.73 (0.31)
+ Sentence generator	43.97 (0.30)	18.28 (0.11)	38.32 (0.22)
+ $\mathcal{L}_{\text{MSE}}$ (= Sentence planner)	**44.40** (0.14)	**18.31** (0.13)	**38.69** (0.10)

Table 4: Ablation study showing ROUGE scores on Curation Corpus when adding the individual components of our model. Mean and std (in brackets) over 5 runs.

Model	Parameters	ROUGE			Novel Bigrams
		R-1	R-2	R-L	
BSEA (Liu and Lapata, 2019, $L_{\text{dec}} = 6$, $\text{ff}_{\text{dec}} = 2048$)	180M	43.13	17.80	37.63	36.83%
BSEA (our implementation, $L_{\text{dec}} = 6$, $\text{ff}_{\text{dec}} = 2048$)	182M	43.21	17.69	37.54	37.12%
BSEA (our implementation, $L_{\text{dec}} = 6$, $\text{ff}_{\text{dec}} = 3072$)	191M	43.12	17.84	37.53	37.34%
BSEA (our implementation, $L_{\text{dec}} = 8$, $\text{ff}_{\text{dec}} = 2048$)	198M	43.41	17.91	37.79	37.09%
BSEA (our implementation, $L_{\text{dec}} = 8$, $\text{ff}_{\text{dec}} = 3072$)	210M	43.68	18.06	38.06	37.77%
Sentence planner	208M	**44.40**	**18.31**	**38.69**	**39.29%**

Table 5: Number of parameters of each model (M = million) together with ROUGE scores and novel bigrams on Curation Corpus.

test set. It shows that the attribution to r_{sent} with the sentence generator alone is about a quarter, while three quarters are attributed to the cross-attention. This is already a substantial amount, considering that the alternative is to directly look at the document. r_{sent}'s attribution share further increases to more than a third with the addition of the guidance loss $\mathcal{L}_{\text{MSE}}$, making r_{sent} even more useful.

While we expect that the sentence representation is mostly used as an outline for the next summary sentence, we are curious to see how much information of the source document is present in r_{sent}. We use the conductance (Dhamdhere et al., 2019) via r_{sent} with respect to the encoder outputs, and compare it to the conductance via the cross-attention. We ignore the encoder's computation as it is the same for both paths. Since it is computationally expensive to compute gradients over every neuron in r_{sent}, we sum over just 5 integration steps and average the result over the first 10 examples of the test set. From Table 3, we see that almost a third of the document's information is passed through the sentence representation. The addition of the guidance loss decreases this number, which means that r_{sent} serves more as an outline than an additional condensed representation of the document.

4.3 Model Ablation

Table 4 shows an ablation study for the two components we introduced in the hierarchical decoder. Both the sentence generator network and the guidance loss provide a steady increase in ROUGE performance as well as a reduction in variance. This demonstrates the efficacy of our additions.

4.4 Number of Parameters

To verify that the improved performance of the sentence planner is not just a result of the increased number of parameters, we perform an experiment where we increase the base model's capacity. BERTSUMEXTABS consists of a 12-layer Transformer encoder, and a 6-layer decoder. Our model has additional parameters in the 2-layer Transformer that serves as the sentence generator. We therefore increase the BERTSUMEXTABS decoder's parameters such that the total model sizes match. Specifically, we increase the number of layers L_{dec} and the inner dimension of the feed-forward sublayer ff_{dec}. The comparison is shown in Table 5. While increasing the number of parameters improves BERTSUMEXTABS's ROUGE scores, they are still far behind the sentence planner's scores. Similarly, the share of novel bigrams rises a bit with additional parameters. However, it still stays behind the abstractiveness of the sentence planner, showing that the inductive bias of our hierarchical decoder is very effective.

4.5 Results on CNN/DailyMail

For comparison with previous work, we now report the results on the more extractive CNN/DailyMail corpus. Table 6 shows the results for BERTSUMEXTABS and the sentence planner. The first

Model	ROUGE			Sentences		Novel Bigrams	Corefs
	R-1	R-2	R-L	Num	Len		
Gold summaries	-	-	-	*3.88*	*14.08*	*54.33%*	*0.105*
BSEA (Liu and Lapata, 2019, their checkpoint)	42.16	19.49	39.16	3.33	19.1	7.40%	0.124
BSEA (Liu and Lapata, 2019, our training)	41.17	18.82	38.27	3.07	18.5	8.14%	0.126
BSEA (our implementation)	41.48	18.86	38.41	2.99	19.6	7.18%	0.104
Sentence planner	41.87	19.37	39.02	3.82	17.8	**10.65%**	**0.132**

Table 6: Results on CNN/DailyMail. Best result with our own training underlined.

Quality	BSEA	SP	p-value
Non-redundancy	4.05	**4.08**	0.408
Fluency	3.70	**3.75**	0.343
Structure/coherence	3.68	**3.85**	0.102
Informativeness	3.57	**3.77**	0.069
Abstractiveness	3.45	**3.65**	0.047
Semantic similarity	2.98	**3.18**	0.043

Table 7: Mean score for each quality in the human evaluation for BSEA and the sentence planner (SP). Scores range from 1 (worst) to 5 (best). The p-value is determined with a paired bootstrap test.

line evaluates the model checkpoint that Liu and Lapata (2019) provide. When we train both the extractive initialization and the abstractive model ourselves with the hyperparameters suggested, we are not quite able to achieve the same results. With our own implementation of the decoder, we are able to close the gap in ROUGE scores somewhat. The sentence planner performs best out of the models we trained ourselves. As on the Curation Corpus, it is also much more abstractive than BERTSUMEXTABS. This could well account for the remaining difference in ROUGE scores.

The mean number of generated sentences by the sentence planner is almost identical with the reference summaries, and again a lot larger than for BERTSUMEXTABS. The generated sentences are also shorter, in line with the references. The number of coreference links across sentence boundaries are similar across models, with the sentence planner producing those links most often. We conclude that even on the more extractive CNN/DailyMail corpus, the sentence planner generates more abstractive and coherent summaries at high ROUGE.

4.6 Human Evaluation

We perform a human evaluation to verify the results found by our automatic metrics. We compare outputs of BERTSUMEXTABS (our implementation) with the sentence planner. The annotators are presented with the source article, the reference summary as well as the candidate summaries for both systems. The systems are labeled *1* and *2*, and their order is randomized for each example. For each candidate summary, the annotators then have to select a score from 1 to 5 for six qualities, which are presented with a descriptive question (in brackets). The qualities are non-redundancy (*Is information stated only once?*), fluency (*Is the summary grammatical and good to read?*), structure/coherence (*Do the sentences build on each other?*), informativeness (*Is the important information captured?*), abstractiveness (*How much of the summary is rephrased (instead of copied)?*), and semantic similarity (*How semantically similar is the candidate summary to the gold summary?*).

We randomly draw 20 examples from the Curation Corpus test set. We limit the number of words of source articles to be above 100 and below 700 (includes 70% of examples), to remove extreme examples and keep the workload for annotators reasonable. We divide our 6 annotators, which are all NLP experts, into two groups, who review 10 examples each, resulting in 3 annotations per example, of which we take the mean. The results are reported in Table 7. The sentence planner is evaluated favorably compared to BERTSUMEXTABS in all categories. The non-redundancy and fluency categories show a smaller gap. This is expected, as we did not change the word generator, which impacts these categories the most. On the other categories, the sentence planner achieves larger improvements, showing that the introduction of a hierarchical decoder improves the planning capabilities of the model.

To determine statistical significance of the results, we follow the guidelines in Dror et al. (2018) and select the non-parametric paired bootstrap test (Efron and Tibshirani, 1994). We find that the two models are not significantly different for the first four categories, while they are for the abstractiveness and semantic similarity categories when selecting a threshold of $p = 0.05$. Additionally, we quantify the inter-annotator reliability with the intraclass correlation coefficient (ICC), according to Shrout and Fleiss (1979). The reliability is moderate with an ICC of 0.56 and a 95% confidence interval of [0.46, 0.65]. Given the moderate annotator agreement and our relatively small sample size of the human evaluation, it is possible that a more extensive (and therefore expensive) human evaluation could show a significant difference in informativeness and structure/coherence.

Finally, we are curious whether the Corefs evaluation can serve as an automatic evaluation of the structure/coherence category. We therefore compute the Pearson ρ for the correlation between the human and the metric's scores. The correlation is weak at 0.098 (p-value: 0.549). Thus there seems to be a mismatch between what the metric measures (discourse coherence by counting the number of coreference links across sentence boundaries) and the open way the question was formulated in the human evaluation (*Do the sentences build on each other?*). Nevertheless, the Corefs metric showed its value by very clearly distinguishing the CNN/DailyMail's summaries from the Curation Corpus's summaries. We therefore leave its optimal use for future work.

5 Related Work

Our proposal is the first hierarchical decoder for a Transformer-based text summarization model. We survey previous work on hierarchical attention in summarization on the encoder side, and sentence-level planning on the decoder side.

5.1 Hierarchical Attention

Nallapati et al. (2016) use hierarchical attention in the encoder with a word- and a sentence-level RNN. The attention weights at the word level are re-weighted by the sentence-level attention weights. Celikyilmaz et al. (2018) divide the document into paragraphs, which are encoded separately by agents. Each agent performs attention within its paragraph, and the decoder attends to the agents. Gehrmann et al. (2018) first employ a content selector at the word level to decide which words are candidates for copying. They then use a pointer-generator network with just the admissible tokens to generate the summary. Miculicich et al. (2018) use hierarchical attention networks (Yang et al., 2016) to encode the context of previous sentences, which is used to inform the translation of the next word. In contrast to these methods, we employ hierarchy on the decoder side, and generate a sentence representation for the *next* sentence.

5.2 Sentence Planning

Tan et al. (2017) use word- and sentence-level RNNs in both encoder and decoder. They also predict a next sentence embedding, but use a graph model as importance for the encoded sentences instead of attention. The word-level decoder RNN is conditioned by initializing the first hidden state with the sentence embedding. Perez-Beltrachini et al. (2019) use a CNN word encoder/decoder and an LSTM sentence decoder for multi-document summarization. They predict a next sentence embedding with attention, which they add to the input of each convolutional decoder layer. An auxiliary loss pushes sentence embeddings to be close to LDA topics of summary sentences. Both models do not employ Transformers, and consequently their conditioning is very different from ours.

Several papers have investigated sentence-level language modeling. Ippolito et al. (2020) pick the most likely continuation from a set of candidate sentences. Their task provides a context of four sentences and requires to pick a single following sentence. A pretrained BERT model generates a target sentence representation, and the candidate with the highest cosine similarity is selected. Huang et al. (2020) address the task of sentence infilling, where context on both sides of the missing sentence is provided. They learn sentence representations with a denoising autoencoder, predict the representation of the missing sentence with a separate Transformer, and then use the autoencoder's decoder to generate the missing sentence from that representation. Deutsch and Roth (2019) propose the *summary cloze* task. Given the beginning of a summary, the topic and the reference document, their model has to continue with a single sentence supported by the reference document. These approaches only predict a single sentence, and are given substantial context. In our approach, we generate sentence representations with variable context (or no context for the first summary sentence).

Hua and Wang (2020) receive a prompt and a set of keyphrases, which they position and then fill in the gaps around them. Similarly, Jhamtani and Berg-Kirkpatrick (2020) generate a keyword per sentence to be generated, and then generate its left and right context. In contrast to these approaches, our sentence generator outputs a latent representation r_{sent} for the entire sentence, which is used to condition the word generator. We do not tie this representation to specific words.

6 Conclusion

We presented the sentence planner, an encoder-decoder model with a hierarchical decoder, consisting of a sentence and a word generator. Our sentence generator computes a plan for the next summary sentence. The word generator is then conditioned on this plan when generating the sentence's words. An additional loss term, which guides the sentence planner towards producing the embedding of the target next sentence, improves the sentence generator's plan. When comparing the sentence planner to a state-of-the-art model without a hierarchical decoder, it generates more abstractive and coherent summaries at higher ROUGE scores.

In future work, we aim to apply our model to other generation tasks, such as machine translation or dialogue generation.

References

Jimmy Lei Ba, Jamie Ryan Kiros, and Geoffrey E Hinton. 2016. Layer normalization. *arXiv preprint arXiv:1607.06450*.

Steven Bird, Edward Loper, and Ewan Klein. 2009. *Natural Language Processing with Python*. O'Reilly Media, Inc.

Asli Celikyilmaz, Antoine Bosselut, Xiaodong He, and Yejin Choi. 2018. Deep communicating agents for abstractive summarization. In *Proceedings of the 2018 Conference of the North American Chapter of the Association for Computational Linguistics: Human Language Technologies, Volume 1 (Long Papers)*, pages 1662–1675.

Curation. 2020. Curation corpus base.

Daniel Deutsch and Dan Roth. 2019. Summary cloze: A new task for content selection in topic-focused summarization. In *Proceedings of the 2019 Conference on Empirical Methods in Natural Language Processing and the 9th International Joint Conference on Natural Language Processing (EMNLP-IJCNLP)*, pages 3711–3720.

Jacob Devlin, Ming-Wei Chang, Kenton Lee, and Kristina Toutanova. 2019. Bert: Pre-training of deep bidirectional transformers for language understanding. In *Proceedings of NAACL-HLT 2019*, pages 4171–4186.

Kedar Dhamdhere, Mukund Sundararajan, and Qiqi Yan. 2019. How important is a neuron. In *International Conference on Learning Representations*.

Rotem Dror, Gili Baumer, Segev Shlomov, and Roi Reichart. 2018. The hitchhiker's guide to testing statistical significance in natural language processing. In *Proceedings of the 56th Annual Meeting of the Association for Computational Linguistics (Volume 1: Long Papers)*, pages 1383–1392.

Bradley Efron and Robert J Tibshirani. 1994. *An introduction to the bootstrap*. CRC press.

Sebastian Gehrmann, Yuntian Deng, and Alexander Rush. 2018. Bottom-up abstractive summarization. In *Proceedings of the 2018 Conference on Empirical Methods in Natural Language Processing*, pages 4098–4109.

Karl Moritz Hermann, Tomas Kocisky, Edward Grefenstette, Lasse Espeholt, Will Kay, Mustafa Suleyman, and Phil Blunsom. 2015. Teaching machines to read and comprehend. In *Advances in Neural Information Processing Systems*, pages 1693–1701.

Xinyu Hua and Lu Wang. 2020. PAIR: Planning and iterative refinement in pre-trained transformers for long text generation. In *Proceedings of the 2020 Conference on Empirical Methods in Natural Language Processing (EMNLP)*.

Yichen Huang, Yizhe Zhang, Oussama Elachqar, and Yu Cheng. 2020. INSET: Sentence infilling with inter-sentential transformer. In *Proceedings of the 58th Annual Meeting of the Association for Computational Linguistics*, pages 2502–2515.

Ryu Iida and Takenobu Tokunaga. 2012. A metric for evaluating discourse coherence based on coreference resolution. In *24th International Conference on Computational Linguistics*.

Daphne Ippolito, David Grangier, Douglas Eck, and Chris Callison-Burch. 2020. Toward better storylines with sentence-level language models. In *Proceedings of the 58th Annual Meeting of the Association for Computational Linguistics*, pages 7472–7478.

Harsh Jhamtani and Taylor Berg-Kirkpatrick. 2020. Narrative text generation with a latent discrete plan. In *Findings of the Association for Computational Linguistics: EMNLP 2020*.

Mike Lewis, Yinhan Liu, Naman Goyal, Marjan Ghazvininejad, Abdelrahman Mohamed, Omer Levy, Ves Stoyanov, and Luke Zettlemoyer. 2019. BART: Denoising sequence-to-sequence pre-training for natural language generation, translation, and comprehension. *arXiv preprint arXiv:1910.13461*.

Chin-Yew Lin. 2004. ROUGE: A package for automatic evaluation of summaries. In *Text Summarization Branches Out*, pages 74–81. Association for Computational Linguistics.

Yang Liu and Mirella Lapata. 2019. Text summarization with pretrained encoders. In *Proceedings of the 2019 Conference on Empirical Methods in Natural Language Processing*.

Lesly Miculicich, Dhananjay Ram, Nikolaos Pappas, and James Henderson. 2018. Document-level neural machine translation with hierarchical attention networks. In *Proceedings of the 2018 Conference on Empirical Methods in Natural Language Processing*, pages 2947–2954.

Ramesh Nallapati, Bowen Zhou, Cicero dos Santos, Caglar Gulcehre, and Bing Xiang. 2016. Abstractive text summarization using sequence-to-sequence rnns and beyond. In *Proceedings of The 20th SIGNLL Conference on Computational Natural Language Learning*, pages 280–290.

Shashi Narayan, Shay B Cohen, and Mirella Lapata. 2018. Don't give me the details, just the summary! topic-aware convolutional neural networks for extreme summarization. In *Proceedings of the 2018 Conference on Empirical Methods in Natural Language Processing*, pages 1797–1807.

Laura Perez-Beltrachini, Yang Liu, and Mirella Lapata. 2019. Generating summaries with topic templates and structured convolutional decoders. In *Proceedings of the 57th Annual Meeting of the Association for Computational Linguistics*, pages 5107–5116.

Alexander M Rush, Sumit Chopra, and Jason Weston. 2015. A neural attention model for abstractive sentence summarization. In *Proceedings of the 2015 Conference on Empirical Methods in Natural Language Processing*, pages 379–389.

Abigail See, Peter J Liu, and Christopher D Manning. 2017. Get to the point: Summarization with pointer-generator networks. In *Proceedings of the 55th Annual Meeting of the Association for Computational Linguistics (Volume 1: Long Papers)*, pages 1073–1083.

Patrick E Shrout and Joseph L Fleiss. 1979. Intraclass correlations: uses in assessing rater reliability. *Psychological bulletin*, 86(2):420.

Simeng Sun, Ori Shapira, Ido Dagan, and Ani Nenkova. 2019. How to compare summarizers without target length? pitfalls, solutions and re-examination of the neural summarization literature. In *Proceedings of the Workshop on Methods for Optimizing and Evaluating Neural Language Generation*, pages 21–29.

Mukund Sundararajan, Ankur Taly, and Qiqi Yan. 2017. Axiomatic attribution for deep networks. In *Proceedings of the 34th International Conference on Machine Learning-Volume 70*, pages 3319–3328.

Jiwei Tan, Xiaojun Wan, and Jianguo Xiao. 2017. Abstractive document summarization with a graph-based attentional neural model. In *Proceedings of the 55th Annual Meeting of the Association for Computational Linguistics (Volume 1: Long Papers)*, pages 1171–1181.

Ashish Vaswani, Noam Shazeer, Niki Parmar, Jakob Uszkoreit, Llion Jones, Aidan N Gomez, Łukasz Kaiser, and Illia Polosukhin. 2017. Attention is all you need. In *Advances in neural information processing systems*, pages 5998–6008.

Thomas Wolf, Lysandre Debut, Victor Sanh, Julien Chaumond, Clement Delangue, Anthony Moi, Pierric Cistac, Tim Rault, Rémi Louf, Morgan Funtowicz, Joe Davison, Sam Shleifer, Patrick von Platen, Clara Ma, Yacine Jernite, Julien Plu, Canwen Xu, Teven Le Scao, Sylvain Gugger, Mariama Drame, Quentin Lhoest, and Alexander M. Rush. 2019. Huggingface's transformers: State-of-the-art natural language processing. *ArXiv*, abs/1910.03771.

Stratos Xenouleas, Prodromos Malakasiotis, Marianna Apidianaki, and Ion Androutsopoulos. 2019. Sum-qe: A bert-based summary quality estimation model. In *Proceedings of the 2019 Conference on Empirical Methods in Natural Language Processing and the 9th International Joint Conference on Natural Language Processing (EMNLP-IJCNLP)*, pages 6007–6013.

Zichao Yang, Diyi Yang, Chris Dyer, Xiaodong He, Alex Smola, and Eduard Hovy. 2016. Hierarchical attention networks for document classification. In *Proceedings of the 2016 conference of the North American chapter of the association for computational linguistics: human language technologies*, pages 1480–1489.

Jingqing Zhang, Yao Zhao, Mohammed Saleh, and Peter J. Liu. 2020. PEGASUS: Pre-training with extracted gap-sentences for abstractive summarization. In *Proceedings of the 37th International Conference on Machine Learning*.

A Alternative Approaches

In the following, we discuss alternative approaches which we tried but did not achieve as good results as the proposed model.

Separate encoders for document and summary. We conjectured that encoding a document for cross-attention in the word generator, and encoding a summary for generating the next summary sentence representation require extracting different pieces of information. We therefore added a second encoder for the summary generated so far, and initialized it with BERT. This change did not improve over sharing the encoder weights for the article and the summary. However, it introduced many additional parameters, so we discarded this idea.

Same preprocessing for the summary. BERTSUMEXTABS uses different preprocessing formats for the source document and the summary. For the document, every sentence is surrounded by a leading `CLS` token and a trailing `SEP` token. The summary is preceded by a *beginning of summary* token, the summary sentences are separated by a sentence separator token and the end is marked with an *end of summary* token.

We tried homogenizing the preprocessing formats for the document and the summary, such that the encoder does not need to deal with different inputs. We surround every sentence with a `CLS` and `SEP` token. The end of the summary is still marked with an *end of summary* token to tell the decoder to stop.

We did not reach the results of the preprocessing used in BERTSUMEXTABS with this format. Interestingly, the generated summaries consistently contained fewer sentences on average. We conjecture that this could be an artefact of decoding with beam search, but cannot substantiate this presumption.

Contextual sentence representations. In our model, we encode summary sentences individually, without self-attention to the surrounding sentences. It is not possible to allow representations to see future ground-truth sentences, as that would serve as a shortcut for the model and prevent proper learning of the task. While it is possible for the sentence representations to encode information of previous summary sentences, experiments showed no improvements with this change.

Attention to the sentence representation. A different way to integrate the sentence representation in the word generator is to perform attention over it. We experimented with two methods. On the one hand, we specialized an attention head to exclusively look at the sentence representation, while the others attend to the source document. This method performed slightly worse than the base model on ROUGE scores. On the other hand, we concatenated the sentence representation to the encoder outputs, and jointly attended to it in the word generator's cross-attention. When analyzing the attention weights, we realized that the sentence representation was mostly ignored. As a remedy, we separated training into two phases. In the first phase, we trained our model without attention to the document, such that the sentence planner gets a chance to learn meaningful sentence representations and is not ignored from the start. We then finetuned the model with attention to the document. While this increased the attention weights of the sentence representation substantially, the results did not improve over the baseline with the same number of total training steps (pretraining and finetuning combined).

B Preprocessing on Curation Corpus

We follow the instructions in the Curation Corpus Github repository[7] to download the 40000 article-summary pairs. After filtering examples where either the article or the summary are empty, we are left with 39911 examples. We split them into train/validation/test sets as 80/10/10 to arrive at split sizes of 31929/3991/3991.

Since the text extractor from the HTML websites inserts a lot of newlines (probably due to the website layout), we replace them with spaces in order to not split sentences in the middle.

We use the NLTK tokenizer (Bird et al., 2009) to split the article text into sentences. We then preprocess the data in the same way as Liu and Lapata (2019) processed the CNN/DailyMail corpus, except that we do not filter examples based on the number of tokens in the article or summary, but instead keep them irrespective of their length.

We are happy to assist with reconstructing the dataset as we have used it in this paper.

[7] `https://github.com/CurationCorp/curation-corpus`

Model	ROUGE		
	R-1	R-2	R-L
BSEA (Liu and Lapata, 2019)	42.95 (0.14)	17.67 (0.19)	37.46 (0.21)
BSEA (our implementation)	43.37 (0.37)	17.92 (0.17)	37.73 (0.31)
Sentence planner	**44.40** (0.14)	**18.31** (0.13)	**38.69** (0.10)

Table 8: Comparison of generated with reference summaries on Curation Corpus. Mean and std (in brackets) over 5 runs. Best result in bold.

Model	Sentences		Novel Bigrams	Corefs
	Number	Length		
Gold summaries	*3.46*	*28.0*	*69.22%*	*0.441*
BSEA (Liu and Lapata, 2019)	2.73 (0.09)	27.3 (0.5)	36.77% (0.94%)	0.267 (0.011)
BSEA (our implementation)	2.76 (0.10)	28.5 (0.8)	37.29% (1.32%)	0.283 (0.026)
Sentence planner	3.15 (0.11)	28.2 (0.5)	**39.29%** (2.00%)	**0.289** (0.023)

Table 9: Properties of generated summaries on Curation Corpus. Mean and std (in brackets) over 5 runs.

Dataset / Model	Focus	Coherence
CNN/DailyMail	*0.654*	*0.298*
Curation Corpus	*0.848*	*0.563*
BSEA (Liu and Lapata, 2019)	0.838	0.547
BSEA (our implementation)	0.850	0.563
Sentence planner	0.859	0.562

Table 10: Focus and coherence scores of SUM-QE. Models are trained and evaluated on Curation Corpus. Mean over 5 runs.

C Full Results on Curation Corpus

Tables 8 and 9 show the mean and standard deviation (in brackets) over 5 runs of each model, with random seeds from 1 to 5.

D SUM-QE Evaluation

In line with our evaluations, SUM-QE (Xenouleas et al., 2019) evaluates the linguistic quality of a summary. In particular, the two qualities *focus* and *coherence* are desired properties for natural summaries. However, we found the metric to give non-discriminative scores to all summaries (including reference summaries). We therefore only provide the results for completeness.

SUM-QE automatically evaluates summaries with regard to linguistic quality questions asked in the DUC-05/06/07 tasks. We select the qualities regarding focus and coherence, described as follows:

Q4 – Focus. The summary should have a focus; sentences should only contain information that is related to the rest of the summary.

Q5 – Structure and Coherence. The summary should be well-structured and well-organized. The summary should not just be a heap of related information, but should build from sentence to sentence to a coherent body of information about a topic.

The raters were asked to judge summaries on an integer scale of 1 to 5, which is normalized to $(0, 1)$ by the SUM-QE model. It is trained on the raters' judgments and achieves high correlations on a held-out test set. We use the model trained on DUC-05/06 (and evaluated on DUC-07) with the "multi-task-5" setting, producing one output per linguistic quality.

Table 10 holds the SUM-QE scores for the reference summaries of CNN/DailyMail and Curation Corpus. There is an evident difference in scores between the two datasets, with Curation Corpus's summaries being judged more focused and coherent by the model. When comparing the scores of Curation Corpus's reference summaries with the models' scores, there are only minimal differences. The same holds true for a comparison between models. We therefore decided to remove this evaluation from the main text of the paper.

E Example Summaries

Tables 11 and 12 show example summaries from the Curation Corpus validation set for the sentence planner and BERTSUMEXTABS (our implementation), alongside the source article and the reference summary.

Source article
Theresa May's plans for a post-Brexit trade deal with the US will be put at risk if she retains EU protections for food and drink such as Champagne and Parma Ham, a senior ally of Donald Trump has warned. The Telegraph has learned that Liam Fox, the International Trade Secretary, has written to David Davis, the Brexit Secretary, warning him not to concede over the issue during negotiations with Brussels. During a recent visit to the US he was told by Paul Ryan, a senior Republican and Speaker of the House of Representatives, that the UK must be able to "diverge" from EU protected status standards to reach a free trade deal. The US produces its own Feta, Parmesan and Champagne and has strongly resisted attempts to ban the sale of American products in the past. Its refusal to compromise on the issue led to the collapse of a major trade deal between the EU and the US. However Michel Barnier, the EU's chief Brexit negotiator, is demanding that Britain must recognise 3,300 protected food and drink products after Brexit. The products are protected under a system of "geographical indications", meaning that they cannot be produced elsewhere.

Reference summary
A post-Brexit trade deal with the US may be jeopardised if the UK continues to recognise EU protected status standards for food and drink. The US has resisted calls to adopt protections for products such as feta, Parmesan and Champagne, and would expect the UK to also diverge from them. However, the EU's chief Brexit negotiator, Michel Barnier, says Britain must retain the protections.

Candidate summary (sentence planner)
uk prime minister theresa may ' s plans for a post - brexit trade deal with the us will be placed at risk if she retains eu protections for food and drink products such as champagne and parma ham , according to unnamed sources . european trade secretary liam fox has written to david davis , the eu ' s chief brexit negotiator michel barnier , to call for britain to recognise 3 , 300 protected food and drinks products after brexit . the uk produces its own feta , parmesan and champagne imports , and called for the uk to " diverge " from eu protected status standards .

Candidate summary (BERTSUMEXTABS, our implementation)
brexit negotiator liam fox has written to david davis , the uk ' s brexit negotiator , calling for britain to recognise 3 , 300 protected food and drink products after brexit . the uk produces its own feta , parmesan and champagne and has strongly opposed attempts to ban the sale of us products in the past . michel barnier , the eu ' s chief brexit negotiator for brexit negotiator michel barnier is calling for the uk to recognise three , 300 products following brexit .

Table 11: Hard example from the Curation Corpus. The sentence planner correctly calls "a senior ally of Donald Trump" an "unnamed source". It nicely includes the Speaker of the House's demand to "diverge" from EU standards as a call by the US. It gets confused with the International Trade Secretary, the Brexit Secretary and the EU's chief Brexit negotiator. It also mistakes the US for the UK when talking about a country producing its own products. BERTSUMEXTABS does these same mistakes, but gets even more confused with the Brexit negotiator. It repeats the call to recognize the protected products by the Brexit negotiator, and misses the main point of the article, namely that this issue jeopardizes the post-Brexit trade deal.

Source article
FILE PHOTO: U.S. President Donald Trump talks to reporters as he heads to the Marine One helicopter to depart the White House for travel to Florida in Washington, U.S. October 8, 2018. REUTERS/Jonathan Ernst/File PhotoWASHINGTON (Reuters) - President Donald Trump's administration on Thursday for a second time asked the U.S. Supreme Court to put the brakes on a lawsuit filed by young activists who have accused the U.S. government of ignoring the perils of climate change. In the lawsuit, 21 activists, ages 11 to 22, said federal officials violated their rights to due process under the U.S. Constitution by failing to adequately address carbon pollution such as emissions from the burning of fossil fuels. The lawsuit was filed in 2015 against former President Barack Obama and government agencies in a federal court in Eugene, Oregon. Both the Obama and Trump administration have failed in efforts to have the lawsuit thrown out. On July 30, the high court rejected an earlier application by the Trump administration, saying it was premature. Eugene, Oregon-based federal judge Ann Aiken on Monday issued another ruling allowing the case to move forward to trial on Oct. 29 if either the high court or the San Francisco-based 9th U.S. Circuit Court of Appeals do not intervene. Reporting by Lawrence Hurley; Editing by Will Dunham
Reference summary
President Trump's administration on 18 October failed in its attempt to halt a climate change lawsuit filed in 2015 by 21 activists, aged between 11 and 22, which accuses the US government of ignoring the risks of climate change. The Obama administration had also attempted unsuccessfully to have the lawsuit thrown out, while the high court rejected a previous application by the Trump administration to have the case dismissed on 30 July. The latest ruling from the Supreme Court means the case can proceed to trial on 29 October if neither the high court or Court of Appeals intervenes.
Candidate summary (sentence planner)
president donald trump ' s administration has asked the us supreme court to put the brakes on a lawsuit filed by young activists who have accused the us government of ignoring the perils of climate change . in 2015 , 21 activists claimed federal officials violated their rights to due process under the constitution by failing to address carbon pollution , including emissions from the burning of fossil fuels . on 30 july , the high court rejected an earlier application by the trump administration , saying it was premature .
Candidate summary (BERTSUMEXTABS, our implementation)
president donald trump ' s administration for a second time has asked the us supreme court to put the brakes on a lawsuit filed by 21 activists who have accused the us government of ignoring the perils of climate change . the case , which was filed in 2015 against former president barack obama and government agencies in a federal court in oregon , is being brought forward by the high court on 30 july .

Table 12: Example from the Curation Corpus. The sentence planner manages to get all facts correct, and summarizes the important content very well by removing phrases such as "on Thursday for a second time", "U.S." in "U.S. Constitution" and "adequately" in "adequately address". It also uses the information that the lawsuit was filed in 2015 from a later sentence to include in the sentence about the origin of the lawsuit. BERTSUMEXTABS also nicely fuses information in its first generated sentence. In the second one, however, it mistakenly believes that the case will be handled on July 30, instead of October 29. It is again a bit shorter on information compared to the sentence planner.

Template-aware Attention Model for Earnings Call Report Generation

Yangchen Huang, Seyed Danial Mohseni Taheri and **Prashant K Dhingra**
J.P.Morgan Chase & Co., New York, NY
{yangchen.huang, seyeddanial.mohsenitaheri, prashant.k.dhingra}@jpmchase.com

Abstract

Earning calls are among important resources for investors and analysts for updating their price targets. Firms usually publish corresponding transcripts soon after earnings events. However, raw transcripts are often too long and miss the coherent structure. To enhance the clarity, analysts write well-structured reports for some important earnings call events by analyzing them, requiring time and effort. In this paper, we propose TATSum (**T**emplate-**A**ware a**T**tention model for **Sum**marization), a generalized neural summarization approach for structured report generation, and evaluate its performance in the earnings call domain. We build a large corpus with thousands of transcripts and reports using historical earnings events. We first generate a candidate set of reports from the corpus as potential soft templates which do not impose actual rules on the output. Then, we employ an encoder model with margin-ranking loss to rank the candidate set and select the best quality template. Finally, the transcript and the selected soft template are used as input in a seq2seq framework for report generation. Empirical results on the earnings call dataset show that our model significantly outperforms state-of-the-art models in terms of informativeness and structure.

1 Introduction

Earnings Calls, conference calls held by public companies to disclose their performance of a specific period, are key resources in providing signals for financial analysts' decision-making process. Analysts, investors, and the mass media can learn about a company's financial results, operation details, and future guidance by listening to these conference calls. Previous works have highlighted the importance of earnings calls in modeling analysts' behavior (Frankel et al., 1999; Keith and Stent, 2019).

As nowadays firms disclose more and more information (Dyer et al., 2017), earnings call transcripts are usually longer and contain more information than before, resulting in challenges in efficiently analyzing these unstructured documents and detecting informative facts. Some financial analysts write well-structured reports (Figure 1) (Refinitiv) for earnings calls after attending the event or reading the transcript. However, writing such reports usually takes time and effort. In addition, reports are not available for every company and event. Therefore, generating earnings reports quickly and automatically can fill the gap for no-report-available conferences and strongly accelerate the research process in the financial industry.

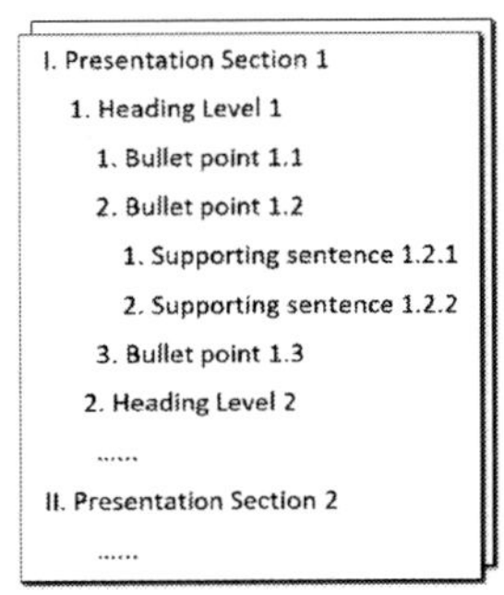

Figure 1: Example of an analyst report. Generated reports of our system follow the same structure.

To fulfill this goal, we aim to develop an effective text summarization system to automatically generate reports with a hierarchical structure. Text summarization (Maybury, 1999), as an important field of Natural Language Processing, attracts considerable interest from researchers. Various datasets for summarization tasks have been built, most of which contains small to middle-sized document and short summary, e.g., CNN/Daily Mail (Hermann et al., 2015; Nallapati et al., 2016), WikiHow (Koupaee and Wang, 2018), Reddit (Kim et al., 2019), etc. Researchers design innovative architectures and benchmark the model performance on these mainstream datasets, yet extending summarization framework to the domain of earnings call

Proceedings of the Third Workshop on New Frontiers in Summarization, pages 15–24
November 10, 2021.

transcripts, has never been explored.

In contrast to popular summarization tasks, structured earnings report generation has several challenges due to the special properties of data. First, earnings call conferences usually take a few hours, and transcripts contain thousands of words. This feature makes it impossible for popular pre-trained models such as BERT (Devlin et al., 2019) and BART (Lewis et al., 2020) to provide high-quality summaries since these approaches partition the long documents into smaller sequences within 512 tokens to meet the input limit, resulting in loss of cross-partition information. Second, generated reports are required to be clearly organized and well-formatted. In addition to summarization, it is important for the model to recognize and output the explicit logical structure of the earnings call presentation. To the best of our knowledge, the structure quality of generated summaries from lengthy documents, in terms of logic and format, has rarely been examined in literature.

In this paper, we formally conceptualize report generation as an extension of summarization tasks and propose a novel approach, **T**emplate-**A**ware a**T**tention model for **Sum**marization (TATSum), to produce hierarchically-structured reports. Inspired by traditional template-based summarization (Zhou and Hovy, 2004), and soft template-based sentence summarization (Cao et al., 2018), we use historical reports as soft templates to provide supplemental structure information for a summarization system. We use soft templates as they do not enforce an actual rule in the generated summaries. To deal with the long sequence problem, we leverage the advantage of Long-Documents-Transformer (Longformer) (Beltagy et al., 2020), which reduces the complexity of the self-attention mechanism in Transformers (Vaswani et al., 2017) and allow for longer input sequences.

We collect historical earnings call transcripts and reports, and divide them into speaker sections with fewer words. The combination of a transcript section and a report section serves as an individual data point in the corpus. Our proposed framework consists of three modules as illustrated in Figure 2: (i) *Candidate Generation*, which generates a set of potential soft template candidates for a transcript section, (ii) *Candidate Ranking*, which ranks candidates through a Siamese-architected (Bromley et al., 1993) Longformer Encoder and selects the candidate with the highest rank as the final soft template for the transcript, and (iii) *Report Generation*, which generates the report using the soft template together with the raw transcript through a Longformer-Encoder-Decoder (LED) model (Beltagy et al., 2020). Figure 1 illustrates the structure of reports generated by our algorithm.

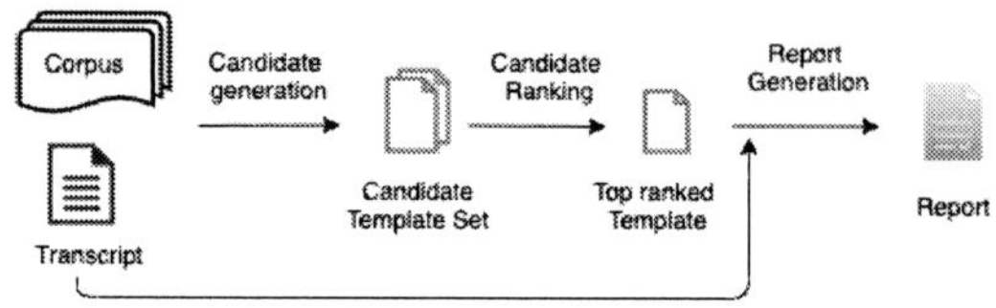

Figure 2: Flowchart of the report generation system

We evaluate the proposed framework on hundreds of earnings call events. Experiments show that TATSum significantly outperforms the state-of-the-art summarization models in terms of informativeness, format, and logical structure. Besides, extensive experiments are conducted to analyze the effect of different components of our framework on the performance of the model.

The contributions of this work are summarized as follows:

- We introduce a section-based soft template as supplemental information to the encoder-decoder framework to generate structured and readable earnings call reports.
- We design a Siamese-architected Longformer encoder for better template selection and further improve the quality of generated reports.
- Our algorithm adopts and extends the LED to provide template-aware summarization and overcome the challenge of long sequence encoding and long document generation.
- We conduct experiments on earnings call transcripts for the first time and evaluate the impact of different components of the proposed system. Results show that TATSum achieves superior performance compared with state-of-the-art baselines.

The paper is organized as follows: in Section 2, we review the relevant prior literature. Section 3 presents the novel architecture of TATSum. We conduct extensive experiments on the earnings call dataset and analyze the results in Section 4. Section 5 concludes the paper and provides future directions.

2 Related Work

Earlier studies of neural abstractive summarization employ encoder-decoder architecture to generate a shorter version of a sentence (Rush et al., 2015). Nallapati et al. (2016) extend previous work to summarize documents with more than one sentence using hierarchical attention. A variety of studies focus on building advanced attention mechanism for better summarization, e.g., convolutional attention (Chopra et al., 2016), graph-based attention (Tan et al., 2017), Bottom-up attention (Gehrmann et al., 2018), etc. See et al. (2017) propose a hybrid pointer-generator network and a coverage mechanism to keep track of already-summarized words. Paulus et al. (2018) introduce a deep reinforced model with a novel intra-attention mechanism and show improved performance for long document summarization.

Recently, pre-trained language models, which are trained to learn contextual representations from large-scale corpora, have been proved to be successful in summarization tasks. Popular pre-trained models like BERT (Devlin et al., 2019) and BART (Lewis et al., 2020) are adopted to build summarization-specific architecture. BERTSum (Liu and Lapata, 2019) proposes a novel document-level BERT-based encoder and an auto-regressive decoder with Trigram Blocking techniques and shows strong performance in both extractive and abstractive summarization. Aghajanyan et al. (2020) integrate BART with the Robust Representations through Regularized Finetuning (R3F) method to perform better fine-tuning for pre-trained models and achieve the state-of-the-art performance on CNN/Daily Mail.

Longformer (Beltagy et al., 2020) significantly reduces the time and space complexity of the attention mechanism and allows for much longer input sequences. It achieves this goal by replacing the self-attention in traditional Transformers (Vaswani et al., 2017) with windowed attention and introducing new task-oriented global attention. Longformer-Encoder-Decoder (LED) (Beltagy et al., 2020), a variant of Longformer, is also introduced for supporting long document seq2seq tasks. LED-large 16K, a BART-pretrained LED model with no additional pretraining, outperformed Bigbird summarization (Zaheer et al., 2020), a modified Transformer for long sequences with Pegasus pretraining (Zhang et al., 2020), and achieved the state-of-the-art performance on arXiv dataset (Cohan et al., 2018). In this paper, LED is adopted as the base model and a strong baseline benchmark.

In the domain of earnings calls, there is limited work exploring the potential of applying text summarization techniques. Cardinaels et al. (2019) generate an automatic summary for earnings releases using off-the-shelf unsupervised summarization methods such as KLSum (Haghighi and Vanderwende, 2009), LexRank (Erkan and Radev, 2004), etc., and conduct experiments to analyze the impact of automatic and management summaries on the investors' judgment. However, comprehensive experiments on the performance of summarization techniques are missing. In this work, we develop a novel summarization algorithm for report generation, provide extensive experiments on the earnings call dataset, and compare it with the state-of-the-art models in the literature.

An important feature of our system is to generate well-structured and formatted reports. Template-based summarization (Zhou and Hovy, 2004) is a traditional technique to summarize sentences. With a manually designed incomplete sentence template, the method fills the template using some input text, following pre-defined rules. This method can guarantee that the output sentence follows a specific format. However, constructing templates for long documents and large-scale datasets still remains challenging and requires domain knowledge. Cao et al. (2018) extended the template-based summarization and introduced a soft template, which is a summary sentence selected from the training set, to resolve this issue. Re3Sum (Cao et al., 2018) selects the soft template through an Information Retrieval (IR) platform and jointly learns template quality as well as generates the summary through a seq2seq framework. In this paper, we select historical reports from the corpus and form candidate sets.

To further improve template quality, our Candidate Ranking Module is inspired by MatchSum (Zhong et al., 2020). Zhong et al. (2020) formulates extractive summarization as a semantic text matching problem, and architect a Siamese-BERT network with margin-ranking loss to select the best candidate summary.

3 Method

Our goal is to generate hierarchically structured reports from long documents. The automatic generation system, TATSum, consists of three modules: *Candidate Generation*, *Candidate Ranking*, and *Report Generation*. Given an earnings call transcript, we divide it into different sections and consider each section as an input sequence T. This helps in the tractability of the summarization process by considering fewer tokens and results in well-structured reports since each section usually follows a coherent structure that is different from others. Similarly, human-written reports are divided into sections, R, and mapped to the document sections in the training phase.

For each document section T, the *Candidate Generation* module filters a candidate set of top i soft templates $\mathcal{C}^T := \{R_1, \cdots, R_i\}$ from a built corpus. We rank the candidate set $\mathcal{C}^T$ using the *Candidate Ranking* module to select the best soft template $\hat{R}^T$ to use. Finally, in the *Report Generation* module, the best soft template $\hat{R}^T$ and the raw document section T together are encoded into hidden states. A decoder takes the combination of encoded hidden states as well as decoder inputs to generate the abstractive report. Figure 3 illustrates *Candidate Ranking* and *Candidate Generation* modules. The three modules will be described in detail in the following subsections.

3.1 Candidate Generation

This module finds soft templates from the training corpus and forms a set of candidates. Our corpus, P, includes all document sections $\mathcal{T}$ and report sections $\mathcal{R}$ in the training set. To find the set of template candidates, we consider two assumptions: (i) similar transcripts should have similar reports, and (ii) a good template should give instructions about the format while not adding misleading information.

Since our dataset includes thousands of documents, we use an information retrieval technique, TF-IDF, to efficiently find the set of candidates. TF-IDF is a traditional unsupervised learning technique that can convert document text into a bag of words and quickly vectorize it. Since transcripts and reports have different styles, we consider the similarity between transcripts following assumption (i). Therefore, we first compute the similarity between section T and the other transcript sections in the corpus P using TF-IDF cosine similarity. Then, we select the top 5 scored document sections and use their corresponding reports in the corpus to form the candidate set $\mathcal{C} = \{R_1, \cdots, R_5\}$.

Although TF-IDF is a quick and easy method to calculate similarities and select candidates, it may not always provide candidates that resemble gold reports. We test this hypothesis by calculating the ROUGE average score (average of ROUGE-1, ROUGE-2, and ROUGE-l F1 score) between a sample of candidate sets and the human-written reports. We find that only 17.4% of the best TF-IDF candidates have the highest ROUGE average score among all the candidates, indicating that TF-IDF is not sufficient for retrieving the best soft-template. Thus, we add the second module, *Candidate Ranking*, to rank the candidate set and predict the best candidate that has the highest ROUGE score with the human-written report.

3.2 Candidate Ranking

The purpose of this module is to precisely select the best template, i.e., the template which has the highest ROUGE score with the human-written report. To train this module, we first calculate the ROUGE average score between each candidate template in the candidate set, $\mathcal{C}^T$, and the human-written report, R^{*T}, and store them in the descending order in $\tilde{C}^T$ as a label.

Inspired by Siamese network (Bromley et al., 1993) and Siamese-BERT structure (Zhong et al., 2020), we construct a Siamese-Longformer architecture to rank the candidate set. Longformer, a.k.a Long-Document Transformer,(Beltagy et al., 2020) is a model that successfully addresses the input length limitation of Transformer-based models by reducing the time complexity of the attention mechanism. The Siamese-Longformer model consists of two Longformer encoders with tied weights and a cosine similarity layer to compute comparable output vectors. One Longformer network encodes transcripts, T, and the other one encodes reports, R. We use the encoded hidden state of the bos_token '$< s >$' from the final Longformer layer to extract the transcript and report embedding vectors, e_T and e_R, respectively. The cosine-similarity layer connects these representation vectors and obtains the semantic similarity between the two documents.

$$S(T, R) = cosine(e_T, e_R)$$

If two documents have a higher ROUGE score, we expect them to have higher predicted semantic similarity.

We use margin-ranking loss to update the weights, and the model is expected to predict the correct rank of the candidate set based on the ROUGE score. Specifically, the loss function is

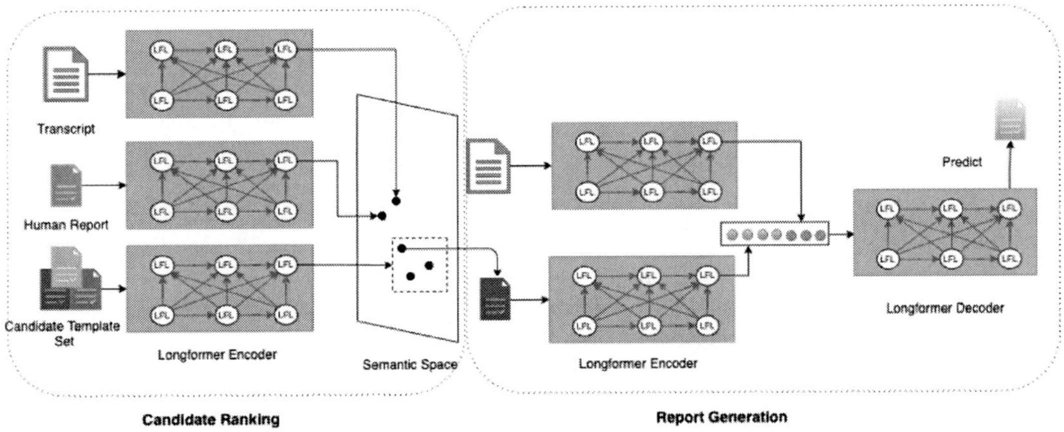

Figure 3: Illustration of different components of the *Candidate Ranking* module (left) and the *Report Generation* module (right). First, we learn parameters of the Longformer layers (LFL) in the *Candidate Ranking* to rank existing reports in the candidate set. Then, we encode the representations of the transcript and the top candidate using Longformer Encoder and decode their embeddings to generate reports.

designed from the following criteria.

- Human-written report should be the most semantically similar with the transcript
- A candidate template that has a higher rouge score with the human-written report should have a higher semantical similarity with the transcript.

Based on the first criteria, we derive the construction of the first loss function:

$$L_1 = \sum_{R \in C^T} \max(0, S(T, R) - S(T, R^{*T}))$$

Where R^{*T} is the human-written report, and $R \in C^T$ denotes all the candidate templates for transcript T.

Based on the second criteria, we use sorted candidate set ranking in $\tilde{C}^T$ and design a margin-ranking loss as follows:

$$L_2 = \sum_{\{i,j\} \in \tilde{C}^T} \max(0, S(T, R_j^T) - S(T, R_i^T) + (j - i)\epsilon) \quad (i < j)$$

where R_i denotes the candidate template ranked i, and ϵ is a hyperparameter that distinguishes between candidates with good, i, and bad, j, rankings. As described in criteria 2, the construction aims to measure the loss of any mis-ranking within the candidate set. Finally, the margin-ranking loss we use to train the Siamese-Longformer network is a combination of the two loss functions.

$$L_R = L_1 + L_2 \quad (1)$$

During the inference phase, the model will predict the similarity scores of candidates in the candidate set, and the candidate with the highest score will be set as the best soft template $\hat{R}^T$ for the transcript for further report generation.

$$\hat{R}^T := \arg\max_{R \in C^T} S(T, R)$$

3.3 Report Generation

This module aims to generate the final report based on the soft template and the transcript. To generate an abstractive report, we design a soft-template-based encoder-decoder architecture to conduct seq2seq generation. We employ a pretrained LED as the base encoder-decoder model. The model takes a transcript section T and a soft template $\hat{R}^T$ as the input. They are tokenized and encoded by a Longformer encoder respectively. Similar to module 2, we use the encoded hidden state of '$< s >$' from the top Longformer layer as the representation of the corresponding transcript/template in the semantic space. The hidden states of the encoded transcript H_t and template H_s are concatenated as the final encoding outputs.

$$H_T = LongformerEncoder(T)$$
$$H_{\hat{R}^T} = LongformerEncoder(\hat{R}^T)$$
$$H_e = [H_T; H_{\hat{R}^T}]$$

The combined encoding outputs are then fed into a Longformer Decoder, and the decoding hidden state, H_d, is generated auto-regressively at position k based on the previous report tokens y_{k-1}:

$$H_{d,k} = Decoder(H_{d,k-1}, y_{k-1}, H_e)$$

Finally, a softmax layer predicts the probability vector of words at position k in the report:

$$\mathbf{P}_k = softmax(H_{d,k} W^P),$$

where W^P is learnable matrix. In cases in which the template includes too many tokens, we truncate it to ensure that we get more information from the transcript than the template since the main content in the report should source from the transcript, and templates should only provide information for formatting. Generally, the tokens from a template are about 25% of the transcript.

The whole encoder-decoder architecture is fine-tuned during training. A beam search is conducted during the test to generate an abstractive report that has the highest overall probability.

$$R = Beam(\mathbf{P}_1, \mathbf{P}_2, ..., \mathbf{P}_k)$$

3.4 Optimization

We use two sets of loss functions in generating the reports of the earning calls. In *Candidate Ranking* module, we aim to train the parameters of Siamese-Longformer to find the best template in the candidate set. We use ranking loss, L_R, defined in equation (1) to achieve this goal.

In *Report Generation* module, our learning goal is to maximize the negative log-likelihood of the probability of the actual report.

$$L_G = -\sum_k log(p_{y_k})$$

We optimize the two losses separately over their respective parameters using gradient-based approaches (see section 4.4 for more details).

4 Experiment

We evaluate TATSum on Earnings call reports. We aim to answer the two following questions.

- Q1: How does TATSum perform compared to the state-of-the-art summarization systems?
- Q2: How do different components of TATSum such as soft-template and template ranking affect the performance of the model?

4.1 Dataset

We collected transcripts and human-written reports for 3655 earnings call events from 2017 to 2020, hosted by 1948 listed companies. Most selected companies are listed in NYSE or NASDAQ. For better generalization of our model, we also select a few companies from world-wide exchanges, such as TSX, FWB, Euronext, etc. These transcripts and reports are divided into 11141 sections, and each section is treated as an individual sequence. The statistics of our dataset is shown in Table 1. In our dataset, transcript lengths are significantly larger than the majority of public datasets such as Daily Mail and NYTimes and similar to long documents such as arXiv (Cohan et al., 2018). However, the reports in our dataset are substantially longer than the summaries of existing datasets, indicating that instead of doing lots of condensation, analysts tend to retain most of the information by paraphrasing and restructuring the oral transcript. Therefore, generating long sequences in natural language with a well-organized structure, is the most critical part for automatic earnings call reports.

Dataset	#docs	avg.doc. len(words)	avg. report len(words)
Docs	3655	3621	2524

Table 1: Statistics of the built earnings call dataset

We retain about 20% of the dataset as validation and use the rest for training. To prevent data leakage or utilizing future information, we test the performance of TATSum on 2000 transcript sections extracted from 666 earnings events in late 2020 and early 2021. In this setting, when generating the report for an earnings call transcript, TATSum only leverage a historical report that is available prior to the event. The entire dataset is shown in Table 2.

Dataset	Transcripts/Reports	Sections
Training Set	2929	8786
Validation Set	726	2265
Test Set	666	2000

Table 2: Document and section number information of the dataset

4.2 Evaluation Metrics

We employ ROUGE (Lin and Hovy, 2003) as the automatic evaluation metric. ROUGE has been used as the standard evaluation metric for machine translation and automatic summarization since 2004. The commonly adopted ROUGE metrics are ROUGE-1 (overlap of unigram), ROUGE-2 (overlap of bigrams), and ROUGE-l (Longest Common Subsequence, or LCS). In the Candidate Ranking module, we use an average of ROUGE-1, ROUGE-2, and ROUGE-3 F1 score as labels for training. Through testing of the whole system, we calculate and report all these metrics.

ROUGE can measure how much information

the generated report maintains compared with the human-written report. However, correctness, which can not be captured by ROUGE, is another important metric for the generated report in the domain of earnings calls. We manually review the rendered result, especially focusing on important financial statistics, trends, and sentiment, to evaluate whether it reports correct information from the earnings call.

4.3 Baselines

To compare the performance of our proposed model with others, we consider following state-of-the-art neural summarization baselines:

- **BERTSum**(Liu and Lapata, 2019): It uses document-level BERT-based encoder and an autoregressive decoder with Trigram Blocking for summarization.
- **LED** (Beltagy et al., 2020): It modifies the self-attention in Transformers with windowed attention for long document summarization.

4.4 Implementation Details

We implement our model with Pytorch and adopt the pretrained LED-base model in *Candidate Ranking* and *Report Generation* modules. In particular, we use LEDs with 768 hidden state and 3072 feed-forward layer dimensionality. We use dropout with probability 0.1 and a customized Adam optimizer (Kingma and Ba, 2014) ($\beta_1 = 0.9, \beta_2 = 0.999, \epsilon - 1e - 9$) during training. The learning rates through optimization follow Noam decay scheme (Vaswani et al., 2017) with a warmup step of 500 and are set to be:

1. Module Candidate Ranking:

$$Lr = 3\text{e}{-}3{*}\min(step^{-0.5}, step{*}wrm.steps^{-1.5})$$

2. Module Report Generation:

$$Lr = 3\text{e}{-}5{*}\min(step^{-0.5}, step{*}wrm.steps^{-1.5})$$

We save a model checkpoint every 5000 steps and choose the best-performed checkpoint on the validation set. In *Report Generation* module, we use the Block Trigram technique (Liu and Lapata, 2019) to reduce potential redundancy. However, we find this approach ineffective for some reports and observe repetitions of words with punctuations in between. Therefore, we add a new Block Tri-word method that forces the decoder never to output the exact same three words in a predicted sequence with all punctuations deleted. When the decoder creates the same three words that exist in the previous pure word sequence, the probability of the beam is set to be 0.

Although we employ the Longformer architecture to deal with long sequences, we still face memory challenges in *Report Generation* module when the earnings call section is too long. To increase the performance for earnings call sections of arbitrary length, we divide a long section into several short sub-sections and generate reports for each sub-section. We then combine each sub-section and report them in the same hierarchical structure. This method is proved to perform well when a transcript section exceeds the sequence length limit.

We search for best hyperparameters for baselines, and use optimization schemes suggested by authors. Models are trained on Tesla-V100 GPUs.

4.5 Experiment Results

Table 3 shows the ROUGE F1 score for different methods.

Metrics	ROUGE1	ROUGE2	ROUGE-l
BERTSum	36.89	22.16	35.40
LED	65.17	53.07	64.93
TATSum	**76.20**	**61.89**	**75.94**

Table 3: Results of TATSum and Baseline models

Due to the small input length limit in the architecture of BertSum, it is not able to generate fluent and readable reports by partitioning the long document and combining the output. Taking advantage of the modified attention mechanism and huge sequence length limit, LED, on the contrary, achieves quite good performance. All three Rouge-F scores are above 50, indicating that reports generated by LED can extract critical information from earnings presentations similar to human beings. By adding a precisely-selected soft template to LED, our proposed system, TATSum, boosts the report quality even more, with a significant improvement over the performance of LED by 17%.

As discussed in section 4.1, earnings call reports contain much more words than summaries in popular summarization datasets. Therefore, the ROUGE scores are higher than those observed from CNN/DM and arXiv correspondingly. In order to guarantee the quality of generated reports for real use cases, in terms of structure and accuracy, we further conduct manual checking on a small sample of earnings events selected from the test set. We read their transcripts, human-written reports, and automatic report generated by TATSum, and compare the content in these documents. Generated reports mimic the analyst report well in format and structure. For information accuracy, we primarily focus on the numbers, trends, and sentiment in generated reports. Our observation shows that except in a few cases where some parts are missing, information within the generated report is accurate and coherent.

4.6 Ablation Study

In this section, we analyze variants of our model to find the effect of different components on the model performance. We consider variations as follows: (1) *No template*: we remove the first and second modules and consider a pure LED architecture for report generation and (2) *NoRanking*: We forgo *Candidate Ranking* module and use the template with the highest TF-IDF cosine similarity in *Candidate Generation*.

In table 4, we report the average ROUGE score of generated reports on the test set under different experiment setting.

Metrics	ROUGE1	ROUGE2	ROUGE-l
NoTemplate	65.17	53.07	64.93
NoRanking	75.90	61.48	75.63
TATSum	**76.20**	**61.89**	**75.94**

Table 4: Ablation study of design choices in TATSum

Effect of soft template: To capture the impact of soft templates on the performance of our model, we compare the results of *NoTemplate* and *NoRanking*. As illustrated in Table 4, A soft template based seq2seq model achieves significantly higher ROUGE scores. In addition to boosting the performance, incorporating the template stabalize the training process and results in faster convergence, indicating that the model can better learn to write reports in a quicker manner with supplemental information. We also compare several reports generated by the two models, and find that the report of *NoRanking* model has better format and logical structure. The report is clearly organized, with good heading levels and correct serial numbers. In contrast, the report of *NoTemplate* contains more incorrect indentations, levels, and serial numbers. It proves that adding a soft template do provide the model with more information on how to write a report logically like a human.

Effect of template ranking: Similarly, results of *NoRanking* and TATSum are compared to study whether ranking the candidate set of templates improves the performance. As shown in Table 4, ranking the candidate set and selecting a template of better quality can slightly increase all three ROUGE scores of generated reports. It is worth mentioning that unlike adding a soft template, ranking the candidate set can take a longer time for labeling and training. For labeling, ROUGE scores need to be calculated for each template in the candidate set with the human-written report, and all data points in the training set should be labeled. For training, a Siamese-Longformer encoder is constructed to predict the rank of the candidate set, which also requires long training and validation time. Therefore, further thoughts on balancing the tradeoff between performance and training time are necessary for each dataset.

5 Conclusions

This paper proposes an innovative neural summarization system, TATSum, with three modules, Candidate Generation, Candidate Ranking, and Report Generation, to generate structured reports automatically. In Candidate Generation module, we build a corpus of historical documents and reports, and for each document, we generate a candidate set using quick and easy similarity-based criteria. The candidate set is then ranked in the Candidate Ranking module, following the predicted result of an encoder model with margin-ranking loss. We choose the candidate with the highest rank as the soft template. In the final Report Generation module, we encode both template and document into hidden states and feed the combined hidden states into a decoder to generate the report. Extensive experiments are conducted on the earning call dataset and show that our model can generate reports with high informativeness (ROUGE) and high accuracy (numbers, trends, etc.). We also prove that adding a template can significantly improve the quality of the generated report, and finely selecting a template with good quality can increase performance even more.

We mainly test TATSum on automatic report generation for earnings call events. However, the advantage of Longformer architecture for long sequence tasks, as well as the significant power of adding soft templates for structured document generation, can extend our proposed framework to various domains, e.g., medical report, employee annual review, call center record, etc. We would like to take advantage of this proved architecture to explore more potential in structured report generation.

References

Armen Aghajanyan, Akshat Shrivastava, Anchit Gupta, Naman Goyal, Luke Zettlemoyer, and Sonal Gupta. 2020. Better fine-tuning by reducing representational collapse. *arXiv preprint arXiv:2008.03156.*

Iz Beltagy, Matthew E Peters, and Arman Cohan. 2020. Longformer: The long-document transformer. *arXiv preprint arXiv:2004.05150.*

Jane Bromley, Isabelle Guyon, Yann LeCun, Eduard Säckinger, and Roopak Shah. 1993. Signature verification using a" siamese" time delay neural network. *Advances in neural information processing systems*, 6:737–744.

Ziqiang Cao, Wenjie Li, Furu Wei, Sujian Li, et al. 2018. Retrieve, rerank and rewrite: Soft template based neural summarization. Association for Computational Linguistics (ACL).

Eddy Cardinaels, Stephan Hollander, and Brian J White. 2019. Automatic summarization of earnings releases: attributes and effects on investors' judgments. *Review of Accounting Studies*, 24(3):860–890.

Sumit Chopra, Michael Auli, and Alexander M Rush. 2016. Abstractive sentence summarization with attentive recurrent neural networks. In *Proceedings of the 2016 Conference of the North American Chapter of the Association for Computational Linguistics: Human Language Technologies*, pages 93–98.

Arman Cohan, Franck Dernoncourt, Doo Soon Kim, Trung Bui, Seokhwan Kim, Walter Chang, and Nazli Goharian. 2018. A discourse-aware attention model for abstractive summarization of long documents. In *Proceedings of the 2018 Conference of the North American Chapter of the Association for Computational Linguistics: Human Language Technologies, Volume 2 (Short Papers)*, pages 615–621.

Jacob Devlin, Ming-Wei Chang, Kenton Lee, and Kristina Toutanova. 2019. Bert: Pre-training of deep bidirectional transformers for language understanding. In *Proceedings of the 2019 Conference of the North American Chapter of the Association for Computational Linguistics: Human Language Technologies, Volume 1 (Long and Short Papers)*, pages 4171–4186.

Travis Dyer, Mark Lang, and Lorien Stice-Lawrence. 2017. The evolution of 10-k textual disclosure: Evidence from latent dirichlet allocation. *Journal of Accounting and Economics*, 64(2-3):221–245.

Günes Erkan and Dragomir R Radev. 2004. Lexrank: Graph-based lexical centrality as salience in text summarization. *Journal of artificial intelligence research*, 22:457–479.

Richard Frankel, Marilyn Johnson, and Douglas J Skinner. 1999. An empirical examination of conference calls as a voluntary disclosure medium. *Journal of Accounting Research*, 37(1):133–150.

Sebastian Gehrmann, Yuntian Deng, and Alexander M Rush. 2018. Bottom-up abstractive summarization. In *Proceedings of the 2018 Conference on Empirical Methods in Natural Language Processing*, pages 4098–4109.

Aria Haghighi and Lucy Vanderwende. 2009. Exploring content models for multi-document summarization. In *Proceedings of human language technologies: The 2009 annual conference of the North American Chapter of the Association for Computational Linguistics*, pages 362–370.

Karl Moritz Hermann, Tomáš Kočiský, Edward Grefenstette, Lasse Espeholt, Will Kay, Mustafa Suleyman, and Phil Blunsom. 2015. Teaching machines to read and comprehend. In *Proceedings of the 28th International Conference on Neural Information Processing Systems-Volume 1*, pages 1693–1701.

Katherine A Keith and Amanda Stent. 2019. Modeling financial analysts' decision making via the pragmatics and semantics of earnings calls. *arXiv preprint arXiv:1906.02868.*

Byeongchang Kim, Hyunwoo Kim, and Gunhee Kim. 2019. Abstractive summarization of reddit posts with multi-level memory networks. In *Proceedings of the 2019 Conference of the North American Chapter of the Association for Computational Linguistics: Human Language Technologies, Volume 1 (Long and Short Papers)*, pages 2519–2531.

Diederik P Kingma and Jimmy Ba. 2014. Adam: A method for stochastic optimization. *arXiv preprint arXiv:1412.6980.*

Mahnaz Koupaee and William Yang Wang. 2018. Wikihow: A large scale text summarization dataset. *arXiv preprint arXiv:1810.09305.*

Mike Lewis, Yinhan Liu, Naman Goyal, Marjan Ghazvininejad, Abdelrahman Mohamed, Omer Levy, Veselin Stoyanov, and Luke Zettlemoyer. 2020. Bart: Denoising sequence-to-sequence pre-training for natural language generation, translation, and comprehension. In *Proceedings of the 58th Annual Meeting of the Association for Computational Linguistics*, pages 7871–7880.

Chin-Yew Lin and Eduard Hovy. 2003. Automatic evaluation of summaries using n-gram co-occurrence statistics. In *Proceedings of the 2003 Human Language Technology Conference of the North American Chapter of the Association for Computational Linguistics*, pages 150–157.

Yang Liu and Mirella Lapata. 2019. Text summarization with pretrained encoders. In *Proceedings of the 2019 Conference on Empirical Methods in Natural Language Processing and the 9th International Joint Conference on Natural Language Processing (EMNLP-IJCNLP)*, pages 3721–3731.

Mani Maybury. 1999. *Advances in automatic text summarization.* MIT press.

Ramesh Nallapati, Bowen Zhou, Cicero dos Santos, Caglar Gucehre, and Bing Xiang. 2016. Abstractive text summarization using sequence-to-sequence rnns and beyond. In *Proceedings of The 20th SIGNLL Conference on Computational Natural Language Learning*, pages 280–290.

Romain Paulus, Caiming Xiong, and Richard Socher. 2018. A deep reinforced model for abstractive summarization. In *International Conference on Learning Representations*.

Refinitiv. `https://www.refinitiv.com/en/financial-data`.

Alexander M Rush, Sumit Chopra, and Jason Weston. 2015. A neural attention model for abstractive sentence summarization. In *Proceedings of the 2015 Conference on Empirical Methods in Natural Language Processing*, pages 379–389.

Abigail See, Peter J Liu, and Christopher D Manning. 2017. Get to the point: Summarization with pointer-generator networks. In *Proceedings of the 55th Annual Meeting of the Association for Computational Linguistics (Volume 1: Long Papers)*, pages 1073–1083.

Jiwei Tan, Xiaojun Wan, and Jianguo Xiao. 2017. Abstractive document summarization with a graph-based attentional neural model. In *Proceedings of the 55th Annual Meeting of the Association for Computational Linguistics (Volume 1: Long Papers)*, pages 1171–1181.

Ashish Vaswani, Noam Shazeer, Niki Parmar, Jakob Uszkoreit, Llion Jones, Aidan N Gomez, Łukasz Kaiser, and Illia Polosukhin. 2017. Attention is all you need. *Advances in Neural Information Processing Systems*, 30:5998–6008.

Manzil Zaheer, Guru Guruganesh, Kumar Avinava Dubey, Joshua Ainslie, Chris Alberti, Santiago Ontanon, Philip Pham, Anirudh Ravula, Qifan Wang, Li Yang, et al. 2020. Big bird: Transformers for longer sequences. In *NeurIPS*.

Jingqing Zhang, Yao Zhao, Mohammad Saleh, and Peter Liu. 2020. Pegasus: Pre-training with extracted gap-sentences for abstractive summarization. In *International Conference on Machine Learning*, pages 11328–11339. PMLR.

Ming Zhong, Pengfei Liu, Yiran Chen, Danqing Wang, Xipeng Qiu, and Xuan-Jing Huang. 2020. Extractive summarization as text matching. In *Proceedings of the 58th Annual Meeting of the Association for Computational Linguistics*, pages 6197–6208.

Liang Zhou and Eduard Hovy. 2004. Template-filtered headline summarization. In *Text summarization branches out*, pages 56–60.

Knowledge and Keywords Augmented Abstractive Sentence Summarization

Shuo Guan[1], **Ping Zhu**[2] and **Zhihua Wei**[2]
[1]New York University
[2]Tongji University, College of Electronic and Information Engineering
[1]shuo.guan@cs.nyu.edu
[2]{pingzhu,zhihua_wei}@tongji.edu.cn

Abstract

In this paper, we study the knowledge-based abstractive sentence summarization. There are two essential information features that can influence the quality of news summarization, which are topic keywords and the knowledge structure of the news text. Besides, the existing knowledge-augmented methods have poor performance on sentence summarization since the sparse knowledge structure problem. Considering these, we propose **KAS**, a novel Knowledge and Keywords Augmented Abstractive Sentence Summarization framework. Tri-encoders are utilized to integrate contexts of original text, knowledge structure and keywords topic simultaneously, with a special linearized knowledge structure. Automatic and human evaluations demonstrate that KAS achieves the best performances.[1]

1 Introduction

With the increasing of computing power and model capacity, it is possible to generate mostly grammatical summarization of natural language text. In general, there are two essential information features of summarization: (1) topic keywords in text (2) the knowledge structure of the text. These features can basically cover all the information in summary generation, especially in sentence or short text summarization. Therefore, considering this reason, we are building a neural network model that integrates both topic keyword context and knowledge structure context.

Knowledge augmented summarization has been intensively studied recently, most of which are about document summarization. However, there is not much research on knowledge-based sentence summarization. The main reason is that the existing methods are not applicable to sentence summarization. The knowledge-based summarization frameworks usually use GNN (Graph Neural Networks) as the knowledge structure encoder. GNN is designated for encoding graph structure, and it has gained good performances on integrating knowledge graph contexts for document and multi-paragraph summarization. However, the knowledge graph of sentence is usually sparse, and GNN has poor performance in sparse knowledge structure. Specifically, GNNs may cause over-smoothing problem when training on the sparse graphs(Alon and Yahav, 2021), especially for GCNs (Graph Convolutional Networks) (Kipf and Welling, 2017), decreasing the robustness and performance of the model. Therefore, we are creating a new knowledge-augmented sentence summarization model considering these problems. Besides, considering most of the knowledge based summarization models are only applicable to English, we are aiming at making our model applicable to multiple languages.

In order to address these issues, we propose a special linearized knowledge sequence structure that are applicable to sentence summarization. Correspondingly, we propose a novel tri-encoder framework KAS integrating three separate encoders, considering contexts of original text, topic keywords and knowledge structure simultaneously based on their salience. Evaluations demonstrate that KAS framework and the corresponding linearized knowledge structure enhances the performances significantly. Besides, the structure of KAS can be applied to summarization on multiple languages. We have conducted experiments on English and Chinese corpus and achieved best performances on both.

2 Related Work

Knowledge-based Summarization The existing method for utilizing knowledge graph into text generation and summarization is adding a separate encoder to encode the vectorized knowledge graph for context integration. Ribeiro et al. (2020) in-

[1]Code is in https://github.com/SeanG-325/KAS

Proceedings of the Third Workshop on New Frontiers in Summarization, pages 25–32
November 10, 2021.

Algorithm 1 Knowledge Sequence Construction

Require: Text Sequence $\mathcal{S}$; Triples Extractor $\mathcal{E}$; Knowledge Graph $\mathcal{G}_k[*][*] = 0$.
  $T = \mathcal{E}(\mathcal{S})$
  for all $e \in T$ **do**
    if $\mathcal{E}(e.E) \neq \phi$ **then**
      $e.E = \mathcal{E}(E).E$
      $T = T \cup \mathcal{E}(E)$
    end if
  end for
  for $e \in T$ **do**
    $\mathcal{G}_k[e.E_1][e.R] = \mathcal{G}_k[e.R][e.E_2] = 1$
  end for
  Collect the occurance locations in $\mathcal{S}$ for all vertices in $\mathcal{G}_k$ as $L = \{l_1, ..., l_m\}$
  $S_{KG} = \text{DFS}_{KGL}(\mathcal{G}_k, L)$
  return S_{KG}

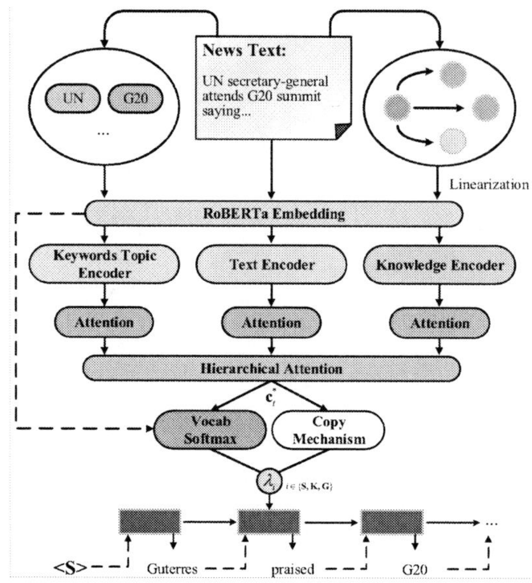

Figure 1: The Model Structure of KAS. The λ_i are soft gates for distributing copy probabilities.

troduced a knowledge graph encoding strategy for graph-to-text generation model. Koncel-Kedziorski et al. (2019), Huang et al. (2020) proposed a text generation (summarization) model integrated with a GNN encoder (Veličković et al., 2018) using encoded graph data preprocessed from the input text. Aiming at solving the possible sparse problem of graphs, Konstas et al. (2017) and Fan et al. (2019) proposed methods of graph linearization, and used LSTM/transformer encoders to encode the graph structure.

The Pointer Mechanism Pointer Mechanism has drawn much attention in text generation(Miao and Blunsom, 2016; Nallapati et al., 2016; Gulcehre et al., 2016; Eric and Manning, 2017). In text summarization, Pointer-Generator Network model (See et al., 2017) is proposed to keep the generation ability while using pointer mechanism. Sun et al. (2018) proposed a method for using pointer mechanism with multiple separate encoders. The idea of Pointer Mechanism is setting soft or hard gates to select from predefined vocabulary or input sequences to generate tokens.

3 Summarization Framework

3.1 Knowledge and Keywords Construction

The whole linearized knowledge graph constructing process is presented in Algorithm 1. For $\mathcal{E}$, we use OLLIE (Mausam et al., 2012) to extract triples from English news texts. As few established tools are for open domain Chinese triple extraction, we extract triples from semantic rules using Language Technology Platform (Che et al., 2010). As shown in the algorithm, fact triples in different granularity will be re-extracted until the granularity of the entities and relationships (i.e. remove all attributes and duplicate nouns redundancy) all triples is minimized, and we keep reconstructing the triples to enhance the connectivity of the knowledge graph. We assume each triple e has 3 elements: E_1, R and E_2. The E in $e.E$ denotes E_1 and E_2, which is $\{E_1, E_2\}$. Then all edges (relationships) will be converted to vertices.

We then generate the linearized knowledge graph sequence by a modified DFS algorithm. The DFS is modified on the start vertex selection and priorities of different traversal paths. When traversal starts or the current vertex has more than one path, we select the vertex whose token first appear in the source text as the next. It reduces text redundance effectively and makes the framework focus more on the key logic instead of other irrelevant information.

In order to construct keywords topic sequences, we use TextRank(Mihalcea and Tarau, 2004) algorithm to extract keywords from source text, and make them in the order in which they appears in the original text. This brings priori topic knowledge to the model and makes the model explicitly consider the keywords topic information of the text.

3.2 Architecture

KAS takes as input a news text $\boldsymbol{S} = \{x_i\}$, a keywords topic sequence $\boldsymbol{K} = \{k_i\}$ and a knowledge sequence $\boldsymbol{G} = \{v_i\}$, and let $\mathcal{D} = \{\boldsymbol{S}, \boldsymbol{K}, \boldsymbol{G}\}$. The tri-encoder structure shown in Figure 1 integrates the context of original source text, keywords topic and internal knowledge. The RoBERTa (Liu et al., 2019) is utilized for word embedding pre-training, and we use the outputs of the last RoBERTa layer as the input embedding for all encoders. We build encoders to the generate hidden states $\boldsymbol{h}_t^{\boldsymbol{S}}, \boldsymbol{h}_t^{\boldsymbol{K}}, \boldsymbol{h}_t^{\boldsymbol{G}}$, which is $\boldsymbol{h}_t^{\boldsymbol{x}} = g(\boldsymbol{h}_{t-1}^{\boldsymbol{x}})(\boldsymbol{x} \in \mathcal{D})$, in which function g is a bi-directional LSTM. The hidden states in the final time step of the three encoders, $\boldsymbol{h}_{l_1}^{\boldsymbol{S}}, \boldsymbol{h}_{l_2}^{\boldsymbol{K}}, \boldsymbol{h}_{l_3}^{\boldsymbol{G}}$, should be transformed into the decoder initial state $\boldsymbol{d}_0 = \tanh(\boldsymbol{W}_m \cdot [\boldsymbol{h}_{l_1}^{\boldsymbol{S}} || \boldsymbol{h}_{l_2}^{\boldsymbol{K}} || \boldsymbol{h}_{l_3}^{\boldsymbol{G}}])$.

The attentions of the source text, keywords and knowledge are computed as($\boldsymbol{\alpha}_t^{\boldsymbol{S}}$), ($\boldsymbol{\alpha}_t^{\boldsymbol{K}}$) and ($\boldsymbol{\alpha}_t^{\boldsymbol{G}}$) (Bahdanau et al., 2015). The context vectors are computed as $\boldsymbol{c}_t^{\boldsymbol{x}} = \sum_{i=0}^{t} \alpha_i^{\boldsymbol{x}} \boldsymbol{h}_i^{\boldsymbol{x}}, \quad \boldsymbol{x} \in \mathcal{D}$.

We decode with an attention-based decoder, the decoder hidden state at timestep t $\boldsymbol{d}_t$ is $\boldsymbol{d}_t = f(\boldsymbol{d}_{t-1}, \boldsymbol{c}_{t-1}^{\boldsymbol{S}}, \boldsymbol{c}_{t-1}^{\boldsymbol{K}}, \boldsymbol{c}_{t-1}^{\boldsymbol{G}}, \boldsymbol{y}_{t-1})$, in which $\boldsymbol{d}_{t-1}$ is the decoder hidden state, $\boldsymbol{y}_{t-1}$ is the decoder input, $\boldsymbol{c}_{t-1}^{\boldsymbol{x}}$ are the context vectors. The function f denotes to an unidirectional LSTM.

Hierarchical Attention The salience for the three contexts should be automatically adjusted. Therefore, besides the word-level attention in each encoder, we further utilize a encoder-level hierarchical attention mechanism for ensemble context. We compute the ensemble attention as

$$b^{\boldsymbol{x}} = \boldsymbol{u}^T \tanh(\boldsymbol{W}_{hc}^{\boldsymbol{x}} \boldsymbol{c}_t^{\boldsymbol{x}} + \boldsymbol{W}_{hd}^{\boldsymbol{x}} \boldsymbol{d}_t + \boldsymbol{b}_h^{\boldsymbol{x}})$$

$$\beta^{\boldsymbol{x}} = \text{softmax}(b^{\boldsymbol{x}}), \quad \boldsymbol{x} \in \mathcal{D}$$

$\beta^{\boldsymbol{x}}$ is the hierarchical attention weight of the three contexts in the ensemble context. We then compute the ensemble context $\boldsymbol{c}_t^*$ as

$$\boldsymbol{c}_t^* = \sum_{\boldsymbol{x} \in \mathcal{D}} \beta^{\boldsymbol{x}} \boldsymbol{c}_t^{\boldsymbol{x}}$$

The ensemble context $\boldsymbol{c}_t^*$ is a fixed length vector encoding salient information from the three contexts of the tri-encoder model.

$P_{vocab}(w)$ is calculated by scaling $[\boldsymbol{h}_t || \boldsymbol{c}_t^*]$ to the vocabulary size and taking a softmax:

$$P_{vocab}(w) = \text{softmax}(\boldsymbol{W}_s[\boldsymbol{h}_t || \boldsymbol{c}_t^*] + b_s)$$

To allow $\boldsymbol{W}_s$ to reuse the linguistic in input embedding and decrease the number of parameters, we integrate weight-sharing mechanism (Paulus et al., 2018) in the model as $\boldsymbol{W}_s = \tanh(\boldsymbol{W}_{emb} \cdot \boldsymbol{W}_{sh})$, in which $\boldsymbol{W}_{emb}$ is input embedding matrix.

Tri-Copy Mechanism We compute p_{cpy}, which is overall copy probability and will be distributed to the three encoders:

$$p_{cpy} = \sigma(\boldsymbol{W}_{cpy}[\boldsymbol{h}_t || \boldsymbol{c}_t^*] + \boldsymbol{b}_{cpy})$$

$P_{cpy}(w)$ is distributed to the tri-encoders with soft gates λ_S, λ_K, λ_G. Here, $\lambda_i (i \in \mathcal{D})$ automatically adjust $\boldsymbol{d}_t$, $\boldsymbol{y}_{t-1}$, and the context vector $\boldsymbol{c}_t^i$. We define λ_i as:

$$\lambda_i = \frac{\sigma(\boldsymbol{w}_{di}^T \boldsymbol{d}_t + \boldsymbol{w}_{yi}^T \boldsymbol{y}_{t-1} + \boldsymbol{w}_{ci}^T \boldsymbol{c}_t^i)}{\sum_{\boldsymbol{x}} \sigma(\boldsymbol{w}_{d\boldsymbol{x}}^T \boldsymbol{d}_t + \boldsymbol{w}_{y\boldsymbol{x}}^T \boldsymbol{y}_{t-1} + \boldsymbol{w}_{c\boldsymbol{x}}^T \boldsymbol{c}_t^{\boldsymbol{x}})} \cdot p_{cpy} \qquad (i, \boldsymbol{x} \in \mathcal{D})$$

The training loss can be defined as the the negative log likelihood of the target sequence:

$$\mathcal{L} = -\sum_{t=0}^{T} \log p(y_t = w_t^* | P_{vocab}, \boldsymbol{S}, \boldsymbol{K}, \boldsymbol{G}, y_{<t})$$

in which w_t^* is the target word at step t, T is the length of the target sequence. The multi-copy mechanism can make the model more inclined to generate informative words.

4 Experiments

4.1 Dataset

We use LCSTS dataset (Hu et al., 2015), which contains a training set of 2.4M online Chinese short news texts in Chinese social media SinaWeibo. We choose 725 pairs from the test set with high annotation scores as our test set. Besides, we consider the annotated Gigaword corpus (Rush et al., 2015), which leads to around 3.8M training samples and 1951 test samples for evaluation.

4.2 Experiment Settings

The model is mainly implemented in Tensorflow[2]. In the data preprocess step, we use Jieba[3] for Chinese words segmentation and topic keywords extraction, and LTP(Che et al., 2010) for knowledge extraction. For English we use OLLIE to extract knowledge triples. For our model, we have 512-dimensional hidden states and word embedding. We use a predefined vocabulary of 60k words for

[2]https://www.tensorflow.org/

[3]https://github.com/fxsjy/jieba

Models	RG-1	RG-2	RG-L
PGEN+COV(See et al., 2017)	38.22	25.80	35.46
GLOBAL(Lin et al., 2018)	39.40	26.90	36.50
NCLS(Zhu et al., 2019)	39.71	27.45	37.13
CATT(Duan et al., 2019)	44.35	30.65	40.58
LEXICON(Wan et al., 2020)	42.3	29.8	38.4
KAS			
+Kw	40.74	27.30	36.96
+KG	43.04	30.01	38.82
+KwKG	**44.42**	**31.07**	**40.71**

Table 1: F_1 scores on the LCSTS dataset in terms of the full-length RG-1, RG-2, and RG-L. **Bold** means the best. "+KG" and "+Kw" means the model augmented by knowledge and keywords separately.

Models	RG-1	RG-2	RG-L
SEASS(Zhou et al., 2017)	36.15	17.54	33.63
GLOBAL(Lin et al., 2018)	36.30	18.00	33.80
GENPARSE(Song et al., 2020)	36.61	18.85	34.33
CPDS(Wang et al., 2019)	37.01	17.10	34.87
KAS			
+Kw	36.74	17.51	33.73
+KG	37.01	18.02	34.47
+KwKG	**37.46**	**18.89**	**35.01**

Table 2: F_1 scores on the Gigaword dataset in terms of the full-length RG-1, RG-2, and RG-L. **Bold** means the best.

Case Study

ST: 中石化计划推进下游油品销售业务的产权重整，被誉为央企发展混合所有制、打破垄断的一大突破。民企老板直言，如不放开加油站的油源垄断，股权层面出让部分空间的意义有限：“不解决油源，让民资参股只是个花活。”

ST: Sinopec plans to promote the property right reorganization of downstream oil sales business, which is known as a breakthrough for central enterprises to develop mixed ownership and break monopoly. The private enterprise boss said frankly that if the monopoly of oil sources in gas stations is not released, the significance of transferring part of the space at the equity level is limited: "it's meaningless to let private capital participate in the shares without solving the problem of oil source."

Ref: 民营油企负责人：不解决油源让民资参股只是个花活

Ref: Private oil enterprises boss: it's meaningless to let private capital participate in shares without solving the problem of oil sources

+Kw: 民企老板：让民资参股只是个花活

+Kw: Private oil enterprise boss: it's meaningless to let private capital participate in shares .

+KwKG: 民企老板炮轰中石化计划：不解决油源让民资参股只是个花活

+KwKG: Private oil enterprise boss bombards Sinopec plan: it's meaningless to let private capital participate in shares without solving the problem of oil sources.

Figure 2: A case study on the LCSTS dataset. **ST** is source text; **Ref** is reference summary; **+Kw** is keywords augmented; **+KwKG** is keywords and knowledge augmented.

Models	Inf.↑	Flu.↑	Div.↑	HE.↓	LE.↓
PGEN+COV	2.92	3.43	3.52	18%	35%
KAS					
+Kw	2.97	3.92*	3.47	10%	31%
+KwKG	3.82*	4.47*	4.15*	**3%***	12%*
HUMAN	**4.30**	**4.63**	**4.48**	17%	**2%**

Table 3: Human evaluation on informativeness (Inf.), fluency (Flu.) and diversity (Div.) (1-to-5), and hallucination error(HE.) and logical error (LE.) (0-to-1). **Bold** are the bests. ⋆ : Significantly different from all other models. ($p < 0.05$)

both source and target in word-level inputs. Adagrad optimizer is used with learning rate 0.15 and an initial accumulator value of 0.1. All models are trained on a single NVIDIA RTX 2080 Ti GPU, with a batch size of 64 on inputs.

4.3 Automatic and Human Evaluation

The model is evaluated with the standard ROUGE metric (Lin, 2004), shown in Table 1 and 2. We use the F_1 scores for ROUGE-1, ROUGE-2 and ROUGE-L.

Besides the automatic evaluation, we further conduct human evaluation for the framework. We randomly sample 100 articles from LCSTS test set and ask 3 Chinese native speakers to rate summaries of our systems and the baseline (PGEN+COV), along with outputs by human-written summaries. After reading the articles, each judge scores summaries on a Likert scale from 1 (worst) to 5 (best) on (1)*informativeness* and (2)*fluency*. Besides, in the experiment we noticed that the outputs of KAS are more diversified and attractive to readers, so we test (3)*diversity*: whether the summary arouses annotators' reading interest. We consider two types of unfaithful errors: (i) *hallucination error* and (ii) *logical error*. We ask the annotators to label each type as 1 for existence of errors and 0 otherwise.

4.4 Analysis

The automatic evaluation scores show that KAS achieves bests on LCSTS and Gigaword. The Table 3 shows that KAS augmented by both keywords topic and knowledge achieves the best results in all indicators, with significant enhancements.

A case study on LCSTS is shown in Figure 2. The words marked green are the key information of the sentence, and the words marked blue are the diversified and eye-catching words generated by KwKG model, which is augmented by both keywords and knowledge. We can see that the model only augmented by keywords (+Kw) mistakenly ignored some key points in the sentence, while the KwKG model contains all summary points.

Further, we find that diversity indicator of summaries is enhanced significantly, which is reflected in Table 3. Specifically, in the experiment we found the KwKG model may usually generate diversified words, as showed in the figure (marked blue). As LCSTS is a dataset of social media news in an eye-catching style, we speculate while the knowledge structure may enhance the understanding ability of the framework, it can implicitly enhance the memory of the writing styles of the training set.

5 Conclusion

In this work, we propose KAS, an abstractive summarization framework augmented by knowledge and topic keywords that supports multiple languages. Experimental results show that KAS generates more qualified summaries and achieves the best performances. In the future, we aim at enhancing attractiveness of sentence summarization based on our structure.

Acknowledgments

This work was partially supported by CIMS, and partially supported by National Natural Science Foundation of China (No.61976160).

References

Uri Alon and Eran Yahav. 2021. On the bottleneck of graph neural networks and its practical implications. In *9th International Conference on Learning Representations, ICLR 2021, Virtual Event, Austria, May 3-7, 2021*.

Dzmitry Bahdanau, Kyunghyun Cho, and Yoshua Bengio. 2015. Neural machine translation by jointly learning to align and translate. In *3rd International Conference on Learning Representations, ICLR 2015, San Diego, CA, USA, May 7-9, 2015, Conference Track Proceedings*.

Wanxiang Che, Zhenghua Li, and Ting Liu. 2010. LTP: A Chinese language technology platform. In *Coling 2010: Demonstrations*, pages 13–16, Beijing, China. Coling 2010 Organizing Committee.

Xiangyu Duan, Hongfei Yu, Mingming Yin, Min Zhang, Weihua Luo, and Yue Zhang. 2019. Contrastive attention mechanism for abstractive sentence summarization. In *Proceedings of the 2019 Conference on Empirical Methods in Natural Language Processing and the 9th International Joint Conference on Natural Language Processing (EMNLP-IJCNLP)*, pages 3044–3053, Hong Kong, China. Association for Computational Linguistics.

Mihail Eric and Christopher Manning. 2017. A copy-augmented sequence-to-sequence architecture gives good performance on task-oriented dialogue. In *Proceedings of the 15th Conference of the European Chapter of the Association for Computational Linguistics: Volume 2, Short Papers*, pages 468–473, Valencia, Spain. Association for Computational Linguistics.

Angela Fan, Claire Gardent, Chloé Braud, and Antoine Bordes. 2019. Using local knowledge graph construction to scale Seq2Seq models to multi-document inputs. In *Proceedings of the 2019 Conference on Empirical Methods in Natural Language Processing and the 9th International Joint Conference on Natural Language Processing (EMNLP-IJCNLP)*, pages 4186–4196, Hong Kong, China. Association for Computational Linguistics.

Caglar Gulcehre, Sungjin Ahn, Ramesh Nallapati, Bowen Zhou, and Yoshua Bengio. 2016. Pointing the unknown words. In *Proceedings of the 54th Annual Meeting of the Association for Computational Linguistics (Volume 1: Long Papers)*, pages 140–149, Berlin, Germany. Association for Computational Linguistics.

Baotian Hu, Qingcai Chen, and Fangze Zhu. 2015. LCSTS: A large scale Chinese short text summarization dataset. In *Proceedings of the 2015 Conference on Empirical Methods in Natural Language Processing*, pages 1967–1972, Lisbon, Portugal. Association for Computational Linguistics.

Luyang Huang, Lingfei Wu, and Lu Wang. 2020. Knowledge graph-augmented abstractive summarization with semantic-driven cloze reward. In *Proceedings of the 58th Annual Meeting of the Association for Computational Linguistics*, pages 5094–5107, Online. Association for Computational Linguistics.

Thomas N. Kipf and Max Welling. 2017. Semi-Supervised Classification with Graph Convolutional Networks. In *Proceedings of the 5th International Conference on Learning Representations*, ICLR '17.

Rik Koncel-Kedziorski, Dhanush Bekal, Yi Luan, Mirella Lapata, and Hannaneh Hajishirzi. 2019. Text Generation from Knowledge Graphs with Graph Transformers. In *Proceedings of the 2019 Conference of the North American Chapter of the Association for Computational Linguistics: Human Language Technologies, Volume 1 (Long and Short Papers)*, pages 2284–2293, Minneapolis, Minnesota. Association for Computational Linguistics.

Ioannis Konstas, Srinivasan Iyer, Mark Yatskar, Yejin Choi, and Luke Zettlemoyer. 2017. Neural AMR: Sequence-to-sequence models for parsing and generation. In *Proceedings of the 55th Annual Meeting of the Association for Computational Linguistics (Volume 1: Long Papers)*, pages 146–157, Vancouver, Canada. Association for Computational Linguistics.

Chin-Yew Lin. 2004. ROUGE: A package for automatic evaluation of summaries. In *Text Summarization Branches Out*, pages 74–81, Barcelona, Spain. Association for Computational Linguistics.

Junyang Lin, Xu Sun, Shuming Ma, and Qi Su. 2018. Global encoding for abstractive summarization. In *Proceedings of the 56th Annual Meeting of the Association for Computational Linguistics (Volume 2: Short Papers)*, pages 163–169, Melbourne, Australia. Association for Computational Linguistics.

Yinhan Liu, Myle Ott, Naman Goyal, Jingfei Du, Mandar Joshi, Danqi Chen, Omer Levy, Mike Lewis, Luke Zettlemoyer, and Veselin Stoyanov. 2019. Roberta: A robustly optimized bert pretraining approach. *arXiv e-prints*, arXiv:1907.11692.

Mausam, Michael Schmitz, Stephen Soderland, Robert Bart, and Oren Etzioni. 2012. Open language learning for information extraction. In *Proceedings of the 2012 Joint Conference on Empirical Methods in Natural Language Processing and Computational Natural Language Learning*, pages 523–534, Jeju Island, Korea. Association for Computational Linguistics.

Yishu Miao and Phil Blunsom. 2016. Language as a latent variable: Discrete generative models for sentence compression. In *Proceedings of the 2016 Conference on Empirical Methods in Natural Language Processing*, pages 319–328, Austin, Texas. Association for Computational Linguistics.

Rada Mihalcea and Paul Tarau. 2004. TextRank: Bringing order into text. In *Proceedings of the 2004 Conference on Empirical Methods in Natural Language Processing*, pages 404–411, Barcelona, Spain. Association for Computational Linguistics.

Ramesh Nallapati, Bowen Zhou, Cicero dos Santos, Çağlar Gulçehre, and Bing Xiang. 2016. Abstractive text summarization using sequence-to-sequence RNNs and beyond. In *Proceedings of The 20th SIGNLL Conference on Computational Natural Language Learning*, pages 280–290, Berlin, Germany. Association for Computational Linguistics.

Romain Paulus, Caiming Xiong, and Richard Socher. 2018. A deep reinforced model for abstractive summarization. In *International Conference on Learning Representations*.

Leonardo F. R. Ribeiro, Yue Zhang, Claire Gardent, and Iryna Gurevych. 2020. Modeling global and local node contexts for text generation from knowledge graphs. *Transactions of the Association for Computational Linguistics*, 8:589–604.

Alexander M. Rush, Sumit Chopra, and Jason Weston. 2015. A neural attention model for abstractive sentence summarization. In *Proceedings of the 2015 Conference on Empirical Methods in Natural Language Processing*, pages 379–389, Lisbon, Portugal. Association for Computational Linguistics.

Abigail See, Peter J. Liu, and Christopher D. Manning. 2017. Get to the point: Summarization with pointer-generator networks. In *Proceedings of the 55th Annual Meeting of the Association for Computational Linguistics (Volume 1: Long Papers)*, pages 1073–1083, Vancouver, Canada. Association for Computational Linguistics.

Kaiqiang Song, Logan Lebanoff, Qipeng Guo, Xipeng Qiu, Xiangyang Xue, Chen Li, Dong Yu, and Fei Liu. 2020. Joint parsing and generation for abstractive summarization. In *The Thirty-Fourth AAAI Conference on Artificial Intelligence, AAAI 2020, The Thirty-Second Innovative Applications of Artificial Intelligence Conference, IAAI 2020, The Tenth AAAI Symposium on Educational Advances in Artificial Intelligence, EAAI 2020, New York, NY, USA, February 7-12, 2020*, pages 8894–8901. AAAI Press.

Fei Sun, Peng Jiang, Hanxiao Sun, Changhua Pei, Wenwu Ou, and Xiaobo Wang. 2018. Multi-source pointer network for product title summarization. In *Proceedings of the 27th ACM International Conference on Information and Knowledge Management*, CIKM '18, pages 7–16, New York, NY, USA. Association for Computing Machinery.

Petar Veličković, Guillem Cucurull, Arantxa Casanova, Adriana Romero, Pietro Lió, and Yoshua Bengio. 2018. Graph attention networks. In *International Conference on Learning Representations*.

Boyan Wan, Zhuo Tang, and Li Yang. 2020. Lexicon-constrained copying network for chinese abstractive summarization. *CoRR*, abs/2010.08197.

Wenbo Wang, Yang Gao, Heyan Huang, and Yuxiang Zhou. 2019. Concept pointer network for abstractive summarization. In *Proceedings of the 2019 Conference on Empirical Methods in Natural Language Processing and the 9th International Joint Conference on Natural Language Processing (EMNLP-IJCNLP)*, pages 3076–3085, Hong Kong, China. Association for Computational Linguistics.

Qingyu Zhou, Nan Yang, Furu Wei, and Ming Zhou. 2017. Selective encoding for abstractive sentence summarization. In *Proceedings of the 55th Annual Meeting of the Association for Computational Linguistics (Volume 1: Long Papers)*, pages 1095–1104, Vancouver, Canada. Association for Computational Linguistics.

Junnan Zhu, Qian Wang, Yining Wang, Yu Zhou, Jiajun Zhang, Shaonan Wang, and Chengqing Zong. 2019. NCLS: Neural cross-lingual summarization. In *Proceedings of the 2019 Conference on Empirical Methods in Natural Language Processing and the 9th International Joint Conference on Natural Language Processing (EMNLP-IJCNLP)*, pages 3054–3064, Hong Kong, China. Association for Computational Linguistics.

Appendices

A Details of Human Evaluation

Here we show the details of the indicators in human evaluation.

Informativeness It is the indicator reflecting whether the generated summary covers all important information points in the input text.

Fluency The indicator reflecting whether the summary is grammatically correct, clear and coherent.

Diversity The indicator reflecting whether the summary arouses annotators' reading interest(which is a key quality indicator of social media news summaries).

Logical Error The error for model of generating summaries whose logic structures contradicting with which in the original text (such as summarizing "A is B's dog" as "B is A's dog").

Hallucination Error The error for model of generating summaries containing the facts that are not in or cannot be inferred from original text.

B Case Study

For details and case study, we randomly pick an example of generated summaries in Figure 2. The original examples (in Chinese) are shown and all the texts are carefully translated into English for reading convenience. The words marked in green are key information points in original text, and the words marked in blue are diversified phrase. The examples demonstrate that the combination of knowledge graphs and keywords sequence can increase logicality and diversity in Chinese summarization tasks.

Examples of summary

ST: 中石化计划推进下游油品销售业务的产权重整，被誉为央企发展混合所有制、打破垄断的一大突破。民企老板直言，如不放开加油站的油源垄断，股权层面出让部分空间的意义有限："不解决油源，让民资参股只是个花活。"

ST: Sinopec plans to promote the property right reorganization of downstream oil sales business, which is known as a breakthrough for central enterprises to develop mixed ownership and break monopoly. The private enterprise boss said frankly that if the monopoly of oil sources in gas stations is not released, the significance of transferring part of the space at the equity level is limited: "it's meaningless to let private capital participate in the shares without solving the problem of oil source."

Ref: 民营油企负责人：不解决油源让民资参股只是个花活

Ref: Private oil enterprises boss: it's meaningless to let private capital participate in shares without solving the problem of oil sources

+Kw: 民企老板：让民资参股只是个花活

+Kw: Private oil enterprise boss: it's meaningless to let private capital participate in shares

+KwKG: 民企老板炮轰中石化计划：不解决油源让民资参股只是个花活

+KwKG: Private oil enterprise boss bombards Sinopec plan: it's meaningless to let private capital participate in shares without solving the problem of oil sources

ST: 教育部要求每所学校、幼儿园都要制订防止餐桌浪费的具体办法，提倡小份多次管饱的文明用餐方式。各地中小学还要开展餐饮消费、办公用纸、家庭用水等情况的社会调查，到节粮、节水、环保等方面的社会实践基地参与体验活动。

ST: The Ministry of education requires schools and kindergartens to formulate specific measures to prevent table waste, and to promote the civilized way of eating with small portions and full meals for many times. Primary and secondary schools around the country also need to carry out social surveys on catering consumption, office paper and household water consumption, and participate in experience activities in social practice bases of grain saving, water saving and environmental protection.

Ref: 关于在中小学幼儿园广泛深入开展节约教育的意见

Ref: Opinions on extensive and in-depth development of thrift education in primary and secondary school kindergartens

+Kw: 教育部：学校要制订防止餐桌浪费的具体办法

+Kw: Ministry of Education: schools should formulate specific measures to prevent table waste

+KwKG: 教育部要求:学校引导学生勤俭节约

+KwKG: Requirements of the Ministry of Education: schools guide students to be diligent and thrifty

Figure 3: An example of generated summaries on the LCSTS dataset. **ST** is source text; **Ref** is reference summary; **+Kw** is keywords topic augmented; **+KwKG** is keywords topic and knowledge augmented.

Rewards with Negative Examples for Reinforced Topic-Focused Abstractive Summarization

Khalil Mrini
University of California, San Diego
La Jolla, CA 92093
khalil@ucsd.edu

Can Liu
Amazon Alexa
Seattle, WA 98101
liuca@amazon.com

Markus Dreyer
Amazon Alexa
Seattle, WA 98101
mddreyer@amazon.com

Abstract

We consider the problem of topic-focused abstractive summarization, where the goal is to generate an abstractive summary focused on a particular topic, a phrase of one or multiple words. We hypothesize that the task of generating topic-focused summaries can be improved by showing the model what it must *not* focus on. We introduce a deep reinforcement learning approach to topic-focused abstractive summarization, trained on rewards with a novel negative example baseline. We define the input in this problem as the source text preceded by the topic. We adapt the CNN-Daily Mail and New York Times summarization datasets for this task. We then show through experiments on existing rewards that the use of a negative example baseline can outperform the use of a self-critical baseline, in ROUGE, BERTSCORE, and human evaluation metrics.

1 Introduction

Topic-focused summarization is the task of generating a summary given a source text and a specific query or topic. Approaches to topic-focused summarization include query relevance and importance (Gupta et al., 2007), multi-modality manifold ranking (Wan et al., 2007; Wan, 2008; Wan and Xiao, 2009), and query attention (Nema et al., 2017). The DUC 2005 and 2006 datasets (Dang, 2005, 2006) are examples of datasets that are widely used for this task. These datasets are much smaller than benchmark datasets for generic summarization, resulting in fewer research work to train topic-focused summarization on state-of-the-art systems (Deutsch and Roth, 2019).

In parallel, there has been growing work in recent years on reinforcement learning approaches to (generic) abstractive summarization. Proposed rewards aim to optimize non-differentiable summarization metrics like ROUGE (Lin, 2004) and BERTSCORE (Zhang et al., 2019), or to encourage desirable summary aspects like semantic cohesion (Celikyilmaz et al., 2018) and entity coherence (Sharma et al., 2019). Many reinforced abstractive summarization methods use the self-critical baseline or SCST (Rennie et al., 2017) to cap their rewards. This self-critical baseline is obtained by greedily searching for a sequence that maximizes the likelihood probability of the current model.

In this work, we propose a reinforcement learning-based approach to topic-focused summarization. First, we adapt widely used generic summarization benchmarks to this task, such that we aim to generate only one out of three summary sentences, given a corresponding topic. Then, instead of using the self-critical baseline, we introduce a novel baseline that uses negative examples: a sentence that contains information that the summarization model should *not* focus on.

We run experiments on two existing generic summarization datasets adapted to our task: CNN-Daily Mail (Hermann et al., 2015; Nallapati et al., 2017) and New York Times (Sandhaus, 2008). Our experiments span two existing rewards: the popular ROUGE-L reward and the Distributed Semantic Reward (DSR) of Li et al. (2019), inspired by BERTSCORE (Zhang et al., 2019). Our results show that using our negative example baseline outperforms the self-critical baseline across both datasets and both rewards. We obtain improvements on both datasets in ROUGE and BERTSCORE metrics, and human annotators find that summaries generated with our negative baseline for rewards are generally more relevant to the given topic.

2 Related Work

2.1 Topic-Focused Summarization

There are different definitions of topic-focused summarization. The DUC datasets (Dang, 2005, 2006) propose summarization of documents given a question, also called a query. Vanderwende

Proceedings of the Third Workshop on New Frontiers in Summarization, pages 33–38
November 10, 2021.

et al. (2007) propose SumFocus, a system for topic-focused multi-document extractive summarization. SumFocus is comprised of four components: a generic extractive summarization system, a topic-focusing component, sentence simplification, and lexical expansion of topic words.

Deutsch and Roth (2019) define the task of *summary cloze* as the problem of deciding which content to select in topic-focused summarization, given a context (partial summary). They propose a neural model with separate encoders for the topic and the partial summary.

2.2 Reinforcement Learning for Summarization

There is a growing body of work that use reinforcement learning (RL) methods to optimize non-differentiable rewards. ROUGE scores remain a popular RL reward. Other rewards include sentence selection to improve ROUGE scores (Chen and Bansal, 2018; Pasunuru and Bansal, 2018), optimizing question answering metrics (Scialom et al., 2019), and adding desirable custom features to generated summaries (Böhm et al., 2019; Sharma et al., 2019).

Li et al. (2019) find that rewards based on BERTSCORE (Zhang et al., 2019) and ROUGE each optimize their own metric, but decrease the other one.

Wang et al. (2018) introduce a topic-aware reinforced summarization model. The authors experiment with generic – not topic-focused – summarization datasets, and infer topics using LDA (Blei et al., 2003). Information about the topics is then infused into the model using a topic-aware attention mechanism and topic embeddings.

Whereas a few (Narayan et al., 2018; Li et al., 2018) use the REINFORCE algorithm (Williams, 1992), many RL-based summarization approaches (Paulus et al., 2018; Pasunuru and Bansal, 2018; Li et al., 2018; Celikyilmaz et al., 2018; Yang et al., 2018; Li et al., 2019) use the self-critical sequence training approach (SCST) (Rennie et al., 2017).

3 Problem Statement

We tackle the task of topic-focused abstractive summarization as the problem of producing an abstractive summary focused on a given topic, a phrase of one or multiple words. The generated summary should include information from the input text that is related to the topic, and exclude all other information. Consequently, different topics with the same input text should yield different summaries.

More formally, given an input text $\mathbf{x}$, a topic $\mathbf{t}$ and a corresponding reference summary $\mathbf{y}$, we aim to maximize the probability that we generate the right summary:

$$p(\mathbf{y}|\mathbf{x},\mathbf{t}) > p(\mathbf{y}'|\mathbf{x},\mathbf{t}) \quad (1)$$

for all $\mathbf{y}' \neq \mathbf{y}$.

4 Rewards with a Negative Example

In self-critical sequence learning (Rennie et al., 2017; Wang et al., 2018), the RL loss formula is as follows for our task:

$$\mathcal{L}_{\text{RL}} = -\left(r(\mathbf{y}^s) - b\right) \sum_{i=1}^{N} \log P(y_i^s | y_1^s, ..., y_{i-1}^s, \mathbf{x}, \mathbf{t}) \quad (2)$$

where b is the RL baseline, and $b = r(\hat{\mathbf{y}})$ in self-critical sequence learning. $\mathbf{y}^s$ is a sampled summary, and $\hat{\mathbf{y}}$ is a summary obtained greedily by maximizing the probability of the overall sequence.

In our particular task, we propose to use a baseline with a negative example. The intuition is that we encourage the model to generate summaries that are more similar to the reference summary than the negative example. This negative example is an independent sentence from the summary of the corresponding source text, but which does not contain the topic. The negative example acts as a sample of undesirable information, and helps the summarization model learn what kind of information to exclude.

Given a reference summary $\mathbf{y}$, and a negative summary $\bar{\mathbf{y}}$, our RL loss with negative examples is defined as in equation 2, where we define the RL baseline: $b = r(\bar{\mathbf{y}})$.

4.1 Rewards

We apply our method on two popular rewards for summarization: rewards based on the ROUGE and BERTSCORE metrics between the sampled summary and the reference summary.

ROUGE-L reward. Given a sampled summary $\mathbf{y}^\mathbf{s}$ and a reference summary $\mathbf{y}$, we define the ROUGE-L reward as follows:

$$r_{\mathbf{R}}(\mathbf{y}^\mathbf{s}) = \text{ROUGE}(\mathbf{y}^\mathbf{s}, \mathbf{y}) \quad (3)$$

BERTSCORE Reward. We adopt the Distributed Semantic Reward (DSR) definition of Li et al.

(2019). This reward measures the semantic similarity with the reference summary. It is defined as follows:

$$r_{\mathrm{s}}(\mathbf{y}^{\mathrm{s}}) = \mathrm{F_{BERT}}(\mathbf{y}^{\mathrm{s}}, \mathbf{y}) \tag{4}$$

where $\mathrm{F_{BERT}}$ is the F1 formula of BERTScore (Zhang et al., 2019). It is defined as:

$$\mathrm{F_{BERT}} = 2 * \frac{\mathrm{P_{BERT}} * \mathrm{R_{BERT}}}{\mathrm{P_{BERT}} + \mathrm{R_{BERT}}} \tag{5}$$

where the precision $\mathrm{P_{BERT}}$ and recall $\mathrm{R_{BERT}}$ are defined as follows for a given reference y and candidate y':

$$\mathrm{P_{BERT}} = \frac{1}{|y'|} \sum_{\hat{x}_j \in y'} \max_{x_i \in y} \mathbf{x}_i^{\top} \hat{\mathbf{x}}_j \tag{6}$$

$$\mathrm{R_{BERT}} = \frac{1}{|y|} \sum_{x_i \in y} \max_{\hat{x}_j \in y'} \mathbf{x}_i^{\top} \hat{\mathbf{x}}_j \tag{7}$$

4.2 Loss Formula

Whereas Pasunuru and Bansal (2018) train by alternating multiple rewards, Li et al. (2019) propose a single loss formula combining DSR and ROUGE rewards. However, their results show that combining DSR and ROUGE does not yield better results in either ROUGE or $\mathrm{F_{BERT}}$ scores, compared to using only one reward at a time, along with the summarization loss. We decide to also use only one reward at a time.

We aim to optimize the following loss function:

$$\begin{aligned}\mathcal{L} = &-(1-\gamma) * \log p(\mathbf{y}|\mathbf{x}, \mathbf{t}) \\ &+\gamma * \mathcal{L}_{\mathrm{RL-N}}(\mathbf{y}^{\mathrm{s}}, \mathbf{y}, \bar{\mathbf{y}})\end{aligned} \tag{8}$$

where γ is a hyperparameter, and the first term is the negative log-likelihood loss with the reference summary as the target.

5 Experiments and Results

5.1 Datasets

In our experiments, we use two popular summarization benchmarks: the non-anoymized CNN-Daily Mail dataset (Hermann et al., 2015; Nallapati et al., 2017) and the New York Times (NYT) dataset (Sandhaus, 2008).

In the CNN-Daily Mail dataset, summaries are usually 3 independent sentences, corresponding to the "highlights" at the top of the article on the original website. We consider each sentence separately as a reference summary, thereby creating on average 3 datapoints from 1 datapoint in the original dataset.

DATASET	SET	# DATAPOINTS
CNN-Daily Mail	Train	748,170
	Dev	20,705
	Test	31,815
NYT	Train	139,497
	Dev	9,911
	Test	16,021

Table 1: Statistics for our focused version of the CNN-Daily Mail and NYT datasets.

We filter the large NYT dataset to only get articles with 3-sentence summaries. Similarly to the CNN-Daily Mail dataset, summary sentences are independent, making them fit for topic-focused abstractive summarization.

We use TopicRank (Bougouin et al., 2013), a keyphrase extraction algorithm, to get the 10 most popular keyphrases of the input text. Out of these 10 keyphrases, we pick the highest-scoring one which only appears in the specific summary sentence $\mathbf{y}_i$ to be the topic of $\mathbf{y}_i$. We consider one of the other reference summary sentences of the same input text as the negative example. Therefore, each datapoint in our version of the datasets contains an input text, a reference summary, a negative summary, and a topic. We make sure that no same input text (article) appears in more than one data split. We show the statistics of the dataset used in Table 1.

5.2 Training Details

We set $\gamma = 0.9984$ following Paulus et al. (2018) to balance the magnitude difference. We adopt the BART Large architecture (Lewis et al., 2019) as it set a state of the art in the generic summarization of the CNN-Daily Mail dataset, among other tasks. We use a learning rate of $3e-5$. We start training from the best model trained on the cross-entropy objective only, on our topic-focused summarization datasets.

We prepend the topic and a separator token to the input text of each datapoint. As the average reference summary is shorter (on average 13 tokens), we set the length of generated summaries at test time between 10 and 20 tokens.

DATASET		CNN-DAILY MAIL				NEW YORK TIMES			
METRIC		R1 F1	R2 F1	RL F1	F_{BERT}	R1 F1	R2 F1	RL F1	F_{BERT}
EXTRACTIVE SUMMARIZATION BASELINE MODELS									
Lead-1		19.94	6.54	16.33	69.08	22.22	9.89	18.44	69.48
BM25		22.92	9.71	19.79	69.95	30.38	15.80	26.45	73.23
SumFocus		32.08	15.82	28.14	73.92	29.00	14.64	25.27	72.86
Oracle-1		47.52	29.85	44.10	79.47	53.34	36.15	49.49	80.64
NEURAL ABSTRACTIVE SUMMARIZATION MODELS									
REWARD	RL b								
None	–	38.88	21.91	35.10	76.71	45.84	30.93	40.83	79.32
ROUGE	Self-critical	39.64	22.78	37.10	74.82	46.52	32.43	42.49	77.69
ROUGE	Negative (Ours)	**39.97**	**23.22**	**37.87**	74.12	**47.02**	**32.87**	**43.12**	78.03
BERTSCORE	Self-critical	39.10	21.83	36.77	77.34	45.67	31.62	41.70	79.93
BERTSCORE	Negative (Ours)	39.38	22.41	37.29	**77.65**	45.51	31.25	41.57	**80.35**

Table 2: Summarization experiment results on the test sets with the ROUGE and BERTSCORE rewards. The model with no reward is a summarizer model trained only on the cross-entropy objective.

DATASET		CNN-DAILY MAIL			NEW YORK TIMES		
REWARD	CRITERIA	Negative	Self-Critical	Tie	Negative	Self-Critical	Tie
ROUGE	Relevance to Topic	25	21	34	21	14	45
	Fluency	17	21	42	14	12	54
BERTSCORE	Relevance to Topic	19	15	46	22	18	40
	Fluency	16	11	51	18	15	47

Table 3: Human evaluation ratings of two annotators on 40 sampled summaries from each dataset, comparing reinforced summarization models trained with the negative baseline (ours) vs. the self-critical baseline.

5.3 Baseline Models

We train four extractive baseline models and three abstractive summarization baseline models.

The four extractive baseline models are common summarization baselines, that are meant to give an idea about the difficulty of the task. The first baseline model is **Lead-1**, which chooses the first sentence from the source article as the generated summary. The second baseline model is **BM25** (Robertson et al., 1995), an IR-based score to rank search results given the query. In our case, BM25 ranks sentences of the source article given the topic, and outputs the most relevant sentence as the generated summary. The third baseline model is **SumFocus** (Vanderwende et al., 2007), an unsupervised probabilistic model for topic-focused summarization. The fourth baseline is **Oracle-1**, which greedily searches for the sentence with the highest ROUGE score with the reference summary. This baseline model is meant as an upper-bound for extractive summarization models.

We experiment with three abstractive summarization baseline models that use BART Large. The first baseline model is trained on cross-entropy only. The second and third baseline models are trained with the **ROUGE** and **BERTSCORE** (DSR) rewards respectively, with the self-critical method.

5.4 Results and Discussion

We show the results of our experiments in Tables 2. Our proposed approach outperforms the cross-entropy-only BART baseline, but also the two self-critical approaches across both datasets. This shows that negative examples are a good reward baseline in topic-focused summarization. We notice a significant jump in performance in ROUGE-L F1 especially (about 2.5 points), and an increase in ROUGE-1 and ROUGE-2 as well, compared to the cross-entropy-only baseline. Our BERTSCORE-rewarded model achieves the highest F_{BERT} scores, with a slight increase from its self-critical counterpart.

We hire two annotators to judge the fluency and topic relevance of the 40 sampled summary pairs, and therefore get 80 evaluations for each criterion. We ask the two annotators to compare our models with their self-critical counterparts. The annotators are not informed about which model generated which summary. Results in Table 3 show that our model's summaries are generally more relevant to the topic, and that our BERTScore models are more fluent.

6 Conclusions

We propose a deep reinforcement learning approach to topic-focused abstractive summarization, where we aim to generate summaries focused on a given phrase of one or multiple words. We introduce a new baseline for rewards, based on negative examples collected from independent summary sentences. We show through experiments that our proposed approach outperforms the baseline of self-critical reinforcement learning in the optimized reward metric, and human annotators find our model generates summaries that are more relevant to the topic.

References

David M Blei, Andrew Y Ng, and Michael I Jordan. 2003. Latent dirichlet allocation. *the Journal of machine Learning research*, 3:993–1022.

Florian Böhm, Yang Gao, Christian M Meyer, Ori Shapira, Ido Dagan, and Iryna Gurevych. 2019. Better rewards yield better summaries: Learning to summarise without references. In *Proceedings of the 2019 Conference on Empirical Methods in Natural Language Processing and the 9th International Joint Conference on Natural Language Processing (EMNLP-IJCNLP)*, pages 3101–3111.

Adrien Bougouin, Florian Boudin, and Béatrice Daille. 2013. Topicrank: Graph-based topic ranking for keyphrase extraction.

Asli Celikyilmaz, Antoine Bosselut, Xiaodong He, and Yejin Choi. 2018. Deep communicating agents for abstractive summarization. In *Proceedings of the 2018 Conference of the North American Chapter of the Association for Computational Linguistics: Human Language Technologies, Volume 1 (Long Papers)*, pages 1662–1675.

Yen-Chun Chen and Mohit Bansal. 2018. Fast abstractive summarization with reinforce-selected sentence rewriting. In *Proceedings of the 56th Annual Meeting of the Association for Computational Linguistics (Volume 1: Long Papers)*, pages 675–686.

Hoa Trang Dang. 2005. Overview of duc 2005. In *Proceedings of the document understanding conference*, pages 1–12.

Hoa Trang Dang. 2006. Overview of duc 2006. In *Proceedings of the document understanding conference.*

Daniel Deutsch and Dan Roth. 2019. Summary cloze: A new task for content selection in topic-focused summarization. In *Proceedings of the 2019 Conference on Empirical Methods in Natural Language Processing and the 9th International Joint Conference on Natural Language Processing (EMNLP-IJCNLP)*, pages 3711–3720.

Surabhi Gupta, Ani Nenkova, and Dan Jurafsky. 2007. Measuring importance and query relevance in topic-focused multi-document summarization. In *Proceedings of the 45th Annual Meeting of the Association for Computational Linguistics Companion Volume Proceedings of the Demo and Poster Sessions*, pages 193–196.

Karl Moritz Hermann, Tomas Kocisky, Edward Grefenstette, Lasse Espeholt, Will Kay, Mustafa Suleyman, and Phil Blunsom. 2015. Teaching machines to read and comprehend. In *Advances in neural information processing systems*, pages 1693–1701.

Mike Lewis, Yinhan Liu, Naman Goyal, Marjan Ghazvininejad, Abdelrahman Mohamed, Omer Levy, Ves Stoyanov, and Luke Zettlemoyer. 2019. Bart: Denoising sequence-to-sequence pre-training for natural language generation, translation, and comprehension. *arXiv preprint arXiv:1910.13461.*

Piji Li, Lidong Bing, and Wai Lam. 2018. Actor-critic based training framework for abstractive summarization. *arXiv preprint arXiv:1803.11070.*

Siyao Li, Deren Lei, Pengda Qin, and William Yang Wang. 2019. Deep reinforcement learning with distributional semantic rewards for abstractive summarization. In *Proceedings of the 2019 Conference on Empirical Methods in Natural Language Processing and the 9th International Joint Conference on Natural Language Processing (EMNLP-IJCNLP)*, pages 6038–6044, Hong Kong, China. Association for Computational Linguistics.

Chin-Yew Lin. 2004. Rouge: A package for automatic evaluation of summaries. In *Text summarization branches out*, pages 74–81.

Ramesh Nallapati, Feifei Zhai, and Bowen Zhou. 2017. Summarunner: a recurrent neural network based sequence model for extractive summarization of documents. In *Proceedings of the Thirty-First AAAI Conference on Artificial Intelligence*, pages 3075–3081.

Shashi Narayan, Shay B Cohen, and Mirella Lapata. 2018. Ranking sentences for extractive summarization with reinforcement learning. In *Proceedings of the 2018 Conference of the North American Chapter of the Association for Computational Linguistics: Human Language Technologies, Volume 1 (Long Papers)*, pages 1747–1759.

Preksha Nema, Mitesh M Khapra, Anirban Laha, and Balaraman Ravindran. 2017. Diversity driven attention model for query-based abstractive summarization. In *Proceedings of the 55th Annual Meeting of the Association for Computational Linguistics (Volume 1: Long Papers)*, pages 1063–1072.

Ramakanth Pasunuru and Mohit Bansal. 2018. Multi-reward reinforced summarization with saliency and entailment. In *Proceedings of the 2018 Conference of the North American Chapter of the Association for Computational Linguistics: Human Language Technologies, Volume 2 (Short Papers)*, pages 646–653.

Romain Paulus, Caiming Xiong, and Richard Socher. 2018. A deep reinforced model for abstractive summarization. In *International Conference on Learning Representations*.

Steven J Rennie, Etienne Marcheret, Youssef Mroueh, Jerret Ross, and Vaibhava Goel. 2017. Self-critical sequence training for image captioning. In *Proceedings of the IEEE Conference on Computer Vision and Pattern Recognition*, pages 7008–7024.

Stephen E Robertson, Steve Walker, Susan Jones, Micheline M Hancock-Beaulieu, Mike Gatford, et al. 1995. Okapi at trec-3. *Nist Special Publication Sp*, 109:109.

Evan Sandhaus. 2008. The new york times annotated corpus. *Linguistic Data Consortium, Philadelphia*, 6(12):e26752.

Thomas Scialom, Sylvain Lamprier, Benjamin Piwowarski, and Jacopo Staiano. 2019. Answers unite! unsupervised metrics for reinforced summarization models. *arXiv preprint arXiv:1909.01610*.

Eva Sharma, Luyang Huang, Zhe Hu, and Lu Wang. 2019. An entity-driven framework for abstractive summarization. In *Proceedings of the 2019 Conference on Empirical Methods in Natural Language Processing and the 9th International Joint Conference on Natural Language Processing (EMNLP-IJCNLP)*, pages 3271–3282.

Lucy Vanderwende, Hisami Suzuki, Chris Brockett, and Ani Nenkova. 2007. Beyond sumbasic: Task-focused summarization with sentence simplification and lexical expansion. *Information Processing & Management*, 43(6):1606–1618.

Xiaojun Wan. 2008. Using only cross-document relationships for both generic and topic-focused multi-document summarizations. *Information Retrieval*, 11(1):25–49.

Xiaojun Wan and Jianguo Xiao. 2009. Graph-based multi-modality learning for topic-focused multi-document summarization. In *Twenty-First International Joint Conference on Artificial Intelligence*. Citeseer.

Xiaojun Wan, Jianwu Yang, and Jianguo Xiao. 2007. Manifold-ranking based topic-focused multi-document summarization. In *IJCAI*, volume 7, pages 2903–2908.

Li Wang, Junlin Yao, Yunzhe Tao, Li Zhong, Wei Liu, and Qiang Du. 2018. A reinforced topic-aware convolutional sequence-to-sequence model for abstractive text summarization. In *Proceedings of the 27th International Joint Conference on Artificial Intelligence*, pages 4453–4460.

Ronald J Williams. 1992. Simple statistical gradient-following algorithms for connectionist reinforcement learning. *Machine learning*, 8(3-4):229–256.

Min Yang, Qiang Qu, Ying Shen, Qiao Liu, Wei Zhao, and Jia Zhu. 2018. Aspect and sentiment aware abstractive review summarization. In *Proceedings of the 27th international conference on computational linguistics*, pages 1110–1120.

Tianyi Zhang, Varsha Kishore, Felix Wu, Kilian Q Weinberger, and Yoav Artzi. 2019. Bertscore: Evaluating text generation with bert. In *International Conference on Learning Representations*.

A Novel Wikipedia based Dataset for Monolingual and Cross-Lingual Summarization

Mehwish Fatima and **Michael Strube**
Heidelberg Institute for Theoretical Studies gGmbH, Heidelberg, Germany
(mehwish.fatima|michael.strube)@h-its.org

Abstract

Cross-lingual summarization is a challenging task for which there are no cross-lingual scientific resources currently available. To overcome the lack of a high-quality resource, we present a new dataset for monolingual and cross-lingual summarization considering the English-German pair. We collect high-quality, real-world cross-lingual data from *Spektrum der Wissenschaft*, which publishes human-written German scientific summaries of English science articles on various subjects. The generated *Spektrum* dataset is small; therefore, we harvest a similar dataset from the *Wikipedia Science Portal* to complement it. The Wikipedia dataset consists of English and German articles, which can be used for monolingual and cross-lingual summarization. Furthermore, we present a quantitative analysis of the datasets and results of empirical experiments with several existing extractive and abstractive summarization models. The results suggest the viability and usefulness of the proposed dataset for monolingual and cross-lingual summarization.

1 Introduction

The summarization research has recently shifted from monolingual summarization (MS) to cross-lingual summarization (CLS) (Ouyang et al., 2019; Duan et al., 2019; Zhu et al., 2019). However, due to the absence of real cross-lingual datasets, recent CLS studies (Shen et al., 2018; Ouyang et al., 2019; Zhu et al., 2019; Pontes et al., 2020) are conducted on existing monolingual news datasets and off-the-shelf machine translation (MT) systems which may introduce noise into pseudo-cross-lingual summarization (PCLS) data. As these CLS studies rely on only news data, the trained summarization models may not work well for other domains such as scientific texts. Although some efforts have been made for investigating the MS task on scientific papers (Vadapalli et al., 2018b; Nikolov et al., 2018; Cohan et al., 2018; Dangovski et al., 2019); however, there is no study on scientific text for CLS to date. Another aspect of consideration is that most CLS studies intend to generate the summaries in English from a local language but not vice versa to facilitate the local readers.

This paper aims to address this issue by developing a summarization dataset containing scientific texts of the English-German language pair from two resources, *Spektrum der Wissenschaft* (SPEKTRUM) and the *Wikipedia Science Portal* (WSP). The paper explores the CLS task by using scientific English documents to generate German summaries for the local readers. To the best of the authors' knowledge, the collected WSP or WIKIPEDIA dataset represents the largest CLS dataset of the English-German pair so far. We believe that the novel WIKIPEDIA dataset encourages new avenues of research in the less explored areas of CLS.

Contributions: This paper has several contributions, including data collection, dataset generation, statistical analysis of the datasets, and an empirical evaluation of MS and CLS. We collect our primary dataset from SPEKTRUM, consisting of 1,510 English science articles with human-written German summaries. In addition, we propose a novel scoring method, which validates the data present in the SPEKTRUM dataset before data extraction. To complement the SPEKTRUM dataset, we harvest our second dataset from WSP, containing 51,312 English and German science articles. The collection of data from two different resources ensures diversity in the written text and topics. It is worth noting that the WIKIPEDIA dataset can also be used for MS, which distinguishes it from existing datasets. We perform a detailed statistical analysis of the dataset that highlights the interesting patterns. Furthermore, we conduct an empirical evaluation with several extractive baselines and existing abstractive summarization models to validate the usability of

Proceedings of the Third Workshop on New Frontiers in Summarization, pages 39–50
November 10, 2021.

our dataset for MS and CLS. Moreover, linguistic quality is evaluated on a subset of the output summaries of the MS and CLS experiments by human judges.

2 Related Work

2.1 Wikipedia Summarization Datasets

Researchers generally believe that WIKIPEDIA is a viable source for data collection, and generating summaries of WIKIPEDIA text is a challenging task.

2.1.1 Monolingual Datasets

WIKIPEDIA has been widely used for the creation of MS datasets such as English multi-document summarization (Zopf et al., 2016; Antognini and Faltings, 2020; Gholipour Ghalandari et al., 2020), English and German single and multi-document summarization (Hättasch et al., 2020), and German single-document summarization (Frefel, 2020). As these datasets are designed for MS, it makes them inadequate for cross-lingual evaluation.

2.1.2 Multilingual Datasets

The TAC MultiLing shared task is held biennially (2011-15) for multilingual multi-document summarization (Giannakopoulos et al., 2011; Giannakopoulos, 2013; Giannakopoulos et al., 2015). These corpora are composed of English Wikinews and translated into 9 languages. The final corpus (MultiLing'15) size is 1500 documents in total for all languages. Ladhak et al. (2020) also create a multilingual dataset named WikiLingua from WikiHow in 18 languages. However, the author conducted experiments to generate English summaries from non-English articles. Although these datasets are multilingual, they are non-scientific, thus cannot be used for cross-lingual summarization of scientific texts. Moreover, the small size of the MultiLing makes it difficult to use for cross-lingual neural models.

2.2 Scientific Summarization Datasets

Kim et al. (2016) build a dataset of introduction-abstract pairs from ARXIV papers for abstractive summarization. Vadapalli et al. (2018b,a) collect a parallel corpus of 87K pairs of research paper titles, abstracts and corresponding blog titles for title generation. Nikolov et al. (2018) create two datasets from scientific articles, abstract-title pairs from MEDLINE for title generation and body-abstract pairs from PUBMED for abstract generation. Cohan et al. (2018) also collect a scientific dataset from ARXIV (194K) and PUBMED (216K) articles for abstractive summarization. Dangovski et al. (2019) create a corpus of 60K science articles from ScienceDaily for summary generation. The datasets mentioned above consist of scientific papers, but all of them were made for MS, which makes them unsuitable for cross-lingual evaluation.

2.3 Cross-lingual Summarization Datasets

Zhang et al. (2016) perform cross-lingual multi-document sentence summarization for the English and Chinese language pair. They use the LDC news dataset and Google translators to get the parallel sentence pairs. Nguyen and Daumé III (2019) collect a dataset from descriptions of news articles from Global Voices in 15 languages. A few researchers work with MT and existing monolingual datasets to achieve the goal of CLS. Pontes et al. (2020) perform cross-lingual multi-sentence compression for the English-French pair. They use the MultiLing'11 dataset for the French language. The dataset is translated with Google translate to generate the English counterpart. Ouyang et al. (2019) propose a Translate-then-Summarize (TRANS-SUM) based CLS model for an inherent monolingual NYT dataset. They use the round-trip translation (RTT) method to convert the English dataset into Somali, Swahili, and Tagalog and then into noisy English. Zhu et al. (2019) also apply on RTT for CLS considering the English-Chinese language pair. There is limited prior work of CLS by using translation corpus during training. Shen et al. (2018); Duan et al. (2019) perform the cross-lingual headline generation and sentence summarization for the English-Chinese language pair. They use the English Gigaword corpus along with the English-Chinese translation corpus for training.

Though these studies focused on CLS, there is no real cross-lingual dataset except for MultiLing and WikiLingua. The datasets are, however, limited in scope and cannot be used for our experiments. To the best of the authors' knowledge, there is no real dataset created with the sole purpose of cross-lingual abstractive summarization of scientific text.

3 Dataset Construction

3.1 Spektrum Data

SPEKTRUM is the German equivalent of the "Scientific American", which began publishing in 1978[1].

[1] Spektrum.de/das-innere-spektrum

The SPEKTRUM magazine is one of the divisions of the Springer Nature publishing group. It is published on a monthly basis and covers many core areas of science, such as archaeology, astronomy, biology, chemistry, *etc.* The SPEKTRUM science journalists present complex English scientific research to non-scientist common readers in a local language (German). SPEKTRUM is therefore viewed as a mediator between scientific publications and the general public.

3.1.1 Data Collection

We have formally contacted and requested SPEKTRUM to release their data for the research purpose. In response to our request, we have meetings with SPEKTRUM's managing director and head of digital production. As a result, we have received a subset of SPEKTRUM data in XML format. The released SPEKTRUM raw data contains German summaries and URLs to their source documents. It consists of 20,556 summaries for the period of December 2000 to February 2019. To process the data, we develop an XML parser that parses the ids, dates, titles, keywords, summaries, and URLs. In some cases, the provided summaries have only one URL associated with them, while in others, there can be multiple URLs. Multiple URLs make detecting and extracting source articles challenging.

Further discussion with SPEKTRUM and manual inspection of a subset of data indicate that there is only one source URL, and the remaining links are for further reading. Before finding the source URLs, all URLs to social media platforms (Facebook, Twitter, YouTube), German websites and non-functional links are filtered out. As a result of filtering, only 5,590 instances are left with functional URLs. Upon further inspection, it is discovered the functional URLs are either PDF or HTML links.

For the instances with PDF links, the extraction of the source article is straightforward. A script is written for PDF URLs to download, extract and parse the text from the articles. We use Beautiful Soup[2] for extraction, and Tika[3] for parsing the text.

For the instances with multiple HTML links, we devise a novel two-step scoring method to find the best-fitting URLs consisting of scientific structure scoring and keyword matching scoring. *Scientific Structure:* This method checks the structure of text for scientific headings - Abstract, Introduction, Results, Discussion, References and Acknowledgements. The score ranges between 0 to 6 by assigning one point for each heading present in the text. The URLs that score four or higher are selected by assuming that a scientific article has at least four of the six headings. To further validate the selected URLs, a keyword matching scoring method is applied. *Keyword Matching:* This method uses the parsed German keywords from raw SPEKTRUM data and the English title of the HTML page to calculate a ratio for matched keywords. The German keywords are translated into English via Google translate[4]. The ratio of matched keywords is defined as the total number of keyword occurrences in page title divided by the total number of German keywords. The URLs with positive scores were selected for the extraction. After the scoring, the HTML pages are downloaded via the module request and extracted with Beautiful Soup[2]. The final extracted instances from PDF and HTML links are 3,554 in total with their German summaries.

3.1.2 Manual Cleaning

After the extraction, the English articles are further manually inspected to filter the incomplete extractions, garbage text, texts other than English, and shorter than the German summary. We manually cleaned the data by two annotators over a period of two weeks. Following manual cleaning, the final data consists of 1,510 English articles and German summaries written by experts in science journalism.

Furthermore, the data is preprocessed for lower case conversion, word and sentence tokenization with NLTK toolkit[5]. The markup tags are used to preserve the structural information on the section and sentence level. The final version of the dataset is stored in JSON format. Unfortunately, this data is insufficient to train the summarization models. Therefore, we decided to collect a similar nature cross-lingual dataset from WIKIPEDIA. Moreover, SPEKTRUM data cannot be published due to the magazine's policies.

3.2 Wikipedia Data

WIKIPEDIA is considered a reliable source for mono- and multi-lingual data acquisition (Antognini and Faltings, 2020; Gholipour Ghalandari et al., 2020; Hättasch et al., 2020; Frefel, 2020).

[2]Pypi/Beautifulsoup
[3]Pypi/Tika
[4]Pypi/Googletrans
[5]Pypi/Nltk

As well as maintaining a consistent format for the articles[6], data is available in several forms for researchers, including data dumps, databases, DBpedia and WIKI-API[7]. These features make WIKIPEDIA an ideal source for cross-lingual summarization data. As a result, we select WSP for scientific cross-lingual data collection. The WSP is a popular, crowd-sourced science encyclopedia available in many languages and is enormous in volume (≈6M articles in English and 2.4M in German). Numerous articles cover various topics such as biology, agriculture, technology, linguistics, and so on.

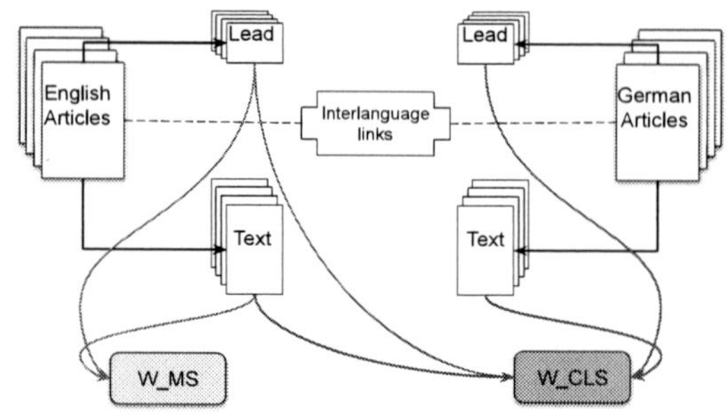

Figure 1: WIKIPEDIA data collection

3.2.1 Data Collection

Figure 1 illustrates the process of collecting monolingual and cross-lingual data from WIKIPEDIA. The Figure 1 shows how English and German articles are connected as well as how they are split to form summaries (lead) and texts. According to WIKIPEDIA's guidelines[6], the lead is the first paragraph of an article that summarizes it. Note that WIKIPEDIA lead is different from a news-style lead or "lede".

WIKI-API[8] is used for data collection which provides an efficient way for extracting an article from a given category, getting existing inter-language links for that article, and extracting sections of that article. Before extraction, the following steps are taken to collect valid data. (i) A list of science subcategories is generated from the main categories. (ii) This list is further processed to generate another list of English and German articles titles. In total, there were 238,766 titles from various science subcategories. (iii) The title list is further checked to find empty titles for both languages. The empty condition is: if the lead is absent, only the lead is present, or only the title is present. Such titles are removed from the list. (iv) Finally, the updated list is used to extract the original articles.

The extracted data is preprocessed to remove the noise and white spaces. The data is converted into lower case and then tokenized for words and sentences with the NLTK toolkit[5]. The markup tags are used to preserve the structural information on the section and sentence level. The final version of the dataset is stored in JSON format. The final dataset is released under the Creative Commons Attribution-ShareAlike 3.0 Unported License for the summarization community[9].

3.2.2 Manual Verification

The majority of corpus construction studies (Antognini and Faltings, 2020; Ladhak et al., 2020; Frefel, 2020) have omitted the manual verification of collected data due to its complexity. Only Hättasch et al. (2020) performed human verification on a subset of 39 summaries from three different parts of the dataset (Harry potter, English and German Star Wars) for one parameter of interest. For cross-lingual science articles, manual verification poses different challenges such as it requires bilingual comprehension of various scientific topics.

To verify the cross-lingual mappings, we randomly select 20 articles from cross-lingual data. The articles with German summaries are given to two native German speakers (judges) who are also fluent in English. They are asked to evaluate the German summaries based on two different parameters, *i.e.*, (i) relevance and (ii) length. The relevance determines if the German summary is related to the English article, and if not, it is given a score of zero. The length refers to how long or short a summary is. Summaries that are long are given a score of one. Zero is assigned to short summaries (one to two sentences). Considering the length parameter is important because our final objective is to summarize the SPEKTRUM dataset, and we want to have a similar dataset. In terms of relevance, both judges agreed that German summaries are relevant to English articles. For the length, the sample German summaries get an average score of 0.74 with a substantial agreement (Fleiss's $\kappa = 0.76$) between judges. It is worth noting that short summaries (≈25%) make the data challenging as such short summaries are used in extreme summarization (Ca-

[6]Wikipedia/Manual_of_Style
[7]Wikimedia/Research:Data
[8]Pypi/Wikiapi
[9]https://github.com/MehwishFatimah/wsd

	WIKIPEDIA			SPEKTRUM	
	EN-TEXT TRAIN/VAL/TEST	EN-SUM TRAIN/VAL/TEST	DE-SUM TRAIN/VAL/TEST	EN-TEXT TEST	DE-SUM TEST
Split	80/10/10	80/10/10	80/10/10	–	–
Total vocabulary	22M/2.7M/2.7M	3.4M/.4M/.4M	2.9M/.3M/.3M	1M	.4M
Total words	64M/8M/7.9M	5.7M/.7M/.7M	4M/.5M/.5M	4.3M	.6M
Avg. words/doc	1572/1562/1542	139/140/140	100/101/101	2337	361
Standard deviation	1961/1935/1906	110/114/112	92/109/124	1510	250
Total sentences	2.5M/.3M/.3M	.2M/.03M/.03M	.2M/.02M/.02M	.19M	.03M
Avg. sentences/doc	61/61/60	06/04/06	05/05/06	102	69
Standard deviation	76/74/72	06/05/04	05/06/08	17	13
Compression ratio	–	20/20/20	17/18/17	–	30

Table 1: Statistics of the final version of the dataset.

chola et al., 2020).

3.3 Final Dataset

The extracted English and German articles are used to create the following sets.

1. **W-MS** - WIKIPEDIA monolingual dataset consisting of English texts and corresponding English summaries.
2. **W-CLS** - WIKIPEDIA cross-lingual dataset containing English texts and corresponding German summaries.
3. **S-CLS** - SPEKTRUM manually corrected test set consisting of English texts and corresponding German summaries.

4 Dataset Statistics

4.1 Overview

Table 1 provides statistics for the final version of the monolingual and cross-lingual datasets for train, val(idation), and two test sets (WSP and SPEKTRUM). There are pairs of text and summary in each set. Total articles are 41,049 (80%) in the train, 5,131 (10%) in the val, 5,132 (10%) in the W-CLS and 1,510 in the S-CLS test sets.

Table 2 presents a comparison of the proposed dataset with some of existing summarization datasets. Based on our observations, our datasets differ from existing datasets in various aspects, particularly cross-linguality.

4.2 Compression Ratio

The compression ratio is defined as the word ratio between a text and its summary (Grusky et al., 2018). Table 1 presents the compression ratio of English and German summaries. An English summary is typically 20% as long as an English text, and a German summary is 17.5% as long as an English text. It is important to note that while both languages belong to the Germanic family, they differ in inflection and compound words. Therefore, judging from these averages, it is difficult to determine whether English summaries are in fact longer than those in German.

4.3 Novel *N*-grams in Summaries

Table 3 presents the percentage of n-grams in the summaries that do not appear in the corresponding text for W-MS. The percentage of novel n-grams in the summaries serves as a measure of their abstractiveness. Approximately 25% of the summary unigrams for the train, val, and test sets are novel. The train, val, and test sets have almost 70% novel bigrams. The percentage of novel n-grams also increases as n $(1-5)$ increases and reaches up to 93% for 5-grams. Furthermore, the Table 3 shows that the summaries have more novel words in them and that the dataset tends to be abstractive.

5 Experiments

5.1 Datasets and Baselines

We conduct an empirical evaluation of W-MS, W-CLS and S-CLS for the summarization task. For MS, we apply both extractive and abstractive methods to W-MS, with the extractive methods serving as baselines. For CLS, we apply the abstractive models to W-CLS and evaluate the models with two test sets: WIKIPEDIA and SPEKTRUM. For CLS baselines, we apply two existing pipeline methods to create PCLS data from W-MS by us-

Dataset	Newswire DM	CNN	NYT	NR	Scientific ARXIV	PM	W-MS	W-CLS	S-CLS
Avg. words/text	653	760	549	659	4900	3000	1559	1559	2337
Avg. words/sum	55	46	40	27	220	203	140	100	361
Compression ratio	12	16.5	13.8	24	22.5	15	20	18	30
Cross-lingual	No	No	No	No	No	No	No	**Yes**	**Yes**

Table 2: Comparison of W-MS, W-CLS and S-CLS to existing summarization datasets.

	1-g	2-g	3-g	4-g	5-g
Train	24.6	69.3	87.6	92.1	93.0
Val	24.5	69.1	87.4	91.9	92.7
Test	24.7	69.4	87.5	92.1	92.9

Table 3: Percentage of novel n-grams in W-MS summaries.

ing FairSeq[10]: (i) TRANS-SUM - Translate-then-Summarize, and (ii) SUM-TRANS - Summarize-then-Translate.

5.2 Methods

The following extractive methods are selected: (i) SUM-BASIC, (ii) LUHN, (iii) KL-SUM, (iv) LSA, (v) LEX-RANK, (vi) TEXT-RANK, and (vii) BERT[11,12].

The following abstractive models are chosen: (i) Attention based sequence to sequence model (S2S) (Bahdanau et al., 2015), (ii) Pointer generator network (PGN) (See et al., 2017), and (iii) Transformer based sequence to sequence model (TRF) (Vaswani et al., 2017). We select these models because these models show good results in previous studies (See et al., 2017; Ouyang et al., 2019; Duan et al., 2019). Moreover, we want to evaluate the performance of these models on our proposed dataset, therefore skipping the pre-trained embeddings and models.

The S2S and PGN models are applied with almost the same hyper-parameters as in See et al. (2017). Word embeddings are configured with 128 dimensions and hidden layers with 256 dimensions. The vocabulary size is 100K and 50K at the encoder and decoder sides, without the OOV words handling as used in the PGN model. In order to solve the OOV words, we choose BPE instead of the n-gram vocabulary. The Adam optimizer is used with a learning rate of 0.15 and a mini-batch of size 16. The models are trained for 40 epochs, and the validation loss is calculated to determine the best-trained model.

Almost the same hyper-parameters are applied for TRF as in Vaswani et al. (2017). Word embeddings have dimensions of 512 and hidden layers have dimensions of 786. The model consists of encoder and decoder stacks, each having 6 layers and 8 multi-attention heads at the decoder side. To make the results comparable among all models, the same vocabulary size of 100K and 50K at the encoder and decoder sides are selected. The Adam optimizer is used at a learning rate of 0.0001 and with a residual dropout of 0.1. For all abstractive models, a beam search of size 4 is applied in the inference phase. For all abstractive models, the encoder and decoder length is fixed to 400 and 100 words as in See et al. (2017). All abstractive models are trained on a single Tesla P40 GPU with 24GB RAM. For training and inference, the S2S and TRF models take around 6 days, and the PGN model takes 3 days.

5.3 Evaluation

For automatic evaluation, ROUGE metric is used for F-score, Precision and Recall. ROUGE relies on different metrics that include n-gram (R-N) and Longest Common Sub-sequence - LCS (R-L) overlap (Lin, 2004). Unigram and bigram overlap (R-1,2) provide a reasonable estimation of informativeness, while R-L estimates the summaries' fluency.

In order to further investigate the linguistic quality of system summaries, two native German speakers with fluent English have evaluated the summaries for two parameters (details are present in Section 6.3). It is worth to be noted that previous monolingual scientific summarization studies (Cohan et al., 2018; Dangovski et al., 2019) have not considered the human evaluations due to its demanding nature. For human evaluation of scientific articles, human judges must read and comprehend long domain-specific articles with summaries

[10]Github.com/fairseq
[11](i-vi)Pypi/Sumy
[12](vii)Pypi/Bertext

	R-1			R-2			R-L		
	F	P	R	F	P	R	F	P	R
				Extractive models					
SUM-BASIC	28.67	22.82	38.68	07.15	05.53	10.12	**25.24**	20.06	34.02
TEXT-RANK	26.29	18.82	43.57	07.11	04.86	13.27	22.98	16.43	38.19
KL-SUM	24.96	17.73	42.13	06.40	04.42	11.58	21.64	15.35	36.65
LUHN	25.67	19.25	38.50	06.75	04.86	11.03	22.54	16.88	33.89
LEX-RANK	26.53	20.11	38.95	06.69	04.92	10.47	23.22	17.58	34.18
RANDOM	28.05	21.20	41.45	**07.51**	05.44	12.13	24.55	18.52	36.39
LSA	26.51	18.97	44.01	07.40	05.03	13.96	23.09	16.50	38.45
BERT	**28.74**	23.56	36.83	**07.51**	06.02	09.98	25.03	20.51	32.10
				Abstractive models					
PGN	22.25	47.88	14.49	05.34	11.90	03.44	20.58	44.52	13.38
S2S	20.94	54.98	12.93	04.75	11.67	02.98	19.31	51.40	11.89
TRF	**25.53**	40.95	18.55	**06.29**	07.03	05.69	**22.76**	36.83	16.47

Table 4: Monolingual results of ROUGE evaluation of W-MS with different extractive and abstractive methods.

to evaluate the linguistic qualities of system summaries. It is more challenging to conduct cross-lingual evaluations as it requires bilingual comprehension for articles tailored to various science topics.

6 Results and Discussion

6.1 Monolingual Results

Table 4 presents the MS results of different extractive and abstractive models with the W-MS. For extractive methods, the BERT achieves the highest results for R-1 and R-2, whereas the SUM-BASIC performs well for R-L. Overall, all extractive techniques yield similar results. All abstractive models perform fairly well for R-1, R-2 and R-L. Nevertheless, the abstractive models have a slightly lower performance than the extractive models. In general, all the summarization methods perform worse for R-2 than R-1 and R-L.

We consider two factors when comparing monolingual extractive and abstractive results: (i) the impact of novel n-grams in the reference summaries, and (ii) the length of output summaries. Regarding the impact of novel n-grams, extractive methods are not impacted by the presence/absence of novel n-grams. For example, if we consider novel unigrams, as mentioned in Table 3, approximately 25% of the summary unigrams are not present in the corresponding text, but the remaining 75% unigrams can overlap. As the extractive methods extract the sentences from the actual text and maintain a good percentage of overlapped words. However, as abstractive models do not rely on extraction, their results can be influenced by the presence/absence of novel n-grams. Based on observation, the extractive results show that Recall is higher than Precision, indicating that the system summaries are longer than the reference summaries. From abstractive results, it can be observed that Precision is higher than Recall indicating that the system summaries tend to be shorter than reference summaries in contrast to extractive methods. Ideally, the system summaries should be similar to reference summaries. Nevertheless, since the models were evaluated on news datasets, they tend to produce short summaries.

6.2 Cross-lingual Results

Table 5 presents the CLS results with different abstractive models. We cannot compare our results with those of recent CLS studies since they used pseudo-cross-lingual data from the news domain. We overcome this problem by using two baselines, TRANS-SUM and SUM-TRANS, which have been used in recent studies. Among the baselines, the SUM-TRANS models perform better than the TRANS-SUM models. However, these baseline models do not perform well in comparison with real CLS data models (W-CLS). The CLS models show significantly ($p < 0.05$) improved results with W-CLS data as compared to SUM-TRANS and TRANS-SUM models ($p < 1\times10^{-6}$). The results supported our hypothesis (as mentioned in Section 1) that MT introduced noise to pseudo-cross-lingual data (PCLS). Consequently, the data noise acts as a bias and affects the neural models. The CLS models

	R-1			R-2			R-L		
	F	P	R	F	P	R	F	P	R
TRANS-SUM									
S2S	14.18	30.49	09.24	01.51	02.55	01.07	12.77	27.67	08.30
PGN	15.81	31.35	10.57	02.86	05.58	01.92	14.69	29.14	09.82
TRF	16.15	32.56	11.41	03.66	05.84	02.72	15.25	32.06	09.29
SUM-TRANS									
S2S	15.04	32.85	09.75	01.48	02.56	01.04	13.64	28.03	08.82
PGN	18.24	28.62	13.38	04.14	10.98	02.55	16.04	30.45	11.11
TRF	19.31	26.77	14.18	04.23	11.67	02.84	17.37	31.74	12.18
W-CLS test set									
S2S†	18.37	37.93	12.12	04.04	09.91	02.54	16.55	34.57	10.88
PGN†	20.72	30.34	15.73	03.79	05.93	02.79	18.68	27.48	14.15
TRF†	**21.61**	26.81	18.10	**04.37**	05.16	03.79	**18.10**	22.42	15.18
S-CLS test set									
S2S†*	16.47	26.42	11.97	03.42	03.43	03.41	11.87	25.47	07.74
PGN†*	18.64	29.74	13.54	03.83	04.05	03.63	15.65	26.42	11.12
TRF†*	**20.81**	31.39	14.47	**04.19**	05.43	03.41	**17.54**	21.73	15.29

Table 5: Cross-lingual results of ROUGE evaluation with different abstractive methods. † denotes a significant improvement in the results and * denotes a significant difference in the results.

learn the mappings between encoder and decoder sides language distributions along with compression. Therefore, distortion in language distributions (*e.g.*, wrong translated tokens, UNK tokens) can affect mappings' learning. Therefore, it is better to train a CLS model with real cross-lingual data rather than PCLS. Overall, the abstractive models perform well for R-1, R-2 and R-L with the W-CLS.

We extend CLS experiments to S-CLS using the same models trained for W-CLS. In these experiments, we examine how on-the-ground cross-lingual summarization models perform on a real-world dataset. The CLS models under-perform on S-CLS set ($p < 1 \times 10^{-4}$) with p-value ($p < 0.05$). The slight drop in performance is probably due to the fact that the decoder is a conditional model that learns contextual representations from training data. Moreover, it seems that BPE vocabulary caters to the unseen words of S-CLS set, as both test sets (W-CLS and S-CLS) have not been used in vocabulary construction.

The CLS results suggest that neural models can learn cross-lingual mappings as well as compression. Using WIKIPEDIA dataset, the models learn the structural mappings between English and German languages and tend to maintain a logical structure of sentences in summaries. Comparatively, all models perform poorly with R-2 compared to R-1 and R-L. Due to the short summaries produced by the models, Precision is higher than Recall, which in turn affects the F-score. Earlier, we noted that these models are designed for news datasets, which do not require long summaries. We selected these neural models because they have demonstrated good performance in machine translation and summarization. However, their implementation has not been tested for cross-lingual texts that are long compared to the use-cases previously mentioned.

Both tasks are different in nature, so there can be no direct comparison between the MS and CLS. In Appendix A, Figures 2 and 3 show the examples of monolingual and cross-lingual system-generated summaries and their reference summary. In abstractive models, blue color represents the creation of new words by the models, red represents the incorrect information, yellow depicts the extractive parts and bold shows the repetition of words/phrases.

6.3 Human Evaluation

Our human judges evaluate the linguistic quality of output summaries. They are native Germans speakers with fluent English skills. For evaluation of the models, we randomly select 20 output summaries, their reference summaries, and the input articles (10 from PGN_MS and 10 from PGN_CLS). The evaluation is performed for two parameters: (i) correctness and ii) fluency on a scale of 1−3 as scale range used by Ouyang et al. (2019). Correctness measure defines whether the original message is preserved coherently (relevance) in a non-redundant manner. Fluency measure determines the structural and grammatical properties of summaries. For MS, the average score for correctness is 2.10, and fluency is 2.65, with a moderate agreement (Fleiss's $\kappa = 0.60$ and 0.58) between judges. For CLS, the average score for correctness is 1.65, and fluency is 1.96, with a substantial agreement (Fleiss's $\kappa = 0.70$) for both scores between judges. From these results, it can be observed that the fluency of the models is good in maintaining an appropriate structure of the output summaries, while the correctness of the models is modest. The cross-lingual models tend to produce irrelevant content in some summaries.

7 Conclusions

Lack of cross-lingual experimental datasets impedes the progress of CLS research. In this paper, we present a new MS and CLS dataset extracted from SPEKTRUM and WIKIPEDIA. Our empirical investigation demonstrates the viability and amenability of the proposed dataset and also highlights the challenging nature of the dataset for recent summarization models. Our results demonstrate the significance of constructing real cross-lingual datasets for CLS. Furthermore, the English and German summaries scored reasonably well in terms of correctness and fluency based on human evaluations. We anticipate that the proposed dataset will encourage the study and research of MS and CLS. In the future, we will scale the CLS experiments using science domain pre-trained models.

Acknowledgments

We thank *Spektrum der Wissenschaft* for providing us their data. We would also like to acknowledge the assistance of Nadia Arslan, Fabian Düker and Jason Brockmeyer in the data extraction and manual evaluation. This work is carried out at the Heidelberg Institute for Theoretical Studies (supported by the Klaus Tschira Foundation), Heidelberg, Germany. In addition, the first author is funded by the Higher Education Commission of Pakistan (HEC) - the Deutscher Akademischer Austausch Dienst (DAAD).

References

Diego Antognini and Boi Faltings. 2020. GameWikiSum: a novel large multi-document summarization dataset. In *Proceedings of the 12th Language Resources and Evaluation Conference*, pages 6645–6650, Marseille, France. European Language Resources Association.

Dzmitry Bahdanau, Kyunghyun Cho, and Yoshua Bengio. 2015. Neural machine translation by jointly learning to align and translate. In *3rd International Conference on Learning Representations, ICLR 2015, San Diego, CA, USA, May 7-9, 2015, Conference Track Proceedings*.

Isabel Cachola, Kyle Lo, Arman Cohan, and Daniel Weld. 2020. TLDR: Extreme summarization of scientific documents. In *Findings of the Association for Computational Linguistics: EMNLP 2020*, pages 4766–4777, Online. Association for Computational Linguistics.

Arman Cohan, Franck Dernoncourt, Doo Soon Kim, Trung Bui, Seokhwan Kim, Walter Chang, and Nazli Goharian. 2018. A discourse-aware attention model for abstractive summarization of long documents. In *Proceedings of the 2018 Conference of the North American Chapter of the Association for Computational Linguistics: Human Language Technologies, Volume 2 (Short Papers)*, pages 615–621, New Orleans, Louisiana. Association for Computational Linguistics.

Rumen Dangovski, Li Jing, Preslav Nakov, Mićo Tatalović, and Marin Soljačić. 2019. Rotational unit of memory: A novel representation unit for RNNs with scalable applications. *Transactions of the Association for Computational Linguistics*, 7:121–138.

Xiangyu Duan, Mingming Yin, Min Zhang, Boxing Chen, and Weihua Luo. 2019. Zero-shot cross-lingual abstractive sentence summarization through teaching generation and attention. In *Proceedings of the 57th Annual Meeting of the Association for Computational Linguistics*, pages 3162–3172, Florence, Italy. Association for Computational Linguistics.

Dominik Frefel. 2020. Summarization corpora of Wikipedia articles. In *Proceedings of the 12th Language Resources and Evaluation Conference*, pages 6651–6655, Marseille, France. European Language Resources Association.

Demian Gholipour Ghalandari, Chris Hokamp, Nghia The Pham, John Glover, and Georgiana Ifrim. 2020. A large-scale multi-document summarization dataset from the Wikipedia current events portal. In *Proceedings of the 58th Annual Meeting of the Association for Computational Linguistics*, pages 1302–1308, Online. Association for Computational Linguistics.

George Giannakopoulos. 2013. Multi-document multilingual summarization and evaluation tracks in ACL 2013 MultiLing workshop. In *Proceedings of the*

MultiLing 2013 Workshop on Multilingual Multi-document Summarization, pages 20–28, Sofia, Bulgaria. Association for Computational Linguistics.

George Giannakopoulos, Mahmoud El-Haj, Benoît Favre, Marina Litvak, Josef Steinberger, and Vasudeva Varma. 2011. TAC2011 MultiLing Pilot Overview. In *Proceedings of the Fourth Text Analysis Conference, TAC 2011*, Gaithersburg, Maryland, USA. NIST.

George Giannakopoulos, Jeff Kubina, John Conroy, Josef Steinberger, Benoit Favre, Mijail Kabadjov, Udo Kruschwitz, and Massimo Poesio. 2015. MultiLing 2015: Multilingual summarization of single and multi-documents, on-line fora, and call-center conversations. In *Proceedings of the 16th Annual Meeting of the Special Interest Group on Discourse and Dialogue*, pages 270–274, Prague, Czech Republic. Association for Computational Linguistics.

Max Grusky, Mor Naaman, and Yoav Artzi. 2018. Newsroom: A dataset of 1.3 million summaries with diverse extractive strategies. In *Proceedings of the 2018 Conference of the North American Chapter of the Association for Computational Linguistics: Human Language Technologies, Volume 1 (Long Papers)*, pages 708–719, New Orleans, Louisiana. Association for Computational Linguistics.

Benjamin Hättasch, Nadja Geisler, Christian M. Meyer, and Carsten Binnig. 2020. Summarization beyond news: The automatically acquired fandom corpora. In *Proceedings of the 12th Language Resources and Evaluation Conference*, pages 6700–6708, Marseille, France. European Language Resources Association.

Minsoo Kim, Dennis Singh Moirangthem, and Minho Lee. 2016. Towards abstraction from extraction: Multiple timescale gated recurrent unit for summarization. In *Proceedings of the 1st Workshop on Representation Learning for NLP*, pages 70–77, Berlin, Germany. Association for Computational Linguistics.

Faisal Ladhak, Esin Durmus, Claire Cardie, and Kathleen McKeown. 2020. WikiLingua: A new benchmark dataset for cross-lingual abstractive summarization. In *Findings of the Association for Computational Linguistics: EMNLP 2020*, pages 4034–4048, Online. Association for Computational Linguistics.

Chin-Yew Lin. 2004. ROUGE: A package for automatic evaluation of summaries. In *Text Summarization Branches Out*, pages 74–81, Barcelona, Spain. Association for Computational Linguistics.

Khanh Nguyen and Hal Daumé III. 2019. Global Voices: Crossing borders in automatic news summarization. In *Proceedings of the 2nd Workshop on New Frontiers in Summarization*, pages 90–97, Hong Kong, China. Association for Computational Linguistics.

Nikola I Nikolov, Michael Pfeiffer, and Richard HR Hahnloser. 2018. Data-driven Summarization of Scientific Articles. In *Proceedings of the Eleventh International Conference on Language Resources and Evaluation (LREC 2018)*, Miyazaki, Japan. European Language Resources Association (ELRA).

Jessica Ouyang, Boya Song, and Kathy McKeown. 2019. A robust abstractive system for cross-lingual summarization. In *Proceedings of the 2019 Conference of the North American Chapter of the Association for Computational Linguistics: Human Language Technologies, Volume 1 (Long and Short Papers)*, pages 2025–2031, Minneapolis, Minnesota. Association for Computational Linguistics.

Elvys Linhares Pontes, Stéphane Huet, Juan-Manuel Torres-Moreno, and Andréa Carneiro Linhares. 2020. Compressive Approaches for Cross-language Multi-document Summarization. *Data & Knowledge Engineering*, 125:101763.

Abigail See, Peter J. Liu, and Christopher D. Manning. 2017. Get to the point: Summarization with pointer-generator networks. In *Proceedings of the 55th Annual Meeting of the Association for Computational Linguistics (Volume 1: Long Papers)*, pages 1073–1083, Vancouver, Canada. Association for Computational Linguistics.

Shi-qi Shen, Yun Chen, Cheng Yang, Zhi-yuan Liu, and Mao-song Sun. 2018. Zero-shot Cross-lingual Neural Headline Generation. *IEEE/ACM Transactions on Audio, Speech, and Language Processing*, 26(12):2319–2327.

Raghuram Vadapalli, Bakhtiyar Syed, Nishant Prabhu, Balaji Vasan Srinivasan, and Vasudeva Varma. 2018a. Sci-blogger: A step towards automated science journalism. In *Proceedings of the 27th ACM International Conference on Information and Knowledge Management, CIKM 2018, Torino, Italy, October 22-26, 2018*, pages 1787–1790. ACM.

Raghuram Vadapalli, Bakhtiyar Syed, Nishant Prabhu, Balaji Vasan Srinivasan, and Vasudeva Varma. 2018b. When science journalism meets artificial intelligence : An interactive demonstration. In *Proceedings of the 2018 Conference on Empirical Methods in Natural Language Processing: System Demonstrations*, pages 163–168, Brussels, Belgium. Association for Computational Linguistics.

Ashish Vaswani, Noam Shazeer, Niki Parmar, Jakob Uszkoreit, Llion Jones, Aidan N. Gomez, Lukasz Kaiser, and Illia Polosukhin. 2017. Attention is all you need. In *Advances in Neural Information Processing Systems 30: Annual Conference on Neural Information Processing Systems 2017, December 4-9, 2017, Long Beach, CA, USA*, pages 5998–6008.

Jiajun Zhang, Yu Zhou, and Chengqing Zong. 2016. Abstractive Cross-language Summarization via Translation Model Enhanced Predicate Argument Structure Fusing. *IEEE/ACM Transac-*

tions on Audio, Speech, and Language Processing, 24(10):1842–1853.

Junnan Zhu, Qian Wang, Yining Wang, Yu Zhou, Jiajun Zhang, Shaonan Wang, and Chengqing Zong. 2019. NCLS: Neural cross-lingual summarization. In *Proceedings of the 2019 Conference on Empirical Methods in Natural Language Processing and the 9th International Joint Conference on Natural Language Processing (EMNLP-IJCNLP)*, pages 3054–3064, Hong Kong, China. Association for Computational Linguistics.

Markus Zopf, Maxime Peyrard, and Judith Eckle-Kohler. 2016. The next step for multi-document summarization: A heterogeneous multi-genre corpus built with a novel construction approach. In *Proceedings of COLING 2016, the 26th International Conference on Computational Linguistics: Technical Papers*, pages 1535–1545, Osaka, Japan. The COLING 2016 Organizing Committee.

A Example Summaries

Monolingual Article: united nations conference on sustainable development background in 1992 , the first conference of its kind , the united nations conference on environment and development (unced) , commonly referred to as the rio conference or earth summit , succeeded in raising public awareness of the need to integrate environment and development . the conference drew 109 heads of state to rio de janeiro , brazil , to address what were dubbed urgent problems of environmental protection and socio-economic development . [...]

Reference: the united nations conference on sustainable development (uncsd) , also known as rio 2012 , or earth summit 2012 was the third international conference on sustainable development aimed at reconciling the economic and environmental goals of the global community. hosted by brazil in rio de janeiro from 13 to 22 june 2012 , [...]

BERT: united nations conference on sustainable development background in 1992 , the first conference of its kind , the united nations conference on environment and development (unced) , commonly referred to as the rio conference or earth summit , succeeded in raising public awareness of the need to integrate environment and development . [...]

LEX-RANK: the world conference on human rights , for example , focused on the right of people to a healthy environment and the right to development ; controversial demands that had met with resistance from some member states until the earth summit . it also created new international institutions , among them the commission on sustainable development , tasked with the follow-up to the rio conference and led to the reform of the global environment facility . [...]

PGN: the united nations environment programme (unep–1898) is an international non-governmental organization devoted to the united nations convention on climate change in the united states . it is the world 's fourth-largest programme in the united states and **the united nations environment programme (unep) and the united nations environment programme (unep)** . the international commission on climate change is the **world 's fourth-largest programme .**

TRF: the first conference of its kind , the united nations conference on environment and development (unced) was held in 1992 . the conference drew heads of state to rio de janeiro , brazil to address what were dubbed urgent problems of environmental protection and socio-economic development . the earth summit influenced subsequent un conferences and set the global green agenda .

Figure 2: Example of monolingual system-generated summaries.

Cross-lingual Article: d' arrest discovered ngc525 using his 11-inch refractor telescope at copenhagen . he located the galaxy 's position with a total of two observations . as he also noted the mag 11-12 star just 2' northwest , his position is fairly accurate . the galaxy was later catalogued by john louis emil dreyer in the new general catalogue , where it was described as very faint , very small , 11th or 12th magnitude star 5 seconds of time to west . the galaxy appears very dim in the sky as it only has an apparent visual magnitude of 13.3 and thus can only be observed with telescopes . [...]

Reference: ngc525 ist eine linsenförmige galaxie vom hubble - typ s0 im sternbild fische auf der ekliptik . sie ist schätzungsweise 99 millionen lichtjahre von der milchstraße entfernt und hat einen durchmesser von etwa 40 . 000 lichtjahren . im selben himmelsareal befinden sich u.a. die galaxien ngc516 , ngc524 , ic101, ic102 . das objekt wurde am 25 . september 1862 von dem deutsch-dänischen astronomen heinrich ludwig d' arrest entdeckt .
Translation: ngc525 is a lenticular galaxy of the hubble type s0 in the constellation pisces on the ecliptic . it is estimated to be 99 million light years from the milky way and about 40 , 000 light years across. the galaxies ngc516 , ngc524 , ic101 , ic102 are located in the same area of the sky . the object was discovered on september 25 , 1862 by the german danish astronomer heinrich ludwig d' arrest .

TRANS-SUM-PGN: ngc142 ist eine unregelmäßige galaxie im sternbild eridanus . sein d <unk> l wurde mit hilfe der kugelsternhaufenluminosität auf 31 , 01 ± 0 , 21 geschätzt , was etwa 52 ms entspricht . er ist das hellste <unk> <unk> .
Translation: ngc142 is an irregular galaxy in the constellation of eridanus . its d<unk>l was estimated with the help of the globular cluster luminosity to 31 . 01 ± 0 . 21 , which corresponds to about 52 ms . it is the brightest <unk> <unk> .

W-CLS-PGN: ngc499 ist eine elliptische galaxie mit aktivem galaxienkern vom hubble - typ e0 im sternbild fische am nordsternhimmel . sie ist schätzungsweise 22 millionen lichtjahre von der milchstraße entfernt und hat einen durchmesser von etwa 70 . 000 lichtjahren .
Translation: ngc499 is an elliptical galaxy with an active galaxy core of the hubble type e0 in the constellation pisces in the north star sky . it is an estimated 22 million light years from the milky way and has a diameter of around 70 , 000 light years .

W-CLS-TRF: d' arrest entdeckte ngc990 mit seinem 11 - zoll - refraktorteleskop . die galaxie wurde von john ratter im neuen katalog katalogisiert , wo sie als sehr kleiner stern beschrieben wurde .
Translation: d' arrest discovered ngc990 with its 11 - inch refractor telescope . the galaxy was cataloged by john ratter in the new catalog , where it was described as a very small star .

Figure 3: Example of cross-lingual system-generated summaries.

Evaluation of Summarization Systems across Gender, Age, and Race

Anna Jørgensen*
Findest
anna.jorgensen@findest.eu

Anders Søgaard
Department of Computer Science
University of Copenhagen
soegaard@di.ku.dk

Abstract

Summarization systems are ultimately evaluated by human annotators and raters. Usually, annotators and raters do not reflect the demographics of end users, but are recruited through student populations or crowdsourcing platforms with skewed demographics. For two different evaluation scenarios – evaluation against gold summaries and system output ratings – we show that summary evaluation is sensitive to protected attributes. This can severely bias system development and evaluation, leading us to build models that cater for some groups rather than others.

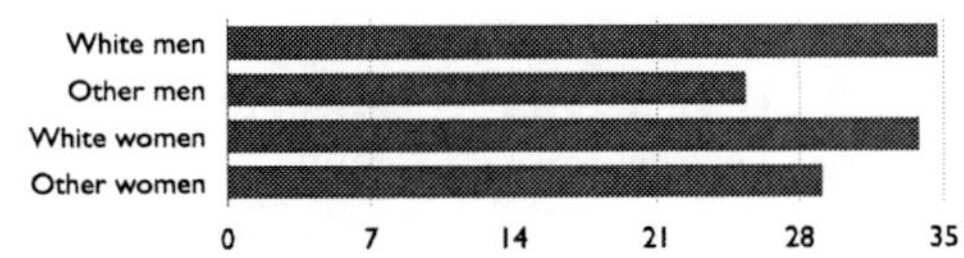

Figure 1: **Social bias in automatic summarization**: We take steps toward evaluating the impact of the gender, age, and race of the humans involved in the summarization system evaluation loop: the authors of the summaries and the human judges or raters. We observe significant group disparities, with lower performance when systems are evaluated on summaries produced by minority groups. See §3 and Table 1 for more details on the Rouge-L scores in the bar chart.

1 Introduction

Summarization – the task of automatically generating brief summaries of longer documents or collections of documents – has, so it seems, seen a lot of progress recently. Progress, of course, is relative to how performance is measured. Generally, summarization systems are evaluated in two ways: by comparing machine-generated summaries to human summaries by text similarity metrics (Lin, 2004; Nenkova and Passonneau, 2004) or by human rater studies, in which participants are asked to rank system outputs. While using similarity metrics is controversial (Liu and Liu, 2008; Graham, 2015; Schluter, 2017), the standard way to evaluate summarization systems is a combination of both.

Both comparison to human summaries and the use of human raters naturally involve human participants, and these participants are typically recruited in some way. In Liu and Liu (2008), for example, the human subjects are five undergraduate students in Computer Science. Undergraduate students in Computer Science are not necessarily representative of the population at large, however, or of the end users of the technologies we develop. In this work, we ask whether such sampling bias when recruiting participants to evaluate summarization systems, is a problem? In other words, do different demographics exhibit different preferences in rater studies of summarization systems? NLP models are only fair if they do not put certain demographics at a disadvantage (Larson, 2017), and it is therefore crucial our benchmarks reflect preferences and judgments across those demographics (Ethayarajh and Jurafsky, 2020).[1]

Contributions We present the, to the best of our knowledge, first in-detail evaluations of summarization systems across demographic groups, focusing on two very different extractive summarization systems – TextRank (Mihalcea and Tarau, 2004) and MatchSum (Zhong et al., 2020). The groups are defined by the three protected attributes: gender, age, and race. While the systems are reported to perform very differently, we show that the system rankings induced by performance scores or user preferences differ across these groups of human summary authors and summary raters. We analyze what drives

*The work was done while the author was at the University of Amsterdam.

[1]We thereby challenge the widely held position that lay people cannot be used for summary evaluation, because they exhibit divergent views on summary quality (Gillick and Liu, 2010). We, in contrast, believe such variance is a product of social differences and something we need to worry about in NLP.

Proceedings of the Third Workshop on New Frontiers in Summarization, pages 51–56
November 10, 2021.

these differences and provide recommendations for future evaluations of summarization systems.

2 Experiments

We present two evaluations in this short paper: an **automated scoring against human summaries** (EXP. A) and a **human rater study** (EXP. B). In both experiments, we use Amazon Mechanical Turk to recruit annotators from different demographic groups, and the first paragraphs of biographies from English Wikipedia as our input data, using the Wikidata API for extraction.[2] We create a dataset of biographies of women and men, obtain human summaries, and generate summaries of these biographies using two out-of-the-box extractive summarization systems. In EXP. A, we compare the system summaries directly to the human summaries (from different groups); in EXP. B, we let human raters compare and rate the two system summaries. To ensure differences between the two summarization systems, we use the 2004 graph-based TextRank (Mihalcea and Tarau, 2004) and the 2020 state-of-the-art, BERT-based MatchSum (Zhong et al., 2020).[3] We follow the MatchSum guidelines described in (Zhong et al., 2020) and limit the length of the input biographies to a maximum 5 sentences and force the output summaries to be between 2-3 sentences long. Our final dataset consists of the original 975 biographies (700 men and 275 women), along with two automatic summaries, as well as human 3 sentence summaries, and is made freely available.[6]

Our evaluations rely on annotations and ratings from Amazon Mechanical Turk. For quality control, we rely on a control question, as well as analyzing annotation time: If a task is completed faster than one standard deviation of the average time spent, the answers in that task are discarded. We collected one manual summary and two system rankings per biography, resulting in 3,135 annotations.

Gender	Race	Rouge-1	Rouge-L
♀		0.407	0.326
♂		0.417	0.326
♀	White	0.418	0.338
	Other	0.371	0.291
♂	White	**0.436**	**0.347**
	Other	0.347	0.254

Table 1: Automated scoring of MatchSum (Zhong et al., 2020) across self-reported protected attributes: **gender**, with values ♀, ♂, and other (all our annotators identified as either male or female), **race**, binarized here as white and other (in order to achieve rough size balance). The ROUGE scores of MatchSum are clearly higher when evaluated against reference summaries created by white men. We also considered **age** (binarized as ±30, to achieve size balance): Here we see slightly better performance when evaluated against summaries of older participants across all genders annotators identified with.

Human summaries In EXP. A, participants were asked to enter the three most important sentences in the document and in three blank text fields; for quality control, we check that these sentences occur in the input document. We collect a total of 1,185 summaries, 53% of which are written by women (0.5% identified neither as male or female). 74% of summaries are written by participants older than 30 years of age. 76% identified as white; 11% as Blacks; 5% as American Indians; 4% as Asians, and 4% as Hispanics.[7] We binarize race as white and other to achieve rough size balance across groups. Aggregating scores across multiple races is not ideal, but by doing so, we compensate for poor representation of some demographics.

Rater study In EXP. B, we present participants with two 2-3 sentence machine summaries and ask them to a) pick their preferred summary and b) rank the two summaries on 4-point forced Likert scales, for fluency, informativeness and usefulness. 40.2% of our raters identified as female. 37.5% were below 30 years of age. 70.8% of ratings identified as white, the rest as American Indians (2.3%), Asians (3.5%), Blacks (19.1%), Hispanics

[2]https://query.wikidata.org/

[3]We use the implementation of TextRank by Barrios et al. (2016)[4] and the original MatchSum implementation.[5] MatchSum obtains state-of-the-art performance across a range of benchmarks by learning to produce summaries whose document encoding is similar to that of the input document. TextRank is a much simpler extractive algorithm; it adopts PageRank to compute node centrality recursively based on a Markov chain model. While MatchSum obtains a Rouge-1 score of .44 on CNN/Daily Mail, TextRank obtains a Rouge-1 score of .33 (Zheng and Lapata, 2019). We use both systems with recommended parameters, as was done in Zheng and Lapata (2019). Note that TextRank, in contrast to MatchSum, is unsupervised. Our Rouge-1 scores below for Wikipedia biographies are generally comparable.

[6]https://github.com/ajoer/summary_preferences

[7]Our race taxonomy was standard, based on https://www.census.gov/prod/2001pubs/cenbr01-1.pdf, but all annotators identified as either American Indian, Asian, black, Hispanic, or white.

Gender	Age	TextRank	MatchSum	N/A
♀	≥30	0.379	0.565	0.056
	<30	**0.481**	**0.454**	0.065
♂	≥30	0.397	0.511	0.092
	<30	0.396	0.531	0.073

Table 2: System ratings across participant gender and age. We highlight the outlier: Younger women significantly preferred TextRank over MatchSum ($p < 0.01$).

Age	Race	TextRank	MatchSum	N/A
<30	ASIAN	34.1	39.0	26.8
	BLACK	**49.0**	**43.1**	7.8
	HISPANIC	40.7	59.3	0.0
	WHITE	43.6	53.5	2.9
≥30	AMER. IND.	40.0	51.3	8.7
	WHITE	43.6	53.5	2.9

Table 3: System ratings across participant race and age. We highlight the outlier: Young blacks significantly preferred TextRank over MatchSum ($p < 0.01$).

		Informative		Useful		Fluent	
	Age	T	M	T	M	T	M
ALL	≥30	0.94	0.96	0.94	0.96	0.9	0.95
	<30	0.77	0.81	0.72	0.79	0.81	0.83
♂	≥30	0.88	0.92	0.86	0.91	0.84	0.89
	<30	0.86	0.9	0.82	0.89	0.85	0.91
♀	≥30	0.89	0.91	0.88	0.92	0.88	0.91
	<30	0.83	0.84	0.8	0.83	0.86	0.83

Table 4: Rater study results with respect to age, on all biographies, as well as on biographies of men (♂) and women (♀) only.

	Informative		Useful		Fluent	
Race	T	M	T	M	T	M
AMER. INDIAN	0.5	0.6	0.7	0.7	**1.2**	1.0
ASIAN	0.7	1.0	0.8	0.9	1.0	0.8
BLACK	0.7	0.8	1.0	0.8	0.9	0.8
HISPANIC	**1.4**	0.9	**1.5**	**1.2**	0.9	1.0
WHITE	0.8	0.7	0.8	0.8	0.9	0.8

Table 5: Rater study results on ALL for race

(2.0%), or as others (2.2%).

We ask all participants to voluntarily submit their race and gender information, and require that they be US-based. We asked the participants in the rater study to also include age information.

Results In Table 1, we present the results of EXP. A: Rouge-1 and Rouge-L results are significantly better when evaluated on summaries produced by white men than when evaluated on summaries produced by any other group. MatchSum summaries also align better with those written by white women compared to those written by non-white women. Generally, MatchSum aligns better with men than with women.

EXP. 2 includes three demographic variables (gender, age, and race). Table 2 presents ratings across gender and age. Most participants prefer the reportedly superior system (with a Rouge-1 advantage of 0.11 on a standard benchmark; see §2), but younger women significantly preferred TextRank over MatchSum ($p < 0.01$). Table 3 presents the ratings across age and race. Here, we again find a single outlier group: Younger blacks significantly prefer TextRank over MatchSum ($p < 0.01$). Our results imply that our standard evaluation methodologies do not align with the subjective evaluations of younger women and younger blacks.

We try to explain these two observations in §5.

We checked for significant group rating differences using bootstrap tests (Efron and Tibshirani, 1994; Dror et al., 2018). Across 1000 rounds, with Bonferroni correction, we find significant ($p < 0.05$) differences in preferences for these groups: ≥30, AMERICAN INDIAN, WHITE ♂, AMERICAN INDIAN ♀, ≥30 ♂, ASIAN< 30, ASIAN< 30♂, WHITE≥30♂, and AMERICAN INDIAN ≥ 30♀. All these subdemographics exhibit significantly different ranking behavior from their peers. So, for example, our results show a significant difference between young and old raters.

We also bin our results by gender of the subjects of the biographies. We rely on Wikidata gender information to make this classification. There are 1409 preferences and ratings of men's biographies (MEN), and 585 of biographies of women (WOMEN). This of course means we see fewer significant differences in ratings of female biographies. For MEN, we find significant differences across a wide range of groups, and with stronger effects for some demographics, suggesting that the gender of the subject of the biography *does* impact ratings differently across subdemographics. We find significant results for WOMEN only for the subdemographic WHITE ($p = 0.004$). This result is interesting, though, since it shows that on female biographies, white and non-white annotators prefer different systems.

Finally, we also asked our annotators to rank the two systems based on fluency, informativeness and usefulness. We used a 4-point forced Likert scale.

One observation is that even across fine-grained dimensions, younger annotators rate summaries lower; see Table 4. Interestingly, however, this difference is only observed with female biographies (rows 3–6). See Table 5 for the results on ALL across race. While ratings are generally low, we see clear differences, with Hispanics finding TextRank significantly more informative and useful, and American Indians finding TextRank significantly more fluent. Interestingly, Hispanics exhibit significant differences across WOMEN and MEN, finding TextRank summaries of female biographies significantly more informative and useful than TextRank summaries of male biographies.

3 Analysis

In order to analyze the differences between the rating behavior of subdemographics, we learn which features are significant for each demographic by training a simple logistic regression text classifier trained on the summaries ranked by each of the subdemographics with significantly different ranking behavior. As task representation, we represent each ranking instance as a vector of 2*149 features, one 149-sized subspace for each summary. Each subspace is made up of a one-hot vector of 145 frequent words (from the English stop words list in NLTK[8]), as well as four task specific features: the summary's average word length, whether the first sentence of the biography is included in the summary, the type/token ratio, and the text complexity of the summaries. We concatenate the 149 features from each system and scale them. We extract the top 20 most salient features for each demographic group and analyze them manually:

The **average word length** of the MatchSum system correlates positively to annotators preferring MatchSum across several demographics, e.g., OVER 30 and MALE WHITE, but this effect is absent with female annotators. Since the inductive bias of TextRank does not explicitly prohibit redundancy (Mihalcea and Tarau, 2004), this finding indicates that MatchSum is preferred among older men, especially whites, when it is informative, introduces main entities, etc. However, other subdemographics seem less sensitive to this variation. MatchSum is *not* generally rated more informative and useful across demographics (Table 5). In other subdemographics, e.g., AMERICAN INDIAN, MatchSum summaries with **pronouns** are rated higher, indicating it is better than TextRank at extracting sentences with pronouns without breaking coreference chains. Referential clarity, e.g., dangling pronouns, is a known source of error in summarization (Pitler et al., 2010; Durrett et al., 2016). TextRank summaries are often preferred by AMERICAN INDIAN and ASIAN, when they include **negation**. This is unsurprising, since negated sentences can often be very informative, and may seem more sophisticated in the context of machine-generated summaries. Negation is also a known source of error (Fiszman et al., 2006). In our data, however, this effect varies across subdemographics.

Our main observation is that female and black participants under 30 prefer TextRank over MatchSum. What drives this? The main predictors in our logistic regression analysis are a) TextRank extracting the **first sentence** of the biography (*twice* as frequently than MatchSum, in more than half of its summaries); and b) TextRank sentences containing **negation**. The former suggests a need for anchoring or framing of the summary, as initial sentences tend to provide this; the latter could suggest that young female or black participants are less prone to the common bias of evaluating negated sentences as less important (Kaup et al., 2013).

4 Conclusion

Our paper is, as far as we know, the first to evaluate summarization systems across different subdemographics. We did so in two different evaluation scenarios: automatic evaluation against gold summaries and system output ratings by human evaluators. We made the gold summaries and the ratings available for future research.

What did we learn from our experiments? Most importantly, of course, we learned that performance numbers differ when evaluated on summaries written by different subdemographics, and that the preferences of rathers from different subdemographics differ. In our experiments with automatic evaluation against gold summaries written by different subdemographics, we saw that summarization systems achieve higher performance scores when evaluated on summaries produced by white men, highlighting an unfortunate bias in these systems. In our rater studies, we also saw significant differences across subdemographics. Most surprisingly, perhaps, we saw that a summarization system from 2004 was rated better than a state-of-the-art system from 2020 by some subdemographics, and effect

[8]nltk.org

that was found to relate to the occurrence of first sentences (providing anchoring or framing of summaries) and negation (often evaluated as less important by majority groups). For now, we can only speculate what a summarization system optimized to perform well across *all* subdemographics would look like, e.g., a system minimizing the worst-case loss across subdemographics rather than the average loss. Our results show very clearly, however, the current state of the art in summarization is biased toward some demographics and therefore fundamentally unfair.

Acknowledgement

We thank the anonymous reviewers, the workshop organizers, and our colleagues at CoAStaL for their helpful comments on early drafts of this paper. The second author was funded by Innovation Fund Denmark.

Ethics Statement

We present two evaluations of summarization systems in which we bin participants by gender, age, and race. All demographic information was self-reported, and we payed annotators equally who chose *not* to report this information. Our work highlights the importance of recruiting balanced pools of participants in evaluations of summarization systems, an issue that has previously been ignored. A major limitation of this work is the under-representation of some groups, which led us to binarize all three social variables. We think of this study as a first attempt to highlight an important issue and hope that others will follow up with large-scale studies with better representation for more groups. Such studies could include many other social variables, e.g., income or level of education.

References

Federico Barrios, Federico López, Luis Argerich, and Rosa Wachenchauzer. 2016. Variations of the similarity function of textrank for automated summarization. *CoRR*, abs/1602.03606.

Rotem Dror, Gili Baumer, Segev Shlomov, and Roi Reichart. 2018. The hitchhiker's guide to testing statistical significance in natural language processing. In *Proceedings of the 56th Annual Meeting of the Association for Computational Linguistics (Volume 1: Long Papers)*, pages 1383–1392, Melbourne, Australia. Association for Computational Linguistics.

Greg Durrett, Taylor Berg-Kirkpatrick, and Dan Klein. 2016. Learning-based single-document summarization with compression and anaphoricity constraints. In *Proceedings of the 54th Annual Meeting of the Association for Computational Linguistics (Volume 1: Long Papers)*, pages 1998–2008, Berlin, Germany. Association for Computational Linguistics.

Bradley Efron and Robert J Tibshirani. 1994. *An introduction to the bootstrap*. CRC Press.

Kawin Ethayarajh and Dan Jurafsky. 2020. Utility is in the eye of the user: A critique of NLP leaderboards. In *Proceedings of the 2020 Conference on Empirical Methods in Natural Language Processing (EMNLP)*, pages 4846–4853, Online. Association for Computational Linguistics.

Marcelo Fiszman, Thomas C Rindflesch, and Halil Kilicoglu. 2006. Summarizing drug information in medline citations. *AMIA ... Annual Symposium proceedings. AMIA Symposium*, page 254—258.

Dan Gillick and Yang Liu. 2010. Non-expert evaluation of summarization systems is risky. In *Proceedings of the NAACL HLT 2010 Workshop on Creating Speech and Language Data with Amazon's Mechanical Turk*, pages 148–151, Los Angeles. Association for Computational Linguistics.

Yvette Graham. 2015. Re-evaluating automatic summarization with BLEU and 192 shades of ROUGE. In *Proceedings of the 2015 Conference on Empirical Methods in Natural Language Processing*, pages 128–137, Lisbon, Portugal. Association for Computational Linguistics.

Barbara Kaup, Rolf Zwaan, and Jana Lüdtke. 2013. The experiential view of language comprehension: How is negation represented?

Brian Larson. 2017. Gender as a variable in natural-language processing: Ethical considerations. In *Proceedings of the First ACL Workshop on Ethics in Natural Language Processing*, pages 1–11, Valencia, Spain. Association for Computational Linguistics.

Chin-Yew Lin. 2004. ROUGE: A package for automatic evaluation of summaries. In *Text Summarization Branches Out*, pages 74–81, Barcelona, Spain. Association for Computational Linguistics.

Feifan Liu and Yang Liu. 2008. Correlation between ROUGE and human evaluation of extractive meeting summaries. In *Proceedings of ACL-08: HLT, Short Papers*, pages 201–204, Columbus, Ohio. Association for Computational Linguistics.

Rada Mihalcea and Paul Tarau. 2004. TextRank: Bringing order into text. In *Proceedings of the 2004 Conference on Empirical Methods in Natural Language Processing*, pages 404–411, Barcelona, Spain. Association for Computational Linguistics.

Ani Nenkova and Rebecca Passonneau. 2004. Evaluating content selection in summarization: The pyramid method. In *Proceedings of the Human Language Technology Conference of the North American Chapter of the Association for Computational Linguistics: HLT-NAACL 2004*, pages 145–152, Boston, Massachusetts, USA. Association for Computational Linguistics.

Emily Pitler, Annie Louis, and Ani Nenkova. 2010. Automatic evaluation of linguistic quality in multi-document summarization. In *Proceedings of the 48th Annual Meeting of the Association for Computational Linguistics*, pages 544–554, Uppsala, Sweden. Association for Computational Linguistics.

Natalie Schluter. 2017. The limits of automatic summarisation according to ROUGE. In *Proceedings of the 15th Conference of the European Chapter of the Association for Computational Linguistics: Volume 2, Short Papers*, pages 41–45, Valencia, Spain. Association for Computational Linguistics.

Hao Zheng and Mirella Lapata. 2019. Sentence centrality revisited for unsupervised summarization. In *Proceedings of the 57th Annual Meeting of the Association for Computational Linguistics*, pages 6236–6247, Florence, Italy. Association for Computational Linguistics.

Ming Zhong, Pengfei Liu, Yiran Chen, Danqing Wang, Xipeng Qiu, and Xuanjing Huang. 2020. Extractive summarization as text matching. In *Proceedings of the 58th Annual Meeting of the Association for Computational Linguistics*, pages 6197–6208, Barcelona, Spain. Association for Computational Linguistics.

Evaluation of Abstractive Summarisation Models with Machine Translation in Deliberative Processes

Miguel Arana-Catania[1,2], Rob Procter[1,2], Yulan He[1,2], Maria Liakata[2,3]
[1]Department of Computer Science, University of Warwick, UK
[2]Alan Turing Institute, UK
[3]Queen-Mary University of London, UK

Abstract

We present work on summarising deliberative processes for non-English languages. Unlike commonly studied datasets, such as news articles, this deliberation dataset reflects difficulties of combining multiple narratives, mostly of poor grammatical quality, in a single text. We report an extensive evaluation of a wide range of abstractive summarisation models in combination with an off-the-shelf machine translation model. Texts are translated into English, summarised, and translated back to the original language. We obtain promising results regarding the fluency, consistency and relevance of the summaries produced. Our approach is easy to implement for many languages for production purposes by simply changing the translation model.

1 Introduction

The processes of deliberation and collective intelligence production have evolved radically thanks to the possibility of carrying them out digitally. However, this often results in large amounts of generated content in the deliberations, causing information overload that prevents their potential from being fully realised (Arana-Catania et al., 2021; Davies and Procter, 2020; Davies et al., 2021). To address this, we evaluate the potential value of abstractive summarisation models when combined together with a machine translation system in synthesising and filtering information collected through such processes. Whereas the current technology of language models is mostly limited to a few languages, which creates a barrier to their more widespread use, our approach can be deployed for many languages just by changing the translation model without the need to generate new, ad-hoc corpora for the task or costly retraining for each new language. The current evaluation is done in a Spanish deliberation dataset.

We have carried out an evaluation with 6 abstractive summarisation models: BART (Lewis et al., 2019), T5 (Raffel et al., 2019), BERT (PreSumm – BertSumExtAbs: Liu and Lapata, 2019), PG (Pointer-Generator with Coverage Penalty) (See et al., 2017), CopyTransformer (Gehrmann et al., 2018), and FastAbsRL (Chen and Bansal, 2018). Those models are applied in combination with the machine translation system MarianMT (Junczys-Dowmunt et al., 2018) using the Opus-MT models (Tiedemann and Thottingal, 2020). We have evaluated the quality of the summaries for each model and their comparison.

Early research on the problem of text summarisation in low resourced languages (although not focused on deliberation) Orăsan and Chiorean (2008) demonstrated the limitations of machine translation systems at that time. Recently, Ouyang et al. (2019) revisited the problem of low quality translations in low resourced languages and successfully demonstrated the possibility of using abstractive summarisation by retraining their model on corpora that have gone through the same machine translation process. In this study, we complete the cycle, translating from the original language to English, summarising, and translating back to the original language, thus avoiding the need for retraining.

Using other approaches, Yao et al. (2015) studied English-to-Chinese summarisation combining an extractive approach with a process of sentence compression that effectively abstracts the results. Duan et al. (2019), following Shen et al. (2018), exploited the capability of a resource-rich language summariser in a teacher-student framework that connects it to the target language summariser.

2 Dataset

The evaluation has been carried out with a dataset from deliberative processes in Spanish, which was translated into English to carry out the summarisation. The generated summaries were then translated back into Spanish for evaluation. Thus, the evaluators evaluated summaries of Spanish texts.

Proceedings of the Third Workshop on New Frontiers in Summarization, pages 57–64
November 10, 2021. ©2021 Association for Computational Linguistics

The dataset is available in the Madrid City Council 'Datos Abiertos' repository[1], called 'Comentarios'. It contains public deliberations in relation to citizen proposals submitted to the participation platform of the city council. The dataset has been selected due to the great success of the participation platform, which has led to $26,400$ proposals and $125,135$ comments being submitted. This is one of the most successful cases of digital participation in the world and is therefore a perfect case study for evaluating the information overload problem in deliberative processes (Arana-Catania et al., 2021).

Each proposal presents a debate space where public comments can be found. Forty debates were selected covering different deliberation scenarios in the dataset. These represent three cases: 20 debates with ($n = 10$) comments, the most common case of debates with few comments; 15 debates with ($20 \leq n \leq 30$) comments, for the medium case; and 5 debates with ($60 \leq n \leq 70$) comments, the large number of comments case.

The debates were also selected to cover three different comment scenarios, i.e., from very short to very lengthy comments. In the first scenario from $1,000$ to $5,000$ total characters; in the medium scenario from $3,000$ to $13,000$; and in the large scenario from $10,000$ to $18,000$ characters. For each debate the text to summarise was created by concatenating its comments into a single text.

By using debates from all scenarios regarding the number of comments and comment length we ensure that the selection is not biased to a specific scenario of deliberation that could skew our results. Examples of the debates can be found in the Appendix, illustrating the combination of multiple narratives through the different comments and the poor grammatical quality of the texts.

3 Abstractive Summarisation Methodology

Different models were selected, covering some of the best available summarisers, but also different model architectures:

- BART (Lewis et al., 2019)[2]. This combines a bidirectional transformer as an encoder, similar to the following T5 and BERT cases, with a left-to-right autoregressive decoder similar as GPT (Radford et al., 2018). The 'large-cnn' pre-trained model[2] has been used here.
- T5 (Raffel et al., 2019)[2]. This uses an encoder-decoder transformer architecture, trained in the Colossal Clean Crawled Corpus. The 't5-small' pre-trained model[2] has been used.
- BERT (PreSumm – BertSumExtAbs: Liu and Lapata, 2019)[3]. This uses a BERT (Devlin et al., 2018) encoder and a randomly initialized transformer as a decoder, fine-tuning it first as an extractive summariser and then as an abstractive one. The BertSumExtAbs pre-trained model[3] has been used.
- PG (Pointer-Generator with Coverage Penalty) (See et al., 2017)[4]. This uses a 1-layer bidirectional LSTM encoder and a 1-layer unidirectional LSTM decoder with attention, with the possibility of switching between copying words or generating them (Pointer-Generator) and including a coverage mechanism adding up attention distributions of previous steps to minimise repetitions. The 'OpenNMT BRNN (2 layer, emb 256, hid 1024)' pre-trained model[4] has been used.
- CopyTransformer (Gehrmann et al., 2018)[5]. This uses the transformer architecture, but one attention head defines the copy distribution. The 'OpenNMT Transformer' pre-trained model[4] has been used.
- FastAbsRL (Chen and Bansal, 2018)[6]. An extractor agent is used to select sentences (using LSTM layers to represent and copy sentences) and an abstractor network is used to compress and paraphrase the selected sentences. Both are trained separately and then the full model is trained with reinforcement learning by using A2C (Mnih et al., 2016).

The reported Rouge scores of these models (Lin, 2004) are shown in Table 1. None of the pre-trained models used were retrained.

Additional models were also evaluated: Adversarial Reinforce GAN (Wang and Lee, 2018), using Generative Adversarial Networks; Contextual

[1] https://datos.madrid.es

[2] Implementation by HuggingFace https://github.com/huggingface/transformers

[3] Implementation by the authors https://github.com/nlpyang/PreSumm

[4] Implementation by OpenNMT https://opennmt.net/OpenNMT-py/examples/Summarization.html

[5] OpenNMT implementation thanks to https://github.com/sebastianGehrmann/bottom-up-summary

[6] Implementation by the authors https://github.com/ChenRocks/fast_abs_rl

Model	R1	R2	RL
BART - large-cnn	44.16	21.28	40.90
T5 - t5-small	41.12	19.56	38.35
BERT - BertSumExtAbs	42.13	19.60	39.18
PG - OpenNMT – BRNN	39.12	17.35	36.12
CopyT - OpenNMT	39.25	17.54	36.45
FastAbsRL	40.88	17.80	38.54

Table 1: Rouge scores reported on the CNN/DailyMail dataset (Hermann et al., 2015).

Matching (Zhou and Rush, 2019), joining ELMo with a domain fluency model; PoDA (Wang et al., 2019), denoising autoencoder transformer with a pointer-generator layer; and GenParse (Song et al., 2018), combining sequential word generation with tree-based parsing. Our initial qualitative evaluation found that none of them were competitive enough with the selected models. Several of these models work at the sentence level, which may impact their relevance in our deliberative case, where texts are composed of multiple authors' comments.

The machine translation system used was MarianMT (Junczys-Dowmunt et al., 2018) using its HuggingFace implementation, with Opus-MT models[7] developed by the Helsinki-NLP group.

Machine translation was first applied to the original text of the deliberations before applying the summarisers, and then to the summary generated to convert back to the original language (see Appendix). Thus, even when the summarisation models are trained with English datasets, the full system can be used in deliberations of any language supported by the machine translation system. The Opus-MT models used in this work count currently with pre-trained models for 1738 language pairs. It is left for future work to evaluate the effect of the translation model, and to apply it to other languages to determine their quality. The models used here show a good performance (see BLEU scores in OpusMTen; OpusMTes) for the languages used.

4 Evaluation Design

We developed a protocol for the human evaluation of the summaries generated by the different models, following designs used in previous studies (Amplayo and Lapata, 2020; Liu and Lapata, 2019; Narayan et al., 2018; Paulus et al., 2017; Yoon et al., 2020; Song et al., 2018). First, the different models were compared regarding their relative overall quality using the Best-Worst scaling (Louviere et al., 2015), shown to be more accurate than a generic individual scoring model, and simultaneously reducing the number of assessments required (Kiritchenko and Mohammad, 2017).

For each debate, 6 different summaries were generated, one for each of the models to be evaluated. These summaries were organised in 9 tuples of 4 elements each, where each summary appeared in 6 of the tuples in random order not allowing the evaluator to identify each model used. In total, considering all the debates, 360 tuples were produced. Each of these tuples was evaluated by 5 independent evaluators (native Spanish speakers with a minimum education level of a Bachelor's degree), producing a total of $1,800$ evaluations. The score for each summary consisted of the percentage of times it was evaluated as Best, minus the percentage of times it was evaluated as Worst.

In addition, a second evaluation was carried out for two summaries in each debate. The models were selected randomly in each case, while ensuring that each model had the same number of evaluations. Here, we were interested in whether the models produce results of sufficient quality to be useful to participants in the debate. Thus, we we used an absolute rather than a relative score. We asked evaluators to rate the following (definitions were shared with evaluators) on a Likert scale from 1 (Strongly disagree) to 4 (Strongly agree):

- Informativeness/Relevance. The summary contains the most relevant ideas and positions of the debate.
- Fluency/Readability/Grammaticality. The summary sentences are grammatically correct, easy to read and understand (considering as a baseline the fluency of the original debate).
- Consistency/Faithfulness. The ideas or facts contained in the summary appear in the original debate.
- Creativity. The summary has been written with its own words and sentences (instead of copying sentences directly from the debate).

5 Evaluation Results

The results obtained for the overall comparison between models are shown in Table 2, which reports the average scores of all the evaluators.

Paired Student's t-tests were performed between all pairs of models to confirm that the difference was statistically significant. This is not the case for the BERT and BART models ($p = 0.09$), showing

[7] https://github.com/Helsinki-NLP/Opus-MT

Model	comp	σ	$comp_{[0,100]}$	$\sigma_{[0,100]}$
BART	33.08	11	66.54	5
BERT	23.33	10	61.67	5
PG	6.25	13	53.13	6
T5	-16.08	14	41.96	7
CopyT	-16.42	5	41.79	2
FastAbsRL	-30.17	10	34.92	5

Table 2: Comparison scores using the Best-Worst scaling (and thus in the range $[-100, 100]$) with its standard deviation, and normalised to the $[0, 100]$ range.

Model	Informative	σ	Fluent	σ
BART	2.58	0.8	2.85	0.8
BERT	2.53	0.8	2.65	0.9
PG	2.33	0.7	2.28	0.8
T5	2.50	0.8	2.30	0.8
CopyT	2.14	0.6	2.02	0.8
FastAbsRL	2.02	0.7	1.73	0.6
	Consistent	σ	**Creative**	σ
BART	2.88	0.8	2.08	0.7
BERT	2.72	0.9	1.98	0.6
PG	2.67	0.8	2.02	0.6
T5	2.63	0.9	1.97	0.6
CopyT	2.46	0.9	1.81	0.6
FastAbsRL	2.13	0.7	1.82	0.7

Table 3: Rating and SD for each model on a scale from 1 (Strongly disagree) to 4 (Strongly agree).

very close results. There is also a clear overlap between T5 and CopyTransformer. All the other combination pairs are found to have a statistically significant difference ($p < 0.05$).

These results are in line with the previous results on English datasets that BART and BERT are the top two summarisers (Lewis et al., 2019; Liu and Lapata, 2019). However, in the present evaluation the performance of a state-of-the-art model (T5) falls below that of a much older model (PG).

The results for the evaluation of the qualitative aspects of each summariser are shown in Table 3. It is important to note that in this case the standard deviation is larger compared to the first case, which is due to the smaller number of evaluations, and thus the following comments should take into account their statistical significance.

In this individual evaluation of each model, it can be seen again how BART obtains the best ratings in all four categories evaluated. BERT is the second best for the categories of '*Informativeness*', '*Fluency*' and '*Consistency*', while PG jumps to the second position for '*Creativity*'. T5 is in the third position for the categories '*Informativeness*' and '*Fluency*' and PG is the third best for '*Consistency*'.

This confirms the best results of BART and BERT, and a close result for T5 for generating informative summaries, but a poorer result for fluency. This may be the reason why the T5 model performed worse in the general overall comparison.

BART and BERT perform well in terms of '*consistency*', with scores close to 3. They perform a bit worse for '*fluency*' and '*informativeness*', around the middle of the possible rating 2.5. Regarding '*creativity*', the models have a poor performance, with a score of around 2, meaning that they tend to copy instead of paraphrase.

6 Conclusions

In this study we have evaluated the application of state-of-the-art, abstractive summarisation models to deliberative processes in Spanish using an off-the-shelf machine translation model. Although we focused on Spanish in this study, our proposed pipeline can be easily deployed without additional effort to many other languages. This offers significant benefits for production applications (especially cases dealing with wide ranges of languages) that are rarely available in other approaches that usually need to be tuned for each language. However, the evaluation of the quality for other languages is left for future work. We have done a comparative evaluation of the overall quality of the models, and an evaluation of each model with respect to different qualitative aspects: *informativeness, fluency, consistency*, and *creativity*.

As a general conclusion, from the models evaluated BART and BERT produced the best results, and satisfactory results are obtained in the proposed pipeline for the quality of the summaries. With regard to the most important aspects, the models show a good result for the categories of *fluency* and *consistency*, and an average result regarding the *informativeness*. These results are especially promising considering the complexity and low grammatical fluency and consistency involved in texts typical of deliberative processes. BART and BERT are the only models that score above the middle score in each of the three categories, and thus we argue perform sufficiently well to be used in practice.

Acknowledgements

This work was funded in part by the UK Engineering and Physical Sciences Research Council (grant no. EP/V048597/1). RP is supported by a Turing Fellowship (grant no. EP/N510129/1). YH and ML are supported by Turing AI Fellowships (grant no. EP/V020579/1, EP/V030302/1, respectively).

References

Reinald Kim Amplayo and Mirella Lapata. 2020. Unsupervised opinion summarization with noising and denoising. *arXiv preprint arXiv:2004.10150*.

Miguel Arana-Catania, Felix-Anselm Van Lier, Rob Procter, Nataliya Tkachenko, Yulan He, Arkaitz Zubiaga, and Maria Liakata. 2021. Citizen participation and machine learning for a better democracy. *Digital Government: Research and Practice*, 2(3):1–22.

Yen-Chun Chen and Mohit Bansal. 2018. Fast abstractive summarization with reinforce-selected sentence rewriting. *arXiv preprint arXiv:1805.11080*.

Jonathan Davies, Miguel Arana-Catania, Rob Procter, Felix-Anselm van Lier, and Yulan He. 2021. Evaluating the application of nlp tools on mainstream participatory budgeting processes in scotland. In *Proceedings of the International Conference on Theory and Practice of Electronic Governance*, pages 317–320.

Jonathan Davies and Rob Procter. 2020. Online platforms of public participation: a deliberative democracy or a delusion? In *Proceedings of the 13th International Conference on Theory and Practice of Electronic Governance*, pages 746–753.

Jacob Devlin, Ming-Wei Chang, Kenton Lee, and Kristina Toutanova. 2018. Bert: Pre-training of deep bidirectional transformers for language understanding. *arXiv preprint arXiv:1810.04805*.

Xiangyu Duan, Mingming Yin, Min Zhang, Boxing Chen, and Weihua Luo. 2019. Zero-shot cross-lingual abstractive sentence summarization through teaching generation and attention. In *Proceedings of the 57th Annual Meeting of the Association for Computational Linguistics*, pages 3162–3172.

Sebastian Gehrmann, Yuntian Deng, and Alexander M Rush. 2018. Bottom-up abstractive summarization. *arXiv preprint arXiv:1808.10792*.

Karl Moritz Hermann, Tomáš Kočiský, Edward Grefenstette, Lasse Espeholt, Will Kay, Mustafa Suleyman, and Phil Blunsom. 2015. Teaching machines to read and comprehend. *arXiv preprint arXiv:1506.03340*.

Marcin Junczys-Dowmunt, Roman Grundkiewicz, Tomasz Dwojak, Hieu Hoang, Kenneth Heafield, Tom Neckermann, Frank Seide, Ulrich Germann, Alham Fikri Aji, Nikolay Bogoychev, et al. 2018. Marian: Fast neural machine translation in c++. *arXiv preprint arXiv:1804.00344*.

Svetlana Kiritchenko and Saif M Mohammad. 2017. Best-worst scaling more reliable than rating scales: A case study on sentiment intensity annotation. *arXiv preprint arXiv:1712.01765*.

Mike Lewis, Yinhan Liu, Naman Goyal, Marjan Ghazvininejad, Abdelrahman Mohamed, Omer Levy, Ves Stoyanov, and Luke Zettlemoyer. 2019. Bart: Denoising sequence-to-sequence pre-training for natural language generation, translation, and comprehension. *arXiv preprint arXiv:1910.13461*.

Chin-Yew Lin. 2004. Rouge: A package for automatic evaluation of summaries. In *Text summarization branches out*, pages 74–81.

Yang Liu and Mirella Lapata. 2019. Text summarization with pretrained encoders. *arXiv preprint arXiv:1908.08345*.

Jordan J Louviere, Terry N Flynn, and Anthony Alfred John Marley. 2015. *Best-worst scaling: Theory, methods and applications*. Cambridge University Press.

Volodymyr Mnih, Adria Puigdomenech Badia, Mehdi Mirza, Alex Graves, Timothy Lillicrap, Tim Harley, David Silver, and Koray Kavukcuoglu. 2016. Asynchronous methods for deep reinforcement learning. In *International conference on machine learning*, pages 1928–1937. PMLR.

Shashi Narayan, Shay B Cohen, and Mirella Lapata. 2018. Ranking sentences for extractive summarization with reinforcement learning. *arXiv preprint arXiv:1802.08636*.

OpusMTen. 2020. https://huggingface.co/helsinki-nlp/opus-mt-en-es.

OpusMTes. 2020. https://huggingface.co/helsinki-nlp/opus-mt-es-en.

Constantin Orăsan and Oana Andreea Chiorean. 2008. Evaluation of a cross-lingual romanian-english multi-document summariser. *Proceedings of the 6th International Conference on Language Resources and Evaluation, LREC 2008*.

Jessica Ouyang, Boya Song, and Kathleen McKeown. 2019. A robust abstractive system for cross-lingual summarization. In *Proceedings of the 2019 Conference of the North American Chapter of the Association for Computational Linguistics: Human Language Technologies, Volume 1 (Long and Short Papers)*, pages 2025–2031.

Romain Paulus, Caiming Xiong, and Richard Socher. 2017. A deep reinforced model for abstractive summarization. *arXiv preprint arXiv:1705.04304*.

Alec Radford, Karthik Narasimhan, Tim Salimans, and Ilya Sutskever. 2018. Improving language understanding by generative pre-training (2018).

Colin Raffel, Noam Shazeer, Adam Roberts, Katherine Lee, Sharan Narang, Michael Matena, Yanqi Zhou, Wei Li, and Peter J Liu. 2019. Exploring the limits of transfer learning with a unified text-to-text transformer. *arXiv preprint arXiv:1910.10683*.

Abigail See, Peter J Liu, and Christopher D Manning. 2017. Get to the point: Summarization with pointer-generator networks. *arXiv preprint arXiv:1704.04368*.

Shi-qi Shen, Yun Chen, Cheng Yang, Zhi-yuan Liu, Mao-song Sun, et al. 2018. Zero-shot cross-lingual neural headline generation. *IEEE/ACM Transactions on Audio, Speech, and Language Processing*, 26(12):2319–2327.

Kaiqiang Song, Lin Zhao, and Fei Liu. 2018. Structure-infused copy mechanisms for abstractive summarization. *arXiv preprint arXiv:1806.05658*.

Jörg Tiedemann and Santhosh Thottingal. 2020. Opus-mt–building open translation services for the world. In *Proceedings of the 22nd Annual Conference of the European Association for Machine Translation*, pages 479–480.

Liang Wang, Wei Zhao, Ruoyu Jia, Sujian Li, and Jingming Liu. 2019. Denoising based sequence-to-sequence pre-training for text generation. *arXiv preprint arXiv:1908.08206*.

Yau-Shian Wang and Hung-Yi Lee. 2018. Learning to encode text as human-readable summaries using generative adversarial networks. *arXiv preprint arXiv:1810.02851*.

Jin-ge Yao, Xiaojun Wan, and Jianguo Xiao. 2015. Phrase-based compressive cross-language summarization. In *Proceedings of the 2015 conference on empirical methods in natural language processing*, pages 118–127.

Wonjin Yoon, Yoon Sun Yeo, Minbyul Jeong, Bong-Jun Yi, and Jaewoo Kang. 2020. Learning by semantic similarity makes abstractive summarization better. *arXiv preprint arXiv:2002.07767*.

Jiawei Zhou and Alexander M Rush. 2019. Simple unsupervised summarization by contextual matching. *arXiv preprint arXiv:1907.13337*.

A Appendix

We present below an example of a debate used in the evaluation in Spanish and its machine translation to English. Following them we present the summaries generated using T5, FastAbsRL, BART, and BERT. Finally, we include the translations of these summaries.

The texts are presented in the same order used in the project. We start with a debate in Spanish, which is translated into English. This translated debate is summarised, and finally the summary is translated back into Spanish. The evaluators analysed only the original debate in Spanish and the final summaries in Spanish.

A.1 Original Spanish debate

- ademas proponemos tranvía.
- el casco no es obligatorio para mayores de 15 años mientras circulan en ciudad. lo dice la dgt.por lo demás, te doy la razón. deben cumplir la normativa de circulación. pero, eh!... los conductores de coches y motos también. hay demasiados que no respetan a los ciclistas... ¿sabias que en ciudad, un ciclista debe ocupar 1 carril de circulación... y no ir por el borde?.
- se deberían sancionar las bicis que van por las aceras o fuera de los carriles bicis.
- si las bicis van por las aceras es porque es muy peligroso ir por los carriles de los coches aunque estén marcados. no existe concienciación todavía por parte de los usuarios conductores. por otro lado, el hecho en sí de ir por la acera no es peligroso, siempre que se vaya "a paso de peatón". lo que no se puede es ir rápido.para mí el verdadero peligro es en las horas nocturnas, en que muchos ciclistas van sin luz alguna y no se ven hasta que estás prácticamente encima de ellos... eso en amsterdam está rigurosamente prohibido y se multa. aquí he visto a la policía municipal pasar de todo al verlos....
- obviamente quien dice eso no ha cogido una bici en su vida, el casco en bici no salva vidas, es un hecho, salva vidas el conductor respetuoso.
- nunca,pero nunca jamás he visto parar un ciclista en un semáforo rojo,o se suben a la acera para cruzar sorteando a los peatones o directamente se lo saltan,en un paso de peatones menos se paran.¿qué pasa,que las norma no son para todos por igual? si un coche se salta un semáforo,la multa es bestial! un poco más de respeto,sobre todo cuando circulan por la acera a la velocidad que les da la gana,con el peligro que conlleva.se creen que todo vale y la calle es suya.
- se puede circular por la calzada, aunque haya carril bici vecin@.
- no me lo creo....nunda digas nunca!.
- ¿no cree que está generalizando demasiado? no todos van con auriculares, no todos se saltan los semáforos, y los coches se tienen que aconstumbrar a la presencia de las bicis....es un medio de transporte más, y se merece respeto.
- la obligación del casco desincentiva el uso d ela bicicleta, que en el caso de mardid está mejorando la movilidad sin aumentar la contaminación

A.2 Machine translated debate

- and we're proposing a tram.
- the helmet is not mandatory for more than 15 years as they travel in the city. says dgt. otherwise, I give you the reason. they must comply with the traffic regulations. but, uh!... the drivers of cars and motorcycles also. there are too many that do not respect cyclists... did you know that in the town, a cyclist must occupy 1 lane of traffic... and not go by the edge?.
- bikes that go along the sidewalks or off the bike lanes should be sanctioned.
- if the bikes go through the sidewalks it is because it is very dangerous to go down the lanes of the cars even if they are marked. there is no awareness yet on the part of the users drivers. On the other hand, the fact itself of going down the sidewalk is not dangerous, as long as it goes "by foot".What you can not do is go fast.For me the real danger is in the night hours, in which many cyclists go without any light and you don't see until you are practically above them... that in Amsterdam is rigorously forbidden and is fined. here I have seen the municipal police pass everything when you see them....
- obviously whoever says that hasn't taken a bike in his life, the bike helmet doesn't save lives, it's a fact, it saves lives the respectful driver.
- never, but I've never seen a cyclist stop at a red light, or get on the sidewalk to cross by

shooting pedestrians or directly jump him, at a pace of pedestrians less stop.What happens, that the rules are not for everyone alike? if a car jumps a light, the ticket is best! a little more respect, especially when they circulate along the sidewalk at the speed that gives them the desire, with the danger that it carries. they believe that everything is good and the street is theirs.

- you can drive along the road, even if there is a nearby bicycle lane.
- I don't believe it... never say it!
- Don't you think it's generalizing too much? Not everyone goes with headphones, not everyone jumps the traffic lights, and cars have to settle for the presence of bikes....it's one more means of transport, and it deserves respect.
- the obligation of the helmet to discourage the use of bicycles, which in the case of Tuesday is improving mobility without increasing pollution

A.3 Generated summaries

- **T5**. the rules are not for everyone alike. not everyone jumps the traffic lights, not everyone goes with headphones, and not everybody jumps traffic lights. a little more respect, especially when they circulate along the street at the speed that gives them the desire, with the danger that it carries. I don't believe it... never say it! Don't you think it's generalizing too much? Don'
- **FastAbsRL**. the helmet is not mandatory for more than 15 years ." the real danger is in which many cyclists go without any light and you don't see until you are practically above them... that in amsterdam is rigorously forbidden . otherwise, i give you the reason. . they must comply with the traffic
- **BART**. Bikes that go along the sidewalks or off the bike lanes should be sanctioned. The real danger is in the night hours, in which many cyclists go without any light. Not everyone goes with headphones, not everyone jumps the traffic lights, and cars have to settle for the presence of bikes. It's one more means of transport, and it deserves respect.
- **BERT**. the helmet is not mandatory for more than 15 years as they travel in the city it is because it is very dangerous to go down the lanes of the cars even if they are marked there is no awareness yet on the part of the users drivers drivers

A.4 Machine translated summaries

- **T5**. las reglas no son para todos por igual. no todos saltan los semáforos, no todos van con auriculares, y no todo el mundo salta semáforos. un poco más de respeto, especialmente cuando circulan por la calle a la velocidad que les da el deseo, con el peligro que conlleva. No lo creo... nunca lo digo! ¿No crees que está generalizando demasiado?
- **FastAbsRL**. el casco no es obligatorio durante más de 15 años. " el verdadero peligro es en el que muchos ciclistas van sin ninguna luz y no se ve hasta que usted está prácticamente por encima de ellos... que en amsterdam está rigurosamente prohibido. Si no, te doy la razón. deben cumplir con el tráfico.
- **BART**. Las bicicletas que van por las aceras o fuera de los carriles bici deben ser sancionadas. El verdadero peligro es en las horas de la noche, en las que muchos ciclistas van sin ninguna luz. No todos van con auriculares, no todos saltan los semáforos, y los coches tienen que conformarse con la presencia de bicicletas. Es un medio de transporte más, y merece respeto.
- **BERT**. el casco no es obligatorio por más de 15 años ya que viajan por la ciudad es porque es muy peligroso ir por los carriles de los coches, incluso si están marcados todavía no hay conciencia por parte de los conductores de los usuarios

Capturing Speaker Incorrectness: Speaker-Focused Post-Correction for Abstractive Dialogue Summarization

Dongyub Lee[1] Jungwoo Lim[2*] Taesun Whang[3*] Chanhee Lee[2]
Seungwoo Cho[4] Mingun Pak[5] Heuiseok Lim[2]
[1]Kakao Corp.
[2]Korea University
[3]Wisenut Inc.
[4]Kakao Enterprise
[5]Microsoft

Abstract

In this paper, we focus on improving the quality of the summary generated by neural abstractive dialogue summarization systems. Even though pre-trained language models generate well-constructed and promising results, it is still challenging to summarize the conversation of multiple participants since the summary should include a description of the overall situation and the actions of each speaker. This paper proposes self-supervised strategies for speaker-focused post-correction in abstractive dialogue summarization. Specifically, our model first discriminates which type of speaker correction is required in a draft summary and then generates a revised summary according to the required type. Experimental results show that our proposed method adequately corrects the draft summaries, and the revised summaries are significantly improved in both quantitative and qualitative evaluations.

1 Introduction

Research on abstractive dialogue summarization recently have achieved remarkable improvements (Chen and Yang, 2020; Malykh et al., 2020; Chen and Yang, 2021; Wu et al., 2021; Zhu et al., 2021) in diverse domains such as daily dialogue, interview, and movie. Despite the promising performance of the pre-trained language models (e.g., UniLM (Dong et al., 2019) and BART (Lewis et al., 2020)), the capability of summarizing the multi-party conversation is still limited. Due to its difficulty of considering all the actions of every speaker for describing a scene is quite challenging. Specifically, Chen and Yang (2020) emphasize dealing with multi-party situation in dialogue summarization based on several criteria, such as role & language change, referral & coreference, and multiple turns & participants.

*These authors equally contributed to this work.

Dialogue 1 (D1)
Isabella: Hi Betty! Isabella: It was very nice to listen about your work yesterday. Thank you for sharing that! Isabella: If you wanted to do sth together, let me know. Betty: Thank you! **Draft Summary (BART$_{base}$)** *Betty was listening to Isabella's work yesterday. If she wanted to do something together, she should let her know.*
Dialogue 2 (D2)
Molly: listen I've got a free ticket to the Muse concert in Cracow, want to come with me? Hannah: nah, I don't like them Molly: what about you Anna Anna: yassss please. let's go! <3" **Draft Summary (BART$_{base}$)** *Molly has a free ticket to the Muse concert in Cracow. Hannah and Anna don't like them.*

Table 1: Examples of the incorrect summaries that contain speaker-related errors. More examples are in Appendix A.1.

Based on this perspective, we have performed human evaluation[1] on the summaries generated by BART$_{base}$ model to figure out whether they adequately include the contents of the conversation. The results showed that only 47% of the samples can be regarded as correct summaries. The rest mainly contain incorrect contents w.r.t. references, reasoning, and gendered pronouns. One interesting finding is that nearly half of the incorrect summaries have speaker-related errors. As shown in Table 1, even though the generated summaries are well-constructed and seem plausible, they are obviously wrong since they describe participants' actions with incorrect speakers. Specifically, the speakers in D1 (i.e., *Betty* and *Isabella*) should be replaced, and one of the speakers in D2 (i.e., *Anna*) should be removed to make the draft summaries correct.

To address the aforementioned finding, this paper mainly focuses on improving the quality of the dialogue summary in terms of correcting speakers. Existing works proposed post-editing methods for abstractive text summarization (Cao et al.,

[1]We choose 100 test set samples provided by Chen and Yang (2020).

Proceedings of the Third Workshop on New Frontiers in Summarization, pages 65–73
November 10, 2021. ©2021 Association for Computational Linguistics

2020; Dong et al., 2020) and table-to-text (Iso et al., 2020), but they mainly focus on correcting summary of the general corpora (e.g., news articles) or facts in a knowledge base, which are somewhat different from the multi-party conversation. Some researches for dialogue summarization (Zhao et al., 2020, 2021) utilized utterance-level representations by constructing dialogue graph, but they lack in leveraging speaker information explicitly.

In this work, we propose a speaker-focused post-correction model for abstractive dialog summarization. We first construct the dataset by using self-supervised speaker manipulation strategies, which corrupt the speakers in summary on purpose. During training, our model predicts whether the speakers are corrupted or not by using the speaker correction type discriminator and then generates a corrected summary according to the correction type via the speaker-focused correction generator.

Our main contributions are as follows. 1) We show that the existing dialogue summarization model often generates incorrect summaries that contain speaker-related errors (i.e., insertion, deletion, and replacement) through human evaluation. Based on this, we design self-supervised speaker manipulation strategies to construct the post-editing data without extra annotations. 2) We propose the highly effective speaker-focused post-correction model not only to capture speaker incorrectness but also adequately revise the draft summary. To the best of our knowledge, it is the first attempt to adopt the post-editing method w.r.t. the speakers in abstractive dialogue summarization. 3) Experimental results show that the revised summaries are significantly improved compared to the draft summaries in both quantitative and qualitative evaluations.

2 Proposed Approach

2.1 Problem Definition

Given a dialogue context $D = \{w_1, w_2, ..., w_n\}$, where n denotes the number of tokens, an abstractive summarization model aims to generate a draft summary $Y^d = \{w_1, w_2, ..., w_m\}$, which is conditioned on the likelihood of $p(Y^d|D)$. However, a draft summary might contain incorrect speaker information, which is caused by the conditional maximum-likelihood objective (Li et al., 2018).

Our proposed model generates a corrected summary $Y^c = \{w_1, w_2, ..., w_k\}$ as follows. First, we corrupt a reference summary Y^r using the self-supervised speaker manipulation strategies to obtain a corrupted summary Y^s. Second, given the dialogue context D and a draft summary Y^d, the required speaker correction type C is predicted, which can be formulated as $p(C|D, Y^d)$. Finally, the speaker-focused correction generator is trained to maximize the conditional distribution of $p(Y^c|D, Y^d, C)$. During training, we use either Y^s or Y^r as input summary and train the model to recover them to Y^r (i.e., Both corrupted and uncorrupted summaries are utilized to prevent over-correction (Section 2.2)).

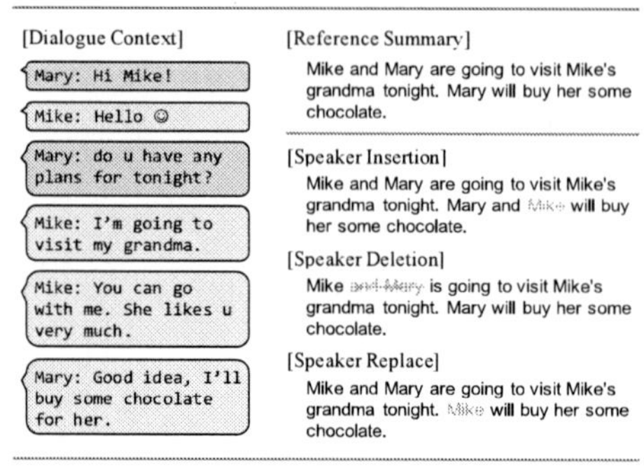

Figure 1: A corruption example with the speaker manipulation strategies. Words in orange represent modified speakers.

2.2 Data Creation with Self-Supervised Speaker Manipulation Strategies

Given a reference summary Y^r, we obtain a corrupted summary Y^s by conducting the self-supervised speaker manipulation strategies: speaker *insertion*, *deletion*, and *replacement*. Figure 1 represents an example of the proposed strategies. First, we extract a list of the speakers from the dialogue context. Second, we randomly choose any speaker to be corrupted and apply speaker insertion, deletion, or replacement functions at a random rate. For the *speaker insertion*, we arbitrarily select a speaker and add it to another speaker with a conjunction or comma. Likewise, for the *speaker deletion*, we remove a speaker followed by a comma and conjunction with other speakers. In the case of *speaker replacement*, we randomly choose a speaker and replace it with another speaker. We also adjust the subject-verb agreement using heuristics as the number of speakers change.

Finally, we label the required correction type according to the speaker manipulation function that is used. For example, if the *speaker insertion* is conducted on a reference summary, we label the required correction type as *deletion*. The required correction type label is used to train the speaker correction type discriminator in Section 2.3. Among the training set, we set the ratio of uncorrupted and corrupted examples to 1:1 to prevent over-correction (Section 2.4). The whole procedure of the speaker manipulation strategies is described in Appendix A.3.

2.3 Speaker Correction Type Discriminator

We utilize the BART$_{large}$ encoder-decoder (Lewis et al., 2020) to discriminate which type of speaker correction is required on a draft summary. Given a dialogue context D and a draft summary Y^d, our speaker correction type discriminator (SCTD) aims to predict required correction type C, where $C \in \{NO, INS, DEL, REP\}$. Each correction type denotes *no needs to be changed, the speaker needs to be inserted, deleted,* and *replaced*, respectively.

The input to the BART is a concatenation of a dialogue context D and a draft summary Y^d, which is represented as $[\textit{<BOS>}, D, \textit{<EOS>}, Y^d, \textit{<EOS>}]$. Then, the output representation of the last *<EOS>* token $h_{\textit{<EOS>}} \in \mathbb{R}^{d_h}$, where d_h denotes a size of output representation, is used to classify the required correction type. We utilize a single-layer feed-forward neural network (FFNN), denoted as,

$$\begin{aligned} Z &= (W_1 h_{\textit{<EOS>}} + b_1) \\ \hat{C} &= \text{softmax}(W_2 Z + b_2), \end{aligned} \tag{1}$$

where $W_1 \in \mathbb{R}^{d_h \times d_h}$ and $W_2 \in \mathbb{R}^{4 \times d_h}$ are trainable parameters. The parameters of the shared BART are represented as Θ_{shd} and those of a single-layer FFNN are represented as Θ_{disc}. The objective is minimizing the negative log-likelihood (NLL) loss: $\mathcal{L}_{\text{SCTD}}(\Theta_{shd}, \Theta_{disc}) = -\sum \log p(C|D, Y^d)$. Another objective of the SCTD is to impose interpretability to the draft summary, which leads to preventing the SCG (Section 2.4) from making a false-positive correction.

2.4 Speaker-focused Correction Generator

Speaker-focused Correction Generator (SCG) utilize the shared BART$_{large}$ to generate a speaker-focused corrected summary. Given a dialogue context D, a draft summary Y^d, and a required correction type C, the input to the BART is represented as $[\textit{<BOS>}, \textit{<COR>}, D, \textit{<EOS>}, Y^d, \textit{<EOS>}]$. Here, we construct the special correction token $\textit{<COR>} \in \{\textit{<NO>}, \textit{<INS>}, \textit{<DEL>}, \textit{<REP>}\}$, which is predicted by SCTD. In this manner, the SCG conditionally generates a corrected summary based on the required speaker correction type. We optimize the model by minimizing the NLL loss: $\mathcal{L}_{\text{SCG}}(\Theta_{shd}, \Theta_{gen\_cor}) = -\sum \log p(Y^c|D, Y^d, C)$.

2.5 Speaker Generator

To make the model more robust, we devise an auxiliary task of generating speakers who appeared in the reference summary. Given a dialogue context D and a draft summary Y^d, speaker generator constructs the list of speakers S, where speakers S appeared in the reference summary. We optimize the model by minimizing the NLL loss: $\mathcal{L}_{\text{SG}}(\Theta_{shd}, \Theta_{gen\_spe}) = -\sum \log p(S|D, Y^d)$. This gives an inductive bias to explicitly generates the list of speakers, which guides the SCG to generate more accurate eventually. Note that we utilize this task as an auxiliary task only in training time.

2.6 Joint Learning Procedure

All the proposed tasks are jointly trained, and the final objective is defined as, $\mathcal{L} = \mathcal{L}_{\text{SCTD}} + \mathcal{L}_{\text{SCG}} + \mathcal{L}_{\text{SG}}$. Note that the shared parameters Θ_s are optimized for all tasks.

3 Experiments

3.1 Dataset

We evaluate our proposed methods on the SAMSUM (Gliwa et al., 2019) dialogue summarization dataset. The SAMSUM dataset is a recently proposed English dataset regarding real-life messenger conversations such as chit-chats, meetings, politics, etc. The dataset consists of 14,732, 818, and 819 dialogue–summary pairs for training, validation, and testing, respectively.

3.2 Quantitative Results

We evaluate our proposed model on the test set by using the standard ROUGE (Lin and Och, 2004) metric. For the draft summarization models, we choose BART$_{base}$ and BART$_{large}$, which are powerful baselines for abstractive dialogue summarization. In Table 2, we compare the ROUGE scores of the draft summaries and those of corrected summaries. Overall, the corrected summaries show significantly higher ROUGE-2 and ROUGE-L scores than those of the draft summaries. Specifically, our correction model shows significant improvements

Draft Model	Speaker Generator	Correction Rate (%)	ROUGE-1		ROUGE-2		ROUGE-L	
			Draft	Corrected	Draft	Corrected	Draft	Corrected
$BART_{base}$	✗	9.8	0.488	**0.493**	0.234	**0.261**	0.447	**0.460**
	✓	9.5	**0.477**	0.473	0.225	**0.251**	0.434	**0.437**
$BART_{large}$	✗	5.4	0.472	**0.475**	0.213	**0.233**	0.428	**0.442**
	✓	3.9	**0.454**	0.444	0.186	**0.194**	0.405	**0.417**

Table 2: ROUGE scores on the test set. "Correction Rate" indicates the rate of the corrections that have been conducted by the model.

Draft Model	Speaker Generator	Correction Rate (%)	After Correction		
			Better	Worse	Same
$BART_{base}$	✗	9.8	60%	21%	19%
	✓	9.5	**61%**	19%	20%
$BART_{large}$	✗	5.4	47%	24%	29%
	✓	3.9	**54%**	26%	20%

Table 3: Human Evaluation results on the test set.

Speaker Generator	F1-Score				
	NO	*INS*	*DEL*	*REP*	Micro AVG
✗	94.67	87.30	95.40	**89.44**	93.03
✓	**95.23**	**92.91**	**96.47**	89.27	**93.89**

Table 4: Automatic Evaluation of the SCTD for each correction type.

Speaker Generator	F1-Score				
	NO	*INS*	*DEL*	*REP*	Micro AVG
✗	98.36	93.10	95.08	96.67	95.83
✓	**100.0**	**96.55**	**98.36**	**98.36**	**98.32**

Table 5: Human Evaluation of the SCG w.r.t. the conditional generation for each correction type.

in ROUGE-2 on $BART_{base}$ draft model (absolute improvements of 2.7%).

3.3 Human Evaluation

We also conduct a human evaluation to validate the corrected summaries generated by our proposed model. Given a dialogue context, reference summary, draft summary, and corrected summary, we asked five annotators from Amazon Mechanical Turk (AMT) to judge a corrected summary is either better, worse, or same compared to a draft summary. An example given to annotators and more details are described in Appendix A.4. As reported in Table 3, the corrected summaries show significantly better results for both $BART_{base}$ and $BART_{large}$ draft models after corrections. Specifically, the speaker generator has little effect on the model when the draft summaries are generated by $BART_{base}$, but shows a performance improvement when the draft model is $BART_{large}$ (Better: 47% → 54%). The reason why the ratio of better results is lower in $BART_{large}$ compared to that of $BART_{base}$ is that the $BART_{large}$ draft model mostly produces more complete summaries than $BART_{base}$ with fewer speaker errors.

3.4 Conditional Generation Analysis

In this analysis, we verify the performance of SCTD and how SCG conditionally generates a corrected summary based on the predicted speaker correction type.

For the SCTD evaluation, we corrupt a reference summary following Section 2.2 and use a corrupted summary as a draft summary. Then, the SCTD predicts which type of speaker correction is required on the draft summary. As reported in Table 4, when utilizing the speaker generator objective as an auxiliary task, the SCTD shows higher F1 scores for all correction types except *REP*. We also observe that the SCTD with speaker generator shows 95.23 in F1 score for *NO* label. This result leads to prevent the SCG from producing false-positive corrections while saving the amount of computation since the summary that predicted as *NO* label is not corrected.

For the SCG evaluation, we sampled 120 (30 for each of four correction type) examples and asked four annotators to judge which operation (*e.g., NO, INS, DEL, REP*) is actually performed when generating a corrected summary given the speaker correction type from SCTD and the draft summary. Then, we measure how well the predicted and actual correction types align using the F1-score. From Table 5, we observe that the SCG with speaker generator shows higher F1 scores for every correction type (98.32% on average). This suggests that our SCG can conditionally generate a well-corrected summary based on the required speaker correction type.

4 Conclusion

In this paper, we pointed out that current dialogue summarization models have problems summarizing the multi-party conversation. To address these problems, we proposed the speaker-focused post-correction model, which can be applied to any abstractive dialogue summarization model. Experimental results show that our model adequately corrects a draft summary.

Acknowledgements

This research was supported by the MSIT (Ministry of Science and ICT), Korea, under the ITRC (Information Technology Research Center) support program (IITP-2018-0-01405) supervised by the IITP (Institute for Information Communications Technology Planning Evaluation).

This work was supported by Institute for Information communications Technology Planning Evaluation (IITP) grant funded by the Korea government (MSIT) (No. 2020-0-00368, A Neural-Symbolic Model for Knowledge Acquisition and Inference Techniques)

References

Meng Cao, Yue Dong, Jiapeng Wu, and Jackie Chi Kit Cheung. 2020. Factual error correction for abstractive summarization models. In *Proceedings of the 2020 Conference on Empirical Methods in Natural Language Processing (EMNLP)*, pages 6251–6258.

Jiaao Chen and Diyi Yang. 2020. Multi-view sequence-to-sequence models with conversational structure for abstractive dialogue summarization. In *Proceedings of the 2020 Conference on Empirical Methods in Natural Language Processing (EMNLP)*, pages 4106–4118.

Jiaao Chen and Diyi Yang. 2021. Structure-aware abstractive conversation summarization via discourse and action graphs. *arXiv preprint arXiv:2104.08400*.

Li Dong, Nan Yang, Wenhui Wang, Furu Wei, Xiaodong Liu, Yu Wang, Jianfeng Gao, Ming Zhou, and Hsiao-Wuen Hon. 2019. Unified language model pre-training for natural language understanding and generation. In *Advances in Neural Information Processing Systems*, volume 32.

Yue Dong, Shuohang Wang, Zhe Gan, Yu Cheng, Jackie Chi Kit Cheung, and Jingjing Liu. 2020. Multi-fact correction in abstractive text summarization. In *Proceedings of the 2020 Conference on Empirical Methods in Natural Language Processing (EMNLP)*, pages 9320–9331.

Bogdan Gliwa, Iwona Mochol, Maciej Biesek, and Aleksander Wawer. 2019. SAMSum corpus: A human-annotated dialogue dataset for abstractive summarization. In *Proceedings of the 2nd Workshop on New Frontiers in Summarization*, pages 70–79.

Hayate Iso, Chao Qiao, and Hang Li. 2020. Fact-based Text Editing. In *Proceedings of the 58th Annual Meeting of the Association for Computational Linguistics*, pages 171–182.

Diederik P Kingma and Jimmy Ba. 2014. Adam: A method for stochastic optimization. *arXiv preprint arXiv:1412.6980*.

Mike Lewis, Yinhan Liu, Naman Goyal, Marjan Ghazvininejad, Abdelrahman Mohamed, Omer Levy, Veselin Stoyanov, and Luke Zettlemoyer. 2020. BART: Denoising sequence-to-sequence pre-training for natural language generation, translation, and comprehension. In *Proceedings of the 58th Annual Meeting of the Association for Computational Linguistics*, pages 7871–7880.

Haoran Li, Junnan Zhu, Jiajun Zhang, and Chengqing Zong. 2018. Ensure the correctness of the summary: Incorporate entailment knowledge into abstractive sentence summarization. In *Proceedings of the 27th International Conference on Computational Linguistics*, pages 1430–1441.

Chin-Yew Lin and Franz Josef Och. 2004. Automatic evaluation of machine translation quality using longest common subsequence and skip-bigram statistics. In *Proceedings of the 42nd Annual Meeting of the Association for Computational Linguistics (ACL-04)*, pages 605–612.

Valentin Malykh, Konstantin Chernis, Ekaterina Artemova, and Irina Piontkovskaya. 2020. SumTitles: a summarization dataset with low extractiveness. In *Proceedings of the 28th International Conference on Computational Linguistics*, pages 5718–5730.

Adam Paszke, Sam Gross, Francisco Massa, Adam Lerer, James Bradbury, Gregory Chanan, Trevor Killeen, Zeming Lin, Natalia Gimelshein, Luca Antiga, Alban Desmaison, Andreas Kopf, Edward Yang, Zachary DeVito, Martin Raison, Alykhan Tejani, Sasank Chilamkurthy, Benoit Steiner, Lu Fang, Junjie Bai, and Soumith Chintala. 2019. Pytorch: An imperative style, high-performance deep learning library. In *Advances in Neural Information Processing Systems*, pages 8026–8037.

Thomas Wolf, Lysandre Debut, Victor Sanh, Julien Chaumond, Clement Delangue, Anthony Moi, Pierric Cistac, Tim Rault, Rémi Louf, Morgan Funtowicz, Joe Davison, Sam Shleifer, Patrick von Platen, Clara Ma, Yacine Jernite, Julien Plu, Canwen Xu, Teven Le Scao, Sylvain Gugger, Mariama Drame, Quentin Lhoest, and Alexander M. Rush. 2020. Transformers: State-of-the-art natural language processing. In *Proceedings of the 2020 Conference on Empirical Methods in Natural Language Processing: System Demonstrations*, pages 38–45.

Chien-Sheng Wu, Linqing Liu, Wenhao Liu, Pontus Stenetorp, and Caiming Xiong. 2021. Cordial: Coarse-to-fine abstractive dialogue summarization with controllable granularity.

Lulu Zhao, Weiran Xu, and Jun Guo. 2020. Improving abstractive dialogue summarization with graph structures and topic words. In *Proceedings of the 28th International Conference on Computational Linguistics*, pages 437–449.

Lulu Zhao, Zeyuan Yang, Weiran Xu, Sheng Gao, and Jun Guo. 2021. Improving abstractive dialogue summarization with conversational structure and factual knowledge.

Chenguang Zhu, Yang Liu, Jie Mei, and Michael Zeng. 2021. Mediasum: A large-scale media interview dataset for dialogue summarization. *arXiv preprint arXiv:2103.06410*.

A Appendix

Dialogue Index: 116
luke: Hey, was just thinking, we should avail ourselves for team selection tomorrow regardless of our injuries
martial: thats what i was thinking also
luke: we should let Jose know that tomorrow
martial: the first thing in the morning infact
luke: the fixtures are really piling up and we need to help the team
martial: yeah, thats for sure, we are a family
luke: we will the coach know that we are ready to play
martial: despite the little pain, me i'm ready
luke: me too
martial: so we meet up at carrington and go to his office very early
luke: yeah, both of us
martial: ok, we'll go together
luke: cool
martial: ok
Draft Summary (BART$_{base}$)
Lukeke, Martial and Jose are going to meet at Carrington and go to the coach's office very early tomorrow.
⇒ Jose is the coach.
↪ Deletion

Dialogue Index: 158
Dave: Hey, is Nicky still at your place? Her phone is off
Sam: She just left
Dave: Thanks!
Draft Summary (BART$_{base}$)
Nicky left Dave's place and her phone is off.
⇒ Nicky left Sam's place.
↪ Replacement

Table 6: Examples of the incorrect summaries that contain speaker-related errors. Dialogue index denotes the index of test set. All the indices are provided by Chen and Yang (2020). ⇒ represents the explanations why the summary is incorrect and ↪ represents the required speaker correction type.

A.1 Draft Summary Evaluation

We describe more examples of the draft summary evaluation in Table 6. They are all generated by BART$_{base}$, and we focus on analyzing the examples that contain speaker-related errors.

A.2 Implementation Details

We implemented our model using the PyTorch (Paszke et al., 2019) library. For the BART-based correction model, we adopt the pre-trained language model BART$_{large}$ based on the hugging face open source[2] (Wolf et al., 2020). For fine-tuning, we trained the correction model using Adam optimizer (Kingma and Ba, 2014) with a batch size of 32 and an initial learning rate of 3e-05. We also utilized the pre-trained BART$_{base}$ and BART$_{large}$ as the draft summarization models. We trained both models using Adam optimizer with a batch size of 32 and an initial learning rate of 3e-05. The correction model is trained for 5 epochs, and BART$_{base}$ and BART$_{large}$ based draft models are trained for 8 epochs and 4 epochs, respectively, showing the best performance on the validation set. The average runtime of each epoch was about 20 minutes. All experiments were conducted with 4 Tesla V100 GPUs. Our code is publicly available[3].

[2] https://github.com/huggingface/transformers

```
Inputs:
  D - dialogue context
  Y^r - reference summary
  FLAG- corruption flag
Outputs:
  Y^s- corrupted summary
  C- required correction type

function SPEAKER_MANIPULATION(D, Y^r, FLAG)
  if FLAG then
    speaker_list ← EXTRACT_SPEAKERS(D)
    func_type ← random.choices[ins, del, rep]
    if func_type == ins then
      Y^s ← SPEAKER_INS(Y^r, speaker_list)
      C ← del
    else if func_type == del then
      Y^s ← SPEAKER_DEL(Y^r, speaker_list)
      C ← ins
    else if func_type == rep then
      Y^s ← SPEAKER_REP(Y^r, speaker_list)
      C ← rep
    end if
  else
    Y^s ← Y^r
    C ← no
  end if
  return Y^s, C
end function
```

Table 7: Procedure to create dataset with self-supervised speaker manipulation strategies.

A.3 An algorithm of Speaker Manipulation Strategies

Table 7 represents the procedure of data creation with our self-supervised speaker manipulation strategies. Here, we decide whether or not to corrupt the reference summary through FLAG.

A.4 Annotations for Human Evaluation

We first showed Turkers a draft summary and corrected summary by our models. In order to focus on the evaluation of speaker corrections, we asked Turkers to count the number of speakers that changed appropriately, badly, or the same as in Figure 2. By counting the number of speakers, the overall assessment of the speaker corrections was

[3] Github repository will be available upon paper acceptance.

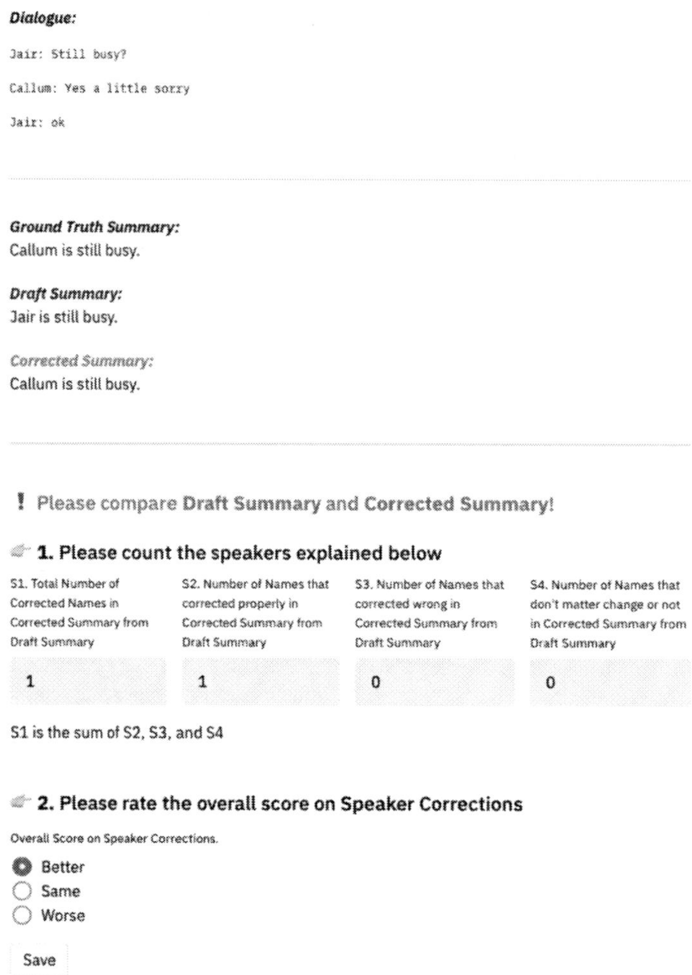

Figure 2: An example given to AMT annotators.

evaluated with Turkers' objectivity. The average Fleiss' Kappa represents moderate level of inter-rater agreement.

A.5 Qualitative Analysis

We also conduct qualitative analysis w.r.t each correction type (i.e., speaker insertion, deletion, and replacement). As illustrated in Table 8, our speaker-focused post-correction model adequately corrects draft summaries for all correction types.

Correction Type	Examples	
Insertion	**Dialogue** Andy: Hi nephew! Paul: Hi uncle! Andy: Are you home? I'm nearby and thought I would drink coffee with you :) Paul: Yup. I'm home. Feel free to come! Andy: If that is ok I will visit you in about 1 hour. Paul: Sure. A lot of political cases for us to talk about :D Andy: Haha. No. Andy: Too much politics with Hannah's father. Andy: I have enough arguments over politics forever. Paul: Hahah. Ok. Waiting for you then. Andy: See you.	**Ground Truth Summary** Andy is going to visit Paul in about 1 hour. **Draft Summary (BART$_{base}$)** Andy will meet Paul for coffee in 1 hour. Andy has a lot of political issues to discuss. **Corrected Summary** Andy will meet Paul for coffee in 1 hour. Paul and Andy have a lot of political issues to discuss.
Deletion	**Dialogue** Julia: Hey, what time are you getting home? Bert: 8-ish. Why? Julia: I was wondering if we should wait for you with the dinner? Bert: Yeah, that would be nice of you. I'll try to get there on time Julia: Ok. Call me if you're running late Bert: I will. xx	**Ground Truth Summary** Julia will be waiting for Bert with the dinner. Bert is coming home around 8. **Draft Summary (BART$_{base}$)** Julia and Bert will wait for Bert with dinner. **Corrected Summary** Julia will wait for Bert with dinner.
	Dialogue Bradley: haha look a cat invaded the pitch at Goodison <file_other> Jill: hahahaha Julia: what a sweet little black ball of fur Jill: here's the video :D <file_other> Julia: haha Bradley: and the commentary :D Bradley: that's the best entertainment Everton fans have had all season :D	**Ground Truth Summary** A sweet little black cat got into the pitch during the Everton's football match. **Draft Summary (BART$_{base}$)** Bradley, Jill, Julia and Julia are talking about the football match at Goodison. **Corrected Summary** Bradley, Jill and Julia are talking about the football match at Goodison.
Replacement	**Dialogue** Randolph: Honey Randolph: Are you still in the pharmacy? Maya: Yes Randolph: Buy me some earplugs please Maya: How many pairs? Randolph: 4 or 5 packs Maya: I'll get you 5 Randolph: Thanks darling	**Ground Truth Summary** Maya will buy 5 packs of earplugs for Randolph at the pharmacy. **Draft Summary (BART$_{base}$)** Randolph will buy 5 pairs of earplugs for Maya. **Corrected Summary** Maya will buy 5 pairs of earplugs for Randolph.
	Dialogue Paula: Why do they make this game with super hard levels? Stew: No idea. I hate those. Paula: It really makes it not fun at all. Stew: Yep. Paula: I just can get past 637 no matter what I do. Stew: Did you try looking up the cheats online? Paula: Brilliant!	**Ground Truth Summary** Paula cannot get past level 637 in her game. She will look up the cheats online. **Draft Summary (BART$_{base}$)** Paula hates the game with super hard levels. Stewart tries looking up the cheats online. **Corrected Summary** Stew hates the game with super hard levels. Paula tries looking up the cheats online.
	Dialogue Willy: Your car is friggin' awesome!! Vinny: I know ;) No, but seriously, I've always wanted a Mustang, and a red one too! Willy: Maybe you can lend it to me for a day or so :) Vinny: Yeah, right. We can car pool together a couple of days a week. Willy: Ok, deal.	**Ground Truth Summary** Willy and Vinny will car pool with Winny's red Mustang. **Draft Summary (BART$_{base}$)** Willy will lend his car to Ginny for a day or so. They will car pool together a couple of days a week. **Corrected Summary** Vinny will lend his car to Will for a day or so. They will car pool together a couple of days a week.
	Dialogue Jair: Still busy? Callum: Yes a little sorry Jair: ok	**Ground Truth Summary** Callum is still busy. **Draft Summary (BART$_{base}$)** Jair is still busy. **Corrected Summary** Callum is still busy.

Table 8: Qualitative analysis w.r.t each correction type (i.e., Insertion, Deletion, and Replacement). Words in red represent the incorrect speakers that should be corrected and words in blue represent the correction results.

Measuring Similarity of Opinion-bearing Sentences

Wenyi Tay[1,2], **Xiuzhen Zhang**[1], **Stephen Wan**[2] and **Sarvnaz Karimi**[2]
[1]RMIT University, Australia
[2]CSIRO Data61, Australia
{wenyi.tay, xiuzhen.zhang}@rmit.edu.au
{Stephen.Wan, Sarvnaz.Karimi}@data61.csiro.au

Abstract

For many NLP applications of online reviews, comparing two opinion-bearing sentences is the key. We argue that, while general purpose text similarity metrics have been applied for this purpose, there has been limited exploration of their applicability to opinion texts. We address this gap by studying: (1) how humans judge the similarity of pairs of opinion-bearing sentences; and, (2) the degree to which existing text similarity metrics, particularly embedding-based ones, correspond to human judgments. We crowdsourced annotations for opinion sentence pairs and our main findings are: (1) annotators tend to agree on whether or not opinion sentences are *similar* or *different*; and (2) embedding-based metrics capture human judgments of "opinion similarity" but not "opinion difference". Based on our analysis, we identify areas where the current metrics should be improved. We further propose to learn a similarity metric for opinion similarity via fine-tuning the Sentence-BERT sentence-embedding network based on review text and weak supervision by review ratings. Experiments show that our learned metric outperforms existing text similarity metrics and especially show significantly higher correlations with human annotations for differing opinions.

1 Introduction

Online reviews are an integral part of e-commerce platforms. Consumers utilize these reviews to make purchasing decisions, and businesses use this feedback to improve products or services. With the ever-growing number of reviews, NLP research has focused on methods to make sense of this vast data resource, including applications for opinion summarization (Suhara et al., 2020; Bražinskas et al., 2020b; Mukherjee et al., 2020; Chu and Liu, 2019; Angelidis and Lapata, 2018) and opinion search (Poddar et al., 2017).

A key characteristic of text in this domain is that it contains opinion-bearing sentences (hereafter, "opinion sentences"). As in preceding work (Pontiki et al., 2016), we view an opinion as having an aspect (e.g., the feature of a product or dimension of a service) and an appraisal (e.g., a positive or negative sentiment). In many applications, one needs to determine if two related opinion sentences are comparable in meaning. From an applied viewpoint, one might think of two opinions being comparable if they support the same recommendation, with respect to the relevant aspect. To compare two opinions, prior work has employed text similarity metrics, where cosine similarity based on TF-IDF (Angelidis and Lapata, 2018) or embedding representations (Suhara et al., 2020) is used to measure opinion sentence similarity.

We group existing text similarity metrics broadly into two types: lexical- and embedding-based approaches. The lexical-based approaches, such as BLEU (Papineni et al., 2002) and ROUGE (Lin, 2004), evaluate text by capturing the overlap in surface forms, such as n-grams of tokens. However, they are often ineffective when texts employ paraphrases or synonyms. Embedding-based metrics, such as Word Mover's Distance (WMD) (Kusner et al., 2015), MoverScore (Zhao et al., 2019), and Sentence-BERT (SBERT) (Reimers and Gurevych, 2019), typically relax the restriction of strict string matching by comparing continuous representations for words and sentences. Such approaches have shown to work well for various NLP applications, including areas involving comparison of sentence meaning; for example, paraphrase detection, question answering, or summarization (Wang et al., 2018; Lan and Xu, 2018; Suhara et al., 2020). However, a detailed study investigating their relationship to corresponding human judgments of opinion sentences is lacking.

In other text similarity settings, such as summary evaluation (Zhao et al., 2019), caption evaluation (Zhang et al., 2020) and machine translation evaluation (Mathur et al., 2019), embedding-

Proceedings of the Third Workshop on New Frontiers in Summarization, pages 74–84
November 10, 2021.

based metrics out-perform lexical-based metrics, as demonstrated by its increased correlation with human judgment scores. However, embedding-based metrics have not yet been evaluated on opinion texts. The success of these embedding-based metrics in other types of text (such as news) cannot be guaranteed for opinion texts. This is because opinion text can be associated with a sentiment polarity. Opinion bearing words that are opposite in sentiment polarity are semantically related. Yet, many of these embedding-based metrics are often trained on semantic relatedness but not specifically sentiment polarity.

We address the gap of lacking research on similarity for opinion-bearing texts in the literature with the following research questions: (1) how do humans evaluate similarity of two opinion sentences? (2) how well do existing metrics capture similarity in a way similar to humans? and if not well, (3) how do we develop metrics to more effectively measure similarity for opinion sentences? We address the first question by conducting a crowdsourcing task that collects human annotations for the degree of similarity of two opinion sentences.[1] For the second research question, we examine the correlation of the text similarity metrics against our crowdsourced annotations. For the third question, we explore approaches to fine-tune embedding-based metrics for similarity of opinion texts.

We make several contributions: (1) we collect and release a dataset of 1635 sentence pairs with similarity scores; (2) we show that annotators broadly agree on whether an opinion sentence pair is "similar" or "different"; (3) we demonstrate that text similarity metrics have weak correlation to human judgments of opinion similarity, and that they perform poorly with differing opinions in particular; (4) we conduct an analysis of differing opinions to characterize the limitations of such approaches when dealing with opinion sentences; and, (5) we propose to learn a metric for similarity of opinion texts by fine-tuning SBERT via weak supervision by review ratings. Our experiments show that the fine-tuned SBERT model outperforms existing metrics for distinguishing different opinions and for measuring similarity of opinion sentences.

[1]The data is available at `https://github.com/wenyi-tay/sos.git`.

2 Related Work

Our research is related to text similarity metrics, which broadly include lexical-based metrics, embedding-based metrics and learned metrics.

Lexical-based Metrics ROUGE (Lin, 2004) is a commonly used metric for opinion summary evaluation. It measures similarity between texts by counting the overlaps of n-grams. BLEU (Papineni et al., 2002) is the default metric for machine translation evaluation. Similar to ROUGE, it also relies on counting overlaps in n-grams. Such lexical matching methods face the same limitation in evaluating texts that are similar in meaning but expressed with different words (Ng and Abrecht, 2015; Shimanaka et al., 2018). METEOR (Denkowski and Lavie, 2014) is proposed to relax the exact n-gram matching to allow matching words with its synonyms.

Embedding-based Metrics Embedding-based metrics are proposed to overcome the limitations of lexical-based metrics (Zhelezniak et al., 2019; Clark et al., 2019; Zhang et al., 2020). Word Mover's Distance (WMD) (Kusner et al., 2015) and MoverScore (Zhao et al., 2019) measure how similar two texts are by accumulating the distance between word embeddings and contextual embeddings, respectively. Sentence-BERT (SBERT) (Reimers and Gurevych, 2019) is a sentence encoder that can be used with cosine similarity to capture similarity of meaning between sentences.

Metric Learning The objective of metric learning is to learn a task specific similarity measure. There are two broad approaches to metric learning. Supervised metric learning requires a training dataset for the task. For example, machine translation metrics learn to score machine translations against humans translations from previous machine translation datasets with human annotations (Shimanaka et al., 2018; Mathur et al., 2019). Sentence similarity can be learnt using Siamese network of sentence encoders with the Manhattan distance with a semantic relatedness dataset (Mueller and Thyagarajan, 2016). However, this approach to metric learning requires a labelled dataset which is not always available.

Alternatively, metric learning by weak supervision uses related data to guide the learning. During the training phase, the training dataset can be different from the end task and even trained with a different training objective. To get the sentence similarity of a pair of sentences, a Siamese network is trained with Natural Language Inference datasets (SNLI and MNLI) using cross entropy loss (Reimers and Gurevych, 2019). To learn the thematic similarity of sentences, the metric is trained on a Triplet network using triplets of sentences from Wikipedia sections (Ein Dor et al., 2018).

To sum up our discussion, it is notable that the lexical-based metric ROUGE is still widely used in the literature for similarity of opinion texts in tasks like opinion summarization evaluation (Amplayo and Lapata, 2020; Bražinskas et al., 2020a). Although ROUGE correlates well with human judgments at the system level but it performs poorly at the summary text level (Bhandari et al., 2020).

3 Human Comparisons of Opinion Sentences

3.1 Data and Annotations

Our dataset is based on that of the SemEval 2016 Task 5: "Aspect-Based Sentiment Analysis Subtask 1" (Pontiki et al., 2016). The SemEval datasets contain review sentences on laptops and restaurants in English. We selected two sentences from reviews on the same product or business to create a sentence pair, for which we collected human judgments of similarity. We constructed 1800 sentence pairs using sentences of at least 3 and at most 25 tokens. Although our dataset covers only two domains, both domains are either often used or closely related to available review datasets. Yelp reviews (Chu and Liu, 2019; Bražinskas et al., 2020a) are often about restaurants and the Amazon reviews on electronics (Angelidis and Lapata, 2018; Bražinskas et al., 2020a) are closely related to the laptop domain. We leave the investigation of more domains to future research.

To ensure that judgments were not trivially about different features of a product, we kept at least one aspect the same between sentences. In this way, annotations would depend on the expression of the appraisal.

Human judgments were collected using Amazon Mechanical Turk.[2] Only annotators with "Mechanical Turk Masters Qualification" were considered. Annotators were asked to rate the similarity in meaning of each pair of opinion sentences on a 5-level Likert scale, using methodology borrowed from the Semantic Textual Similarity task (STS) shared task (Cer et al., 2017). In our annotation task, the scale ranged from 0 ("completely different opinion") to 4 ("completely same opinion"), with the middle value, 2, indicating a partial match.

Domain	Pairs	Alpha	Avg. #Annot.	Avg. Var
Laptop	621	0.541	3.504	0.483
Restaurant	1014	0.624	3.673	0.414
Total Pairs	1635			

Table 1: Statistics on our annotated dataset. Krippendorff's alpha, average number of annotations and average variance of annotations, per pair for each domain.

#Levels	Grouping	Laptop	Restaurant
2	(0,1) (2,3,4)	0.524	0.665
3	(0,1) (2) (3,4)	0.536	0.624
3	(0) (1,2,3) (4)	0.250	0.312

Table 2: Agreement for different Likert scales.

We processed the annotations based on three quality-based criteria: (1) Filter out annotators with low accuracy on quality control sentence pairs; (2) Identify and filter out anomalous annotators; and, (3) Require a minimum of three annotations per sentence pair after filtering out annotators.

3.2 Analysis

Statistics of our dataset are shown in Table 1. The dataset includes 1635 sentence pairs from reviews on two domains. The inter-annotator agreement is measured using Krippendorff's alpha (reliability coefficient) for ordinal levels (Artstein and Poesio, 2008), with coefficients of 0.541 and 0.624 for Laptop and Restaurant, respectively, indicating a moderate level of agreement.

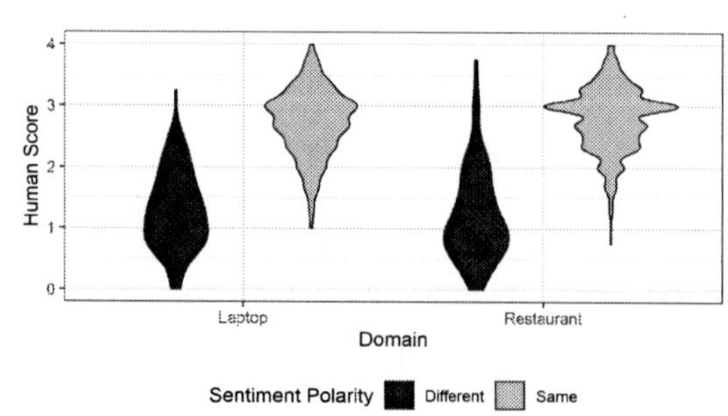

Figure 1: Violin plot of human score of sentence pair by domain and sentiment polarity match.

[2]https://www.mturk.com/

	Laptop		Restaurant	
Metric	P	K	P	K
ROUGE-1	0.078	0.035	0.086	0.068
ROUGE-2	0.102	0.079	0.042	0.027
ROUGE-L	0.070	0.025	0.085	0.070
SPICE	0.074	0.071	0.112	0.116
WMD	0.217	0.184	0.249	0.151
SBERT	**0.430**	**0.311**	**0.450**	**0.331**
MoverScore	0.229	0.172	0.206	0.156

Table 3: Correlation of existing embedding metrics and human scores. The highest correlation is in bold. P: Pearson and K: Kendall.

We investigate the appropriateness of the 5-point Likert scale by comparing the inter-annotator agreement at different levels of Likert scale. Interestingly, while the 5-point scale had the highest level of agreement, a 3-point scale (grouping 0 and 1 together, and 3 and 4 together) led to a similar level of agreement, as shown in Table 2. Grouping the center three levels together led to worse agreement. When grouping levels into 2 bins (0,1 vs 2,3,4), agreement increased for the Restaurant data ($\alpha = 0.665$) but decreased for the laptop data ($\alpha = 0.524$). We refer to the two-level groupings as *broadly different* and *broadly similar* opinions. We draw on this 2-level distinction, also with moderate annotator agreement, later in this paper. Given the moderate level of agreement achieved, we argue that the human judges generally agreed on these similarity judgments. This also suggests that the 5-point scale we collected our annotations on is an appropriate choice.

We explored this agreement further by examining the relationship of these judgments to sentiment polarity. Our selection of sentence pairs were sampled with constraints on aspect but were unconstrained by sentiment, which is already annotated in the SemEval dataset. We grouped sentences pairs with the same polarity and contrasting polarity and examined how humans judged similarity of opinions. We present these results in Figure 1. These violin plots of human scores of sentence pairs with "same" sentiment polarity is spread above level 2 and the violin plots of human scores of sentence pairs with "different" sentiment polarity is below level 2. This is consistent with what one would expect given an ordinal rating of similarity, and supports the use of a 5-point Likert scale.

4 On Metrics and Human Judgments

The following baseline metrics are chosen for our investigation: (1) ROUGE variants, ROUGE-1, ROUGE-2 and ROUGE-L without stemming and without stopword removal, using ROUGE-2.0 (Ganesan, 2018); (2) SPICE (Anderson et al., 2016), an image captioning evaluation metric that compares the scene graph of one text against the reference text; and, (3) WMD, using the implementation of WMD from Gensim (Řehůřek and Sojka, 2010) with the normalized 300-dimension word2vec trained on Google News. We follow Clark et al. (2019) to transform WMD scores to a similarity score using $exp^{-(WMD)}$; (4) SBERT, using sentence-transformers library in python; and (5) MoverScore, using the authors' implementation. These metrics are representative of the different types of metrics. ROUGE is a lexical-based metric, SPICE is a metric that incorporates representations of sentence meaning, and WMD, SBERT and MoverScore are embedding-based metrics.

Pearson and Kendall correlations are reported in Table 3. Pearson correlation is often used for text similarity evaluation. However, Pearson correlation can be misleading because it is a measure of linear relationship, sensitive to outliers and requires the two variables to be approximately normally distributed (Reimers et al., 2016). We therefore include the Kendall correlation, a non parametric correlation that is not limited to linear relationship, less sensitive to outliers and does not make any assumption about the distribution of variable. Amongst the baseline metrics, SBERT has the highest correlation but the correlation is still weak.

4.1 Broadly Different and Broadly Similar

We grouped the data using the binary split (*broadly different* and *broadly similar*) presented in Section 3.2 and calculate the correlations again, presenting these in Table 4. We observe that correlations for *broadly different* are generally lower for baseline metrics (e.g., Pearson correlation ranging from -0.033 to 0.257 for Laptop) than comparable values for the *broadly similar* group. This suggests that the metrics tested have difficulty in determining difference in meaning of opinion sentences.

5 SOS: Sentence-BERT for Opinion Similarity

Our earlier analysis shows that existing embedding-based metrics have low correlation with human

	Laptop		Restaurant	
Metric	**P**	**K**	**P**	**K**
Broadly Different				
ROUGE-1	0.244	**0.180**	0.022	0.034
ROUGE-2	0.082	0.051	0.123	0.102
ROUGE-L	**0.257**	0.166	0.006	0.028
SPICE	−0.006	−0.026	0.014	0.032
WMD	0.038	0.060	**0.233**	**0.110**
SBERT	0.156	0.108	0.119	0.070
MoverScore	−0.033	−0.019	−0.148	−0.073
Broadly Similar				
ROUGE-1	0.053	0.022	0.137	0.076
ROUGE-2	0.104	0.069	0.073	0.036
ROUGE-L	0.058	0.022	0.152	0.088
SPICE	0.132	0.092	0.130	0.104
WMD	0.255	0.177	0.146	0.114
SBERT	**0.391**	**0.272**	**0.399**	**0.276**
MoverScore	0.330	0.230	0.323	0.192

Table 4: Correlation of metric and human scores for *broadly different* or *broadly similar* groups. The highest correlation is in bold. P: Pearson and K: Kendall.

judgments for sentence pairs of opposite sentiment polarity. We hypothesize that the performance of embedding-based metrics can be improved with sentiment polarity information.

A straightforward approach to improving embedding-based metrics for opinion similarity is to use sentimentally trained word embeddings. WMD is based on the Word2Vec word embeddings trained on Google news. For opinion similarity, the sentiment specific word embeddings trained on tweets and the sentiment information associated with emoticons Tang et al. (2014) can be used. We call this baseline approach WMD-SSWE.

Motivated by the observation that BERT-based sentence embeddings has shown superior performance for measuring sentence similarity, we propose to learn a metric for opinion similarity based on SBERT. Our metric is a Siamese network of SBERT that takes in two sentences as inputs and outputs a similarity score. To overcome the problem of costly human annotated similarity score for training, we propose to train the metric through weak supervision based on review ratings. We call our model SOS (SBERT for Opinion Similarity).

Online reviews usually contain a review text and review rating. The review text contains opinion texts and the review rating provides an overall sentiment polarity of review text. For popular review platforms, the review rating typically spans a score of 1 to 5. A review rating of 1 is negative and 5 is positive. We can draw the connection that a review text associated with higher rating is positive. Similarly, a review text associated with lower rating is negative. In our work, we consider positive reviews to have a star rating of 4 and 5, while negative reviews to have a star rating of 1 and 2. We omit reviews of star ratings of 3. For the same product, review texts with the same sentiment polarity (both positive or both negative) are deemed to be similar and review texts with different sentiment polarity (one positive and one negative) are different. This forms the basis of creating the training datasets for fine-tuning our model.

We explore both Siamese networks and Triplet networks for training the opinion similarity model. The Siamese network for fine-tuning SOS, SOS^S, formulates opinion similarity as a classification task with a learning objective to classify a pair of sentences as similar or otherwise. The supervision is a binary signal that a pair is either similar or different. This approach is used by an unsupervised metric for a sentence similarity, where a Siamese network of SBERT is fine-tuned on SNLI and MNLI dataset which is a classification task Reimers and Gurevych (2019). For this work, we create training, development and test datasets of review pairs. Each pair contain reviews from the same product. The pair is either similar (either both positive or both negative) or different (one positive and one negative). We also ensure that the dataset is balanced with similar and different pairs. The training objective is cross entropy loss.

The second variant of our metric is to fine-tune with a triplet network for SOS, SOS^T. Each training instance is a triplet of an anchor example, positive example and negative example. The learning objective is triplet loss, which is to score the distance between anchor example and positive example to be smaller than the distance between anchor example and negative example by a margin. Each triplet is constructed from reviews for the same product. We randomly select a review to form the anchor, and randomly selected another review review that have the same sentiment polarity as the anchor example as the positive example. We then select another review with opposite sentiment polarity to the anchor example as the negative example. For this work, we create training, development and test datasets of review triplets.

Both Siamese and Triplet networks are effective for metric learning, but SOS^T performs better than SOS^S as the training triplets provide context that helps modeling the similarity more effectively. This finding is consistent with the literature for Semantic Text Similarity (Hoffer and Ailon, 2015).

6 Experiments and Results

We examine the performance of our model variants SOS^S and SOS^T on measuring similarity of sentences. Specifically, we compare which training network, the Siamese or Triplet, is more appropriate to fine-tune our model for our task. Apart from comparing the networks, we also included variations in constructing the training pairs or triplets. We constructed pairs and triplets with the entire review text, first sentence of review text or random sentence of review text. We choose to include sentence variations because our task is at a sentence level therefore training examples at sentence level is an appropriate consideration.

We train four variants of SOS: (1) SOS-Siamese-PC (SOS$^S_{PC}$) and SOS-Triplet-PC (SOS$^T_{PC}$)- trained with reviews from Amazon PC dataset[3]; and, (2) SOS-Siamese-Yelp (SOS$^S_{Yelp}$) and SOS-Triplet-Yelp (SOS$^T_{Yelp}$)- trained with reviews from the Yelp Academic dataset[4]. These two review datasets are selected with the intention to train our models on domain related reviews. The models on Amazon PC reviews roughly parallel the Laptop dataset, and models on Yelp reviews roughly parallel the Restaurant dataset. We use python using the code from sentence-transformers library. We use SBERT (stsb-bert-base) model in our metric, and fine-tuned with 10% warm up steps, one epoch and a batch size of eight. We run each model three times and report the average correlation on our opinion similarity evaluation dataset.

The accuracy on the development datasets determines which models to choose. For SOS^S models, SOS$^S_{PC}$ and SOS$^S_{Yelp}$ are both trained with 8000 training examples of entire reviews. Our best SOS^T models are SOS$^T_{PC}$, fine-tuned with 1000 training triplets of entire reviews and margin of 1, and SOS$^T_{Yelp}$, fine-tuned with 3000 training triplets of entire reviews and a margin of seven.

6.1 Main Results

Out of the models we propose, the metric learning models consistently outperform the best embedding-based model (SBERT) (Table 5). Our best model for Restaurant is SOS$^T_{Yelp}$. Although SOS$^T_{Yelp}$ have the highest Pearson correlation for Laptop, its Kendall correlation is comparable to SOS$^T_{PC}$. This suggests that training on Yelp reviews can be generalized to both Laptop and Restaurant opinions. Our models outperform SBERT even when not fine-tuned in a relevant domain. On the other hand, WMD-SSWE have poor correlation with human judgments.

Comparing SOS^S and SOS^T models, triplet trained models achieve higher correlation than the models trained with pairs. A possible explanation is that triplets capture context information that is beneficial to evaluate sentence pairs that are broadly similar. This result is consistent with the observation by Hoffer and Ailon (2015).

For broadly different sentence pairs, almost all

	Laptop		Restaurant	
Metric	**P**	**K**	**P**	**K**
SBERT	0.430	0.311	0.450	0.331
WMD-SSWE	0.128	0.099	0.079	0.188
SOS$^S_{PC}$	0.507	0.354	0.668	0.492
SOS$^S_{Yelp}$	0.515	0.367	0.747	0.535
SOS$^T_{PC}$	0.584	**0.427**	0.634	0.466
SOS$^T_{Yelp}$	**0.606**	0.425	**0.794**	**0.569**

Table 5: Correlation of our metrics and human scores. The highest correlation is in bold. SBERT is the best baseline metric. P: Pearson and K: Kendall.

	Laptop		Restaurant	
Metric	**P**	**K**	**P**	**K**
Broadly Different				
SBERT	0.156	0.108	0.119	0.070
WMD-SSWE	0.244	0.298	0.063	0.171
SOS$^S_{PC}$	0.262	0.176	0.252	**0.196**
SOS$^S_{Yelp}$	0.389	0.273	0.232	0.121
SOS$^T_{PC}$	0.249	0.181	0.268	0.184
SOS$^T_{Yelp}$	**0.396**	**0.299**	**0.275**	0.173
Broadly Similar				
SBERT	0.391	0.272	0.399	0.276
WMD-SSWE	0.141	0.059	0.105	0.104
SOS$^S_{PC}$	0.266	0.215	0.366	0.323
SOS$^S_{Yelp}$	0.284	0.236	0.454	0.365
SOS$^T_{PC}$	**0.478**	**0.346**	0.462	0.333
SOS$^T_{Yelp}$	0.399	0.305	**0.529**	**0.401**

Table 6: Correlation of our metrics and human scores for *broadly different* or *broadly similar* groups. The highest correlation is in bold. SBERT is the best baseline metric. P: Pearson and K: Kendall.

[3]https://s3.amazonaws.com/amazon-reviews-pds/tsv/index.txt

[4]https://www.yelp.com/dataset

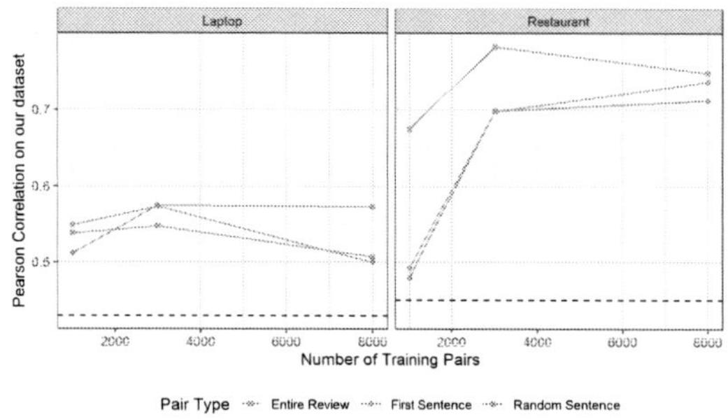

Figure 2: Pearson correlation of SOS^S models on our dataset. The dashed line is SBERT.

our models have a higher correlation than SBERT. This result supports our hypothesis that sentiment polarity information is helpful for opinion similarity and our proposed weak supervision methods (training by pairs and triplets) are effective to learn sentiment polarity information.

For broadly similar sentence pairs, SOS^T models consistently improve both Pearson and Kendall correlation over SBERT. On the other hand, our SOS^S models are not always better. This suggests that the triplet training is more appropriate for "Broadly Similar" pairs. Although the correlation on "Broadly Different" pairs have increased, it is still not as high as correlation on "Broadly Similar" pairs. We discuss this further in Section 7.

6.2 Granularity of Text

Granularity of the text in the training examples can potentially affect the performance of the metric (Ein Dor et al., 2018). We compare the performance of different models trained on training examples constructed by entire reviews, first sentence or random sentence.

The Pearson correlation on the opinion similarity task of the SOS^S models is plotted in Figure 2 and SOS^T models in Figure 3. We present the results for Pearson correlation as Kendall correlation exhibits a similar trend.

Overall, the best models on our opinion similarity dataset are trained on examples of entire reviews except for SOS^S_{PC} which is best with random sentence selection. We initially thought that the sentence examples will be more appropriate as our task is at a sentence level. However, our results show otherwise. One possible reason is that review text contains a mix of positive and negative opinions. Selecting the first sentence or a random sentence might not correspond the overall review rating resulting in a noisy training dataset which eventually reduced the effectiveness of training.

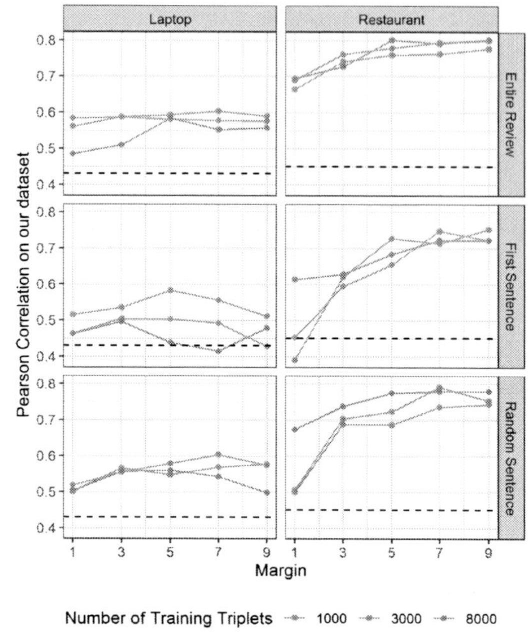

Figure 3: Pearson correlation of SOS^T models on our dataset. The dashed line is SBERT.

Model	Laptop	Restaurant
SBERT	0.430	0.450
Best	0.603	0.801
SOS^T	0.584	0.794

Table 7: Pearson correlation of our selected models and highest correlation amongst all models.

6.3 Optimizing on Development Dataset

We investigate "How much do we fine-tune our model with weak supervision?". Our best models are selected based on the accuracy on the development set. However, is optimizing on the development dataset a good strategy to obtain the model that performs best on the end task?

We observe that optimizing the models on the development set does not lead to the highest correlation on the opinion similarity task (Table 7). However, the performance of these models are not significantly differently (two-sided Permutation Test for paired data at 5%) from the model with highest Pearson correlation. Besides, all our selected models outperform the SBERT model. Hence, model selection based on the development dataset is a reasonable way to select our model for our task.

Sentence Pair	Human	SBERT	SOS^T_{PC}	SOS^T_{Yelp}	Explanation
Restaurant					
S1: Rice is too dry, tuna wasn't so fresh either. S2: Hands down, the best tuna I have ever had.	Q4	Q1	Q2	Q4	Opposite sentiment
S1: It was absolutely amazing. S2: This place is unbelievably over-rated.	Q4	Q1	Q3	Q4	Opposite sentiment and Implicit aspect (S1)
S1: Worst Service I Ever Had. S2: We waited over 30 minutes for our drinks and over 1 1/2 hours for our food.	Q1	Q4	Q4	Q3	Implied opinion (S2)
Laptop					
S1: You will not regret buying this computer! S2: I can't believe people like these computers.	Q4	Q1	Q2	Q4	Opposite sentiment
S1: This is very fast, high performance computer. S2: It wakes in less than a second when I open the lid.	Q1	Q4	Q3	Q3	Implicit aspect (S2) and Implied opinion (S2)

Table 8: Examples of sentence pairs where SBERT scores are inconsistent with human score. We expect the metric scores to be in similar quartiles of human scores. SOS^T_{PC} and SOS^S_{Yelp} are able to score sentence pairs of opposite sentiment more correctly but not sentence pairs of implicit aspect and implied opinion.

Metric	Laptop	Restaurant
Broadly Different Sentence Pairs	116	227
SPICE	0.069	0.062
WMD	0.181	0.172
SBERT	0.052	0.097
MoverScore	0.250	0.198
SOS^T_{PC}	0.000	0.018
SOS^T_{Yelp}	0.017	0.000
Broadly Similar Sentence Pairs	505	787
SPICE	0.000	0.000
WMD	0.028	0.044
SBERT	0.008	0.024
MoverScore	0.022	0.038
SOS^T_{PC}	0.004	0.013
SOS^T_{Yelp}	0.012	0.005

Table 9: Proportion of sentence pairs that are broadly different but scored in Q1 (Top 25%) and broadly similar but scored in Q4 (Bottom 25%) by metric scores.

7 Error Analysis

We examined possible reasons why metrics have difficulty assessing differences in opinion. Table 9 shows how many pairs were deemed similar (in the top quartile (Q1)) when in fact the average human rating indicated they were *different*. For SBERT, the metric correlating best with human judgments (from Table 3), 5-10% of differing opinion pairs show human judgments diametrically oppose to metric scores. SOS variants reduce the percentage of wrongly scored pairs to almost 0%.

Table 8 presents examples for when automatic metrics are confused. Our analysis suggests three possible reasons for the weak correlation: sentence pairs that are opposite in sentiment polarity, implicit aspects, and implied opinions. To better understand the frequency of errors for our dataset, we sampled 100 sentence pairs from each domain and classified the challenges. Our annotations show that on average across both domains, 41% of the sentence pairs contain sentences that are opposite in polarity, 12% contain sentence pairs that contains implicit aspects and 10% contain implied opinions.

Although our SOS models have higher correlation than SBERT for "Broadly Different" pairs, correlations are still not at the same level for "Broadly Similar" pairs. However, SOS models are still not able to do well for opinions that contain implicit aspects or implied opinions. This is a possible reason for the lower correlation in "Broadly Different" pairs. We leave addressing these two challenges to future research.

8 Discussion

Our work have implications for the automatic evaluation of review summaries. ROUGE and its variants are the default automatic metrics for review summary evaluation (Bražinskas et al., 2020a; Suhara et al., 2020; Amplayo et al., 2021). However, ROUGE is shown to be ineffective at evaluating summary pairs with opposite sentiment polarity (Tay et al., 2019). The sentiment agreement is recognized to be important dimension of a review summary and has been included in the human evaluation component of review summaries (Chu and Liu, 2019). This calls for new automatic metrics that considers the agreement of sentiment polarity between summary pairs. Our work fits into this area because we demonstrated that our SOS metric captures the sentiment agreement at sentence level. Future work in this area is to extend the SOS metric to review summary evaluation.

While we focus on investigating text similarity for opinion sentences in this work, an equally interesting direction is to approach this from an inference perspective where one opinion sentence entails the other. We leave this line of investigation to future work.

9 Conclusions

We investigate how humans make similarity judgments over opinion sentences. We contribute a dataset of crowdsourced similarity judgments for opinion sentences. The agreement amongst annotators for judgments is moderate. We study the limitations of current text similarity methods when they are adopted for this task and our analysis show that this is likely due to the inability of current metrics to model *differing* opinions. By fine-tuning Siamese Sentence-BERT using weak supervision, we increase the Pearson correlation with human judgments to 0.606 and 0.794 on Laptop and Restaurant respectively of our opinion similarity dataset.

Acknowledgments

We thank the anonymous reviewers for their thorough and insightful comments. Wenyi is supported by an Australian Government Research Training Program Scholarship and a CSIRO Data61 Top-up Scholarship.

References

Reinald Kim Amplayo, Stefanos Angelidis, and Mirella Lapata. 2021. Unsupervised opinion summarization with content planning. *Proceedings of the AAAI Conference on Artificial Intelligence*, 35(14):12489–12497.

Reinald Kim Amplayo and Mirella Lapata. 2020. Unsupervised opinion summarization with noising and denoising. In *Proceedings of the Annual Meeting of the Association for Computational Linguistics*, pages 1934–1945, Online.

Peter Anderson, Basura Fernando, Mark Johnson, and Stephen Gould. 2016. Spice: Semantic propositional image caption evaluation. In *Computer Vision – ECCV 2016*, pages 382–398, Cham. Springer International Publishing.

Stefanos Angelidis and Mirella Lapata. 2018. Summarizing Opinions: Aspect Extraction Meets Sentiment Prediction and They Are Both Weakly Supervised. In *Proceedings of the Conference on Empirical Methods in Natural Language Processing*, pages 3675–3686, Brussels, Belgium.

Ron Artstein and Massimo Poesio. 2008. Survey article: Inter-coder agreement for computational linguistics. *Computational Linguistics*, 34(4):555–596.

Manik Bhandari, Pranav Narayan Gour, Atabak Ashfaq, Pengfei Liu, and Graham Neubig. 2020. Re-evaluating evaluation in text summarization. In *Proceedings of the Conference on Empirical Methods in Natural Language Processing*, pages 9347–9359, Online.

Arthur Bražinskas, Mirella Lapata, and Ivan Titov. 2020a. Few-shot learning for opinion summarization. In *Proceedings of the Conference on Empirical Methods in Natural Language Processing*, pages 4119–4135, Online.

Arthur Bražinskas, Mirella Lapata, and Ivan Titov. 2020b. Unsupervised opinion summarization as copycat-review generation. In *Proceedings of the Annual Meeting of the Association for Computational Linguistics*, pages 5151–5169, Online.

Daniel Cer, Mona Diab, Eneko Agirre, Iñigo Lopez-Gazpio, and Lucia Specia. 2017. SemEval-2017 task 1: Semantic textual similarity multilingual and crosslingual focused evaluation. In *Proceedings of the International Workshop on Semantic Evaluation*, pages 1–14, Vancouver, Canada.

Eric Chu and Peter Liu. 2019. MeanSum: A neural model for unsupervised multi-document abstractive summarization. In *Proceedings of the International Conference on Machine Learning*, pages 1223–1232, Long Beach, CA.

Elizabeth Clark, Asli Celikyilmaz, and Noah A. Smith. 2019. Sentence mover's similarity: Automatic evaluation for multi-sentence texts. In *Proceedings of the Annual Meeting of the Association for Computational Linguistics*, pages 2748–2760, Florence, Italy.

Michael Denkowski and Alon Lavie. 2014. Meteor Universal: Language Specific Translation Evaluation for Any Target Language. In *Proceedings of the Ninth Workshop on Statistical Machine Translation*, pages 376–380, Baltimore, MD.

Liat Ein Dor, Yosi Mass, Alon Halfon, Elad Venezian, Ilya Shnayderman, Ranit Aharonov, and Noam Slonim. 2018. Learning thematic similarity metric from article sections using triplet networks. In *Proceedings of the Annual Meeting of the Association for Computational Linguistics (Volume 2: Short Papers)*, pages 49–54, Melbourne, Australia.

Kavita Ganesan. 2018. ROUGE 2.0: Updated and improved measures for evaluation of summarization tasks. *CoRR*, abs/1803.01937.

Elad Hoffer and Nir Ailon. 2015. Deep metric learning using triplet network. In *Similarity-Based Pattern Recognition*, pages 84–92, Cham. Springer International Publishing.

Matt J. Kusner, Yu Sun, Nicholas I. Kolkin, and Kilian Q. Weinberger. 2015. From word embeddings to document distances. In *Proceedings of the International Conference on International Conference on Machine Learning - Volume 37*, pages 957–966, Lille, France.

Wuwei Lan and Wei Xu. 2018. Neural network models for paraphrase identification, semantic textual similarity, natural language inference, and question answering. In *Proceedings of the International Conference on Computational Linguistics*, pages 3890–3902, Santa Fe, NM.

Chin-Yew Lin. 2004. ROUGE: A package for automatic evaluation of summaries. In *Text Summarization Branches Out*, pages 74–81, Barcelona, Spain. Association for Computational Linguistics.

Nitika Mathur, Timothy Baldwin, and Trevor Cohn. 2019. Putting evaluation in context: Contextual embeddings improve machine translation evaluation. In *Proceedings of the Annual Meeting of the Association for Computational Linguistics*, pages 2799–2808, Florence, Italy.

Jonas Mueller and Aditya Thyagarajan. 2016. Siamese recurrent architectures for learning sentence similarity. In *Proceedings of the AAAI Conference on Artificial Intelligence*, page 2786–2792, Phoenix, AZ.

Rajdeep Mukherjee, Hari Chandana Peruri, Uppada Vishnu, Pawan Goyal, Sourangshu Bhattacharya, and Niloy Ganguly. 2020. Read what you need: Controllable aspect-based opinion summarization of tourist reviews. In *Proceedings of the International ACM SIGIR Conference on Research and Development in Information Retrieval*, page 1825–1828, Virtual Event, China.

Jun-Ping Ng and Viktoria Abrecht. 2015. Better summarization evaluation with word embeddings for ROUGE. In *Proceedings of the Conference on Empirical Methods in Natural Language Processing*, pages 1925–1930, Lisbon, Portugal.

Kishore Papineni, Salim Roukos, Todd Ward, and Wei-Jing Zhu. 2002. Bleu: a method for automatic evaluation of machine translation. In *Proceedings of the Annual Meeting of the Association for Computational Linguistics*, pages 311–318, Philadelphia, PA.

Lahari Poddar, Wynne Hsu, and Mong Li Lee. 2017. Author-aware aspect topic sentiment model to retrieve supporting opinions from reviews. In *Proceedings of the Conference on Empirical Methods in Natural Language Processing*, pages 472–481, Copenhagen, Denmark.

Maria Pontiki, Dimitris Galanis, Haris Papageorgiou, Ion Androutsopoulos, Suresh Manandhar, Mohammad AL-Smadi, Mahmoud Al-Ayyoub, Yanyan Zhao, Bing Qin, Orphée De Clercq, Véronique Hoste, Marianna Apidianaki, Xavier Tannier, Natalia Loukachevitch, Evgeniy Kotelnikov, Nuria Bel, Salud María Jiménez-Zafra, and Gülşen Eryiğit. 2016. SemEval-2016 task 5: Aspect based sentiment analysis. In *Proceedings of the International Workshop on Semantic Evaluation*, pages 19–30, San Diego, CA.

Radim Řehůřek and Petr Sojka. 2010. Software Framework for Topic Modelling with Large Corpora. In *Proceedings of the LREC Workshop on New Challenges for NLP Frameworks*, pages 45–50, Valletta, Malta.

Nils Reimers, Philip Beyer, and Iryna Gurevych. 2016. Task-oriented intrinsic evaluation of semantic textual similarity. In *Proceedings of the International Conference on Computational Linguistics: Technical Papers*, pages 87–96, Osaka, Japan.

Nils Reimers and Iryna Gurevych. 2019. Sentence-BERT: Sentence embeddings using Siamese BERT-networks. In *Proceedings of the Conference on Empirical Methods in Natural Language Processing and the International Joint Conference on Natural Language Processing*, pages 3982–3992, Hong Kong, China.

Hiroki Shimanaka, Tomoyuki Kajiwara, and Mamoru Komachi. 2018. RUSE: Regressor using sentence embeddings for automatic machine translation evaluation. In *Proceedings of the Conference on Machine Translation: Shared Task Papers*, pages 751–758, Belgium, Brussels.

Yoshihiko Suhara, Xiaolan Wang, Stefanos Angelidis, and Wang-Chiew Tan. 2020. OpinionDigest: A simple framework for opinion summarization. In *Proceedings of the Annual Meeting of the Association for Computational Linguistics*, pages 5789–5798, Online.

Duyu Tang, Furu Wei, Nan Yang, Ming Zhou, Ting Liu, and Bing Qin. 2014. Learning sentiment-specific word embedding for twitter sentiment classification. In *Proceedings of the Annual Meeting of the Association for Computational Linguistics (Volume 1: Long Papers)*, pages 1555–1565, Baltimore, MD.

Wenyi Tay, Aditya Joshi, Xiuzhen Zhang, Sarvnaz Karimi, and Stephen Wan. 2019. Red-faced ROUGE: Examining the suitability of ROUGE for opinion summary evaluation. In *Proceedings of the Annual Workshop of the Australasian Language Technology Association*, pages 52–60, Sydney, Australia.

Alex Wang, Amanpreet Singh, Julian Michael, Felix Hill, Omer Levy, and Samuel Bowman. 2018. GLUE: A multi-task benchmark and analysis platform for natural language understanding. In *Proceedings of the EMNLP Workshop BlackboxNLP:*

Analyzing and Interpreting Neural Networks for NLP, pages 353–355, Brussels, Belgium.

Tianyi Zhang, Varsha Kishore, Felix Wu, Kilian Q. Weinberger, and Yoav Artzi. 2020. Bertscore: Evaluating text generation with bert. In *International Conference on Learning Representations*, Online.

Wei Zhao, Maxime Peyrard, Fei Liu, Yang Gao, Christian M. Meyer, and Steffen Eger. 2019. MoverScore: Text generation evaluating with contextualized embeddings and earth mover distance. In *Proceedings of the Conference on Empirical Methods in Natural Language Processing and the International Joint Conference on Natural Language Processing*, pages 563–578, Hong Kong, China.

Vitalii Zhelezniak, Aleksandar Savkov, April Shen, Francesco Moramarco, Jack Flann, and Nils Y. Hammerla. 2019. Don't settle for average, go for the max: Fuzzy sets and max-pooled word vectors. In *International Conference on Learning Representations*, New Orleans, LA.

EASE: Extractive-Abstractive Summarization End-to-End using the Information Bottleneck Principle

Haoran Li * **Arash Einolghozati*** **Srinivasan Iyer**
Bhargavi Paranjape **Yashar Mehdad** **Sonal Gupta** **Marjan Ghazvininejad**
Facebook
{aimeeli,arashe,sviyer}@fb.com
{bparan,mehdad,sonalgupta,ghazvini}@fb.com

Abstract

Current abstractive summarization systems outperform their extractive counterparts, but their widespread adoption is inhibited by the inherent lack of interpretability. Extractive summarization systems, though interpretable, suffer from redundancy and possible lack of coherence. To achieve the best of both worlds, we propose EASE, an extractive-abstractive framework that generates concise abstractive summaries that can be traced back to an extractive summary. Our framework can be applied to any evidence-based text generation problem and can accommodate various pre-trained models in its simple architecture. We use the Information Bottleneck principle to jointly train the extraction and abstraction in an end-to-end fashion. Inspired by previous research that humans use a two-stage framework to summarize long documents (Jing and McKeown, 2000), our framework first extracts a pre-defined amount of evidence spans and then generates a summary using only the evidence. Using automatic and human evaluations, we show that the generated summaries are better than strong extractive and extractive-abstractive baselines.

1 Introduction

Pretrained sequence-to-sequence language models such as BART (Lewis et al., 2020), T5 (Raffel et al., 2019) and their variants have achieved state-of-the-art results on various tasks such as summarization, machine translation, and data2text tasks (Zhang et al., 2019b; Kale and Rastogi, 2020). Despite the higher fidelity compared with models without pre-training for tasks such as summarization (Maynez et al., 2020), the lack of interpretability in abstractive generation remains an obstacle to their broader adoption. Extractive summarization systems, on the other hand, have the advantage of being interpretable but are too restrictive by forcing the output to be spans from the document, reducing their

Source Document:
(CNN)Mike Rowe is coming to a river near you. "Sometimes, you hear about a person who makes you feel good about humanity, but bad about yourself," Rowe says. **On Thursday's episode of "Somebody's Gotta Do It," Rowe meets up with Chad Pregracke, the founder of Living Lands & Waters, who does just that.** Pregracke wants to clean up the nation's rivers one piece of detritus at a time. His quota? Always "more." Read Mike Rowe's Facebook post on how to break our litter habit. **Since he founded the nonprofit in 1998 at the ripe age of 23, Pregracke and more than 87,000 volunteers have collected 8.4 million pounds of trash from U.S. waterways. Those efforts helped him earn the 2013 CNN Hero of the Year Award, along with numerous other honors.** "Wherever you are, no matter if there's a stream, a creek, a lake, whatever, that needs to be cleaned up, you can do it. Just organize it and do it," he told CNN's Anderson Cooper after his win. Pregracke also gives Rowe a tour of the 150-foot, solar-powered barge that the Living Lands & Waters staff calls home during lengthy cleanups. The part-home, part-office, part-dumpster has seven bedrooms, two bathrooms, a classroom and a kitchen – and just happens to be made from a recycled strip club. According to the organization's latest annual report, Pregracke has made it his mission in 2015 to remove 500,000 more pounds of trash. If you'd like to help achieve this goal, visit his website to learn how to help: LivingLandsAndWaters.org/Get-Involved/.

Summary: Mike Rowe meets Chad Pregracke, the founder of Living Lands & Waters. The nonprofit has collected 8.4 million pounds of trash from U.S. waterways. Pregracke was named the 2013 CNN Hero of the Year.

Figure 1: An example of a summary and its evidence (highlighted) as generated by our framework.

naturalness, coherence, and conciseness. In this paper, we propose EASE, a novel framework that combines the two systems to produce natural summaries that can be traced back to an interpretable extractive summary. Our general framework can accommodate different pretrained models and suitable for any evidence-based text generation task.

The existing extractive-abstractive systems can be divided into three main categories: 1- Relying on attention for interpretability (Hsu et al., 2018). Due to the probabilistic nature of the attention mechanism, it falls short of providing usable evidence; 2- Providing word-level evidence for the generated summaries (Gehrmann et al., 2018). Though more useful than attention, this evidence is too granular to be useful for humans; 3- Training the content selector separately using pseudo labels or other heuristics (Liu and Lapata, 2019; Pilault et al., 2020). In contrast, we seek a theoretically-grounded model that can learn the evidence extraction end-to-end.

Perhaps the closest work to ours is Zhao et al. (2020) focusing on long-document summarization by training a joint extractive-abstractive model via weak supervision. Though a complicated and spe-

*Equal contribution.

Proceedings of the Third Workshop on New Frontiers in Summarization, pages 85–95
November 10, 2021.

cific framework, it achieves poor results on benchmarks such as CNN/DM. EASE on the other hand, is based on the Information Bottleneck (IB) principle (Tishby et al., 1999), which formalizes the trade-off between the size of the extracted evidence and the information provided for the generation of the final output. While this method has been successfully adopted by prior work for a simpler discriminative task (Paranjape et al., 2020), we extend it to generative tasks where the extracted evidence can be viewed as a coarse version of the final abstractive output.

We leverage pretrained language models that first extract the necessary evidence from the source document (*extractor*) and then, using only the extracted evidence spans, generate the final output (*abstractor*). Fig. 1 shows an example of the summary and evidence generated by our system.

Our main contributions are as follows:

- We propose EASE, a general-purpose theoretically-grounded Extractive-Abstractive framework for extractive-abstractive text generation that is jointly trained in an end-to-end fashion. We apply EASE to text summarization.
- Our abstractor generates the summary using only the extracted evidence which can be viewed as an extractive summary. We propose a new *sparsity budget* parameter that controls the trade-off between the length of the evidence spans (i.e., the extractive summary)and the final abstractive output's quality
- Our results show that EASE extracts evidence better than the baselines without significantly sacrificing the quality of the generated summary, compared with the state-of-the-art fully abstractive systems on the CNN/DailyMail dataset.

2 Extractive-Abstractive Framework

There exists evidence that humans use a two-stage extractive-abstractive framework to summarize long documents (Jing and McKeown, 2000) by first extracting salient parts and then deciding what to eliminate, reword, and reorganize. Inspired by this, we propose EASE, a framework that learns extraction and abstraction collectively in an end-to-end fashion. This not only provides interpretable evidence for the generated summary, which can be many times smaller than the original document, but also reduces the effective input length used during abstraction. This has been shown to directly correlate with the extent of hallucination in pretrained language models (Yang et al., 2020a).

In order to formalize the problem, we use the IB principle to learn an optimal model between the original document x and the final summary y through a compressed representation z. The IB objective is to minimize the following:

$$L_{IB} = I(x; z) - \beta I(z; y), \quad (1)$$

where $I()$ is the mutual information. This objective encourages z to contain only the information about x that is useful in predicting y. Moreover, β controls the trade-off in z between containing information about x (i.e., sparsity) vs about y (i.e., prediction quality).

We use a relaxation for (1) similar to Paranjape et al. (2020) to make it tractable. As such, z is obtained by masking the original document x to produce a summaries y. We illustrate EASE in Fig. 2. EASE can perform extraction (i.e., masking) either at the token or at the sentence level. We first describe the token-level model and subsequently generalize it for sentence-level extraction. As such, the extractor masks tokens in the original document x to extract a rough summary z, which is used as evidence by the abstractor to produce the summary y. We define $z = m \odot x$ where m is a boolean mask on the input x. This is similar to the masking process used in Masked Language Models (MLM), except that instead of random masking (Devlin et al., 2019) or heuristic-based masking (Zhang et al., 2019b,d), we learn which tokens should be masked in an end-to-end fashion. Using the variational bound (Alemi et al., 2016) on (1), the model is trained using two loss terms. The first loss ensures that the final summary is close to the golden summaries:

$$L_{Task} = E_{m \simeq p(m|x)}[-\log q_\theta(y|m \odot x)], \quad (2)$$

where $q_\theta(y|z)$ is a parametric approximation to the true likelihood $p(y|z)$.

Similar to Paranjape et al. (2020), we assume that the mask variables over individual words are conditionally independent given the input x. This means that the evidence z can contain redundancies, as the extractor chooses evidence individually without conditioning on prior extractions. Since the extracted evidence is not the final summary,

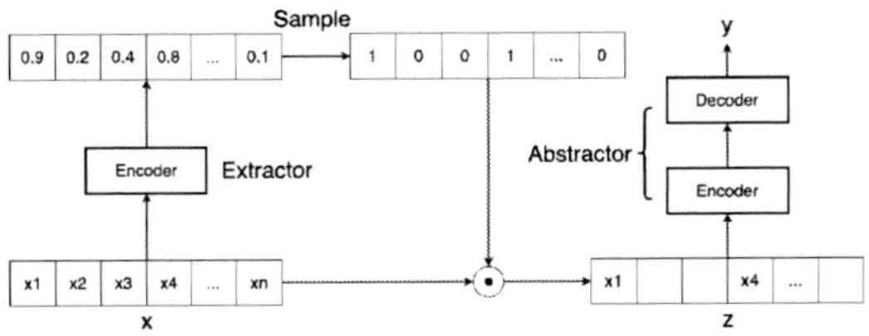

Figure 2: The Extractive-Abstractive model architecture. The extractor samples the evidence from the source which is used by the abstractor.

the abstractor still has the opportunity to eliminate redundancies. Nallapati et al. (2017) explore a modeling approach that keeps track of the current state of the summary, but we leave this direction to future work. Formally,

$$p_\theta(z|x) = \prod_j p_\theta(z_j|x),$$

where $p_\theta(z_j|x) = Bernoulli(\theta_j(x))$.

Optimizing the loss in (2) would result in the extractor masking no tokens and hence, maximizing the mutual information between the input and output of the abstractor. Therefore, the second loss term is a sparsity constraint to ensure that the extractor's output is a measurable subset of input tokens and can be used as evidence for the abstractor output:

$$L_{Sparsity} = \sum_j KL[p_\theta(z_j|x), r(z_j)], \quad (3)$$

where we set the prior distribution $r(z_j) = Bernouli(\pi)$. For summarization tasks π can be small i.e. $0.3 \leq \pi \leq 0.5$. As such, the combined loss can be written as:

$$\begin{aligned} L_{EA} =& E_{m \simeq p(z|x)}[-\log q_\theta(y|m \odot x)] \\ &+ \beta \sum_j KL[p_\theta(z_j|x), Bernouli(\pi)], \end{aligned} \quad (4)$$

where $p_\theta(z|x)$ is the parametric posterior distribution over z and β is a hyperparameter to weigh the performance-sparsity trade-off.

2.1 Soft Masking

The combined loss presented above is not differentiable, as it includes sampling operations from Bernoulli distributions. Since we aim to learn the masking function (unlike random masking), this would not be amenable to end-to-end training using backpropagation. Rather than using the REINFORCE algorithm which suffers from high variance (Bastings et al., 2019), we use the Gumbel Softmax reparameterization trick (Jang et al., 2017) similar to Paranjape et al. (2020). This replaces the sampling step with an argmax: $argmax_{i \in 0,1}(logp(z_j|x) + g_i)$, where g_i is a random sample from the Gumbel$(0, 1)$ distribution. Finally, the argmax is replaced by a weighted softmax:

$$z_j^* = \frac{\exp\left((\log(p(z_j = 1|x) + g_1)/\tau\right)}{\sum_{i \in 0,1} \exp\left((\log(p(z_j = i|x) + g_i)/\tau\right)}.$$

Note that $z_j^* \in (0, 1)$ gets boundary values (i.e., 0 or 1) when $\tau \to 0$ (in practice, we use $\tau = 0.01$).

2.2 Model Architecture

As illustrated in Fig. 2, our model has two parts: the extractor and the abstractor. The extractor is a pretrained transformer encoder similar to BERT (Devlin et al., 2019) with an additional linear layer on top that computes $p_\theta(z_j|x)$. The abstractor on the other hand, is a pretrained seq-to-seq language model like BART (Lewis et al., 2020). From our experiments, we find a BART-base encoder (6 layers) to be adequate as an extractor model, while we use a BART-large abstractor. Note that we can use any other pretrained encoders (e.g., RoBERTa (Liu et al., 2019)) and seq2seq models (e.g., Pegasus (Zhang et al., 2019b)) for the extraction and abstraction task, respectively. Also note that after the evidence extraction, in order to ensure that there is no leakage of information, we need to encode the extracted tokens separately again. Using the same encoded representation would leak information to the abstractor about the masked tokens.

During training, given an input x, the extractor generates a probability for each token in x to be selected (i.e. not masked). Based on these probabilities (p_j), we sample m_j with values in (0,1). We then pass $z = x \odot m$ to the abstractor to generate the output. In our experiments, we tried two different ways of masking the input using m: 1) directly masking the embedding, i.e. $z_j = m_j * x_j + (1 - m_j) * x_{mask}$ where x_{mask} is initialized from the BART's original `<mask>` token, and, 2) using m as an attention mask for both the encoder's self attention as well as the encoder-decoder cross attention, i.e. to block attention to the masked tokens. However, we did not observe a significant difference between these two schemes. During the inference, the extractor deterministically selects the top $\pi\%$ of the source tokens. Such hard masking ensures that the sparsity requirement is exactly met during inference time.

2.3 Sentence-level Extraction

In the previous section, we described token-level extraction where each token in the source document is individually masked or retained. The main drawback of using scattered token-level extraction is that it is difficult to be used as interpretable evidence. While in Section 5.1, we explore a method for improving the interpretability of token-level evidence by encouraging span-level extraction, in this section, we focus on sentence-level extraction as an effective means to achieve interpretability.

In sentence-level extraction approaches, the model first selects the sentences that need to be masked, followed by the masking of all tokens within those sentences. Unlike the token-level model, the extractor's output in this setup is a linguistically plausible (but possibly redundant) extractive summary, i.e., complete sentences from the source. For sentence-level extraction, we add a special `[CLS]` token to the beginning of each sentence and use its representation as the sentence encoding. We also add a segment embedding to each token in the sentence to distinguish between the sentences in a document. The segment embeddings are initialized randomly and learned during training. We use the `[CLS]` token representation to perform soft masking as in the token-level model.

3 Experimental Settings

Datasets: We primarily experiment with the CNN/DailyMail dataset (Hermann et al., 2015) owing to its extractive-like nature; its summaries are typically closely related to the source sentences. We also present results on the XSUM (Narayan et al., 2018) dataset, a highly abstractive dataset in which summaries can be viewed as a title for the source documents.

Model Hyperparameters and evaluation metrics: We initialize the seq-to-seq abstractor with the BART-large model and initialize the extractor with the BART-base encoder.
We use the fairseq codebase[1] for our experiments and use the same hyperparameters as used for fine-tuning BART on CNN/DM and XSum by the official codebase. Specifically, we fine-tune BART using a polynomial decay learning rate scheduler with the Adam optimizer (Kingma and Ba, 2014). We use a learning rate of 3e-5 with 500 warmup steps and train for 20000 steps. During our initial experiments, we observed similar results for values of $\beta \in [1, 10]$ in (4). We use $\beta = 5$ in our reported results. We use ROUGE F1 scores (R1/R2/RL) for the automatic evaluation. ROUGE scores were calculated using the files2rouge toolkit[2].

4 Results

In this section, we report the performance of our model from both automatic and human evaluation perspective, along with ablation studies. Figure 4 shows example summaries along with evidence highlighted from our system at different sparsity levels.

4.1 Automatic Evaluation

In Table 1, we present the performance of our model for CNN/DM and XSum when using a sparsity of 0.5, with a BART-base encoder as the extractor and a BART-large abstractor. We also present the performance of BART and BERTSUM as representative abstractive and extractive systems, respectively. Moreover, they can be considered as EASE's exctractor (BERTSUM) or abstractor (BART) on their own. Note that for BERTSUM, we present the performance of the Ext-large version for CNN/DM and the two-stage ExtAbs version for XSum. We also include results from previous evidence-based extractive-abstractive systems for comparison. For CNN/DM, our token-level and sentence-level models that use around 50% of the source input perform slightly better than BERTSUM, but slightly worse than BART-large. For XSum, our gap with the BART-large baseline is larger. This is expected given that XSum summaries are highly abstractive, making it much harder for the extractor to extract the most important information in an end-to-end fashion.

Moreover, we observe that the sentence-level model performs slightly better than the token-level model for CNN/DM but slightly worse for XSum. We hypothesize that for the more extractive CNN/DM dataset, keeping continuous spans of text is of paramount importance, while for the more abstractive XSum dataset, the sparsity budget

[1]https://github.com/pytorch/fairseq

[2]https://github.com/pltrdy/files2rouge

Model	CNN/DailyMail	XSum
BART-large (Lewis et al., 2019)	44.16/21.28/40.90	45.14/22.27/37.25
BERTSUM (Liu and Lapata, 2019)	43.85/20.34/39.90	38.81/16.50/31.27
Previous evidence-based Extractive-Abstractive systems		
Bottom-Up (Gehrmann et al., 2018)	40.96/18.38/38.16	-
SEAL (Zhao et al., 2020)	39.3/16.5/-	-
EASE (ours)		
Token-level sparsity 0.5	43.96/20.91/40.74	42.70/19.38/33.81
Sentence-level sparsity 0.5	43.98/20.95/40.78	41.82/19.05/33.99

Table 1: ROUGE-1/2/L results for CNN/DailyMail and XSum.

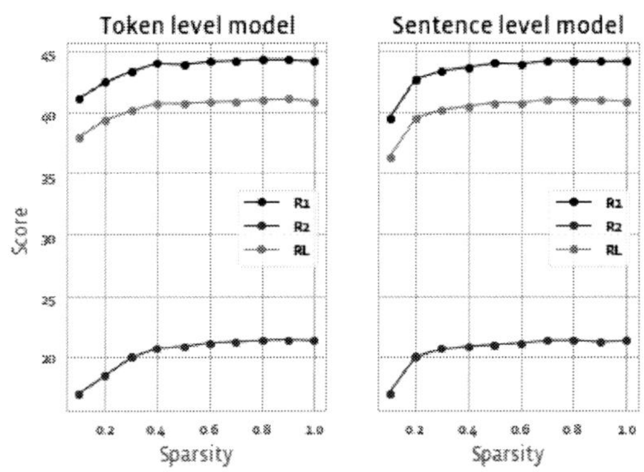

Figure 3: R1/R2/RL vs Sparsity for token level and sentence level models. For sentence level model, we enforce it to extract at least three sentences.

can be better spent on a more scattered extraction of key pieces throughout the document. In section 5, we explore ideas to 1) improve the performance of the token-level model using pre-training; 2) improve the interpretability of token-level models by encouraging the extraction of continuous spans; and 3) improve the performance of both token and sentence level models using semi-supervised learning.

4.2 Model Analysis

Effect of Sparsity Prior: In this section, we investigate the effect of sparsity on the generated summaries. Figure 3 presents ROUGE score of both token-level and sentence-level models, trained with different sparsity priors. As expected, increasing the sparsity ratio improves the ROUGE scores at the cost of more verbose extracted evidence. Moreover, the performance gains flatten after a sparsity of around 0.3. We found that token-level models are more robust to lower sparsity rates, i.e. they can remove functional words without losing document information, but they are not well-suited in terms of interpretability. Note that for the sentence-level models, at inference time we extracted at least three sentences to ensure that short documents would have enough evidence at lower sparsity rates.

Model	Token level	Sentence Level
base Ex + base Ab	42.9/19.8/39.7	42.42/19.7/39.27
base Ex + base Ab shared	42.28/19.37/39.14	42.58/19.81/39.43
base Ex + large Ab	43.96/20.91/40.74	43.98/20.95/40.78

Table 2: Ablation studies on the effect of model size and sharing. All models are trained with 0.5 sparsity.

Effect of model size: We examine the effect of using models of different sizes on summarization performance, and also explore the possibility of sharing the encoder. We consider BART-base and BART-large for the abstractor. We also experimented with using RoBERTa (Liu et al., 2019) and BART-large encoder for the extractor but found it very unstable and hard to tune the relative loss weights. To explore the possibility of reducing the model size, we also experiment with sharing the encoder's parameters between the extractor and abstractor encoders. Table 2 presents results of these settings for both token-level and sentence-level models using a sparsity of 0.5.

We can see that using a large model for the abstractor yields significant improvements. Moreover, sharing the encoder between the extractor and the abstractor does not hurt the performance. However, since using a large abstractor is essential while using a large extractor is unstable during training, we use a BART-base extractor and a BART-large abstractor for our default setting.

Effect of extraction: We evaluate the effect of extraction quality on the final summary for our

Extract Sentences	Sparsity 0.5	Sparsity 0.3
$\pi\%$	43.98/20.95/40.78	43.38/20.57/40.2
Top-3	41.37/18.58/38.18	41.19/18.63/38.01
Lead-3	40.84/18.16/37.71	40.6/18.05/37.46
Random-3	31.46/10.04/28.92	31.34/10.06/28.79

Table 3: Effect of different extraction techniques on the final summary.

sentence-level models. We use our model trained with different sparsity rates but during inference, feed only the top-3 sentences with highest scores to the abstractor for generating the summary. We compare with the baselines of using random-3 and lead-3 sentences as well as using all $\pi\%$ of sentences. Table 3 presents results of our two models with sparsity values of 0.5 and 0.3. We find that for both models, summaries using the top-3 sentences selected by the extractor outperform lead-3 extraction, even though the CNN/DM dataset has a strong lead bias. We conclude that our extractor is indeed extracting important sentences, which we further confirm using human evaluations, described in the next section.

4.3 Human Evaluation

We conduct human evaluation on both the extracted evidence and the generated summaries. For the summaries, we asked annotators to rate them between 1-5 on two qualitative aspects of the summary: Consistency and Relevance. Consistency is the factual alignment between the summary and the source document, measuring whether the summary is changing details or hallucinating. Relevance measures whether the summary captures the key points of the source document. We compared our generated summaries with BART as a baseline. We also evaluate the relevance of extractions from the sentence-level models. To make evaluation easier, we gather the top-3 sentences with the highest extraction scores and ask annotators whether those are the most important sentences in the source document. Here, we compare with Lead-3 extraction as a baseline.

We sampled 200 examples from the CNN/DM test set and conducted human evaluation using Amazon Mechanical Turk with three annotators. We present the average annotators' scores in Table 4, using z-score p-values smaller than 0.01 to measure statistical significance. We find that for extraction relevance, the top-3 sentences from our extractor scored higher than Lead-3, which itself received a high relevance score due to the strong

Models	Summary		Extraction
	Consistency	Relevance	Relevance
BART	**4.89**	**4.13**	-
Token-level model	4.77	**4.16**	-
Sentence-level model	**4.86**	3.80	**4.45**
Lead-3 extraction	-	-	4.38

Table 4: Human Evaluation results on CNN/DM. We evaluate our token-level and sentence-level models, with 0.5 sparsity on summary relevance and consistency and compare with BART. We evaluate extraction relevance of our sentence-level model and compare with Lead-3.

lead bias in the CNN/DM dataset. For abstractive summaries, we find that the sentence-level model achieves a similar consistency score as BART, but slightly better than the token-level model. On one hand, the sentence model achieves a lower relevance score than BART and token model. We hypothesize that the interpretable nature of the sentence model results in a loss of some of the key information in the source document as expected, whereas the token model avoids this by extracting keywords throughout the source. On the other hand, the token-level model can fabricate new details between the extracted keywords, which results in lower consistency. As such, there is an inherent trade-off between relevance and interpretability.

5 Further improvements and Future Work

5.1 Span-level model with Lasso loss

In the previous section, we found that although sentence-level models are interpretable, they can miss out on key parts of the source document. However, token-level models enjoy much more freedom during extraction but yield evidence that is not very useful for humans. To find a compromise between these two, i.e. a span-level model, we attempt to make the evidence extracted by token-level models more contiguous, by adding a lasso loss (Bastings et al., 2019) to the total loss in (4):

$$L_{Lasso} = \sum_{i=0}^{n-1} |z_i - z_{i+1}|, \tag{5}$$

where n is the number of source tokens. The lasso loss ensures that the number of transitions between the masked and unmasked tokens is minimized and hence, the model extracts more contiguous spans of text as evidence. In the first row of Table 5, we observe that the lasso loss mainly improves the

Source Document:
(CNN)Two passengers found dead on a cruise ship in Puerto Rico appear to have died in a murder-suicide, the cruise line said. Holland America Line said two guests were found dead inside their stateroom on the ms Ryndam at 11:30 a.m. Thursday. "The cabin was immediately secured, and the authorities were notified, including the FBI," Holland America said. "We are cooperating fully with the investigation, and the authorities will make the official determination on what occurred." **FBI spokesman Moises Quinones said authorities were on scene investigating.** The ship left Tampa, Florida, on March 29 on a 14-day Southern Caribbean cruise. It's currently in San Juan, Puerto Rico. Puerto Rico Port Authority spokesman Efraín Santiago told El Nuevo Dia newspaper that the cleaning staff on the ship had discovered the deceased passengers after knocking on the cabin's door.
Summary (Sparsity 0.3): Holland America Line said two guests were found dead inside their stateroom on the ms Ryndam at 11:30 a.m. Thursday. The FBI is investigating.

Source Document:
(CNN)Gastrointestinal illness has gripped 100 people on the cruise ship Celebrity Infinity, according to a report from the Centers for Disease Control. Of the ship's 2,117 passengers, 95 have suffered from vomiting, diarrhea and other symptoms, the CDC said. The illness has also affected five members of the 964-person crew. The CDC has yet to determine what's causing the ailments. Two staffers from the agency are scheduled to meet the West Coast-based ship in San Diego on Monday. The Infinity left San Diego on March 29. It made its last stop in Puerto Vallarta, Mexico, on April 10, according to MarineTraffic.com. **Celebrity Cruises has been taking action since the outbreak began, including increasing cleaning and disinfection procedures, keeping passengers informed and taking specimens from the afflicted for testing by the CDC, the agency says.** According to the Maritime Executive, this is the third time the Celebrity Infinity has suffered an outbreak of gastrointestinal illness, with others occurring in 2006 and 2013. The ship was built in 2001 and refurbished in 2011.
Summary (Sparsity 0.5): Of the ship's 2,117 passengers, 95 have suffered from vomiting, diarrhea. The illness has also affected five members of the 964-person crew. Celebrity Cruises has been taking action since the outbreak began.

Figure 4: Summarization outputs with their evidence (highlighted), from our systems at different sparsity levels.

token-level model. This is particularly evident in the improvement in RL which is due to the extraction of contiguous spans as evidence.

5.2 Unlabeled Pretraining

Although we initialize the extractor and abstractor with pretrained language models, the model may benefit from further pretraining suited to the downstream task. To this end, we use our model in an auto-encoding fashion, i.e., the abstractor reconstructs the original text using the extracted pieces selected by the extractor. Our hypothesis is that an extractor capable of extracting the most informative parts from which the source can be reconstructed should be better positioned to extract important parts of the source, resulting in higher-quality summaries. Therefore, we pretrain EASE on the WikiText-103 (Merity et al., 2017) dataset to reconstruct the original unlabeled documents using the same loss as in (4) by setting $Y = X$. This can be viewed as a special case of summarization, where the compression rate is one. We only pretrain the token-level model, since pretraining sentence-level models without measures such as topic guidance (Kang and Hovy, 2020) typically leads to hallucination. Results on the CNN/DM dataset by adding pretraining are presented in the second row of Table 5. Even though pretraining improves the token-level model, results for the span-level model are mixed. Our hypothesis is that the lasso continuity helps with summarization by picking contiguous spans, as evidenced by the high RL. However, during the reconstruction pretraining, the lasso loss can be problematic by masking long spans, which are then prone to hallucinations. We leave pretraining alongside span extraction using techniques such as guided reconstruction to future work.

Model	Token level	Span Level (lasso)
vanilla EASE	43.96/20.91/40.74	44.33/20.67/41.06
+ pretraining	44.12/20.89/40.80	44.06/20.82/40.83

Table 5: CNN/DM results on token-level models trained with lasso loss and pretraining.

Model	Token level	Sentence level
vanilla EASE	43.96/20.91/40.74	43.98/20.95/40.78
+ SSL	44.28/21.21/41.0	44.10/21.12/40.89

Table 6: Results on token level and sentence level models, trained with additional semi-supervised extraction.

5.3 Semi-supervised Training

Multiple recent works (Nallapati et al., 2017; Liu and Lapata, 2019) have explored heuristics to obtain pseudo alignments between target summaries and source sentences for summarization datasets. To evaluate the effect of weakly supervising the extractor in EASE using these pseudo labels, we use the greedy procedure of Liu and Lapata (2019) to obtain oracle extractive annotations for CNN/DM. As such, we maintain an evidence set and greedily add source sentences to the set that yield the maximum increase in its ROUGE score against the target summary. This yields a binary labeling of input sentences and we introduce an additional binary cross entropy loss to our training objective in (4) between this binary labeling and the predicted masking probabilities. By using the sentence-level pseudo labels for the tokens of each sentence, we also add this loss to the token-level models. We have shown the results in Table. 6. We observe improvements in all ROUGE metrics for both sentence-level and token-level models, though the gains on the former are more modest. Studying the interaction of this objective with the aforementioned lasso objectives is left for future work.

6 Related Work

6.1 Pretrained Models for Summarization

Lewis et al. (2020) introduced BART, a general-purpose denoising seq2seq transformer, that achieved the state-of-the-art results on many summarization tasks. Later, Zhang et al. (2019b) extended the MLM denoising objective using sentence masking. Zhang et al. (2019c) introduced a multi-stage encoder for extractive summarization, whereas Zhang et al. (2019a) use a two-stage decoder to generate summaries by creating a draft and refining it using a pretrained language model. In EASE, we use pretrained models, i.e., BART, to initialize the extractive and abstractive modules but after that, use an end-to-end loss that trains both modules simultaneously.

6.1.1 Self-supervised Summarization

Miao and Blunsom (2016) introduced an autoencoder setup for sentence compression to reduce the need for labeled examples. A copy ptr/generator model was used for the compressor which alongside the reconstructor is trained to reconstruct the unlabeled documents. Moreover, REINFORCE (Williams, 1992) was used to train the model end-to-end. Baziotis et al. (2019) introduced a similar autoencoder setup but used the Gumbel Softmax reparametrization for training. (Févry and Phang, 2018) also used a denoising autoencoder to compress sentences and a countdown at the decoder to control summary length.

Inspired by the IB principle, West et al. (2019) introduced a recursive algorithm to prune a document to form an unsupervised extractive summary. These summaries are in turn used to train a self-supervised system using a next-sentence objective is used. In contrast, we use a loss formulation derived directly from the IB and train the model end-to-end. (Saito et al., 2020) used a saliency model to extract important pieces of a document before feeding them to an abstractive seq2seq model. In contrast with our model, the saliency module is trained separately by using heuristics to provide pseudo labels for the extraction. (Yang et al., 2020b) proposed pretraining over millions of news articles using the lead sentence as the self supervision.

6.2 Evidence-based Extractive-Abstractive Summarization

The transformer decoder (Liu* et al., 2018) was first used to accommodate long documents from a coarse extractive summarizer. Later, Zhao et al. (2020) also focus on long-document summarization and train a joint extractive-abstractive model by weakly supervising the extractor through pseudo labels. This model, although interpretable, does poorly on a dataset like CNN/DM. (Pilault et al., 2020) introduce another interpretable summarizing model for long documents by performing a simple extractive step to condition the decoder. They show that this approach produces more abstractive summaries compared with the copy mechanism. Unlike these models, we train both modules jointly using the theoretically grounded IB principle with no pseudo labels. Moreover, we seek consistent models suitable for more extractive datasets and achieve results on par with the abstractive model while only using half of the input. (Gehrmann et al., 2018) trained a content selector separately to tag the words and then use bottom-up attention to only copy words from the tagged set. Similar to our token-level model, this is not useful evidence.

Compressive summarization is another way to have a trade-off between extractive and abstractive methods where extractive summaries are compressed to form the final summary (Mendes et al., 2019). Recently, Desai et al. (2020) use syntactic rules to find a high-recall candidate set and then use the notions of plausibility and salience to ensure the grammaticality and importance of the remaining pieces, respectively. Unlike compressive summarization, we explore an extractive-abstractive framework where a concise abstractive summary can be traced back to the evidence; learned jointly with no manual rules or postprocessing.

7 Conclusion

In this paper, we introduced EASE, an extractive-abstractive framework for summarization tasks that trains an extractor and an abstractor in an end-to-end fashion. The extracted evidence can be viewed as an interpretable extractive summary of the summary from which the final summary is generated by the abstractor. We show that our sentence-level extractive-abstractive summarization systems are better than strong extractive-abstractive baselines and either on-par or only slightly lower in quality compared to strong abstractive baselines.

8 Ethical Considerations

Intellectual Properties and Privacy Rights All of the datasets (CNN/DM and XSum) used in our study are publicly available. Regarding privacy rights, the authors of the paper completed IRB human subject protection training for conducting this study.

Compensation for Annotators We compensated the Turkers approximately $15 per hour. We first annotated examples in-house to determine the required annotation speed. We evaluated 200 examples with 8 annotations per example (including outputs from different models) and typically each example takes around 10 minutes.

Steps Taken to Avoid Potential Problems We interacted closely with the Turkers to ensure that compensation was fair and that the instructions were clear. We did pilot examples with each annotator in the beginning to help them to be better calibrated.

Environmental Cost The experiments described in the paper make use of V100 GPUs with 32GB memory. We used up to 8 GPUs per experiment. The experiments may take several hours. We didn't do a lot of parameter search: we re-used the best parameter reported from BART open-source code and only tuned weight on loss on the validation set. Future work will be able to draw on these insights and models in production may be trained once for use using the most promising settings.

References

Alexander Alemi, Ian Fischer, Joshua Dillon, and Kevin Murphy. 2016. Deep variational information bottleneck. *ICLR*.

Jasmijn Bastings, Wilker Aziz, and Ivan Titov. 2019. Interpretable neural predictions with differentiable binary variables. In *Proceedings of the 57th Annual Meeting of the Association for Computational Linguistics*, pages 2963–2977, Florence, Italy. Association for Computational Linguistics.

Christos Baziotis, Ion Androutsopoulos, Ioannis Konstas, and Alexandros Potamianos. 2019. SEQ^3: Differentiable sequence-to-sequence-to-sequence autoencoder for unsupervised abstractive sentence compression. In *Proceedings of the 2019 Conference of the North American Chapter of the Association for Computational Linguistics: Human Language Technologies, Volume 1 (Long and Short Papers)*, pages 673–681, Minneapolis, Minnesota. Association for Computational Linguistics.

Shrey Desai, Jiacheng Xu, and Greg Durrett. 2020. Compressive summarization with plausibility and salience modeling. In *Proceedings of the 2020 Conference on Empirical Methods in Natural Language Processing (EMNLP)*, pages 6259–6274, Online. Association for Computational Linguistics.

Jacob Devlin, Ming-Wei Chang, Kenton Lee, and Kristina Toutanova. 2019. BERT: Pre-training of deep bidirectional transformers for language understanding. In *Proceedings of the 2019 Conference of the North American Chapter of the Association for Computational Linguistics: Human Language Technologies, Volume 1 (Long and Short Papers)*, pages 4171–4186, Minneapolis, Minnesota. Association for Computational Linguistics.

Thibault Févry and Jason Phang. 2018. Unsupervised sentence compression using denoising autoencoders. In *Proceedings of the 22nd Conference on Computational Natural Language Learning*, pages 413–422, Brussels, Belgium. Association for Computational Linguistics.

Sebastian Gehrmann, Yuntian Deng, and Alexander Rush. 2018. Bottom-up abstractive summarization. In *Proceedings of the 2018 Conference on Empirical Methods in Natural Language Processing*, pages 4098–4109, Brussels, Belgium. Association for Computational Linguistics.

Karl Moritz Hermann, Tomas Kocisky, Edward Grefenstette, Lasse Espeholt, Will Kay, Mustafa Suleyman, and Phil Blunsom. 2015. Teaching machines to read and comprehend. In *Advances in Neural Information Processing Systems*, volume 28, pages 1693–1701. Curran Associates, Inc.

Wan-Ting Hsu, Chieh-Kai Lin, Ming-Ying Lee, Kerui Min, Jing Tang, and Min Sun. 2018. A unified model for extractive and abstractive summarization using inconsistency loss. In *Proceedings of the 56th Annual Meeting of the Association for Computational Linguistics (Volume 1: Long Papers)*, pages 132–141, Melbourne, Australia. Association for Computational Linguistics.

Eric Jang, Shixiang Gu, and Ben Poole. 2017. Categorical reparameterization with gumbel-softmax.

Hongyan Jing and Kathleen McKeown. 2000. The decomposition of human-written summary sentences.

Mihir Kale and Abhinav Rastogi. 2020. Text-to-text pre-training for data-to-text tasks. In *Proceedings of the 13th International Conference on Natural Language Generation*, pages 97–102, Dublin, Ireland. Association for Computational Linguistics.

Dongyeop Kang and Eduard Hovy. 2020. Plan ahead: Self-supervised text planning for paragraph completion task. In *Proceedings of the 2020 Conference on Empirical Methods in Natural Language Processing (EMNLP)*, pages 6533–6543, Online. Association for Computational Linguistics.

Diederik P. Kingma and Jimmy Ba. 2014. Adam: A method for stochastic optimization. Cite arxiv:1412.6980Comment: Published as a conference paper at the 3rd International Conference for Learning Representations, San Diego, 2015.

Mike Lewis, Yinhan Liu, Naman Goyal, Marjan Ghazvininejad, Abdelrahman Mohamed, Omer Levy, Ves Stoyanov, and Luke Zettlemoyer. 2019. Bart: Denoising sequence-to-sequence pre-training for natural language generation, translation, and comprehension.

Mike Lewis, Yinhan Liu, Naman Goyal, Marjan Ghazvininejad, Abdelrahman Mohamed, Omer Levy, Veselin Stoyanov, and Luke Zettlemoyer. 2020. BART: Denoising sequence-to-sequence pretraining for natural language generation, translation, and comprehension. In *Proceedings of the 58th Annual Meeting of the Association for Computational Linguistics*, pages 7871–7880, Online. Association for Computational Linguistics.

Peter J. Liu*, Mohammad Saleh*, Etienne Pot, Ben Goodrich, Ryan Sepassi, Lukasz Kaiser, and Noam Shazeer. 2018. Generating wikipedia by summarizing long sequences. In *International Conference on Learning Representations*.

Yang Liu and Mirella Lapata. 2019. Text summarization with pretrained encoders. In *Proceedings of the 2019 Conference on Empirical Methods in Natural Language Processing and the 9th International Joint Conference on Natural Language Processing (EMNLP-IJCNLP)*, pages 3730–3740, Hong Kong, China. Association for Computational Linguistics.

Yinhan Liu, Myle Ott, Naman Goyal, Jingfei Du, Mandar Joshi, Danqi Chen, Omer Levy, Mike Lewis, Luke Zettlemoyer, and Veselin Stoyanov. 2019. Roberta: A robustly optimized bert pretraining approach. *arXiv preprint arXiv:1907.11692*.

Joshua Maynez, Shashi Narayan, Bernd Bohnet, and Ryan McDonald. 2020. On faithfulness and factuality in abstractive summarization. In *Proceedings of the 58th Annual Meeting of the Association for Computational Linguistics*, pages 1906–1919, Online. Association for Computational Linguistics.

Afonso Mendes, Shashi Narayan, Sebastião Miranda, Zita Marinho, André F. T. Martins, and Shay B. Cohen. 2019. Jointly extracting and compressing documents with summary state representations. In *Proceedings of the 2019 Conference of the North American Chapter of the Association for Computational Linguistics: Human Language Technologies, Volume 1 (Long and Short Papers)*, pages 3955–3966, Minneapolis, Minnesota. Association for Computational Linguistics.

Stephen Merity, Caiming Xiong, James Bradbury, and Richard Socher. 2017. Pointer sentinel mixture models. In *5th International Conference on Learning Representations, ICLR 2017, Toulon, France, April 24-26, 2017, Conference Track Proceedings*. OpenReview.net.

Yishu Miao and Phil Blunsom. 2016. Language as a latent variable: Discrete generative models for sentence compression. In *Proceedings of the 2016 Conference on Empirical Methods in Natural Language Processing*, pages 319–328, Austin, Texas. Association for Computational Linguistics.

Ramesh Nallapati, Feifei Zhai, and Bowen Zhou. 2017. Summarunner: A recurrent neural network based sequence model for extractive summarization of documents. AAAI'17. AAAI Press.

Shashi Narayan, Shay B. Cohen, and Mirella Lapata. 2018. Don't give me the details, just the summary! topic-aware convolutional neural networks for extreme summarization. In *Proceedings of the 2018 Conference on Empirical Methods in Natural Language Processing*, pages 1797–1807, Brussels, Belgium. Association for Computational Linguistics.

Bhargavi Paranjape, Mandar Joshi, John Thickstun, Hannaneh Hajishirzi, and Luke Zettlemoyer. 2020. An information bottleneck approach for controlling conciseness in rationale extraction. In *Proceedings of the 2020 Conference on Empirical Methods in Natural Language Processing (EMNLP)*, pages 1938–1952, Online. Association for Computational Linguistics.

Jonathan Pilault, Raymond Li, Sandeep Subramanian, and Chris Pal. 2020. On extractive and abstractive neural document summarization with transformer language models. In *Proceedings of the 2020 Conference on Empirical Methods in Natural Language Processing (EMNLP)*, pages 9308–9319, Online. Association for Computational Linguistics.

Colin Raffel, Noam Shazeer, Adam Roberts, Katherine Lee, Sharan Narang, Michael Matena, Yanqi Zhou, Wei Li, and Peter Liu. 2019. Exploring the limits of transfer learning with a unified text-to-text transformer.

Itsumi Saito, Kyosuke Nishida, Kosuke Nishida, and Junji Tomita. 2020. Abstractive summarization with combination of pre-trained sequence-to-sequence and saliency models.

Naftali Tishby, Fernando C. Pereira, and William Bialek. 1999. The information bottleneck method. pages 368–377.

Peter West, Ari Holtzman, Jan Buys, and Yejin Choi. 2019. BottleSum: Unsupervised and self-supervised sentence summarization using the information bottleneck principle. In *Proceedings of the 2019 Conference on Empirical Methods in Natural Language Processing and the 9th International Joint Conference on Natural Language Processing (EMNLP-IJCNLP)*, pages 3752–3761, Hong Kong, China. Association for Computational Linguistics.

Ronald J. Williams. 1992. Simple statistical gradient-following algorithms for connectionist reinforcement learning. *Mach. Learn.*, 8(3–4):229–256.

Zixiaofan Yang, Einolghozati Arash, Inan Hakan, Diedrick Keith, Fan Angela, Dulmez Pinar, and Gupta Sona. 2020a. Improving text-to-text pretrained models for the graph-to-text task. In *WebNLG workshop at INLG 2020*.

Ziyi Yang, Chenguang Zhu, Robert Gmyr, Michael Zeng, Xuedong Huang, and Eric Darve. 2020b. TED: A pretrained unsupervised summarization model with theme modeling and denoising. In *Findings of the Association for Computational Linguistics: EMNLP 2020*, pages 1865–1874, Online. Association for Computational Linguistics.

Haoyu Zhang, Jingjing Cai, Jianjun Xu, and Ji Wang. 2019a. Pretraining-based natural language generation for text summarization. In *Proceedings of the 23rd Conference on Computational Natural Language Learning (CoNLL)*, pages 789–797, Hong Kong, China. Association for Computational Linguistics.

Jingqing Zhang, Yao Zhao, Mohammad Saleh, and Peter J. Liu. 2019b. Pegasus: Pre-training with extracted gap-sentences for abstractive summarization. *ArXiv*, abs/1912.08777.

Xingxing Zhang, Furu Wei, and Ming Zhou. 2019c. HIBERT: Document level pre-training of hierarchical bidirectional transformers for document summarization. In *Proceedings of the 57th Annual Meeting of the Association for Computational Linguistics*, pages 5059–5069, Florence, Italy. Association for Computational Linguistics.

Zhengyan Zhang, Xu Han, Zhiyuan Liu, Xin Jiang, Maosong Sun, and Qun Liu. 2019d. ERNIE: Enhanced language representation with informative entities. In *Proceedings of the 57th Annual Meeting of the Association for Computational Linguistics*, pages 1441–1451, Florence, Italy. Association for Computational Linguistics.

Yao Zhao, M. Saleh, and Peter J. Liu. 2020. Seal: Segment-wise extractive-abstractive long-form text summarization. *ArXiv*, abs/2006.10213.

Context or No Context? A preliminary exploration of human-in-the-loop approach for Incremental Temporal Summarization in meetings

Nicole M. Beckage, Shachi Kumar, Saurav Sahay, and Ramesh Manuvinakurike
Intel Labs, USA
firstname.lastname@intel.com

Abstract

Incremental meeting temporal summarization, summarizing relevant information of partial multi-party meeting dialogue, is emerging as the next challenge in summarization research. Here we examine the extent to which human abstractive summaries of the preceding increments (context) can be combined with extractive meeting dialogue to generate abstractive summaries. We find that previous context improves ROUGE scores. Our findings further suggest that contexts begin to outweigh the dialogue. Using keyphrase extraction and semantic role labeling (SRL), we find that SRL captures relevant information without overwhelming the the model architecture. By compressing the previous contexts by $\approx$ 70%, we achieve better ROUGE scores over our baseline models. Collectively, these results suggest that context matters, as does the way in which context is presented to the model.

1 Introduction

In meetings, especially in a virtual setting, distractions are common place and can last anywhere from a few seconds to minutes, impacting concentration and participation in the remainder of the meeting negatively. A note-taking tool designed to provide temporally relevant summaries of what has happened in the last 2-3 minutes may mitigate the negative effects of distractions and interruptions.

Missing a few minutes of content, rather than the whole meeting, provides unique challenges for current summarization tools. Instead of summarizing the main points of the meeting, a temporally-relevant summarization aid must instead capture relevant meeting content given previous events, even if those events would not be included in the full meeting summary. Such a tool may benefit from taking the past notes or summaries from meeting participants as context and incrementally updating the summaries for a specific time interval to capture relevant information that a distracted individual would need to know to reintegrate into the meeting.

The goal of this work is to investigate the ability to incrementally summarize meetings, specifically focusing on how a summarization tool may make use of past summaries to increase the accuracy of temporally-relevant abstractive summarization.

The task of incremental temporal summarization in dialogue has two main aspects to it, i) The content being summarized has a temporal order–the information evolves over time. ii) summaries build upon or use the past context (transcriptions, summaries, or human notes) to generate the summaries for the current dialogue. A new dataset based on incremental temporal summarization of the AMI dataset, which we call the AMI-ITS, provides a means to investigate incremental temporal summarization of meeting dialogues.

Temporal summarization has been studied in the context of summarizing news articles (Dang and Owczarzak, 2008; McCreadie et al., 2014; Aslam et al., 2015). In such a setting, the input news articles that evolve over time are streamed in chunks. The summarizer needs to either summarize the new content or update the earlier generated summary with the new information. While similar to incremental temporal summarization (ITS) in meetings scenario, additional challenges are associated with the properties of human conversation such as disfluencies and dyadic exchanges (questions and answers, acknowledgements, confirmations etc.) where a contributions to the summaries are from multiple interlocutors (Poesio and Rieser, 2010).The information also comes in smaller increments of time, and at a much faster rate than news articles. Limited work has been done on temporal summarization and incremental summarization in multi-party meeting scenarios.

The main contribution of this work is to quantify the impact of previous human generated sum-

Proceedings of the Third Workshop on New Frontiers in Summarization, pages 96–106
November 10, 2021. ©2021 Association for Computational Linguistics

maries in improving meeting summarization. We specifically focus on how to best use previous summaries from earlier temporal summarization. This mimics the use of the meeting notes of individuals to generate up to date summaries of meeting dialogue and provides the basis for an incremental summarization tool that works jointly with meeting participants in real time. We ask fundamental questions about how to use previous summaries by humans including whether meeting summaries or meeting dialogues should be prioritized as input to the model. We then look at how many summaries the model requires to most accurately summarize the most recent temporal chunks and conclude by showing that extracting meaningful information from past summaries through semantic role labeling can further improve temporal summarization. Collectively this work shows that temporal summarization benefits from having a human in the loop and suggests ways to use human input most effectively.

2 Related work

Because of the differences between news articles and human dialogue, incremental summarization for meetings/dialogues provides unique challenges and requires novel approaches. Table 1 compares training examples and summarizations across a standard news corpus (CNN/DailyMail), scientific paper summarization (Pubmed), the AMI meeting corpus, and the temporal version of the AMI meeting corpus (AMI-ITS) which focuses on 100 second incremental temporal sequences from the AMI dataset and will be explained in more detail below. Not only are the meeting corpora much smaller in terms of training examples, the dialogue is much longer compared to news articles, averaging 4757 words in the AMI meeting transcripts compared to 781 words for the news corpus. While meetings tend to be much longer in length than news articles, much of this information is considered non-extractive (i.e. not containing information relevant to the abstract summary). Incremental summarization is a noticeably different task than full meeting summarization, news summarization, and article summarization, with most of the words spoken being labeled as extractive. The summaries in the AMI-ITS dataset are also longer than either the news corpus or the AMI corpus and the summaries are more than 25% of the overall extractive text. The novel challenge in temporal summarization for meeting dialogues is that much of the meeting text is relevant in summarizing key events and concepts of the previous 100 second chunks. These differences suggest that the temporal summarization task is different from news summarization and full meeting summarization in two main ways 1) meetings have different properties than other types of text and 2) temporal summarization is different than summarizing a whole document.

Corpus	doc.	obs.	words	extract	summary (%)
CNN/DM	312K	312K	781	382	56 (7.2%)
Pubmed	133K	278K	3016	-	203 (6.7%)
AMI	137	137	4,757	210	19 (0.4%)
AMI-ITS	49	924	262	162	67 (25.6%)

Table 1: Corpus statistics: number of documents, number examples, average number of words, proportion of extractives and the average number of words in the abstractive summary for each example.

Meeting Summarization. Much of the available summarization datasets exist for news articles summarization scenario (Narayan et al., 2018; Dernoncourt et al., 2018). The news articles and summaries for these news articles have a very different structure than meetings and dialogue. Dialogue summarization corpora (Carletta et al., 2005; Janin et al., 2003; Lacson et al., 2006; Favre et al., 2015; Misra et al., 2015; Barker et al., 2016; Liu et al., 2019a; Gliwa et al., 2019) have helped accelerate the research in the area of conversational summarization. Major differences exist between dialogue summarization and summarization of news articles (Jung et al., 2019). News articles tend to follow a structure in which the most relevant information is contained early in the text. Meetings, by definition, require engagement of multiple participants resulting in transcripts with different styles, perspectives, and roles. Compared to news summarization, labeled training data of meeting summaries is also severely limited. Several models have been developed recently focused on generating summaries for meetings and dialogues and have achieved promising results (See for e.g. See et al. (2017); Chen and Bansal (2018); Zhao et al. (2019); Liu (2019); Zhang et al. (2020); Feng et al. (2020); Zhu et al. (2020); Fabbri et al. (2021b)). These models suggest that altering the input representation, the model architecture and loss function may all play a part in improving accuracy for summarization of meetings.

Incremental Summarization. While meeting summaries are limited by datasets, incremental tem-

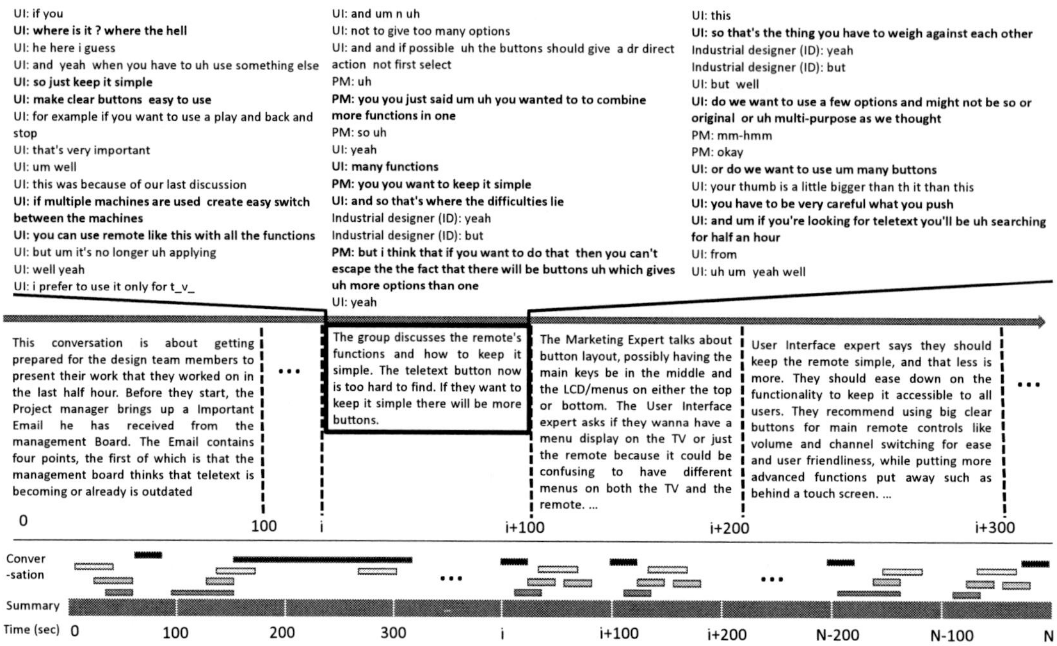

Figure 1: Shows sample incremental temporal summaries from the corpus along with the conversation transcriptions and extractives (in bold) as marked by a crowd-worker.

poral summarizations of meetings is even more limited. Instead of focusing on summarizing the full content of the meeting/dialogue, incremental summarization focuses on building incremental representations of the meetings rather than a full summary at the end. Work in incremental dialogue processing has considered when to add additional information to an existing summary (McCreadie et al., 2014), how representations of individuals and topics can be influenced by time (Chen and Metze, 2012), considerations of turn taking (Zhu et al., 2020) and more (Zhong et al., 2021). While these models consider various aspects of incremental and temporal summarization in the model design choices, evaluation often excludes incremental and temporal aspects.

Recently, deep learning models (Li et al., 2019; Liu et al., 2019b) and especially transformer-based models, have achieved impressive performance in abstractive summarization task (Zhang et al., 2020; Raffel et al., 2020; Lewis et al., 2020; Zhu et al., 2020). Such transformer-based models are typically pre-trained on a large dataset and then fine-tuned on a smaller dataset. In this work, we adopt a current state-of-the-art transformer architecture, BART, and utilize and evaluate transfer learning to generate temporally relevant summaries to meeting dialogue. Recent work focusing on meeting summarization has suggested that a new architecture (HMNet) may improve summarization on meeting dialogue (Zhu et al., 2020). This work extends transformer architectures to include a word level transformer, to process and encode the word-level dialogue, and a turn-based transformer which considers the speaker role and sentence embeddings from the word-level transformer. This model architecture has achieved SOTA performance on the AMI meeting corpus but has not been validated on incremental summarization tasks. Our contribution is not to develop a new model architecture for summarization or to outperform state-of-the-art but rather to examine the role of previous summaries on the ability to improve performance in later summaries. We hope to understand the usefulness of previous summaries (contexts) in accurately summarizing the current temporal information. We leave temporal summarization using such architectures to future work.

3 Data

Our primary focus is on abstractive summarization for incremental temporal scenarios. The incremental temporal summarization module takes the utterances in the current time window as input. In this work, we focus on how best to use the past summaries (context) as input. Models are evaluated on temporal summaries capturing the last 100 seconds of the meeting. While it has been shown that having previous temporal summaries is helpful in accurately summarizing a specific context (Manuvinakurike et al., 2021), we investigate this question further by asking how much context is relevant and how to best use past context. We use these results to draw conclusions about the role of human summarization in model performance.

AMI/AMI-ITS corpus: In this work, we rely heavily on a novel extension to the AMI-meeting dataset (Carletta et al., 2005) which we call the **AMI-ITS** dataset (Manuvinakurike et al., 2021). The meetings in the original AMI dataset consist of conversations between 4 role-playing participants (Project Manager (PM), Industrial Designer (ID), User Interface expert (UI), and Marketing expert (ME)) in a remote-control design scenario. Each group of 4 participants meet 4 times and continue the conversation forward from the previous sessions but often on a new agenda. The AMI corpus consists of extractive and abstractive summaries for the full conversation annotated by experts.

The AMI-ITS dataset provides extractive and abstractive summaries for 100 second time durations on a subset of the AMI meetings. Table 1 indicates the number of 100 second chunks that were labeled in the AMI-ITS corpus and the average number of tokens in the full text, extractive and abstractive summaries. We refer to the original AMI dataset, specifically the extractive and abstractive summaries, as AMI and use the addition of ITS to indicate the *incremental and temporal* meeting dialog corpus. To build the AMI-ITS corpus, individuals were presented with a 100 second dialogue chunk. They also saw up to 3 summaries that captured the 3 preceding dialogue chunks. Participants would check a box next to each line of text indicating whether or not the specific dialogue line was extractive, or relevant to the summary. They then provided a summary of the dialogue which was used as context for down-stream meeting dialogues. Figure 1 shows a sample incremental temporal summary from the AMI-ITS dataset.

We evaluate all models on their ability to predict abstractive summaries from AMI-ITS. In all cases, 3 models of each type were trained to compute average performance and estimate model variability. We select models to optimize ROUGE-1 recall values but also report other measures. In total 42*3 models were trained for this work.

4 Models

Model Input/Output: The input to all models is extractive meeting dialog. For this work, we use human judgements of extractive sentences as labeled by participants in the AMI-ITS data collection pipeline. Previous work by Manuvinakurike et al. (2021) showed that learning a highly accurate automatic extractor given available training data is possible with accuracy above 70%. Role information ($role$, e.g. 'Project Manager (PM):') may be included as part of the input as well. Work on dialog summarization indicates that role information is important in abstractive summarizations (Zhu et al., 2020) and thus we include comparisons of role and non-role labeled dialogues in our experiments.

Context: The main model variants investigate the role of context in improving abstractive summarization. We define context to be the number of previous (human generated) abstractive summaries provided to the model during training and prediction. For example, our summarization model may be asked to summarize the meeting events that happened between 1000 and 1100 seconds of a given meeting. In this case, there are 10 previous contexts that the model can be provided. Because the temporal summaries are focused on only the events of 1000 to 1100 seconds, the summarization model may not benefit from seeing summaries from the first 0 to 100 seconds but may benefit from seeing the summary from 900 to 1000 seconds.

In labeling our models and results, we include the number of past summaries the model saw during training. A context value of 0 indicates that the summarization model was provided no summaries from the past, whereas, a context value of 5 would indicate that summaries for the most recent 5 100-second chunks were included. Because of the redundancy in the transformer model input as context values increase in length, the order of the previous contexts is shuffled. Each context is separated by the end of sentence, start of sentence characters from the model tokenizer.

5 Methods and Results

We focus our exploration on BART as the baseline model as this model has been investigated both in incremental summarization and dialogue summarization. For fine-tuning of abstractive models, we fine-tune for a maximum of 25 epochs and choose the model resulting in the best ROUGE-1 F-measure on the validation set. We use the following configuration for all baseline models: learning rate=0.0001, training batch size=4, and label smoothed negative log-likelihood loss. The maximum sequence length is set to 1024. The models can generate summaries of the max length of 142 tokens. For model training and inference, we use multiple machines with a combination of either an Intel(R) Xeon(R) or Intel(R) Xeon(R) Platinum 8280 CPU and NVIDIA Titan X or Titan Xp GPU. All models were trained on 2 GPUs. For the pretrained models, we use the BART-large-cnn model, from the Huggingface (Wolf et al., 2019) library. We retain the default model configurations. For all experimental conditions, we input the transcriptions of the extractives marked by crowd workers in the AMI-ITS dataset and n previous contexts. The order of the previous contexts are randomly shuffled when building the dataset. We evaluate models on their ability to generate the abstractive summaries similar to those provided by the crowd workers in the AMI-ITS dataset.

5.1 Fine-tuning to dialogue

We first investigate whether incremental temporal summarization is improved by fine-tuning a pretrained summarization model, originally trained on CNN/DailyMail (CNN), to meeting dialogues and their respective abstractive summaries from the AMI corpus. As mentioned, news summarization often emphasize and leverages information from early in the news article; dialogue does not follow any systematic structure and the beginning of meetings may actually contain spurious information such as introductions and technical issues.

Because the task is to summarize small chunks of dialogue, it is possible that the granularity of the AMI summaries, which is significantly less than required for 100 second time slices, not improve the performance over the baseline model. Thus we compare using the pretrained BART-large model, trained on CNN news articles (Hermann et al., 2015; Nallapati et al., 2016) to one that is fine-tuned on the AMI dataset (Carletta et al., 2005) (AMI). In all cases, we fine-tune on the training data portion of the AMI-ITS dataset and evaluate on the AMI-ITS test set. We also consider the importance of speaker role information by using role labels in the AMI dataset and role labels at test and fine-tuning both models on AMI-ITS dialog that contains role information. Baseline models are evaluated by ROUGE scores (R1, R2 and RL)[1] on a testing set of the AMI-ITS dataset.

We conclude from table 2 that fine-tuning on the AMI dataset may hurt performance on the AMI-ITS dataset. It is unclear if role information affects performance. The decrease in performance when fine-tuning on AMI is likely due to the difference in tasks–summarization of a full meeting versus summarization of the last 100 seconds. We thus use the pretrained BART CNN transformer for all subsequent experiments.

model	ROUGE-1	ROUGE-2	ROUGE-L
CNN	47.61/34.14	**15.28/11.21**	29.07/**20.36**
CNN_{role}	**47.85**/33.80	**15.47**/11.01	**29.17**/20.07
AMI	45.27/**35.42**	14.38/11.14	28.16/21.34
AMI_{role}	45.71/33.85	13.89/10.15	27.89/20.10

Table 2: R1, R2, and RL scores (recall/precision) on the AMI-ITS dataset for BART trained on CNN/DailyMail (CNN) or fine-tuned first on AMI (AMI). $role$ indicates speaker role information is part of the input.

5.2 Summaries vs extractive texts

As we add more and more previous contextual information to the model, the input length quickly exceeds the max length that the pretrained model can process. In the case of the BART CNN/DailyMail model, inputs larger than 1024 tokens are ignored. This can be problematic when training and evaluating performance of the BART AMI-ITS model specifically because the model may be using the text and summary information differently. We thus ask whether model performance changes when we truncate the input, preferring to maintain either 1) extractive text information or 2) context information. To investigate this question we consider input representations that include extractive text and up to 10 previous summaries where available. We then test two model variants: one that will maintain the extractive text to the exclusion of the summaries and another than maintains the summaries to the exclusion of the extractive text. Table 3 shows that model performance is positively affected by the availability of the extractive text than models preferring previous summaries over current text in terms of R1 recall. This highlights a difference between human summarization and model summarization as Manuvinakurike et al. (2021) showed

[1]ROUGE scores were calculated via rouge-score version 0.0.4 `pypi.org/project/rouge-score/`

model	ROUGE-1	ROUGE-2	ROUGE-L
T-10	**46.11**/34.39	13.60/10.21	**27.92**/20.37
T-10_{role}	45.35/34.47	13.90/10.78	**27.92**/20.62
C-10	44.23/**36.37**	14.25/**12.12**	27.47/**22.21**
C-10_{role}	44.32/36.12	**14.27**/11.66	27.80/22.00

Table 3: R1, R2, and RL (recall/precision) scores for models that selectively prefer extractive text over contexts (T-10) or contexts over extractive text (C-10) in the case wher 10 contexts are used.

that human summaries were higher quality when previous contexts were supplied. For the rest of our experiments, we keep extractive text over summaries when the input length exceeds the maximum length of the model input.

5.3 The effect of past summaries

Our main research question focuses on to what extent previous (human) generated summaries improve the quality of the summaries. To explore this question, we construct model inputs that include a various number of previous temporal summaries. We consider models trained without and with role labels on the dialogue. Table 4 shows the result from this experiment. Generally, the quality of the summaries from a model trained on input without the role information does not improve with the addition of summary information when evaluated on ROUGE recall. We see a small improvement in ROUGE precision. It may seem non-intuitive that additional contexts does not improve ROUGE recall, but this result may be because the model receives large amounts of context information compared to dialogue, resulting in over-attendance to past summaries rather than current dialogue.

In the case of a model trained with role labels on the dialogue, previous contextual information helps, up until a point. For improving recall, providing the previous 5 summaries improves performance and surpasses model performance when no role labels are provided. Precision is also highest when context information of 3 previous summaries is included as input to the model. These results suggest that previous context is useful to these models but that distinguishing contexts from dialogue is important to model performance.

5.4 Capturing context

Given the challenges of dealing with input length while including past contexts, we explore ways to capture only the relevant information from the past summaries. In this section we describe the methods for capturing the context using keyphrase extraction and semantic role labels from the past summaries.

context	ROUGE-1	ROUGE-2	ROUGE-L
0	**47.61**/34.14	**15.28**/11.21	**29.07**/20.36
1	46.88/34.82	14.05/10.54	28.72/20.59
3	45.89/**35.70**	14.93/**11.55**	28.36/**21.51**
5	46.81/34.55	13.87/10.13	28.50/20.50
10	45.35/34.50	13.93/10.80	27.90/20.62
0_{role}	47.85/33.80	15.47/11.01	29.17/20.07
1_{role}	46.22/35.50	14.14/10.90	28.25/21.08
3_{role}	45.34/**36.58**	14.33/**11.56**	27.70/**21.85**
5_{role}	**48.29**/33.67	**15.66**/10.85	**29.52**/19.88
10_{role}	46.65/34.52	14.28/10.54	28.35/20.44

Table 4: R1, R2, and RL scores (recall/precision) for models trained with different numbers of contexts.

Keyphrase extraction: For keyphrase extraction, we define the context as the 10 most important words or phrases from past summaries. To extract meaningful keyphrases from the human generated summaries, we use a pre-trained BERT model, KeyBERT (Grootendorst, 2020). This technique uses BERT-embeddings (Devlin et al., 2018) and cosine similarity to find sub-phrases in a document that are most similar to the full document itself. We generate top-10 keyphrases (ranging between 1-5 words) for each previous summary and use these keyphrases as past contexts. We use Maximal Margin Relevance (MMR, Carbonell and Goldstein (1998)) to reduce redundancy and increase diversity in the keyphrases. All keywords for each context are concatenated into one string and separated by end/start tokens. Results from table 5 indicate that keyphrase extraction improves ROUGE precision values but does not improve recall.

model	context	ROUGE-1	ROUGE-2	ROUGE-L
baseline	0	47.61/34.14	15.28/11.21	29.07/20.36
$baseline_{role}$	5	48.29/33.67	15.66/10.85	29.52/19.88
Keyphrase	1	44.57/**37.11**	13.35/11.23	26.85/**21.90**
	3	43.51/**36.81**	13.52/**11.61**	27.01/**22.35**
	5	46.61/34.70	14.39/10.86	28.53/20.75
	10	46.66/**35.33**	13.68/10.42	28.42/20.84
$Keyphrase_{role}$	1	46.54/**37.10**	14.96/**12.07**	28.01/**21.74**
	3	44.05/**37.58**	13.65/**11.74**	27.32/**22.84**
	5	46.92/**34.79**	15.52/**11.52**	**29.78/21.45**
	10	42.50/**36.97**	13.03/**11.47**	26.29/**22.26**

Table 5: R1, R2, and RL scores (recall/precison) for models trained with different amounts of past contexts where contexts are defined as the top 10 keyphrases extracted via keyBERT. Bolded values indicate improvement over baseline context models.

Semantic Role labeling: We next consider whether semantic role labels can provide relevant contextual information. Using semantic role labelers (SRL) for extracting semantic role information has shown promise, but remains largely unexplored (Yan and Wan, 2014; Trandabat, 2011). SRL helps extract important semantic information from the text in the form of Verb-Argument (& modifiers) which can serve as keywords to capture context. We extract semantic roles using Allennlp toolkit (Gardner et al., 2018) using a BERT-based model (Shi and Lin, 2019) trained on Ontonotes 5.0 dataset (Pradhan et al., 2013). The model is used out-of-the-box to extract verbs, and for each verb we also extract the verb arguments, including agents, patient, causers, instrument, benefactive, attribute, experiencers, starting point and ending points. These are ARG0-4 tags from the Propbank scheme (Bonial et al., 2010).

For Semantic Role Labeling (SRL) contexts, we try two types of extractions. One uses only the verb arguments as past contexts, another includes the verb, verb argument pairs. In all cases, the SRL output is concatenated into one string which is then separated by a start of sentence, end of sentence tokenizer pair. Results of the SRL extraction can be seen in table 6. We find the best performing model, of all models tested, is a model that uses the verb arguments of the three past contexts as context for the current dialogue. The performance is either better or on par with the baseline model regardless of which type of ROUGE measure and whether one considers recall or precision. Better precision, at the sake of recall, can be attained through SRL verb arguments of the previous 5 contexts. This strongly suggests a benefit of past contexts and that pre-processing the information of past contexts can be useful in increasing model performance.

5.5 Auto-summarization

In all of our experiments, we use human generated summaries as context. However, the transformer architecture trained with no past context information returns summaries of the last 100 seconds. Instead of requiring data collected via human-in-the-loop, we could instead use these automatically generated summaries as context for the model. Table 7 shows performance of 4 model variants trained either using human summaries or those automatically generated from the transformer architecture trained without previous summaries. In terms of recall, the human summaries result in better performance suggesting that a human-in-the-loop approach may result in better overall temporal summaries.

model	context	ROUGE-1	ROUGE-2	ROUGE-L
baseline	0	47.61/34.14	15.28/11.21	29.07/20.36
baseline_{role}	5	48.29/33.67	15.66/10.85	29.52/19.88
SRL	1	47.87/34.77	14.45/10.63	29.18/20.66
	3	**49.38**/33.80	**16.85**/11.41	**30.93**/20.40
	5	44.01/**36.77**	14.56/**12.40**	27.60/**22.56**
	10	47.40/34.06	15.34/11.25	29.10/20.44
SRLverb	1	46.49/36.27	13.66/10.62	28.60/21.64
	3	43.89/**38.88**	14.56/**12.95**	26.96/**23.48**
	5	44.90/**35.41**	13.69/10.93	26.98/20.80
	10	46.79/**35.98**	15.81/**12.14**	28.51/**21.45**
SRL_{role}	1	44.08/**38.32**	14.91/13.07	27.99/**23.74**
	3	44.18/**36.73**	14.36/11.96	27.47/**22.38**
	5	47.98/34.41	15.05/10.85	29.93/20.87
	10	47.64/**36.43**	15.66/**12.14**	28.82/**21.42**
SRLverb_{role}	1	46.47/34.74	14.37/10.91	28.96/**21.10**
	3	47.25/33.70	15.56/11.04	28.80/19.89
	5	46.20/**35.06**	15.26/11.54	28.80/**21.36**
	10	46.73/**36.01**	15.04/11.67	28.57/**21.33**

Table 6: R1, R2, and RL scores (recall/precision) for models that are trained with past contexts from semantic role labeling including verb object pair (SRLverb), with SRL objects (SRL) only.

summaries	context	ROUGE-1	ROUGE-2	ROUGE-L
human	5	46.81/34.55	13.87/10.13	28.50/20.50
auto	5	44.59/35.70	13.89/11.02	27.05/21.06
human_{role}	5	48.29/33.67	15.66/10.85	29.52/19.88
auto_{role}	5	46.67/36.50	14.07/11.18	28.66/21.95

Table 7: R1, R2, and RL scores (recall/precision) comparing human vs transformer generated summaries.

6 Discussion & Future work

In this work we present an analysis of the role of past context on summarizing 100 seconds of temporal meeting dialogue. We explore, in depth, the way in which past summaries can be used by a summarization model to generate abstractive summaries. Our work strongly suggests that context impacts model performance. We also find the way in which we represent previous summaries can impact metrics related to the quality of the abstractive summaries. We show that in certain conditions human generated summaries can improve over models with no contextual information. We then show that extracting meaningful content from past summaries can further boost model performance. Specifically, we found the verb arguments of a semantic role labeler provides the most performance improvement over our baseline models. We believe that this result provides a new direction for temporal summarization by suggesting that contextual information preceding the specific dialogue may be informative for the model in generating summaries.

To further analyze the summaries generated by the models we compare the summaries to the extractive text that was provided as input. Table 8 shows the ROUGE (Recall/Precision) measures for this comparison. We can make several observations from this table. We see that adding role information when there is no context helps improve the recall and precision (b,c in Table 8). We also observe that the human abstractive summaries (a) shows lowest recall and precision when compared to the extractive input text than those achieved via our temporal summarization models. This indicates that humans are generating summaries using tokens not present in the input which presents unique challenge to the summarization models. Another important observation we can make is that the precision of these models is high, suggesting that words in the model's abstract summary appear in the input. Recall, as expected, is low as many of the words in the input do not appear in the summary. We can also observe that adding more context information influences the SRL-based models in achieving better R2 & RL recall compared to the baseline.

model	context	ROUGE-1	ROUGE-2	ROUGE-L
(a) humans		18.73/49.62	5.09/12.91	10.84/28.65
(b) baseline	0	31.18/55.67	15.37/26.82	20.23/34.63
(c) baseline$_{role}$	0	**31.88**/58.16	15.87/28.01	20.38/36.14
(d) Keyword	1	29.79/**65.13**	15.57/33.15	19.30/40.79
	10	27.55/55.47	11.89/23.59	17.65/34.54
(e) Keyword$_{role}$	1	29.50/61.41	14.59/29.71	18.02/36.39
	10	28.33/64.43	14.80/**33.34**	18.89/**41.70**
(f) SRL	1	28.24/54.27	11.73/21.69	17.04/31.95
	10	31.01/59.66	16.07/30.70	19.94/37.29
(g) SRLverb	1	26.51/54.12	10.55/20.67	16.42/32.55
	10	29.25/58.46	15.28/29.84	18.94/36.48
(h) SRL$_{role}$	1	26.91/60.47	14.13/31.16	18.30/39.52
	10	31.69/61.88	**16.90**/32.94	**20.66**/39.37
(i) SRLverb$_{role}$	1	27.79/54.39	11.82/21.66	17.69/33.00
	10	30.74/60.84	14.67/28.74	18.91/36.16

Table 8: R1, R2, and RL scores (recall/precision) comparing model summaries to the extractive text of the meeting transcripts with context of 1 & 10.

There are limitations and clear future directions of this work. First, the model architecture we explored here is the standard BART summarization architecture. More recent models have achieved impressive performance on meeting summarizations (Feng et al., 2020; Zhu et al., 2020; Fabbri et al., 2021b). Exploring these architectures and adapting them for ITS scenario remains a promising avenue for the future work. This work also suggests that an architecture specifically aimed to capitalize on past summary information may be a promising line for our future work. When inspecting model performance, specifically when the role labels were not present, we found that the model tended to over-attend to previous contextual information. This may be mitigated by building an architecture that keeps dialogue and context information separate.

Our work provides a rather simplistic HITL (Human in the loop) approach for summarization. In this work, we integrate the summaries from the past as input to the models. While, the approach is simple, we have demonstrated that such a method of integrating context information could help improve the performance of the summarizer. Integrating human inputs into the inference pipeline is an interesting area for future work. Eventually, this system should be able to integrate human information seamlessly, requiring more experiments and analysis to understand how individuals are generating temporal summaries and how the model makes use of the past context for prediction.

One of the challenges is evaluating the quality of summaries in a scalable and automatic fashion. The ROUGE metrics are widely adopted for the purposes of summary evaluation (Lin, 2004). While numerous automated evaluation metrics exist for measuring how closely the generated summary matches with the ground-truth (Fabbri et al., 2021a) a metric for ITS scenario needs further research. Human evaluations are commonly adopted for measuring the summary quality. However, such an approach can be expensive and could also prove to be noisy when deployed over crowdsourcing environment. Recently Shapira et al. (2021) have highlighted the issue and provided an interactive evaluation of multi-document summaries. We intend to explore other types of evaluations and human judgements on ITS datasets in the future.

Incremental Temporal summarization is an emerging area of research and thus limited by data. We base all our analysis on the AMI-ITS dataset (Manuvinakurike et al., 2021). One aspect of this dataset is that summaries are generated by individuals who are seeing the 3 previous summaries generated by other crowdsource workers. These workers may be influenced by these previous summaries when generating their summaries of the last 100 seconds. Because of this, the summaries themselves may contain information about previous context making the addition of other contexts redundant and altering the extendability of these results. In the future, we intend to analyse and better understand how transformer models use previous context as well as how individuals determine what aspects of a meeting are important for incremental summarization.

References

Javed Aslam, Fernando Diaz, Matthew Ekstrand-Abueg, Richard McCreadie, Virgil Pavlu, and Tetsuya Sakai. 2015. TREC 2014 temporal summarization track overview. Technical report, NIST, Gaithersburg, MD.

Emma Barker, Monica Lestari Paramita, Ahmet Aker, Emina Kurtić, Mark Hepple, and Robert Gaizauskas. 2016. The sensei annotated corpus: Human summaries of reader comment conversations in on-line news. In *Proceedings of the 17th annual meeting of the special interest group on discourse and dialogue*, pages 42–52.

Claire Bonial, Olga Babko-Malaya, Jinho D Choi, Jena Hwang, and Martha Palmer. 2010. Propbank annotation guidelines. *Center for Computational Language and Education Research Institute of Cognitive Science University of Colorado at Boulder.*

Jaime G. Carbonell and Jade Goldstein. 1998. The use of mmr, diversity-based reranking for reordering documents and producing summaries. In *SIGIR '98: Proceedings of the 21st Annual International ACM SIGIR Conference on Research and Development in Information Retrieval, August 24-28 1998, Melbourne, Australia*, pages 335–336.

Jean Carletta, Simone Ashby, Sebastien Bourban, Mike Flynn, Mael Guillemot, Thomas Hain, Jaroslav Kadlec, Vasilis Karaiskos, Wessel Kraaij, Melissa Kronenthal, et al. 2005. The ami meeting corpus: A pre-announcement. In *International workshop on machine learning for multimodal interaction*, pages 28–39.

Yen-Chun Chen and Mohit Bansal. 2018. Fast abstractive summarization with reinforce-selected sentence rewriting. In *Proceedings of the 56th Annual Meeting of the Association for Computational Linguistics (Volume 1: Long Papers)*, pages 675–686.

Yun-Nung Chen and Florian Metze. 2012. Integrating intra-speaker topic modeling and temporal-based inter-speaker topic modeling in random walk for improved multi-party meeting summarization. In *Thirteenth Annual Conference of the International Speech Communication Association.*

Hoa Trang Dang and Karolina Owczarzak. 2008. Overview of the tac 2008 update summarization task. In *TAC.*

Franck Dernoncourt, Mohammad Ghassemi, and Walter Chang. 2018. A repository of corpora for summarization. In *Proceedings of the Eleventh International Conference on Language Resources and Evaluation.*

Jacob Devlin, Ming-Wei Chang, Kenton Lee, and Kristina Toutanova. 2018. Bert: Pre-training of deep bidirectional transformers for language understanding. *arXiv preprint arXiv:1810.04805.*

Alexander R Fabbri, Wojciech Kryściński, Bryan McCann, Caiming Xiong, Richard Socher, and Dragomir Radev. 2021a. Summeval: Re-evaluating summarization evaluation. *Transactions of the Association for Computational Linguistics*, 9:391–409.

Alexander R Fabbri, Faiaz Rahman, Imad Rizvi, Borui Wang, Haoran Li, Yashar Mehdad, and Dragomir Radev. 2021b. Convosumm: Conversation summarization benchmark and improved abstractive summarization with argument mining. *arXiv preprint arXiv:2106.00829.*

Benoit Favre, Evgeny Stepanov, Jérémy Trione, Frédéric Béchet, and Giuseppe Riccardi. 2015. Call centre conversation summarization: A pilot task at multiling 2015. In *Proceedings of the 16th Annual Meeting of the Special Interest Group on Discourse and Dialogue*, pages 232–236.

Xiachong Feng, Xiaocheng Feng, Bing Qin, and Xinwei Geng. 2020. Dialogue discourse-aware graph model and data augmentation for meeting summarization. *Dialogue*, 1:U2.

Matt Gardner, Joel Grus, Mark Neumann, Oyvind Tafjord, Pradeep Dasigi, Nelson F Liu, Matthew Peters, Michael Schmitz, and Luke Zettlemoyer. 2018. Allennlp: A deep semantic natural language processing platform. In *Proceedings of Workshop for NLP Open Source Software*, pages 1–6.

Bogdan Gliwa, Iwona Mochol, Maciej Biesek, and Aleksander Wawer. 2019. Samsum corpus: A human-annotated dialogue dataset for abstractive summarization. *EMNLP-IJCNLP 2019*, page 70.

Maarten Grootendorst. 2020. Keybert: Minimal keyword extraction with bert.

KM Hermann, T Kočiský, E Grefenstette, L Espeholt, W Kay, M Suleyman, and P Blunsom. 2015. Teaching machines to read and comprehend. *Advances in Neural Information Processing Systems*, 28.

Adam Janin, Don Baron, Jane Edwards, Dan Ellis, David Gelbart, Nelson Morgan, Barbara Peskin, Thilo Pfau, Elizabeth Shriberg, Andreas Stolcke, et al. 2003. The icsi meeting corpus. In *2003 IEEE International Conference on Acoustics, Speech, and Signal Processing, 2003. Proceedings.*, volume 1.

Taehee Jung, Dongyeop Kang, Lucas Mentch, and Eduard Hovy. 2019. Earlier isn't always better: Subaspect analysis on corpus and system biases in summarization. In *Proceedings of the 2019 Conference on Empirical Methods in Natural Language Processing and the 9th International Joint Conference on Natural Language Processing*, pages 3315–3326.

Ronilda C Lacson, Regina Barzilay, and William J Long. 2006. Automatic analysis of medical dialogue in the home hemodialysis domain: structure induction and summarization. *Journal of biomedical informatics*, 39(5):541–555.

Mike Lewis, Yinhan Liu, Naman Goyal, Marjan Ghazvininejad, Abdelrahman Mohamed, Omer Levy, Veselin Stoyanov, and Luke Zettlemoyer. 2020. BART: Denoising sequence-to-sequence pre-training for natural language generation, translation, and comprehension. In *Proceedings of the 58th Annual Meeting of the Association for Computational Linguistics*, pages 7871–7880.

Manling Li, Lingyu Zhang, Heng Ji, and Richard J Radke. 2019. Keep meeting summaries on topic: Abstractive multi-modal meeting summarization. In *Proceedings of the 57th Annual Meeting of the Association for Computational Linguistics*, pages 2190–2196.

Chin-Yew Lin. 2004. Rouge: A package for automatic evaluation of summaries. In *Text summarization branches out*, pages 74–81.

Chunyi Liu, Peng Wang, Jiang Xu, Zang Li, and Jieping Ye. 2019a. Automatic dialogue summary generation for customer service. In *Proceedings of the 25th ACM SIGKDD International Conference on Knowledge Discovery & Data Mining*, pages 1957–1965.

Yang Liu. 2019. Fine-tune bert for extractive summarization. *arXiv preprint arXiv:1903.10318*.

Zhengyuan Liu, Angela Ng, Sheldon Lee, Ai Ti Aw, and Nancy F Chen. 2019b. Topic-aware pointer-generator networks for summarizing spoken conversations. In *2019 IEEE Automatic Speech Recognition and Understanding Workshop (ASRU)*, pages 814–821.

Ramesh Manuvinakurike, Saurav Sahay, Wenda Chen, and Lama Nachman. 2021. Incremental temporal summarization in multiparty meetings. In *Proceedings of the 22nd Annual Meeting of the Special Interest Group on Discourse and Dialogue*.

Richard McCreadie, Craig Macdonald, and Iadh Ounis. 2014. Incremental update summarization: Adaptive sentence selection based on prevalence and novelty. In *Proceedings of the 23rd ACM international conference on conference on information and knowledge management*, pages 301–310.

Amita Misra, Pranav Anand, Jean E Fox Tree, and Marilyn Walker. 2015. Using summarization to discover argument facets in online idealogical dialog. In *Proceedings of the 2015 Conference of the North American Chapter of the Association for Computational Linguistics: Human Language Technologies*, pages 430–440.

Ramesh Nallapati, Bowen Zhou, Cicero dos Santos, Çağlar Gulçehre, and Bing Xiang. 2016. Abstractive text summarization using sequence-to-sequence rnns and beyond. In *Proceedings of The 20th SIGNLL Conference on Computational Natural Language Learning*, pages 280–290.

Shashi Narayan, Shay B Cohen, and Mirella Lapata. 2018. Don't give me the details, just the summary! topic-aware convolutional neural networks for extreme summarization. In *Proceedings of the 2018 Conference on Empirical Methods in Natural Language Processing*, pages 1797–1807.

Massimo Poesio and Hannes Rieser. 2010. Completions, coordination, and alignment in dialogue. *Dialogue & Discourse*, 1(1).

Sameer Pradhan, Alessandro Moschitti, Nianwen Xue, Hwee Tou Ng, Anders Björkelund, Olga Uryupina, Yuchen Zhang, and Zhi Zhong. 2013. Towards robust linguistic analysis using ontonotes. In *Proceedings of the Seventeenth Conference on Computational Natural Language Learning*, pages 143–152.

Colin Raffel, Noam Shazeer, Adam Roberts, Katherine Lee, Sharan Narang, Michael Matena, Yanqi Zhou, Wei Li, and Peter J Liu. 2020. Exploring the limits of transfer learning with a unified text-to-text transformer. *Journal of Machine Learning Research*, 21:1–67.

Abigail See, Peter J Liu, and Christopher D Manning. 2017. Get to the point: Summarization with pointer-generator networks. In *Proceedings of the 55th Annual Meeting of the Association for Computational Linguistics*, pages 1073–1083.

Ori Shapira, Ramakanth Pasunuru, Hadar Ronen, Mohit Bansal, Yael Amsterdamer, and Ido Dagan. 2021. Extending multi-document summarization evaluation to the interactive setting. In *Proceedings of the 2021 Conference of the North American Chapter of the Association for Computational Linguistics: Human Language Technologies*, pages 657–677, Online.

Peng Shi and Jimmy Lin. 2019. Simple bert models for relation extraction and semantic role labeling. *arXiv preprint arXiv:1904.05255*.

Diana Trandabat. 2011. Using semantic roles to improve summaries. In *Proceedings of the 13th European Workshop on Natural Language Generation*, pages 164–169.

Thomas Wolf, Lysandre Debut, Victor Sanh, Julien Chaumond, Clement Delangue, Anthony Moi, Pierric Cistac, Tim Rault, Rémi Louf, Morgan Funtowicz, et al. 2019. Huggingface's transformers: State-of-the-art natural language processing. *arXiv preprint arXiv:1910.03771*.

Su Yan and Xiaojun Wan. 2014. Srrank: leveraging semantic roles for extractive multi-document summarization. *IEEE/ACM Transactions on audio, speech, and language processing*, 22(12):2048–2058.

Jingqing Zhang, Yao Zhao, Mohammad Saleh, and Peter Liu. 2020. Pegasus: Pre-training with extracted gap-sentences for abstractive summarization. In *International Conference on Machine Learning*, pages 11328–11339.

Zhou Zhao, Haojie Pan, Changjie Fan, Yan Liu, Linlin Li, Min Yang, and Deng Cai. 2019. Abstractive meeting summarization via hierarchical adaptive segmental network learning. In *The World Wide Web Conference*, pages 3455–3461.

Ming Zhong, Da Yin, Tao Yu, Ahmad Zaidi, Mutethia Mutuma, Rahul Jha, Ahmed Hassan, Asli Celikyilmaz, Yang Liu, Xipeng Qiu, et al. 2021. Qmsum: A new benchmark for query-based multi-domain meeting summarization. In *Proceedings of the 2021 Conference of the North American Chapter of the Association for Computational Linguistics: Human Language Technologies*, pages 5905–5921.

Chenguang Zhu, Ruochen Xu, Michael Zeng, and Xuedong Huang. 2020. A hierarchical network for abstractive meeting summarization with cross-domain pretraining. In *Proceedings of the 2020 Conference on Empirical Methods in Natural Language Processing: Findings*, pages 194–203.

Are We Summarizing the Right Way? A Survey of Dialogue Summarization Data Sets

Don Tuggener[1], Margot Mieskes[2], Jan Deriu[1], and Mark Cieliebak[1]

[1]Zurich University of Applied Sciences (ZHAW), Winterthur, Switzerland, *{tuge, deri, ciel}@zhaw.ch*
[2]University of Applied Sciences, Darmstadt, Germany, *margot.mieskes@h-da.de*

Abstract

Dialogue summarization is a long-standing task in the field of NLP, and several data sets with dialogues and associated human-written summaries of different styles exist. However, it is unclear for which type of dialogue which type of summary is most appropriate. For this reason, we apply a linguistic model of dialogue types to derive matching summary items and NLP tasks. This allows us to map existing dialogue summarization data sets into this model and identify gaps and potential directions for future work. As part of this process, we also provide an extensive overview of existing dialogue summarization data sets.

1 Introduction

Dialogue summarization is a long-standing task in the NLP field and has recently gained traction through the emergence of novel data sets (Gliwa et al., 2019; Zhu et al., 2021) and community efforts like the AutoMin[1] shared task or the SummDial@SIGDial 2021 special session[2]. Dialogues can take a wide variety of forms ranging from formal interviews on a specific topic, political debates to informal conversations over the telephone.[3] Therefore, the question of what is a suitable, appropriate summary of this type of data emerges. While abstractive and extractive summaries have emerged as the de-facto standard for summarization of continuous text (either single or multiple documents), the situation is less clear for dialogue summarization: What is a "proper" summary for the different types of dialogues?

Several dialogue corpora with associated human-written summaries have been created. These summaries differ significantly in type, style, and focus, depending on the instructions that were given to the human annotators. It is usually not clear *why* the particular summary type was chosen for the dialogue corpus at hand. In fact, we are not aware of any well-founded theory that answers this questions.

To close this gap, we leverage the well-established linguistic model of dialogue types by Walton and Krabbe (1995) to identify suitable summary items for the different types of dialogues. This results in a combination of linguistically defined dialogue types, their features, and the suitable summary items. We then place all existing dialogue data sets with summaries that we are aware of into this matrix. This allows us to map the available resources and to identify gaps, which opens up directions for future work.

More precisely, this work presents four contributions:

1. A concise presentation of the linguistically grounded classification of dialogue types by Walton and Krabbe (Section 2)
2. A mapping from dialogue types to potential summary items and associated NLP tasks (Table 2). This indicates which summaries would be appropriate for which dialogue type.
3. An overview of all existing data sets for dialogue summarization that we are aware of (Section 3), which will be useful for researchers in the field even independent from the linguistic model.
4. A mapping from the existing data sets to the linguistic model, and an analysis of potential resource gaps (Section 4).

We also present the overview of existing dialogue summarization data sets in a comprehensive tabular overview in Table A in the Appendix.

[1]`https://elitr.github.io/automatic-minuting/index.html`

[2]`https://elitr.github.io/automatic-minuting/summdial.html`

[3]In this paper we focus on *spontaneous spoken dialogues*, leaving out written dialogues such as Twitter discussion, scripted dialogues, which occur for example in movies, and the summarization of material spoken by single persons only.

Proceedings of the Third Workshop on New Frontiers in Summarization, pages 107–118
November 10, 2021.

2 Dialogue Types in Linguistics

The analysis of dialogues within linguistics is mainly investigated in the fields of conversation analysis and pragmatics. A large body of work investigates speech acts (Searle, 1969; Grice, 1975, inter alia), i.e. dialogues are decomposed into individual turns and their communicative intents are analysed. A smaller body of work focuses on establishing a typology of dialogues. Among these works, Walton and Krabbe (1995) is a well-established model that is often cited and discussed.

2.1 The Walton & Krabbe Model

Walton and Krabbe developed a model of dialogues types and their features which is often picked up in subsequent work in various fields. Table 1 (upper part) shows the model. It features six basic dialogue types: *Persuasion*, *Negotiation*, *Inquiry*, *Deliberation*, *Information-seeking*, and *Eristics*. There are three additional mixed types: *Debate* (*Persuasion* and *Eristics*), *Committee meeting* (mainly *Deliberation*), and *Socratic Dialogue* (mainly *Persuasion*).[4]

Recently, Macagno and Bigi (2018) showed how Walton and Krabbe's model is connected to theories of speech acts, dialect acts, and pragmatic acts and concepts such as "communicative intentions". Walton and Krabbe's dialogue types were explored by research in multi-agent communication in computer science. For example, Reed (1998) applies the model to derive dialogue frames to describe multi-agent interactions.

A related approach to dialogue type categorization is presented in Franke (2010, 2011). The approach develops a taxonomy of (minimal) dialogues. Minimal dialogues are sequences of speech acts in a dialogue that have ended in a conclusion or decision. A naturally-occurring dialogue is then modelled as a sequence of these minimal dialogues.

It is noteworthy that naturally-occurring dialogues are seen as a mixture of multiple dialogue types in both aforementioned models. Still, we find that most of the dialogue corpora we examine in Section 3 can be assigned to one (or two) main dialogue type(s) under the Walton and Krabbe model.

We choose the Walton and Krabbe model as the basis of our analysis of resources in the dialogue summarization space as it is generally the most established one and has been shown to extend well into other domains. Furthermore, the features that Walton and Krabbe attribute to the dialogue types enable us to infer desiderata for the type of summary that suits the dialogue type. For example, if the the main goal of a negotiation is "making a deal", then a suitable summary would present the deal that resulted from the negotiation. Similarly, if the main goal of a debate is "accommodating conflicting points of views", then a suitable summary would list these points of view, and by extension, attribute them to the speakers participating in the debate, and, going further, provide insight into the reasoning of the speakers etc. Finally, the generation of the desirable summary types can then be decomposed naturally into well-established NLP tasks such as topic detection, argument mining, and stance detection, etc.

In summary, the Walton and Krabbe model and its features provide a structured perspective on dialogues that lets us identify suitable connections between dialogue types and summary items, and enables us to pin-point NLP tasks that are applicable for accomplishing such summaries.

2.2 Mapping Dialogue Types to Summary Items

Having selected the model of dialogue types by Walton and Krabbe (1995) as the lens through which we wish to explore the resources in the dialogue summarization domain, we first infer desirable properties of summaries for each of the dialogue types. For this purpose, we examine the dialogue types' features (primarily: *Initial situation* and *Main goal*; secondarily: *Participant's aim* and *Side benefits*) to derive items that an optimal summary would contain in this view. To link the desirable summary items to specific NLP tasks, we note down NLP targets that need to be identified and extracted to enable a summarization system to produce the summary items in its outputs.

The lower part of Table 1 presents the result of this process.[5] The summary items are ordered by importance in relation to our prioritization of the dialogue type features (i.e. Main goals are more important than Side benefits). We exemplify our mapping based on the Persuasion dialogue type:

[4] We omit the mixed dialogue types in Table 1 for brevity, as they are combinations of the other types.

[5] To encourage different takes in this mapping process, the authors of this paper individually performed the task of mapping dialogue types to summary items and NLP tasks and then held a discussion to harmonize the mappings. Overall, the mappings of the authors overlapped to a large extent and complemented each other, i.e., no conflicting points or disagreement emerged

	Persuasion	Negotiation	Inquiry	Deliberation	Information-seeking	Eristics
Initial situation	Conflicting points of view (POVs)	Conflict of interests & need for cooperation	General ignorance	Need for action	Personal Ignorance	Conflict & antagonism
Main goal	Resolution of such conflicts by verbal means	Making a deal	Growth of knowledge & agreement	Reach a decision	Spreading knowledge and revealing positions	Reaching a (provisional) accommodation in a relationship
Participants' aim	Persuade the other(s)	Get the best out of it for oneself	Find a "proof" or destroy one	Influence out-come	Gain, pass on, show, or hide personal knowledge	Strike the other party & win in the eyes of onlookers
Side benefits	Develop and reveal positions, Build up confidence, Influence onlookers, Add to prestige	Agreement, Build up confidence, Reveal position Influence onlookers, Add to prestige	Add to prestige, Gain experience, Raise funds	Agreement, Develop & reveal positions, Add to prestige, Vent emotions	Agreement, Develop & reveal positions, Add to prestige, Vent emotions	Agreement, Develop & reveal positions, Gain experience, Amusement, Add to prestige, Vent emotions
Summary items	POVs, Resolutions, Disagreements, Positions, Arguments, Winners/Losers, Controversies	Final deal, Initial interests, Winners/Losers, Evolution of deal, Arguments	Initial inquiry, Gained/new knowledge, Reached agreement, (Line of) arguments, Mentioned facts	Decision, Initial need for action, Positions of speakers, Evolution of decision, Winners/Losers, Emotions	Initial problem, Solution, Positions, Emotions	Initial conflict, Resolution/agreement, Winners/Losers, Arguments, Emotions
NLP targets	Topics, Stances, Decisions, Arguments, Emotions, Sentiment	Decisions, Stances, Topic tracking, arguments	Topics, Knowledge, Decisions, Arguments, Keyfacts	Decisions, Topics, Stances, Arguments, Topic tracking, Emotions	Topics, Action items, Decisions, Stances, Emotions	Topics, Action items, Decisions, Arguments, Emotions

Table 1: Categorization of dialogue types (columns) and their features (rows) according to Walton and Krabbe (1995), and their mapping to our proposed summary items (sorted by importance) and the applicable NLP tasks' target information.

The main goal of Persuasion dialogues is to revolve a conflict between multiple speakers. Each participant wants to persuade the others. For a summary, we are mainly interested in the different conflicting points of views (POV) and the resolution of the disagreement. However, the arguments used to resolve the conflict, and the final "winner" are also of interest. For each of these summary items, a corresponding NLP task can be used to extract a specific item. For instance, to extract the different POVs, stance detection can be applied. To extract the arguments used to persuade others, argument detection is applicable, etc. That is, summaries of a dialogue under a given dialogue type would ideally include these targets explicitly in a structured manner to facilitate the creation and evaluation of automatic summarization systems.

The list of all NLP targets emerging in the mapping are: *Topics (tracking)*, *Decisions/Action items*, *Arguments*, *Emotions/Sentiment*, *Stances*, *Keyfacts*, and *Knowledge*. We will apply this inventory of NLP targets in Section 4 to map out existing resources and investigate which summary items have been explored for which dialogue types.

3 Data Sets – An Overview

We next provide an overview of existing dialogue summarization data sets. The overview is complemented by Table A in the Appendix which offers a compact and comprehensive outline of the data sets including descriptions, sizes, covered languages, and available summary types. We divide the data sets into the domains that they cover (*Meetings, Broadcast Interviews, Customer and Patient Support, Spontaneous Conversation*) and discuss applicable dialogue types.

Dialogues can be either spoken or written. While several corpora of written or more formal dialogues and their summarization have emerged recently (Gliwa et al., 2019; Chen et al., 2021, inter alia), we here focus on corpora for summarization of (transcripts of) spoken dialogues, which is considerably different than summarization of text, as described for example in Gurevych and Strube (2004).

Work on summarizing spoken dialogues (i.e. involving more than one speaker) started in the late 1990s and early 2000s (see for example Zechner and Waibel (2000b,a)). These already covered a great variety of different types of dialogues, such as TV discussions (NewsHour, CNN CrossFire), phone calls (CALLHOME, CALLFRIEND) and meetings. An overview of these early approaches into summarizing dialogues can be found in Zechner (2002).

At the same time, the VERBMOBIL project, which focused on negotiations dialogues, also worked on summarising these (Reithinger et al., 2000; Alexandersson et al., 2000).[6]

3.1 Meetings

The topic of summarizing meetings gained considerable attraction with extensive work on the ICSI-Corpus (Morgan et al., 2001) and the AMI-Corpus (Murray et al., 2007, e.g.). Murray et al. (2005) presented work on manually summarizing the ICSI meetings, where annotators were instructed to "construct a textual summary [...] aimed at someone who is interested in the research being carried out". Four headlines or questions served as guidelines: 1) Why are they meeting and what do they talk about? 2) Decisions made by the group, 3) progress and achievements and 4) problems described. Liu and Liu (2008) extended this work by creating more human summaries and evaluating the summaries based on a questionnaire to be filled out by humans. Other work looked in more detail into how to detect and summarize action items, their descriptions and their appropriate time frames (Purver et al., 2007, e.g.).

The AMI corpus was also extensively studied in the context of summarization. However, while the ICSI corpus contains actual meetings of the participating research groups, which had a varied number of participants, the AMI corpus contains meetings of four persons with different roles in a product design scenario, which was not a natural scenario for the participants. Additionally, the topic is always the same, whereas the ICSI corpus has a wide variety of topics that were discussed in the meetings, including for example chit-chat among team members waiting for everyone to arrive. Summaries for the AMI corpus were created in an abstractive way, based on dialogue acts supporting the information in the summaries (Murray et al., 2007).

Fernández et al. (2008) aimed at identifying "decision-making sub-dialogues" in the AMI meeting data. The authors state that a decision sub-dialogue consists of three components: a) an issue raised, b) proposals are considered and c) the decision. To that end, they annotate dialogue acts in the data that represent either the issue, or parts of the resolution and the decision.

Similar to the development in the text summarization domain, the dialogue summarization domain moved to using queries to represent the information need of a specific user (Mehdad et al., 2014). Unfortunately, there was not data created for this scenario and the qualitative evaluation was performed on a small subset of the data.

Wang and Cardie (2012) and Wang and Cardie (2013) also work on summarizing meetings, but rather than aiming for a generic summary, they present work on summarizing focused summaries, that are based on specific aspects of a meeting, such as decisions, action items etc.

Following in the footsteps of the AMI corpus Yamamura et al. (2016) present a similar dataset for the Japanese language named "Kyutech Corpus", which also includes reference summaries created in the same fashion as the reference summaries for the AMI corpus.

More recently, Zhong et al. (2021) used queries to represent information need when accessing the ICSI and AMI corpora.

Another type of meeting dialogues occur in the political domain. Political debates from the UK's House of Commons have been used by Vilares and He (2017). The authors aim to produce summaries which give a brief overview on the main viewpoints exchanged and perspectives expressed, which puts it in the area of stance classification and argument mining.

Committee meetings from the Welsh and Canadian Parliament are used by Zhong et al. (2021). Their aim is to create informative summaries based on two types of queries: General queries and specific queries, which included discussion points,

[6]Note that in the following we do not present all existing work in the domain of dialogue summarization, but focus on those that present representative research results or annotations.

opinions, ideas etc. In the discussions elements relevant to the queries have been annotated, as well as informative summaries created.

Dialogue Types The discussed corpora in the meeting domain mainly cover project, team, and committee meetings. Given the Initial situation settings of *Need for action, conflict of interest & need for cooperation*, and the Main goals *Reach a decision, Making a deal*, we assign this domain to the dialogue types *Deliberation* and *Negotiation*.

3.2 Broadcast Interviews

TV discussions were already studied in the early phases of speech summarization. More recent work is presented by Zhu et al. (2021) based on NPR and CNN interviews. Reference summaries are based on the descriptions of the interviews and the list of topics discussed.

Podcasts are another form of exchange, that can be an interview, but it can also be a discussion. Clifton et al. (2020) present a data set of Podcasts used for summarization. Reference summaries are based on creator-generated descriptions, which are most likely rather indicative than informative. Using generic summarization algorithms, summaries are created automatically and evaluated manually.

Dialogue Types While the formats covered in the corpora in this domain are rather open by nature, we map it to the dialogue types *Information-seeking*, e.g. interviews with an experts where ignorance (Initial situation) is remedied by the expert's knowledge (Main goal), and *Debate*, where the Initial situation is the presence of conflicting views that are accommodated and discussed in front of an audience (Main goal).

3.3 Customer and Patient Support

Early work in dialogue summarization also includes call-center dialogues. Higashinaka et al. (2010) present work in this direction, which is unfortunately not based on actual call-center dialogues, but rather on recordings of people who were assigned various roles. Tamura et al. (2011) improved on this by using actual call center data. As the logs available for each dialogue were deemed unsuitable for summarization, two types of summaries were created: 1) Indicative summaries, for agents or managers to grasp the gist of the calls and 2) Informative summaries, that contain the content and allow managers to get necessary details of the calls.

Favre et al. (2015) also present work on summarizing call center dialogues. The aim is to create synopses of the calls, which contain the problem and the suggested solution. As opposed to most other work presented, the data set covered not only English, but French (Decoda Corpus) and Italian (Luna Corpus). Based on the same data sets Danieli et al. (2016) looks into analysing the behavior shown in the conversation, which is an important aspect for quality assurance supervisors.

Liu et al. (2019) present work on the DiDi-corpus, which contains dialogues from customer service centers and summaries created by the respective agents. Their aim is to identify key-point sequences in the dialogues, to which end they devise a tagging system with 51 labels, ranging from "Question Description" to "Solution".

Zhao et al. (2020) present work on the Automobile Master Corpus, which contains data from a customer question and answer scenario. It is unclear what the summaries are aimed at, so we have to assume that they are generic summaries.

Various data sets have been used for summarization that come from the medical domain. Acharya et al. (2019) present work on a data set where patients with a specific condition are interviewed. As the data contains actual interviews it cannot be shared. The summaries created aim to include sentences that motivate patients to get better.

Joshi et al. (2020) and Yim and Yetisgen (2021) work on a data set of medical interviews where reference summaries are created by medical doctors, instructing them to summarize as they would for a "clinical note by including all the relevant information". A specific focus was put on negative utterances such as "does not have symptom X".

Dialogue Types This domain clearly evolves around the need for specific information exchange (Initial setting) and passing knowledge between the speakers (Main goal). We thus assign it the *Information-seeking* dialogue type.

3.4 Spontaneous Conversations

Spontaneous or rather informal conversations were already part of the early work presented by Zechner and Waibel (2000b) and Zechner and Waibel (2000a), which looked at the CALLHOME and CALLFRIEND data, which consists of telephone conversations.

A similar setting is the basis for the Switchboard Corpus, which also contains telephone conversations on specific topics. Gurevych and Strube (2004) required annotators to "select the most important utterances" in a selection of dialogues and formed two types of gold standard: One based on all three annotators and one based on annotations by at least two annotators.

A more recent type of informal dialogues has been presented by Rameshkumar and Bailey (2020) which contains dialogues in the context of pen and paper role-playing games (CD3 data set). Summaries are provided through a wiki and are produced by fans of the associated show.

Dialogue Types This domain is difficult to assert in terms of dialogue types as the features Initial situation and Main goal are not clearly identifiable. While speakers were given a specific topic for a conversation in most cases, they were not specifically instructed to converse in a predefined manner. We can hence only speculate on the dialogue types mirrored in these conversations; the conversations would have to be examined individually to determine a sequence of matching dialogue types, which is infeasible in our study.

4 Mapping Data Sets to Summary Items

Given the overview of dialogue summarization resources and their mapping to dialogue types under the linguistic model in the previous section, and the summary items assigned to the dialogue types in Section 2.2, we are now able to tabulate the corpora and the summary items[7] to see what areas in this space are covered and where there are opportunities for future work.

Specifically, we tabulate corpora and the NLP targets that are mapped to the summary items and insert the paper references that cover the summary item for a given corpus. We perform this mapping under the requirement that a resource explicitly annotates a given NLP target in a structured manner. That is, while a general, abstractive, manual summary of a meeting might include e.g. action items or decisions, they might not be marked explicitly as such in the summaries or the underlying transcripts. In such a setting, the resource would not enable the creation of summarization systems that explicitly extract e.g. action items.[8]

Table 2 shows the result of this mapping. A quick glance reveals that only a small portion of the potential NLP targets are explicitly annotated in the summarization resources. The table also shows where efforts to create resources have been focused in the dialogue summarization space: The corpora in all domains mainly offer topics-related summaries. The meetings domain is an exception, where considerable effort has been put into annotating decisions and action items.

5 Discussion

Early approaches to create resources for dialogue summarization in the 2000's were based on spontaneous conversations. Such dialogues are difficult to map to the Walton and Krabbe types, as the features instantiations, such as *Initial Situation* or *Main Goal*, are hard to determine. The diversity of these conversations also makes it difficult to define clear guidelines for creating summaries: Annotators were mostly guided by a somewhat under-specified *relevancy* criterion and were given a length constraint. In regards to the covered summary items, such extractive summaries might contain e.g. decisions and stances etc., however, they are not marked or labeled in the extracted dialogue segments explicitly.

In the Meetings domain, summarization efforts became more specific and a substantial body of work looked into decisions and action items, which resulted in structured data sets for these summary items. For other summary items that the dialogue types Negotiation and Deliberation yield, such as Stances and Arguments, no structured resources exist, however.

Available summaries in the Broadcast domain consist of content description by the authors/creators of the content, i.e. they were not created by researchers for the purpose of dialogue summarization. The descriptions thus rather follow the (potentially commercially-motivated) goal of raising interest in a audience, rather than providing an informative or indicative summary. The communicative intent of such descriptions can therefore be considered to be substantially different from that of research-oriented summarization data sets. Naturally, such content descriptions do not explicitly make available any specific summary items.

[7]We omit the Knowledge summary item, since no resource covers it. However, Knowledge Discovery might be an interesting task in Inquiry dialogues.

[8]However, it is not always straight-forward to apply the NLP targets to resources. For example, in the QMSum corpus, the most important topics are summarized for all dialogues, but the queries that cover decisions are not guaranteed to be present for all dialogues and are not explicitly labeled as being related to decisions.

Corpus	Topics	Decisions / Action items	Arguments	Emotions / Sentiment	Stances	Keyfacts
Meetings Corpora. Dialogue types: Negotiation, Deliberation						
VerbMobil		Reithinger et al. (2000); Alexandersson et al. (2000)				
ICSI	Murray et al. (2005); Wang and Cardie (2013)	Murray et al. (2005); Purver et al. (2007); Wang and Cardie (2013)				
AMI	Murray et al. (2007)	Fernández et al. (2008); Wang and Cardie (2012, 2013)				
Kyutech		Yamamura et al. (2016)				
QMSum	Zhong et al. (2021)	Zhong et al. (2021)			Zhong et al. (2021)	
Broadcast Corpora. Dialogue types: Information-seeking, Debate						
MediaSum	Zhu et al. (2021)					
Spotify Podcasts	Clifton et al. (2020)					
Customer & Patient Support Corpora. Dialogue types: Information-seeking						
DiDi	Liu et al. (2019)	Liu et al. (2019)				
Call center I	Higashinaka et al. (2010)					
Call center II	Tamura et al. (2011)					
CCCS	Favre et al. (2015)			Favre et al. (2015)		
Telemedicine	Joshi et al. (2020)					
Clinical Encounter Visits	Yim and Yetisgen (2021)					
Spontaneous Conversation Corpora. Dialogue types: N/A						
Callhome corpus	Zechner and Waibel (2000b)					
(televison shows)	Zechner and Waibel (2000a)					
Switchboard	Gurevych and Strube (2004)					
CRD3	Rameshkumar and Bailey (2020)					

Table 2: Mapping of resource papers to corpora and NLP targets that they cover.

In the customer and patient support domain, summarization efforts also leveraged readily available resources such as synopses of call logs or doctor's notes as the summarization targets. Here, the goal of summarization efforts can be mainly described as automating the task of manually producing such notes or synopses. Hence, many linguistically motivated summary items that our approach yields for the Information-seeking dialogue type may simply not apply to the particular use cases that are covered by the existing resources, and are thus not marked explicitly as such.

6 Conclusion

We have provided an overview of existing corpora in the domain of spoken dialogue summarization. We found that topic-related extractive or abstractive summaries are predominant, and are often guided by high-level criteria, i.e. summary guidelines ask for content of "high relevancy" to be included without further specifications.

Furthermore, we have applied a linguistically motivated view on dialogues to the available corpora that yields more specific summary items, such as arguments, stances, or emotions. We found that such specific items are scarcely available in a structured manner in existing corpora. As there are several resources available for e.g. argument mining (Lawrence and Reed, 2020) and stance detection (Küçük and Can, 2020) in dialogues, a potential direction for future work could be an effort to bring together such resources.

While our model-driven view on the dialogue summarization space might be insightful and fruitful for future research, it should not be understood in a normative way: it is not intended to point out that certain directions are misguided. For instance, although our mapping does not yield Emotion as a summary item for Negotiation dialogues, there might be relevant use cases for this line of inquiry. Neither does the approach have any claim to completeness in terms of meeting the information needs of different users. In this regard, query-based approaches seem to hold a large potential to cover a wide variety of information needs (Zhong et al., 2021). However, since summary items are seamlessly embedded in the natural-language responses in such settings, it is uncertain how well query-based methods are able to generate on-the-fly responses for realistic queries like "what are the action items assigned to me and by when do I have to complete them?". Answering such information needs robustly seems to necessitate that the underlying information is extracted in a structured manner (Purver et al., 2007, e.g.) to be able to generate an appropriate and complete response.

Overall, our analysis indicates that the question of what are appropriate summaries of dialogues is a challenging one, and we have presented a view that offers some answers. While emerging query-based approaches seem to be a fruitful direction due to their potential to cover a high variety of information needs, we believe that linguistic considerations, as those outlined in this work, should also be leveraged to support resource creation efforts in the dialogue summarization space in future work.

Future work should also evaluate the summaries resulting from more dialogue-specific annotations as opposed to generic summaries especially with respect to the individual information needs of various users. This of course also leads to developing methods that take the information need into account when creating such summaries automatically.

References

Sabita Acharya, Barbara Di Eugenio, Andrew Boyd, Richard Cameron, Karen Dunn Lopez, Pamela Martyn-Nemeth, Debaleena Chattopadhyay, Pantea Habibi, Carolyn Dickens, Haleh Vatani, and Amer Ardati. 2019. A quantitative analysis of patients' narratives of heart failure. In *Proceedings of the 20th Annual SIGdial Meeting on Discourse and Dialogue*, pages 232–238, Stockholm, Sweden. Association for Computational Linguistics.

Jan Alexandersson, Peter Poller, Michael Kipp, and Ralf Engel. 2000. Multilingual summary generation in a speech-to-speech translation system for multilingual dialogues. In *INLG'2000 Proceedings of the First International Conference on Natural Language Generation*, pages 148–155, Mitzpe Ramon, Israel. Association for Computational Linguistics.

Yulong Chen, Yang Liu, Liang Chen, and Yue Zhang. 2021. DialogSum: A real-life scenario dialogue summarization dataset. In *Findings of the Association for Computational Linguistics: ACL-IJCNLP 2021*, pages 5062–5074, Online. Association for Computational Linguistics.

Ann Clifton, Sravana Reddy, Yongze Yu, Aasish Pappu, Rezvaneh Rezapour, Hamed Bonab, Maria Eskevich, Gareth Jones, Jussi Karlgren, Ben Carterette, and Rosie Jones. 2020. 100,000 podcasts: A spoken English document corpus. In *Proceedings of the 28th International Conference on Computational Linguistics*, pages 5903–5917, Barcelona, Spain (Online). International Committee on Computational Linguistics.

Morena Danieli, Balamurali A R, Evgeny Stepanov, Benoit Favre, Frederic Bechet, and Giuseppe Riccardi. 2016. Summarizing behaviours: An experiment on the annotation of call-centre conversations. In *Proceedings of the Tenth International Conference on Language Resources and Evaluation (LREC'16)*, pages 4430–4433, Portorož, Slovenia. European Language Resources Association (ELRA).

Benoit Favre, Evgeny Stepanov, Jérémy Trione, Frédéric Béchet, and Giuseppe Riccardi. 2015. Call centre conversation summarization: A pilot task at multiling 2015. In *Proceedings of the 16th Annual Meeting of the Special Interest Group on Discourse and Dialogue*, pages 232–236, Prague, Czech Republic. Association for Computational Linguistics.

Raquel Fernández, Matthew Frampton, Patrick Ehlen, Matthew Purver, and Stanley Peters. 2008. Modelling and detecting decisions in multi-party dialogue. In *Proceedings of the 9th SIGdial Workshop on Discourse and Dialogue*, pages 156–163.

Wilhelm Franke. 2010. Elementare Dialogstrukturen. In *Elementare Dialogstrukturen*. Max Niemeyer Verlag.

Wilhelm Franke. 2011. Taxonomie der Dialogtypen. In *Sprachtheorie, Pragmatik, Interdisziplinäres*, pages 213–222. Max Niemeyer Verlag.

Bogdan Gliwa, Iwona Mochol, Maciej Biesek, and Aleksander Wawer. 2019. Samsum corpus: A human-annotated dialogue dataset for abstractive summarization. In *Proceedings of the 2nd Workshop on New Frontiers in Summarization*, pages 70–79.

H Paul Grice. 1975. Speech acts. *Syntax and semantics*, 3:41–58.

Iryna Gurevych and Michael Strube. 2004. Semantic similarity applied to spoken dialogue summarization. In *COLING 2004: Proceedings of the 20th International Conference on Computational Linguistics*, pages 764–770, Geneva, Switzerland. COLING.

Ryuichiro Higashinaka, Yasuhiro Minami, Hitoshi Nishikawa, Kohji Dohsaka, Toyomi Meguro, Satoshi Takahashi, and Genichiro Kikui. 2010. Learning to model domain-specific utterance sequences for extractive summarization of contact center dialogues. In *Coling 2010: Posters*, pages 400–408, Beijing, China. Coling 2010 Organizing Committee.

Anirudh Joshi, Namit Katariya, Xavier Amatriain, and Anitha Kannan. 2020. Dr. summarize: Global summarization of medical dialogue by exploiting local structures. In *Findings of the Association for Computational Linguistics: EMNLP 2020*, pages 3755–3763, Online. Association for Computational Linguistics.

Dilek Küçük and Fazli Can. 2020. Stance detection: A survey. *ACM Computing Surveys (CSUR)*, 53(1):1–37.

John Lawrence and Chris Reed. 2020. Argument mining: A survey. *Computational Linguistics*, 45(4):765–818.

Chunyi Liu, Peng Wang, Jiang Xu, Zang Li, and Jieping Ye. 2019. Automatic dialogue summary generation for customer service. In *Proceedings of the 25th ACM SIGKDD International Conference on Knowledge Discovery & Data Mining*, pages 1957–1965.

Feifan Liu and Yang Liu. 2008. Correlation between ROUGE and human evaluation of extractive meeting summaries. In *Proceedings of ACL-08: HLT, Short Papers*, pages 201–204, Columbus, Ohio. Association for Computational Linguistics.

Fabrizio Macagno and Sarah Bigi. 2018. Types of dialogue and pragmatic ambiguity. In *Argumentation and Language—Linguistic, Cognitive and Discursive Explorations*, pages 191–218. Springer.

Yashar Mehdad, Giuseppe Carenini, and Raymond T. Ng. 2014. Abstractive summarization of spoken and written conversations based on phrasal queries. In *Proceedings of the 52nd Annual Meeting of the Association for Computational Linguistics (Volume 1: Long Papers)*, pages 1220–1230, Baltimore, Maryland. Association for Computational Linguistics.

Nelson Morgan, Don Baron, Jane Edwards, Dan Ellis, David Gelbart, Adam Janin, Thilo Pfau, Elizabeth Shriberg, and Andreas Stolcke. 2001. The meeting project at ICSI. In *Proceedings of the First International Conference on Human Language Technology Research*.

Gabriel Murray, Pei-Yun Hsueh, Simon Tucker, Jonathan Kilgour, Jean Carletta, Johanna D. Moore, and Steve Renals. 2007. Automatic segmentation and summarization of meeting speech. In *Proceedings of Human Language Technologies: The Annual Conference of the North American Chapter of the Association for Computational Linguistics (NAACL-HLT)*, pages 9–10, Rochester, New York, USA. Association for Computational Linguistics.

Gabriel Murray, Steve Renals, Jean Carletta, and Johanna Moore. 2005. Evaluating automatic summaries of meeting recordings. In *Proceedings of the ACL Workshop on Intrinsic and Extrinsic Evaluation Measures for Machine Translation and/or Summarization*, pages 33–40, Ann Arbor, Michigan. Association for Computational Linguistics.

Matthew Purver, John Dowding, John Niekrasz, Patrick Ehlen, Sharareh Noorbaloochi, and Stanley Peters. 2007. Detecting and summarizing action items in multi-party dialogue. In *Proceedings of the 8th SIGdial Workshop on Discourse and Dialogue*, pages 18–25, Antwerp, Belgium. Association for Computational Linguistics.

Revanth Rameshkumar and Peter Bailey. 2020. Storytelling with dialogue: A Critical Role Dungeons and Dragons Dataset. In *Proceedings of the 58th Annual Meeting of the Association for Computational Linguistics*, pages 5121–5134, Online. Association for Computational Linguistics.

C Reed. 1998. Dialogue frames in agent communication. In *Proceedings of the 3rd International Conference on Multi Agent Systems*, page 246.

Norbert Reithinger, Michael Kipp, Ralf Engel, and Jan Alexandersson. 2000. Summarizing multilingual spoken negotiation dialogues. In *Proceedings of the 38th Annual Meeting of the Association for Computational Linguistics*, pages 310–317, Hong Kong. Association for Computational Linguistics.

John R Searle. 1969. *Speech Acts: An Essay in the Philosophy of Language*. Cambridge University Press.

Akihiro Tamura, Kai Ishikawa, Masahiro Saikou, and Masaaki Tsuchida. 2011. Extractive summarization method for contact center dialogues based on call logs. In *Proceedings of 5th International Joint Conference on Natural Language Processing*, pages 500–508, Chiang Mai, Thailand. Asian Federation of Natural Language Processing.

David Vilares and Yulan He. 2017. Detecting perspectives in political debates. In *Proceedings of the 2017 Conference on Empirical Methods in Natural Language Processing*, pages 1573–1582, Copenhagen, Denmark. Association for Computational Linguistics.

Douglas N Walton and Erik CW Krabbe. 1995. *Commitment in dialogue: Basic concepts of interpersonal reasoning*. SUNY press.

Lu Wang and Claire Cardie. 2012. Focused meeting summarization via unsupervised relation extraction. In *Proceedings of the 13th Annual Meeting of the Special Interest Group on Discourse and Dialogue*, pages 304–313, Seoul, South Korea. Association for Computational Linguistics.

Lu Wang and Claire Cardie. 2013. Domain-independent abstract generation for focused meeting summarization. In *Proceedings of the 51st Annual Meeting of the Association for Computational Linguistics (Volume 1: Long Papers)*, pages 1395–1405, Sofia, Bulgaria. Association for Computational Linguistics.

Takashi Yamamura, Kazutaka Shimada, and Shintaro Kawahara. 2016. The Kyutech corpus and topic segmentation using a combined method. In *Proceedings of the 12th Workshop on Asian Language Resources (ALR12)*, pages 95–104, Osaka, Japan. The COLING 2016 Organizing Committee.

Wen-wai Yim and Meliha Yetisgen. 2021. Towards automating medical scribing : Clinic visit Dialogue2Note sentence alignment and snippet summarization. In *Proceedings of the Second Workshop on Natural Language Processing for Medical Conversations*, pages 10–20, Online. Association for Computational Linguistics.

Klaus Zechner. 2002. Automatic summarization of open-domain multiparty dialogues in diverse genres. *Computational Linguistics*, 28(4):447–485.

Klaus Zechner and Alex Waibel. 2000a. DIASUMM: Flexible summarization of spontaneous dialogues in unrestricted domains. In *COLING 2000 Volume 2: The 18th International Conference on Computational Linguistics*.

Klaus Zechner and Alex Waibel. 2000b. Minimizing word error rate in textual summaries of spoken language. In *1st Meeting of the North American Chapter of the Association for Computational Linguistics*.

Lulu Zhao, Weiran Xu, and Jun Guo. 2020. Improving abstractive dialogue summarization with graph structures and topic words. In *Proceedings of the 28th International Conference on Computational Linguistics*, pages 437–449, Barcelona, Spain (Online). International Committee on Computational Linguistics.

Ming Zhong, Da Yin, Tao Yu, Ahmad Zaidi, Mutethia Mutuma, Rahul Jha, Ahmed Hassan Awadallah, Asli Celikyilmaz, Yang Liu, Xipeng Qiu, and Dragomir Radev. 2021. QMSum: A new benchmark for query-based multi-domain meeting summarization. In *Proceedings of the 2021 Conference of the North American Chapter of the Association for Computational Linguistics: Human Language Technologies*, pages 5905–5921, Online. Association for Computational Linguistics.

Chenguang Zhu, Yang Liu, Jie Mei, and Michael Zeng. 2021. MediaSum: A large-scale media interview dataset for dialogue summarization. In *Proceedings of the 2021 Conference of the North American Chapter of the Association for Computational Linguistics: Human Language Technologies*, pages 5927–5934, Online. Association for Computational Linguistics.

A Appendix

Meetings Corpora. Dialogue types: Negotiation, Deliberation			
CORPUS	*DESCRIPTION*	*LANG*	*SUMMARY CONTENTS*
VerbMobil	Negotiations in the domains of scheduling, travel planning, and hotel reservations	DE, EN, JP	- Agreements on locations, dates, hotels, trains (Reithinger et al., 2000). - Agreements on scheduling, accommodation, traveling, entertainment. (Alexandersson et al., 2000).
ICSI Corpus	Informal, natural, and even impromptu meetings at ICSI. 38 meetings for a total of 39 hours, transcribed about 12 hours. 237 participants, 49 unique speakers.	EN	- Summaries answering the following questions: Why are they meeting and what do they talk about? Decisions made by the group? Progress and achievements? Problems described (Murray et al., 2005). - Find dialogue acts that relate to action items (descriptions, time frames, owners, agreements) (Purver et al., 2007). - Abstract summarizing each important output for every meeting. Decision and problem summaries are annotated (Wang and Cardie, 2013).
AMI Corpus	100 hours of meeting recordings.	EN	- Ranking the dialogue acts in terms of being extract-worthy (Murray et al., 2007). - Classify utterances related to decisions: issue (I), resolution (R), and agreement (A). Two authors annotated 9 and 10 dialogues each (Fernández et al., 2008). - An abstract summarizing each decision; dialogue acts that support each decision are annotated (Wang and Cardie, 2012). - Abstract summarizing each important output for every meeting. Decision and problem summaries are annotated (Wang and Cardie, 2013).
Kyutech Corpus	A decision-making task in a virtual shopping mall in a virtual city. 9 conversations.	JP	- Abstractive manual summaries as in the AMI corpus (Yamamura et al., 2016).
QMSum	AMI, ICSI, and 25 committee meetings of the Welsh Parliament and 11 from the Parliament of Canada	EN	- Select and summarize relevant spans of meetings in response to a query (Zhong et al., 2021).
AutoMin	Technical meetings and parliamentary proceedings.	EN, CZ	- Meeting minutes (paper in print; `https://elitr.github.io/automatic-minuting/index.html`)
Broadcast Corpora. Dialogue types: Information-seeking, Debate			
MediaSum	Interview transcripts from NPR and CNN. 49.4K NPR transcripts and 414.2K from CNN.	EN	- Topic descriptions as summaries (Zhu et al., 2021).
Spotify Podcast Dataset	100,000 podcast episodes, comprising ~ 60,000 hours of speech.	EN	- Creator-generated descriptions as reference summaries (Clifton et al., 2020).
Customer & Patient Support Corpora. Dialogue types: Information-seeking			
DiDi	Logs in the DiDi (mobile transportation platform) customer service center.	EN	- Abstractive summaries written by agents. ~300k pairs of dialogues and summaries. "Key point sequences", i.e. a set of 51 a set action/decision items are also annotated (Liu et al., 2019).
Call center I	Simulated contact center dialogues in six domains. 15–20 tasks per domain. ~700 dialogues.	JP	- Scenario texts used as reference data (Higashinaka et al., 2010).
Call center II	4,596 call logs from a Japanese contact center.	JP	- 1. Indicative Summary: Extract utterances to grasp the gist of calls. 2. Informative Summary: Utterances to grasp the details of calls (Tamura et al., 2011).
CCCS	Conversations from the Decoda and Luna corpora of French and Italian call centre recordings. Recordings duration from a few to 15 minutes. 100 conversations in EN, FR each, translated to EN.	FR, IT, EN	- Abstractive summaries about the main events of the conversations, such as the objective of the caller, whether and how it was solved by the agent, and the attitude of both parties. Synopses written by quality assurance experts from call centres (Favre et al., 2015).

Telemedicine	25,000 conversations from a telemedicine platform.	EN	- Medical doctors were asked to summarize the sections of 3000 snippets as they would for a typical clinical note by including all the relevant information (Joshi et al., 2020).
Clinical Encounter Visits	Audio and clinical notes from clinical encounter visits from 500 visits and 13 providers.	EN	- Clinical notes as summary of the patient visit (Yim and Yetisgen, 2021).
Spontaneous Conversation Corpora. Dialogue types: N/A			
Callhome corpus	Spontaneous telephone conversations.	EN, ES	- For 9 English and 14 Spanish dialogues, the most relevant turns were marked (Zechner and Waibel, 2000b).
Televison shows	Four audio excerpts from four television shows.	EN	- Most relevant, meaningful, concise, and informative phrases (Zechner and Waibel, 2000a).
Switchboard	Telephone conversations of at least 10 minutes duration on a given topic. ∼2000 turns.	EN	- 10% of all utterances in the dialogue marked as being relevant (Gurevych and Strube, 2004).
DialogSum	Combination of English learner corpora and dialogue understanding data sets. 13,460 dialogues.	EN	- (1) convey the most salient information; (2) be brief (no longer than 20% of the conversation); (3) preserve important named entities within the conversation; (4) be written from an observer perspective; (5) be written in formal language (Chen et al., 2021).
CRD3	Transcripts of Dungeons and Dragons role-playing game. 398,682 turns.	EN	- Multiple summaries available, e.g. an abstract of the resulting plot/narrative of a game. Includes abstractive summaries collected from the Fandom wiki (Rameshkumar and Bailey, 2020).

Table 3: Overview of existing dialogue summarization data sets. The last column lists papers that provide manually created summaries for a given corpus.

Modeling Endorsement for Multi-Document Abstractive Summarization

Logan Lebanoff[†] **Bingqing Wang**[§] **Zhe Feng**[§] **Fei Liu**[†]

[†]University of Central Florida, Orlando, FL
[§]Robert Bosch LLC, Sunnyvale, CA

loganlebanoff@knights.ucf.edu {bingqing.wang,zhe.feng2}@us.bosch.com
feiliu@cs.ucf.edu

Abstract

A crucial difference between single- and multi-document summarization is how salient content manifests itself in the document(s). While such content may appear at the beginning of a single document, essential information is frequently reiterated in a set of documents related to a particular topic, resulting in an endorsement effect that increases information salience. In this paper, we model the cross-document endorsement effect and its utilization in multiple document summarization. Our method generates a synopsis from each document, which serves as an endorser to identify salient content from other documents. Strongly endorsed text segments are used to enrich a neural encoder-decoder model to consolidate them into an abstractive summary. The method has a great potential to learn from fewer examples to identify salient content, which alleviates the need for costly retraining when the set of documents is dynamically adjusted. Through extensive experiments on benchmark multi-document summarization datasets, we demonstrate the effectiveness of our proposed method over strong published baselines. Finally, we shed light on future research directions and discuss broader challenges of this task using a case study.

1 Introduction

"Repeat a lie often enough and it becomes the truth." This proverb stresses the importance of *repetition* and *frequency* in human comprehension. It causes an endorsement effect that increases the salience of repeated information. In this paper, we leverage the endorsement effect to summarize multiple documents that discuss a particular event or topic (MDS). In the commercial arena, MDS could be used to aggregate search results (Miller, 2020) and distill insights from customer reviews (Bražinskas et al., 2020). Further, MDS is an integral part of the daily work of intelligence analysts who identify important information from raw documents and consolidate it into a summary report to be disseminated to the leadership (Hamilton, 2014).

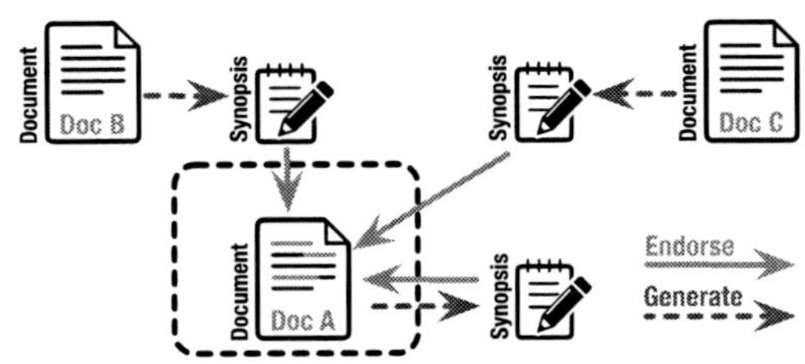

Figure 1: An example of synopsis-document relationships. Synopsis-document endorsements are leveraged to identify important text segments from a source document (e.g., Doc A). Strongly endorsed segments of all documents are consolidated into an abstractive summary.

Multi-document **A**bstractive **S**ummarization, i.e. **MuDAS**, remains a challenging problem compared to its single-document counterpart (See et al., 2017; Chen and Bansal, 2018; Narayan et al., 2018; Raffel et al., 2020; Lewis et al., 2020). The task poses a substantial challenge to modern neural models: when the set of source documents is concatenated into a flat sequence, it may exceed the maximum length allowed by the GPU memory. There are also fewer datasets available to train MuDAS models in an end-to-end fashion. Recent work tackles this problem by selecting representative sentences from the source documents to reduce the task to single-document summarization (Lebanoff et al., 2018; Coavoux et al., 2019; Fabbri et al., 2019).

Nevertheless, there could be substantial information loss if only representative sentences are used for MuDAS. It becomes unclear what information is reiterated and salient, resulting in unimportant sentence parts being included in the summary. E.g., when the sentence "*World leaders join to pledge $8 billion for vaccine, but the U.S. sits out*" is selected from the document set, it is unclear which of its segments, "*$8 billion*" or "*U.S. sits out*," is more salient given the topic of discussion. The neural representations also treat different quantities, e.g., "*$8 billion*" and "*$5 million*," indiscriminately (Rogers et al., 2020). Consequently, there is an urgent need for summarization systems to acquire fine-grained,

Proceedings of the Third Workshop on New Frontiers in Summarization, pages 119–130
November 10, 2021.

segment-level textual salience. Without that, a neural abstractive system can miss out on salient details and favor fluency over information accuracy.

In this paper, we present a conceptual framework that leverages the endorsement effect to model fine-grained segment salience for multi-document summarization. When an analyst reads a document, he retains a synopsis of the key ideas of the document in his mind. The synopsis later serves as an endorser to identify segments in other documents that reiterate the same ideas (Hintzman, 1976). We call the synopsis an "**Endorser**" and the document a "**Candidate**." Segments of the candidate documents that are frequently endorsed by synopses suggest high salience and are to be consolidated into an abstractive summary. Our synopses are generated from a state-of-the-art summarizer (Lewis et al., 2020) and a variety of methods are investigated to quantify the level of endorsement from a text synopsis to a document. Figure 1 provides an overview of synopsis-document endorsement.

Our contributions in this paper include:

- presenting a new conceptual framework to model asynchronous endorsement from text synopses to documents for multi-document summarization;
- devising a novel method to enrich neural encoder-decoder models with fine-grained segment-level endorsement to consolidate strongly endorsed content into an abstractive summary; and
- through extensive experiments on multiple benchmark summarization datasets, we demonstrate the effectiveness of the endorsement method over state-of-the-art baselines. We make our code and models publicly available.[1]

2 Related Work

Redundancy is essential in multi-document summarization. Without repetition and redundancy, even humans cannot agree on what information is salient and should be included in the summary (Daume III and Marcu, 2004). Optimizing summaries for frequency-based saliency has attained success prior to the era of deep learning (Berg-Kirkpatrick et al., 2011; Kulesza and Taskar, 2012; Boudin et al., 2015). These extractive systems strive to include the most frequently occurring concepts in the summary. However, when it comes to abstractive summarization systems, the frequency of concepts is not fully utilized by modern neural models.

Recent studies on MuDAS *implicitly* estimate frequency using hierarchical encoders / decoders. Liu and Lapata (2019) encode the documents using hierarchical Transformers where cross-document relationships are characterized by attention weights. Perez-Beltrachini et al. (2019) explore structured convolutional decoders. Li et al. (2020) leverage similarity and discourse graphs to alter the attention mechanism of encoder-decoder models. Researchers have also attempted optimization algorithms such as maximal margin relevance and determinantal point processes combined with contextualized representations and reinforcement learning (Cho et al., 2019a,b; Mao et al., 2020). Despite promising progress, modeling frequency for multi-document summarization remains an open problem, in part because neural summarization models are often pretrained on single documents that contain little or no redundant content (Kryscinski et al., 2019; Zhang et al., 2019; Jin and Wan, 2020; Laban et al., 2020; Zhang et al., 2020a). Named entities and quantities that represent salient information details are not properly accounted for (Xu and Durrett, 2021). If we do not *explicitly* model frequency, abstractive summarizers may fail to adequately recognize such salient details.

We are particularly interested in reducing multiple input documents to a single document, then consolidate the content into a succinct abstract (Nayeem et al., 2018; Coavoux et al., 2019). Our method enhances the single document with fine-grained segment salience to offset the lead bias (Grenander et al., 2019; Xing et al., 2021), which hinders the development of multiple-document summarization. Our salience estimates are obtained from a frequency-driven endorsement model. Below we present details of the proposed method.

3 Summarization with Endorsement

We approach the MuDAS problem in two stages. First, we obtain fine-grained segment-level endorsement for any candidate document. By excluding unendorsed sentences from consideration, we reduce the set of documents to a single input document. We next present an enhanced abstractive summarization model to consolidate the document into a succinct abstract, analogously to how an editor would consolidate text with emphasis on endorsed segments. This process involves non-trivial design decisions. In this section, we start by presenting the second stage in our approach – the summarization model with endorsement.

[1] https://github.com/ucfnlp/endorser-summ

3.1 The Original Transformer

We choose the encoder-decoder architecture over decoder-only architectures (Radford et al., 2019; Dong et al., 2019; Brown et al., 2020). It allows us to balance the contribution from the source text and its endorsed segments in summary generation. The encoder and decoder each comprise of a stack of L Transformer blocks (Vaswani et al., 2017). Let $\{x\}_{i=0}^{m}$ be the source sequence corresponding to the input document, and $\{y\}_{j=0}^{n}$ the summary sequence. x_0 and y_0 are beginning-of-sequence symbols. Let $\boldsymbol{E}$ be a matrix of token embeddings and $\boldsymbol{P}$ be position embeddings. An encoder produces a set of hidden vectors in its l-th layer (Eq. (1)), $\boldsymbol{H}^{(l)} = \langle \boldsymbol{h}_0^{(l)}, \ldots, \boldsymbol{h}_m^{(l)} \rangle$, where $\boldsymbol{h}_i^{(l)}$ is a hidden vector of the i-th source token. A decoder utilizes top-layer encoder hidden vectors $\boldsymbol{H}^{(L)}$ to decode the summary sequence, where $\boldsymbol{G}^{(l)}$ represents a sequence of hidden vectors of the l-th decoder layer (Eq. (2)). An upper triangular-shaped mask is used by the decoder, so that $\boldsymbol{g}_j^{(l)}$ only depends on summary tokens whose positions are less than j.

$$\boldsymbol{H}^{(l)} = \langle \boldsymbol{h}_0^{(l)}, \ldots, \boldsymbol{h}_m^{(l)} \rangle \quad (1)$$
$$= \begin{cases} \langle \boldsymbol{E}_{x_0} + \boldsymbol{P}_0, \ldots, \boldsymbol{E}_{x_m} + \boldsymbol{P}_m \rangle & l = 0 \\ \text{EncBlock}_l\big(\boldsymbol{H}^{(l-1)}\big) & l > 0 \end{cases}$$

$$\boldsymbol{G}^{(l)} = \langle \boldsymbol{g}_0^{(l)}, \ldots, \boldsymbol{g}_n^{(l)} \rangle \quad (2)$$
$$= \begin{cases} \langle \boldsymbol{E}_{y_0} + \boldsymbol{P}_0, \ldots, \boldsymbol{E}_{y_n} + \boldsymbol{P}_n \rangle & l = 0 \\ \text{DecBlock}_l\big(\boldsymbol{G}^{(l-1)}, \boldsymbol{H}^{(L)}\big) & l > 0 \end{cases}$$

With this architecture, we argue that it is preferable to modify the decoder and cross-attention to steer it towards endorsed content, rather than modifying the encoder representations $\boldsymbol{H}^{(L)}$, as they are often unsupervisedly pretrained. It would be best if such representations remain unaffected by whether a segment of the source text is endorsed or not to provide model flexibility. A decoder layer consists of three main blocks to transform from $\boldsymbol{G}^{(l-1)}$ to $\boldsymbol{G}^{(l)}$ (Eqs. (3-5)).[2] In particular, self-attention allows a summary token to attend to other summary tokens. Cross-attention allows a summary token to attend to all source tokens using $\boldsymbol{H}^{(L)}$. Finally, a feed-forward network with ReLU activation is applied to generate $\mathbf{G}^{(l)}$. Our focus of this work is to improve the cross-attention to emphasize on endorsed content during decoding.

$$\widetilde{\boldsymbol{G}}^{(l-1)} = \text{Self-Attn}(\boldsymbol{G}^{(l-1)}) \quad (3)$$
$$\widehat{\boldsymbol{G}}^{(l)} = \text{Cross-Attn}(\widetilde{\boldsymbol{G}}^{(l-1)}, \boldsymbol{H}^{(L)}) \quad (4)$$
$$\mathbf{G}^{(l)} = \text{FeedForward}(\widehat{\boldsymbol{G}}^{(l)}) \quad (5)$$

The *original* cross-attention head z transforms the j-th decoder state $\widetilde{\boldsymbol{g}}_j^{(l-1)}$ and i-th encoder state $\boldsymbol{h}_i^{(L)}$ into query, key and value vectors (Eqs. (6-8)). It computes attention weights as a normalized dot product between query and key vectors. The output of the head is a weighted sum of value vectors.

3.2 Companion Heads

We introduce a set of *companion heads* for each original head. All companion heads of z share the parameters $\{\boldsymbol{W}_z^Q, \boldsymbol{W}_z^K, \boldsymbol{W}_z^V\}$, but a companion $\text{head}_j^{z,\tau}$ with an endorsement level of τ attends only to source tokens that are endorsed τ times or more. This is achieved with a special binary mask M_i^τ (Eqs. (9-10)). The original heads are believed to copy over source tokens that are deemed relevant to summary tokens according to the dependency syntax (Clark et al., 2019). The companion heads serve a similar purpose but have a narrower focus on endorsed source tokens—frequently endorsed tokens are more likely to be copied over by companion heads. The method thus improves head diversity similar to that of sparse Transformers (Correia et al., 2019; Huang et al., 2021). The hyperparameter τ controls the level of endorsement. Finally, all heads are pooled into a hidden vector $\widehat{\boldsymbol{g}}_j^{(l)}$ (Eq. (11)) to be passed to the feedforward layer.

$$\boldsymbol{q}_j^z = \boldsymbol{W}_z^Q \widetilde{\boldsymbol{g}}_j^{(l-1)} \qquad j \in [n] \quad (6)$$
$$\boldsymbol{k}_i^z = \boldsymbol{W}_z^K \boldsymbol{h}_i^{(L)} \qquad i \in [m] \quad (7)$$
$$\boldsymbol{v}_i^z = \boldsymbol{W}_z^V \boldsymbol{h}_i^{(L)} \qquad i \in [m] \quad (8)$$
$$\text{head}_j^{z,\tau} = \sum_{i=0}^{m} \frac{\exp(\boldsymbol{q}_j^{z\top} \boldsymbol{k}_i^z)}{\sum_{r=0}^{m} \exp(\boldsymbol{q}_j^{z\top} \boldsymbol{k}_r^z)} M_i^\tau \boldsymbol{v}_i^z \quad (9)$$
$$M_i^\tau = \begin{cases} 1 & \text{if Endorse}(x_i) \geq \tau \\ 0 & \text{otherwise} \end{cases} \quad (10)$$
$$\widehat{\boldsymbol{g}}_j^{(l)} = \sum_{z=1}^{n_{\text{head}}} \sum_{\tau=0}^{\tau_{\text{max}}} \text{head}_j^{z,\tau} \boldsymbol{W}_z^\tau \quad (11)$$

When τ_{max} is set to 0, the model reduces to its initial form using the original heads, i.e., $\text{head}_j^{z,0}$. Further, we initialize $\boldsymbol{W}_z^\tau = \lambda^\tau \boldsymbol{W}_z$, where $\boldsymbol{W}_z \in \mathbb{R}^{h_{\text{head}} \times h_{\text{model}}}$ are pretrained model parameters associated with the head z. $\lambda^\tau \in [0, 1]$ is a coefficient

[2] We omit the residual connection and layer normalization associated with each block for brevity.

and $\boldsymbol{W}_z = \sum_{\tau=0}^{\tau_{\max}} \boldsymbol{W}_z^{\tau}$. It indicates that, head z and all of its companion heads are linearly interpolated to produce decoder hidden state $\widehat{\boldsymbol{g}}_j^{(l)}$. If a source token is not endorsed, it will have a reduced impact on the decoder hidden state when companion heads are used. The method has the advantage that, when new documents are dynamically added or removed from the set, it only changes the level of endorsement received by the tokens (τ), thus avoiding costly retraining of the neural encoder-decoder model. We proceed by describing how fine-grained segment-level endorsement is obtained from modeling synopsis-document relationships.

4 Modelling Endorsement

In this section, we present the first stage in our approach – modelling endorsement – whose outputs are passed to the abstractive summarization model in the second stage. Modelling endorsement serves two main purposes. It allows us to identify salient segments of text using a frequency-driven endorsement model, and the level of endorsement guides the summarizer to consolidate salient content. Further, it helps us reduce the source input from multiple documents to a single pseudo-document, whereby any unendorsed sentences are removed from consideration.

A fragment of text is considered to be endorsed if its information is observed in the endorser. We obtain a set of synopses from the source documents; they are used as *endorsers* to identify salient segments from a candidate source document. A segment that is endorsed only once indicates its information is considered important by only one source document. Frequent endorsement by multiple endorsers suggests the information is reiterated in multiple source documents, and reiteration implies increased salience. Any information that is present among multiple sources is likely to be important. Thus, our method identifies salient segments considering both within- and cross-document saliency. Our approach is in spirit similar to those of building semantic concept graphs for multi-document summarization (Bing et al., 2015; Handler and O'Connor, 2018; Falke and Gurevych, 2019) in that frequently reiterated concepts are likely to be captured. However, we do not explicitly construct semantic concept graphs, but focus on modeling synopsis-document endorsement and incorporating it into summary generation, which distinguishes our work from these studies. We investigate two variants to compute segment-level endorsement.

4.1 Synopsis-Document Alignment

Let S be a synopsis serving as the endorser and D a source document, our goal is to estimate whether a token x_i of the document is endorsed by the synopsis. A soft alignment between the synopsis and document is attainable by utilizing text evaluation metrics such as BERTScore (Zhang et al., 2020b), where we build contextualized embeddings for tokens of the document and synopsis, compute the cosine similarity of embeddings, and find a most similar synopsis token for each token of the document to obtain the endorsement score $\mathcal{S}(x_i)$ (Eq. (12)). Albeit a greedy alignment, the method can produce competitive results comparing to methods such as the earth mover's distance (Zhao et al., 2019).

$$\mathcal{S}(x_i) = \max_{y_j \in S} \text{Sim}(x_i, y_j) \qquad (12)$$

Contiguous Segments It is important to endorse segments of text rather than isolated tokens, as segments such as "*\$8 million*" is either included in the abstract in its entirety, or not at all. We transform token-level endorsement scores into binary decisions using the maximum sum subarray algorithm (Eq. (13)), which finds a contiguous subsequence that yields the highest sum of scores. The solution is trivial when all scores are positive. We thus offset the scores by δ before applying the algorithm. Let $\{0.2, 0.3, -0.1, 0.4, -0.5\}$ be an example of a set of adjusted endorsement scores, the algorithm endorses the first four tokens as the sum of their scores is the highest, yielding $\{1, 1, 1, 1, 0\}$, where 1 indicates the token is endorsed and 0 otherwise. We apply the algorithm to each sentence of the document and discard the segment if it has less than 5 tokens. The method endorses salient segments of text, yet is lenient to include gap tokens.

$$\{s, e\} = \arg\max_{\{i,j\} \in m} \sum_{k=i}^{j} (\mathcal{S}(x_k) - \delta) \qquad (13)$$

Soft vs. Hard Alignment A hard alignment between the synopsis and document can be obtained from string matching. A document token receives a score of 1 if it finds a match in the synopsis. Similar to above, we offset the scores by δ to obtain segments of endorsed text. Hard alignment is sensitive to entities and quantities; yet it can miss out on paraphrases. We compare the effectiveness of these alignment methods in the results section.

4.2 Synopses as Endorsers

A synopsis contains the main points of the source document. We employ BART (Lewis et al., 2020), fine-tuned on the CNN/DailyMail dataset, as a single-document abstractive summarizer to produce a synopsis from each document of the input cluster. Synopses as endorsers are superior to whole documents or sentence extracts. Not only are synopses more concise, but they can exclude superfluous information such as quoted material from consideration. We score all sentences of the source documents according to the sum of their token endorsement scores. Highest endorsed sentences are selected and arranged in chronological order to form a pseudo-document, with a limit of $|D|$ tokens, which serves as the input to our summarization module.

When a token is deemed salient by τ endorsers, we set Endorse(x_i)=τ, analogous to a majority vote by the pool of endorsers. We introduce two endorsement patterns. *Reciprocal endorsement* is where a synopsis can endorse every document of the cluster, akin to how every token attends to every other token in Transformer self-attention. *Sequential endorsement* is where source documents are arranged in chronological order and only synopses of the later documents can endorse the earlier documents, akin to how each token can attend only to previous tokens in decoder-only self-attention. Sequential endorsement assumes the first few articles of an event or topic are more important than others. It avoids endorsing redundant content, which is particularly useful when the documents contain redundancy or noise that is typical in the output of clustering algorithms for content aggregation. Importantly, our endorsement framework offers a potential to customize endorsement patterns based on the trustworthiness of news sources, political leanings, content quality, and more.

5 Data

We experiment with a large-scale multi-document summarization dataset (Gholipour Ghalandari et al., 2020) whose data are gathered from the Wikipedia Current Events Portal (WCEP).[3] The dataset contains an archive of important news events happening around 2016–2019. Each event is associated with a succinct summary of 30-40 words written by the editor and an average of 1.2 source articles linked from the event page. Additional source articles are retrieved from the CommonCrawl-News dataset using an event classifier. These articles are published within a window of ±1 day of the event date. We sample from these additional articles to ensure each event has 10 source articles. All summaries and source articles are in English. The dataset contains 8,158, 1,020 and 1,022 clusters respectively in the train, validation and test splits.

Our method aims to produce an abstractive summary from a cluster of news articles discussing a given event or topic. To assess the generality of our method, we apply the model trained on WCEP to three different test sets, i.e., the test split of WCEP and two benchmark multi-document summarization datasets, DUC-04 and TAC-11. The DUC/TAC datasets contain 50 and 44 clusters, respectively. They each comprise a set of news events collected over a period of time, and thus are suitable for evaluation of the model's generality in out-of-domain scenarios. DUC and TAC datasets contain four reference summaries per cluster created by NIST evaluators. WCEP has a single reference summary per cluster written by editors. The target summary length is 100 words for DUC/TAC and 40 words for WCEP, following the convention of previously published results. Endorsement-related statistics for these datasets are presented in Table 1.

6 Experiments

Baseline Systems. We compare our endorsement method to strong multi-document summarization baselines. The extractive summarization systems include (i) *TextRank* (Mihalcea and Tarau, 2004) and *LexRank* (Erkan and Radev, 2004), which are graph-based approaches that perform strongly on this task. (ii) *Centroid* (Hong et al., 2014) computes the importance of a source sentence based on its cosine similarity with the document centroid. (iii) *Submodular* (Lin and Bilmes, 2011) treats multi-document summarization as a submodular maximization problem. (iv) *KL-Sum* (Haghighi and Vanderwende, 2009) is a greedy approach that adds sentences to the summary to minimize KL divergence. (v) *TSR* and *BertReg* (Gholipour Ghalandari et al., 2020) are regression-based sentence ranking methods using averaged word embeddings (TSR) and BERT sentence embeddings (BertReg).

The abstractive summarization systems include: (vi) *PointerGen* (See et al., 2017), which generates a summary by copying source words and predicting new words. The set of documents are concatenated to form the input. (vii) *PG-MMR* (Lebanoff et al., 2018) exploits the maximal marginal relevance method to select sentences and an encoder-decoder model to fuse them into an abstract. (viii)

[3] https://en.wikipedia.org/wiki/Portal:Current_events

Dataset	Synop Len	Num Segs	Seg Len	% Endorse Scores $\geq \tau$ $\tau=0$	$\tau=1$	$\tau=2$
WCEP	61	4.9	14.2	100.0	12.6	5.6
DUC-04	58	6.1	11.7	100.0	9.7	2.3
TAC-11	60	6.7	11.8	100.0	14.5	4.1

Table 1: (LEFT) The average length of synopses (SynopLen), average number of segments in a source document endorsed by a synopsis and average length of endorsed segments (SegLen). (RIGHT) Percentage of tokens with endorsement scores above the threshold value used in each set of companion heads. All tokens with scores below the threshold are masked out.

Hi-MAP (Fabbri et al., 2019) introduces an end-to-end hierarchical attention model to generate abstracts from multi-document inputs. We compare our system to these baselines and report results on WCEP, DUC-04, and TAC-11 datasets[4].

Sequential vs. Reciprocal Endorsement. We investigate two endorsement patterns: (a) *reciprocal endorsement* allows any two documents of the same cluster to endorse each other, and (b) *sequential endorsement* arranges source documents in chronological order and only later documents are allowed to endorse earlier ones. The endorsement mechanism provides the flexibility needed for many domains to exploit cross-document relationships to generate abstractive summaries. For our variants, the highest-scoring sentences are consolidated to form an input document which, along with the endorsement scores, are passed to our endorsement-aware abstractor to be condensed into a summary.

Endorsement-Aware Abstractor. We employ BART, a state-of-the-art encoder-decoder model as our base abstractor (Lewis et al., 2020). The model has 24 layers in the encoder and decoder, a hidden size of 1024, 16 heads, with a total of 406M parameters. It was fine-tuned on the train split of WCEP for an average of two epochs with a batch size of 4. We use the Adam optimizer (Kingma and Ba, 2015) and a learning rate of 3^{-5} with warm-up. At inference time, we use a beam size of K=4, with a minimum decoding length of 10 and a maximum of 50 tokens. Our implementation is based on fairseq[5] and it takes about two hours to train the model on a NVIDIA V100 32GB GPU card.

For the endorsement-aware abstractor, we add two sets of companion heads to the decoder, for a total of 48 attention heads. The τ values for each set of heads are 0/1/2. Table 1 shows the percentage of tokens that receive different levels of attention:

[4]We were unable to compare our method with hierarchical Transformers (Liu and Lapata, 2019) because the authors did not make their ranker available for ranking paragraphs.

[5]`https://github.com/pytorch/fairseq`

System	R-1	R-2	R-SU4
Extractive			
Random Lead	27.6	9.1	–
Random	18.1	3.0	–
TextRank	34.1	13.1	–
Centroid	34.1	13.3	–
Submodular	34.4	13.1	–
TSR	35.3	13.7	–
BertReg	35.0	13.5	–
Our Method (In-Domain)			
Endorser-Reciprocal	43.3	21.9	22.1
Endorser-Sequential	**45.4**	**23.2**	**23.5**

Table 2: A comparison of multi-document summarizers on WCEP's test set.[6] *Endorser-** are our proposed methods.

12% of the tokens receive level-1 attention ($\tau = 1$), 4% receive level-2 attention ($\tau = 2$). The λ^τ values are set to be 0.8, 0.1, and 0.1—this gives more influence to the original attention heads, so the model is not confused by the addition of the new heads that attend to endorsed segments. We use a maximum of 1024 tokens for the input document.

Synopsis-Document Endorsement. To enable soft alignment between a synopsis and a candidate document, we use BERTScore (Zhang et al., 2020b) with the following hash code: roberta-large_L17_no-idf_version=0.3.2(hug_trans=2.8.0)-rescaled. It suggests that the token representations are drawn from the 17th layer of RoBERTa-large. Our maximum sum subarray algorithm requires the scores to contain a mix of positive/negative values. Thus, we subtract all scores by δ. The δ values are 0.85 and 0.8 for the soft and hard alignment, respectively. These values are tuned on validation data, where a larger δ indicates fewer tokens will be endorsed.

We proceed by presenting summarization results on our datasets, including an ablation study to examine the contribution of each part of our method. We also present a case study showcasing the potential of our endorsement method.

6.1 Results

Our methods achieve state-of-the-art results when compared to previous work on WCEP's test set (Table 2). Sequential endorsement outperforms reciprocal endorsement due to the ability of sequential endorsement to remove redundancies introduced in later documents. In news domain, later articles generally review information from previous articles and introduce small developments in the story.

[6]We note that baseline summarizers use a maximum of 100 articles per cluster; these results are obtained from Gholipour Ghalandari et al. (2020). In contrast, our endorsement methods outperform the baselines with only 10 input articles per cluster.

System	R-1	R-2	R-SU4
Extractive			
TextRank	33.16	6.13	10.16
LexRank	34.44	7.11	11.19
Centroid	35.49	7.80	12.02
Neural Abstractive			
Pointer-Gen	31.43	6.03	10.01
PG-MMR	36.88	8.73	12.64
PG-BRNN	29.47	6.77	7.56
Hi-MAP	35.78	8.90	11.43
Our Method (Out-of-Domain)			
Endorser-Sequential	34.74	8.08	12.06
Endorser-Reciprocal	35.24	8.61	12.49
Endorser-Oracle	36.27	8.93	13.04

Table 3: A comparison of multi-document summarizers on the DUC-04 dataset. *Endorser-** are our methods.

System	R-1	R-2	R-SU4
Endorser-HardAlign	44.7	22.4	22.6
Endorser-SoftAlign	45.4	23.2	23.5
- companion heads	**45.8**	**23.5**	**23.8**
- endorse selection	43.6	23.0	22.9
- abstractive module	28.3	9.3	10.9

Table 4: Ablation study on WCEP dataset.

By ordering the documents chronologically and having later articles give endorsement to earlier articles, it encourages the summarizer to pick content from earlier articles and reduce redundancy introduced in later articles. The largest performance increase can be seen in R-2, with *Endorser-Sequential* achieving a 9.7 increase over a BERT-based method. It demonstrates the effectiveness of endorsement for detecting salient segments and stitching them together to form a summary.

We report experimental results on DUC-04 and TAC-11 datasets in Tables 3 and 5. Here, our methods can outperform or perform comparably to previous summarization methods. On the WCEP test set, it corresponds to an ***in-domain*** scenario. On DUC-04 and TAC-11 test sets, it is an ***out-of-domain*** scenario. Due to data scarcity, the model can only be trained on the train split of WCEP and then tested on DUC/TAC datasets. The fact that our system, when used out-of-the-box, can attain better or comparable results to the previous state-of-the-art has demonstrated its strong generalization capability. It suggests that obtaining segment-level endorsement on an outside domain then using it to inform summary generation is meaningful.

We observe that the reciprocal endorsement strategy outperforms sequential endorsement for DUC-04 and TAC-11 test sets. A closer look at the data suggests that this is due to the lower amount of redundancy present in DUC/TAC data. While WCEP documents are *automatically clustered* and contain

System	R-1	R-2	R-SU4
Extractive			
KLSumm	31.23	7.07	10.56
LexRank	33.10	7.50	11.13
Neural Abstractive			
Pointer-Gen	31.44	6.40	10.20
PG-MMR	37.17	10.92	14.04
Our Method (Out-of-Domain)			
Endorser-Sequential	36.11	9.52	13.07
Endorser-Reciprocal	37.43	10.71	13.94
Endorser-Oracle	38.01	11.11	14.61

Table 5: A comparison of multi-document summarizers on the TAC-11 test set. *Endorser-** are our methods.

much redundancy, source documents of DUC/TAC are *manually selected* by NIST assessors, each successive document in a topic cluster presents new developments about the topic. Thus, reciprocal endorsement may lead to better results for domains with less redundancy.

Intuitively, we want to steer the model attention towards endorsed segments if they are of high quality, and away from the segments otherwise. We conduct a set of oracle experiments that set λ^{τ} values to be proportional to the R-2 recall scores of endorsed segments (*Endorser-Oracle*). If the segments obtained for $\tau = 2$ yield a high R-2 recall score, they contain summary content and the model should attend to these endorsed segments by using a high λ^{τ} value. Results are reported in Tables 3 and 5. We find that such a strategy is effective for making the most of companion heads. Future work may associate attention (λ^{τ} values) with the quality of segments obtained at different levels of endorsement ($\tau = \{0, 1, 2\}$).

6.2 Ablation

We perform an ablation study on WCEP to study the effects of each component in our model (Table 4). First, we compare the endorsement methods, denoted by *HardAlign* and *SoftAlign*. SoftAlign achieves consistently better results, showing that it is important to allow flexibility when aligning synopses to documents for endorsement. Next, we remove several components from the best-performing model (SoftAlign) to understand the effect of each. Removing "companion heads" from the abstractive model results in a very small boost in performance. Removing "endorsement selection"—meaning the model uses no information gained from performing endorsement, and is simply a BART model trained to summarize documents—leads to a significant performance drop, especially in R-1. It suggests that using endorsement to identify summary-

(a) Single Synopsis Generated by BART
Opposition leader Sam Rainsy seeks clarification of security guarantees promised by Hun Sen. Hun Sen announced a government guarantee of all politicians' safety Wednesday. The opposition leader was forced to take refuge in a U.N. office in September to avoid arrest. The two parties have formed three working groups to hammer out details of the agreement.
(b) Endorsement from All Synopses
Sam Rainsy, who earlier called Hun Sen's statement "full of loopholes," asked Sihanouk for his help in obtaining a promise from Hun Sen that all members of the Sam Rainsy Party were free from prosecution for their political activities during and after last July's election. Sam Rainsy, a staunch critic of Hun Sen, was forced to take refuge in a U.N. office in September to avoid arrest after Hun Sen accused him of being behind a plot against his life. The alleged assassination attempt came during massive street demonstrations organized by the opposition after Hun Sen's Cambodian People's Party narrowly won the election. The opposition, alleging widespread fraud and intimidation, refused to accept the results of the polls. Fearing for their safety, Sam Rainsy and his then-ally Prince Norodom Ranariddh led an exodus of opposition lawmakers out of Cambodia after parliament was ceremonially opened in late September. Ranariddh, whose FUNCINPEC party finished a close second in the election, returned last week and struck a deal with Hun Sen to form a coalition government. The agreement will make Hun Sen prime minister and Ranariddh president of the National Assembly. The two parties have formed three working groups to hammer out details of the agreement, including the establishment of a Senate to be the upper house of parliament. Sok An, representing Hun Sen's party, said...
(c) Human-Chosen Segments
Sam Rainsy, who earlier called Hun Sen's statement "full of loopholes," asked Sihanouk for his help in obtaining a promise from Hun Sen that all members of the Sam Rainsy Party were free from prosecution for their political activities during and after last July's election. Sam Rainsy, a staunch critic of Hun Sen, was forced to take refuge in a U.N. office in September to avoid arrest after Hun Sen accused him of being behind a plot against his life. The alleged assassination attempt came during massive street demonstrations organized by the opposition after Hun Sen's Cambodian People's Party narrowly won the election. The opposition, alleging widespread fraud and intimidation, refused to accept the results of the polls. Fearing for their safety, Sam Rainsy and his then-ally Prince Norodom Ranariddh led an exodus of opposition lawmakers out of Cambodia after parliament was ceremonially opened in late September. Ranariddh, whose FUNCINPEC party finished a close second in the election, returned last week and struck a deal with Hun Sen to form a coalition government. The agreement will make Hun Sen prime minister and Ranariddh president of the National Assembly. The two parties have formed three working groups to hammer out details of the agreement, including the establishment of a Senate to be the upper house of parliament. Sok An, representing Hun Sen's party, said...

Table 6: An analysis of endorsed segments for a document. **(a)** A synopsis is generated from a candidate document. **(b)** The document also receives endorsement from the other 9 synopses in the cluster. **(c)** We compare to segments chosen by a human using the Pyramid method. Stronger highlighting indicates the segment received endorsement from many synopses.

worthy content from multiple documents is beneficial for an abstractive model.

Moreover, removing the "abstractive model"—meaning summaries are created extractively by selecting the highest-endorsed sentences—results in a large decrease in scores. It indicates that content-selection by endorsement cannot be done alone without an abstractor to create a more concise summary. This is especially the case for WCEP, where human reference summaries are relatively short.

We additionally report BERTScore (Zhang et al., 2020b) to evaluate summaries, in addition to the ROUGE metric (Lin, 2004). BERTScore uses cosine similarity between BERT contextual embeddings of words to detect word overlap between two texts, thus overcoming the problem of lexical variation in summarization. On DUC-04, the F_1 scores are 29.89 and 30.14, respectively for our sequential and reciprocal model. The score for human reference summary is 35.08. They show very similar trends to those in Table 3, suggesting that our method when tested in out-of-domain scenarios can achieve competitive results.

6.3 A Case Study

We present an in-depth analysis of our fine-grained endorsement in Table 6. Soft alignment is used to endorse a candidate document from synopses of the cluster. We compare the resulting endorsements to the text segments chosen by a human using the Pyramid method (Nenkova and Passonneau, 2004), where semantic content units (SCUs) are identified from the reference summaries and are matched to phrases in the candidate document. The segments selected by our endorsement method and those chosen by manual annotation show a great amount of overlap, exemplifying the strength of our method in locating salient content from multi-document inputs. In fact, our endorsement method draws strong parallels with the Pyramid method—in our case, sentences from the automatically-generated synopses act as SCUs, which are then matched to phrases in the candidate document using a soft or hard alignment.

We observe that the endorsement given by a single synopsis is already quite similar to the human segments. However, taking the average endorsement from all ten synopses results in a higher quality set of segments. This shows the inherent value that exists from repetition in multi-document clusters, and it shows the importance of leveraging all of the documents rather than just a single one for salience estimation. Importantly, we observe that named entities, e.g., *"Sam Rainsy," "King Norodom Sihanouk,"* are more readily endorsed than other phrases. These entities are frequently repeated verbatim in all of the documents, thereby increasing their likelihood of being endorsed.

We envision future neural document summarization systems to produce better synopses than BART. They can lead to more accurate estimates for endorsed segments, hence improving the overall performance of our multi-document summarizer. The endorsement mechanism at its core is simple and robust—looking for shared content between a document and a synopsis. It provides great flexibility allowing the summarizer to potentially operate on document clusters containing a varying number of documents, which is a desirable characteristic.

7 Conclusion

We presented a novel framework to model asynchronous endorsement between synopses and documents for multi-document abstractive summarization. We introduced an endorsement method to enrich the encoder-decoder model with fine-grained endorsement. Our method was evaluated on benchmark multi-document datasets and we discussed challenges and shed light on future research.

Acknowledgments

We are grateful to the anonymous reviewers for their helpful comments and suggestions. This research was supported in part by the National Science Foundation grant IIS-1909603.

References

Taylor Berg-Kirkpatrick, Dan Gillick, and Dan Klein. 2011. Jointly learning to extract and compress. In *Proceedings of the 49th Annual Meeting of the Association for Computational Linguistics: Human Language Technologies*, pages 481–490, Portland, Oregon, USA. Association for Computational Linguistics.

Lidong Bing, Piji Li, Yi Liao, Wai Lam, Weiwei Guo, and Rebecca Passonneau. 2015. Abstractive multi-document summarization via phrase selection and merging. In *Proceedings of the 53rd Annual Meeting of the Association for Computational Linguistics and the 7th International Joint Conference on Natural Language Processing (Volume 1: Long Papers)*, pages 1587–1597, Beijing, China. Association for Computational Linguistics.

Florian Boudin, Hugo Mougard, and Benoit Favre. 2015. Concept-based summarization using integer linear programming: From concept pruning to multiple optimal solutions. In *Proceedings of the 2015 Conference on Empirical Methods in Natural Language Processing*, pages 1914–1918, Lisbon, Portugal. Association for Computational Linguistics.

Arthur Bražinskas, Mirella Lapata, and Ivan Titov. 2020. Few-shot learning for opinion summarization. In *Proceedings of the 2020 Conference on Empirical Methods in Natural Language Processing (EMNLP)*, pages 4119–4135, Online. Association for Computational Linguistics.

Tom B. Brown, Benjamin Mann, Nick Ryder, Melanie Subbiah, Jared Kaplan, Prafulla Dhariwal, Arvind Neelakantan, Pranav Shyam, Girish Sastry, Amanda Askell, Sandhini Agarwal, Ariel Herbert-Voss, Gretchen Krueger, Tom Henighan, Rewon Child, Aditya Ramesh, Daniel M. Ziegler, Jeffrey Wu, Clemens Winter, Christopher Hesse, Mark Chen, Eric Sigler, Mateusz Litwin, Scott Gray, Benjamin Chess, Jack Clark, Christopher Berner, Sam McCandlish, Alec Radford, Ilya Sutskever, and Dario Amodei. 2020. Language models are few-shot learners.

Yen-Chun Chen and Mohit Bansal. 2018. Fast abstractive summarization with reinforce-selected sentence rewriting. In *Proceedings of the 56th Annual Meeting of the Association for Computational Linguistics (Volume 1: Long Papers)*, pages 675–686, Melbourne, Australia. Association for Computational Linguistics.

Sangwoo Cho, Logan Lebanoff, Hassan Foroosh, and Fei Liu. 2019a. Improving the similarity measure of determinantal point processes for extractive multi-document summarization. In *Proceedings of the 57th Annual Meeting of the Association for Computational Linguistics*, pages 1027–1038, Florence, Italy. Association for Computational Linguistics.

Sangwoo Cho, Chen Li, Dong Yu, Hassan Foroosh, and Fei Liu. 2019b. Multi-document summarization with determinantal point processes and contextualized representations. In *Proceedings of the 2nd Workshop on New Frontiers in Summarization*, pages 98–103, Hong Kong, China. Association for Computational Linguistics.

Kevin Clark, Urvashi Khandelwal, Omer Levy, and Christopher D. Manning. 2019. What does BERT look at? an analysis of BERT's attention. In *Proceedings of the 2019 ACL Workshop BlackboxNLP: Analyzing and Interpreting Neural Networks for NLP*, pages 276–286, Florence, Italy. Association for Computational Linguistics.

Maximin Coavoux, Hady Elsahar, and Matthias Gallé. 2019. Unsupervised aspect-based multi-document abstractive summarization. In *Proceedings of the 2nd Workshop on New Frontiers in Summarization*, pages 42–47, Hong Kong, China. Association for Computational Linguistics.

Gonçalo M. Correia, Vlad Niculae, and André F. T. Martins. 2019. Adaptively sparse transformers. In *Proceedings of the 2019 Conference on Empirical Methods in Natural Language Processing and the 9th International Joint Conference on Natural Language Processing (EMNLP-IJCNLP)*, pages 2174–2184, Hong Kong, China. Association for Computational Linguistics.

Hal Daume III and Daniel Marcu. 2004. Generic sentence fusion is an ill-defined summarization task. In *Text Summarization Branches Out*, pages 96–103, Barcelona, Spain. Association for Computational Linguistics.

Li Dong, Nan Yang, Wenhui Wang, Furu Wei, Xiaodong Liu, Yu Wang, Jianfeng Gao, Ming Zhou, and Hsiao-Wuen Hon. 2019. Unified language model pre-training for natural language understanding and generation. In H. Wallach, H. Larochelle, A. Beygelzimer, F. d'Alché-Buc, E. Fox, and R. Garnett, editors, *Advances in Neural Information Processing Systems 32*.

Günes Erkan and Dragomir R. Radev. 2004. LexRank: Graph-based lexical centrality as salience in text summarization. *Journal of Artificial Intelligence Research*.

Alexander Fabbri, Irene Li, Tianwei She, Suyi Li, and Dragomir Radev. 2019. Multi-news: A large-scale multi-document summarization dataset and abstractive hierarchical model. In *Proceedings of the 57th Annual Meeting of the Association for Computational Linguistics*, pages 1074–1084, Florence, Italy. Association for Computational Linguistics.

Tobias Falke and Iryna Gurevych. 2019. Fast concept mention grouping for concept map-based multi-document summarization. In *Proceedings of the 2019 Conference of the North American Chapter of the Association for Computational Linguistics: Human Language Technologies, Volume 1 (Long and Short Papers)*, pages 695–700, Minneapolis, Minnesota. Association for Computational Linguistics.

Demian Gholipour Ghalandari, Chris Hokamp, Nghia The Pham, John Glover, and Georgiana Ifrim. 2020. A large-scale multi-document summarization dataset from the Wikipedia current events portal. In *Proceedings of the 58th Annual Meeting of the Association for Computational Linguistics*, pages 1302–1308, Online. Association for Computational Linguistics.

Matt Grenander, Yue Dong, Jackie Chi Kit Cheung, and Annie Louis. 2019. Countering the effects of lead bias in news summarization via multi-stage training and auxiliary losses. In *Proceedings of the 2019 Conference on Empirical Methods in Natural Language Processing and the 9th International Joint Conference on Natural Language Processing (EMNLP-IJCNLP)*, pages 6019–6024, Hong Kong, China. Association for Computational Linguistics.

Aria Haghighi and Lucy Vanderwende. 2009. Exploring content models for multi-document summarization. In *Proceedings of Human Language Technologies: The 2009 Annual Conference of the North American Chapter of the Association for Computational Linguistics*, pages 362–370, Boulder, Colorado. Association for Computational Linguistics.

Jillian Hamilton. A day in the life of an intelligence analyst [online]. 2014.

Abram Handler and Brendan O'Connor. 2018. Relational summarization for corpus analysis. In *Proceedings of the 2018 Conference of the North American Chapter of the Association for Computational Linguistics: Human Language Technologies, Volume 1 (Long Papers)*, pages 1760–1769, New Orleans, Louisiana. Association for Computational Linguistics.

Douglas L. Hintzman. 1976. Repetition and memory. *Psychology of Learning and Motivation*, 10:47–91.

Kai Hong, John M Conroy, Benoit Favre, Alex Kulesza, Hui Lin, and Ani Nenkova. 2014. A repository of state of the art and competitive baseline summaries for generic news summarization. In *Proceedings of the Ninth International Conference on Language Resources and Evaluation (LREC)*.

Luyang Huang, Shuyang Cao, Nikolaus Parulian, Heng Ji, and Lu Wang. 2021. Efficient attentions for long document summarization. In *Proceedings of the 2021 Conference of the North American Chapter of the Association for Computational Linguistics: Human Language Technologies*, pages 1419–1436, Online. Association for Computational Linguistics.

Hanqi Jin and Xiaojun Wan. 2020. Abstractive multi-document summarization via joint learning with single-document summarization. In *Findings of the Association for Computational Linguistics: EMNLP 2020*, pages 2545–2554, Online. Association for Computational Linguistics.

Diederik P. Kingma and Jimmy Ba. 2015. Adam: A method for stochastic optimization. In *Proceedings of the International Conference on Learning Representations (ICLR)*.

Wojciech Kryscinski, Nitish Shirish Keskar, Bryan McCann, Caiming Xiong, and Richard Socher. 2019. Neural text summarization: A critical evaluation. In *Proceedings of the 2019 Conference on Empirical Methods in Natural Language Processing and the 9th International Joint Conference on Natural Language Processing (EMNLP-IJCNLP)*, pages 540–551, Hong Kong, China. Association for Computational Linguistics.

Alex Kulesza and Ben Taskar. 2012. *Determinantal Point Processes for Machine Learning*. Now Publishers Inc.

Philippe Laban, Andrew Hsi, John Canny, and Marti A. Hearst. 2020. The summary loop: Learning to write abstractive summaries without examples. In *Proceedings of the 58th Annual Meeting of the Association for Computational Linguistics*, pages 5135–5150, Online. Association for Computational Linguistics.

Logan Lebanoff, Kaiqiang Song, and Fei Liu. 2018. Adapting the neural encoder-decoder framework from single to multi-document summarization. In *Proceedings of the 2018 Conference on Empirical Methods in Natural Language Processing*, pages 4131–4141, Brussels, Belgium. Association for Computational Linguistics.

Mike Lewis, Yinhan Liu, Naman Goyal, Marjan Ghazvininejad, Abdelrahman Mohamed, Omer Levy, Veselin Stoyanov, and Luke Zettlemoyer. 2020. BART: Denoising sequence-to-sequence pre-training for natural language generation, translation, and comprehension. In *Proceedings of the 58th Annual Meeting of the Association for Computational Linguistics*, pages 7871–7880, Online. Association for Computational Linguistics.

Xintong Li, Aleksandre Maskharashvili, Symon Jory Stevens-Guille, and Michael White. 2020. Leveraging large pretrained models for WebNLG 2020. In *Proceedings of the 3rd International Workshop on Natural Language Generation from the Semantic Web (WebNLG+)*, pages 117–124, Dublin, Ireland (Virtual). Association for Computational Linguistics.

Chin-Yew Lin. 2004. ROUGE: A package for automatic evaluation of summaries. In *Text Summarization Branches Out*, pages 74–81, Barcelona, Spain. Association for Computational Linguistics.

Hui Lin and Jeff Bilmes. 2011. A class of submodular functions for document summarization. In *Proceedings of the 49th Annual Meeting of the Association for Computational Linguistics: Human Language Technologies*, pages 510–520, Portland, Oregon, USA. Association for Computational Linguistics.

Yang Liu and Mirella Lapata. 2019. Hierarchical transformers for multi-document summarization. In *Proceedings of the 57th Annual Meeting of the Association for Computational Linguistics*, pages 5070–5081, Florence, Italy. Association for Computational Linguistics.

Yuning Mao, Yanru Qu, Yiqing Xie, Xiang Ren, and Jiawei Han. 2020. Multi-document summarization with maximal marginal relevance-guided reinforcement learning. In *Proceedings of the 2020 Conference on Empirical Methods in Natural Language Processing (EMNLP)*, pages 1737–1751, Online. Association for Computational Linguistics.

Rada Mihalcea and Paul Tarau. 2004. TextRank: Bringing order into text. In *Proceedings of the 2004 Conference on Empirical Methods in Natural Language Processing*, pages 404–411, Barcelona, Spain. Association for Computational Linguistics.

Ron Miller. 2020. Former salesforce chief scientist announces new search engine to take on google. *https://techcrunch.com/2020/12/08/former-salesforce-chief-scientist-announces-new-search-engine-to-take-on-google/*.

Shashi Narayan, Shay B. Cohen, and Mirella Lapata. 2018. Don't give me the details, just the summary! topic-aware convolutional neural networks for extreme summarization. In *Proceedings of the 2018 Conference on Empirical Methods in Natural Language Processing*, pages 1797–1807, Brussels, Belgium. Association for Computational Linguistics.

Mir Tafseer Nayeem, Tanvir Ahmed Fuad, and Yllias Chali. 2018. Abstractive unsupervised multi-document summarization using paraphrastic sentence fusion. In *Proceedings of the 27th International Conference on Computational Linguistics*, pages 1191–1204, Santa Fe, New Mexico, USA. Association for Computational Linguistics.

Ani Nenkova and Rebecca Passonneau. 2004. Evaluating content selection in summarization: The pyramid method. In *Proceedings of the Human Language Technology Conference of the North American Chapter of the Association for Computational Linguistics: HLT-NAACL 2004*, pages 145–152, Boston, Massachusetts, USA. Association for Computational Linguistics.

Laura Perez-Beltrachini, Yang Liu, and Mirella Lapata. 2019. Generating summaries with topic templates and structured convolutional decoders. In *Proceedings of the 57th Annual Meeting of the Association for Computational Linguistics*, pages 5107–5116, Florence, Italy. Association for Computational Linguistics.

Alec Radford, Jeff Wu, Rewon Child, David Luan, Dario Amodei, and Ilya Sutskever. 2019. Language models are unsupervised multitask learners.

Colin Raffel, Noam Shazeer, Adam Roberts, Katherine Lee, Sharan Narang, Michael Matena, Yanqi Zhou, Wei Li, and Peter J. Liu. 2020. Exploring the limits of transfer learning with a unified text-to-text transformer. *Journal of Machine Learning Research*, 21(140):1–67.

Anna Rogers, Olga Kovaleva, and Anna Rumshisky. 2020. A primer in bertology: What we know about how bert works.

Abigail See, Peter J. Liu, and Christopher D. Manning. 2017. Get to the point: Summarization with pointer-generator networks. In *Proceedings of the 55th Annual Meeting of the Association for Computational Linguistics (Volume 1: Long Papers)*, pages 1073–1083, Vancouver, Canada. Association for Computational Linguistics.

Ashish Vaswani, Noam Shazeer, Niki Parmar, Jakob Uszkoreit, Llion Jones, Aidan N Gomez, Ł ukasz Kaiser, and Illia Polosukhin. 2017. Attention is all you need. In I. Guyon, U. V. Luxburg, S. Bengio, H. Wallach, R. Fergus, S. Vishwanathan, and R. Garnett, editors, *Advances in Neural Information Processing Systems 30*.

Linzi Xing, Wen Xiao, and Giuseppe Carenini. 2021. Demoting the lead bias in news summarization via alternating adversarial learning. In *Proceedings of the 59th Annual Meeting of the Association for Computational Linguistics and the 11th International Joint Conference on Natural Language Processing (Volume 2: Short Papers)*, pages 948–954, Online. Association for Computational Linguistics.

Jiacheng Xu and Greg Durrett. 2021. Dissecting generation modes for abstractive summarization models via ablation and attribution. In *Proceedings of the 59th Annual Meeting of the Association for Computational Linguistics and the 11th International Joint Conference on Natural Language Processing (Volume 1: Long Papers)*, pages 6925–6940, Online. Association for Computational Linguistics.

Jingqing Zhang, Yao Zhao, Mohammad Saleh, and Peter Liu. 2020a. PEGASUS: Pre-training with extracted gap-sentences for abstractive summarization. In *Proceedings of the 37th International Conference on Machine Learning*, volume 119 of *Proceedings of Machine Learning Research*, pages 11328–11339. PMLR.

Tianyi Zhang, Varsha Kishore, Felix Wu, Kilian Q. Weinberger, and Yoav Artzi. 2020b. Bertscore: Evaluating text generation with bert. In *International Conference on Learning Representations*.

Xingxing Zhang, Furu Wei, and Ming Zhou. 2019. HIBERT: Document level pre-training of hierarchical bidirectional transformers for document summarization. In *Proceedings of the 57th Annual Meeting of the Association for Computational Linguistics*, pages 5059–5069, Florence, Italy. Association for Computational Linguistics.

Wei Zhao, Maxime Peyrard, Fei Liu, Yang Gao, Christian M. Meyer, and Steffen Eger. 2019. MoverScore: Text generation evaluating with contextualized embeddings and earth mover distance. In *Proceedings of the 2019 Conference on Empirical Methods in Natural Language Processing and the 9th International Joint Conference on Natural Language Processing (EMNLP-IJCNLP)*, pages 563–578, Hong Kong, China. Association for Computational Linguistics.

SUBSUME: A Dataset for Subjective Summary Extraction from Wikipedia Documents

Nishant Yadav[1]*, Matteo Brucato[1]*, Anna Fariha[2]*,
Oscar Youngquist[1], Julian Killingback[1], Alexandra Meliou[1], and Peter J. Haas[1]
[1]College of Information and Computer Sciences, University of Massachusetts Amherst
[2]Microsoft
annafariha@microsoft.com
{nishantyadav, matteo}@cs.umass.edu
{oyoungquist, jkillingback, ameli, phaas}@cs.umass.edu

Abstract

Many applications require generation of summaries tailored to the user's information needs, i.e., their intent. Methods that express intent via explicit user queries fall short when query interpretation is *subjective*. Several datasets exist for summarization with objective intents where, for each document and intent (e.g., "weather"), a single summary suffices for all users. No datasets exist, however, for subjective intents (e.g., "interesting places") where different users will provide different summaries. We present SUBSUME, the first dataset for evaluation of SUBjective SUMmary Extraction systems. SUBSUME contains 2,200 $(document, intent, summary)$ triplets over 48 Wikipedia pages, with ten intents of varying subjectivity, provided by 103 individuals over Mechanical Turk. We demonstrate statistically that the intents in SUBSUME vary systematically in subjectivity. To indicate SUBSUME's usefulness, we explore a collection of baseline algorithms for subjective extractive summarization and show that (i) as expected, example-based approaches better capture subjective intents than query-based ones, and (ii) there is ample scope for improving upon the baseline algorithms, thereby motivating further research on this challenging problem.

1 Introduction

Traditional non-generic extractive summarization systems allow users to express their summarization intent via a query or a natural-language question (Daumé III and Marcu, 2006; Li and Li, 2014; Verberne et al., 2020). While this simplifies the interaction between the user and the system, queries are not the best means for expressing very *subjective* intents. Consider a user trying to summarize the Wikipedia pages of all US states to find places that would be *interesting* to them. A query such as "interesting places" may report places that are of general interest (e.g., interesting in terms of popularity), thus failing to model the subjectiveness of the concept "interesting". Revising the query (e.g., by adding "art museums" or "surfing spots") can be a complex, iterative process, which is frustrating for the user. Instead, we argue that in cases like this, where the user wants to summarize many documents with the same intent, it is often easier to communicate subjective intents by providing *examples* for a few states, from which the system can infer the intent more effectively.

The example-based paradigm *programming-by-example* (PBE) has been successful for a variety of tasks, such as: code synthesis (Drosos et al., 2020); data wrangling (Gulwani, 2016; FlashFill), integration (Inala and Singh, 2017), and extraction (Le and Gulwani, 2014); text processing and normalization (Yessenov et al., 2013; Kini and Gulwani, 2015); querying relational databases (Fariha and Meliou, 2019), and even creative tasks such as music composition (Frid et al., 2020).

An interface for extractive summarization by example was proposed in SUDOCU (Fariha et al., 2020), offering an easy and natural way for users to annotate documents to construct example summaries: the user browses through the document, optionally performing keyword search, and simply clicks on sentences that should be included in the summary. The system then infers the user's intent from the provided examples, and learns the mechanism to automatically summarize the rest of the unseen documents. Figure 1 contrasts the traditional query-based interface (left) with an example-based one (right). The interface makes it easy for users to construct a few example summaries from a corpus.

Summarization by example is powerful for several reasons: First, it allows the system to access more information than what a query might provide, and, thus, such a paradigm is expected to produce better results than the traditional query-based approaches. Second, it allows users to express very

* Equal contribution.

Proceedings of the Third Workshop on New Frontiers in Summarization, pages 131–141
November 10, 2021. ©2021 Association for Computational Linguistics

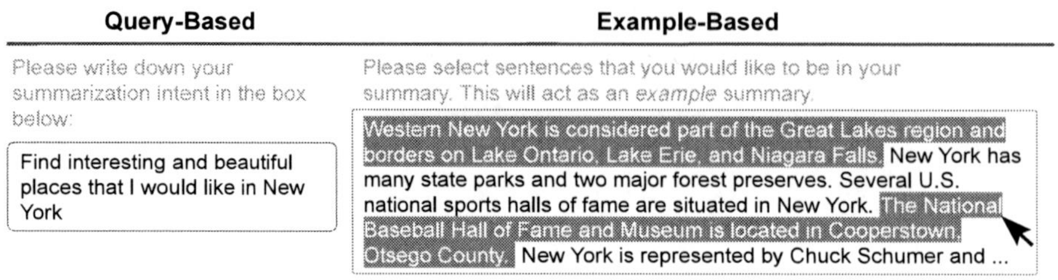

Figure 1: Query-based interface vs. Example-based interface for document summarization.

subjective intents precisely where typical methods fail (e.g., a natural-language query that asks a system to find "places that I like"). Third, it relieves the user from constructing the correct query even for an objective intent: people are often more comfortable in giving a few *examples* of what they want than providing specifications of what they want.

Because an example-based summarization system uses a different input (i.e., the example summaries) than a query-based system (i.e., a query), evaluating an example-based system needs a more complex *evaluation dataset* than those available for query-based systems. Given an intent, we need a few summaries—all produced by the same user—where a subset of the summaries are used as examples and the rest are used to evaluate the summaries that the system produces. Unfortunately, existing summarization datasets provide only one summary per user-intent pair. We present SUBSUME, the first dataset for evaluating SUBjective SUMmary Extraction systems. SUBSUME is suitable for evaluating example-based summarization systems, as it includes 8 different, manually curated summaries, produced by the same user, for every user-intent pair. Further, SUBSUME is the first dataset to include intents with an increasing level of subjectivity. SUBSUME can also be used to evaluate generic (Hong et al., 2014), query-based, question-based, and even abstractive (Nallapati et al., 2016) summarization systems, as the example-driven paradigm *subsumes* them all.

To demonstrate how SUBSUME can be used, we empirically compare several baselines on intents with increasing subjectivity. SUBSUME exposes evidence that (i) as expected, an example-based approach better captures subjective intent than a naive approach that simply inputs an ambiguous intent into a query-based summarizer and (ii) there is ample scope for improving upon the baseline algorithms, thereby motivating further research on this challenging problem.

2 Related Work

Several datasets exist for generic summarization tasks, including the CNN/Daily Mail dataset (Nallapati et al., 2016) which contains 300,000 news article-summary pairs, Webis-TLDR-17, which contains three million document-summary pairs extracted from Reddit forums (Völske et al., 2017), Multi-News dataset, which is a multi-document summarization dataset containing over 50,000 articles-summary pairs (Fabbri et al., 2019), and the Gigaword (Rush et al., 2015) and X-Sum (Narayan et al., 2018) datasets, both of which contain single-sentence summaries of news articles.

ScisummNet (Yasunaga et al., 2019) is a manually annotated corpus for scientific papers on computational linguistics to generate summaries that include the impacts of the articles on the research community. TalkSumm (Lev et al., 2019) is for scientific paper summarization based on conference talks. However, it does not consider personalization, where different people might want different summaries of the same paper. In general, none of the above datasets are suitable for the task of subjective summarization, which is our focus.

A task close to ours is *query* or *topic-based* extractive summarization. Suitable datasets include DUC 2004, DUC 2005, and DUC 2006, which contain query-based (multi-)document summaries (DUC). Webis-Snippet-20 consists of 10M web pages together with their query-based abstractive snippets (Chen et al., 2020). In these datasets, each document (or set of documents) has one or more summaries with respect to a single query. In contrast, SUBSUME contains multiple summaries of each document corresponding to *different intents*. Furthermore, each document-intent pair is summarized by multiple individuals.

Frermann and Klementiev (2019), in the context of "aspect-based" summarization, provide a dataset having multiple topic-focused summaries

Mostly Objective
(I1) How is the weather of the state?
(I2) How is the government structured in this state?
(I3) What is the state's policy regarding education?
(I4) What are the available modes of transport in this state?
Balanced Subjective/Objective
(I5) What drives the economy in this state?
(I6) What are the major historical events in this state?
Mostly Subjective
(I7) What about this state's arts and culture attracts you the most?
(I8) Which places seem interesting to you for visiting in this state?
(I9) What are some of the most interesting things about this state?
(I10) What are the main reasons why you would like living in this state?

Figure 2: Intents used in the SUBSUME dataset.

for each document. The dataset is synthetic, however, and does not involve human annotators. To the best of our knowledge, SUBSUME is the first human-generated dataset for subjective, extractive document summarization, where interpretation of intents varies across individuals.

3 Dataset Description

We now describe our data collection process and design choices, and analyze the statistical properties of the dataset. The dataset is available publicly at `https://github.com/afariha/SubSumE`.

Intents. We devised ten intents with different degrees of subjectiveness, ranging from mostly objective to mostly subjective, as shown in Figure 2. "Objective" intents refer to unambiguous facts (weather, modes of transport), "subjective" intents refer to opinions (interesting, attractive), and the "balanced" intents correspond to a ranking of unambiguous facts according to subjectively estimated importance (drivers, major events) that are expected to vary only moderately between individuals. A statistical analysis (see below) supports our heuristic classification of intents.

Documents. As the source documents, we used English Wikipedia pages of 48 U.S. states. We removed Nebraska and Wyoming as their pages did not have enough content with respect to the chosen intents. We parsed the pages to get text content from paragraph tags, and extracted sentences using Punkt sentence tokenizer from the NLTK library (Loper and Bird, 2002). Our corpus includes homogeneous documents to allow summarization of all documents with respect to all intents. In particular, we chose the Wikipedia pages for the states in the USA because they are homogeneous and contain information on a wide range of topics.

Interface. We collected extractive summaries of the documents using a custom interface on Amazon Mechanical Turk (MTurk). Our interface allowed the workers to search the document for keywords, click on a sentence to include it in the summary, and remove a sentence from the summary. A detailed discussion on the interface is in Appendix B.

Task. Each MTurk task (HIT) required a worker to extract sentences from eight documents to best summarize them according to a given intent, resulting in eight $(document, intent, summary)$ triplets. To generate unique HITs, we partitioned the set of 48 documents into six disjoint sets, each containing eight documents. We then paired each of the six sets with each of the ten intents, resulting in 60 unique HITs. We repeated the above procedure five times to obtain a total of 300 HITs. Out of these 300 HITs, 25 were rejected upon manual inspection (due to poor-quality summaries). The remaining 275 HITs contained eight summaries each, resulting in a total of 2,200 $(document, intent, summary)$ triplets. We allowed workers to participate in multiple HITs as long as they were not identical: either the document-set or the intent was different.

Post-task Survey. We conducted a post-task survey where we asked the workers to provide their interpretation of the intent and any strategies they followed for summarizing. Workers also provided optional demographic information: gender, age, US-residency, English proficiency, and occupation (details are in Appendix E).

Quality Control. We screened noisy workers using MTurk's qualification system. We also inspected the summaries using both automated heuristics and manual inspection to filter out sloppy workers and ensured that the summaries are of good quality and reflect the corresponding intent. A human annotator examined each summary and flagged low-quality ones. For example, for the intent "weather of the state", the annotator flagged a summary as low-quality as it did not contain any weather, but arbitrarily chosen sentences. Additionally, we asked each worker for their interpretation of the task to verify if their task understanding was correct, and excluded summaries in case it was not. Details of our screening test and quality-control mechanisms are in Appendices C and D.

Data Format. We provide SUBSUME in a format to support both query-based and example-driven approaches. Each completed HIT gives us the fol-

Statistic	I1	I2	I3	I4	I5	I6	I7	I8	I9	I10
# Summaries	240	216	232	240	232	224	192	200	208	216
Avg. # sent/summary	11.4	12.7	8.6	10.5	10.8	13.7	11.3	9.3	13.4	11.2
Avg. # words/summary	314	285	227	278	288	380	319	274	375	304
Subjectiveness score	22.7	34.2	35.0	35.6	47.4	58.7	55.7	56.9	74.3	73.2

Table 1: SUBSUME statistics across ten intents.

lowing information and contributes to eight data points in SUBSUME: (1) the intent text (one of I1–I10 in Figure 2), (2) one summary for each of the eight documents in the HIT, (3) interpretation of the intent by the worker, (4) description of summarization strategy followed by the worker, (5) the keywords typed in the search box by the worker while selecting sentences, (6) time-stamps indicating when each sentence was added to the summary, (7) percentage of the document the worker viewed, and (8) optional demographic information of the worker. We include an example datapoint from the dataset in Appendix F.

Dataset Analysis. Table 1 shows statistics of the dataset grouped by intents. We quantify the *subjectiveness* of an intent as follows: Let $\mathcal{S}_{i,d}$ be the set of summaries constructed by all different workers for an intent i and document d. We first compute pair-wise ROUGE-L F_1 scores (normalized between 0 and 100) for all pairs of summaries from $\mathcal{S}_{i,d}$. We define $\texttt{Sim}_{i,d}$ as the average of these scores, measuring the similarity of all pairs of summaries for document d and intent i. We define the *subjectiveness score* (inverse of similarity) for intent i using the following formula: $\texttt{Subj}_i = 100 - \frac{\sum_d \texttt{Sim}_{i,d}}{\sum_d 1}$. The higher the subjectiveness score for a given intent, the lower the similarity among summaries for that intent, thus indicating higher subjectiveness. Our classification of intents in Figure 2 aligns well with this subjectiveness score in Table 1. For instance, "How is the weather of the state?" (**I1**) scores the lowest (22.7) and "What are some of the most interesting things about this state?" (**I9**) scores the highest (74.3).

4 Experiments

In this section, we benchmark existing summarization techniques over SUBSUME in two settings: query-based (QB) and example-driven (EX). Recall that for every user-intent pair, SUBSUME consists of summaries of eight documents. In the EX setting, we use summaries of five documents, chosen at random from the eight summaries, as example summaries to *learn* the user's intent, and evaluate on the remaining three documents. In the QB setting, the baselines summarize the documents using only the query (intent text), and we evaluate on the same set of three documents as in the example-driven setting. We repeat this over ten different splits of the eight document-summary pairs, and average out results across all splits, and over all data points. We report F_1 scores of ROUGE-1, ROUGE-2, and ROUGE-L metrics (Lin, 2004) for all the baselines.

4.1 Baselines

We benchmark the following baselines. We refer the reader to Appendix A for detailed descriptions and implementation details.

KEYWORD first extracts keywords from the example summaries or query text, followed by filtering out sentences with less than t_k keywords. Lastly, a summary is constructed using the top-k sentences with respect to TF-IDF scores.

SBERT embeds example summaries (query text) and sentences in test documents using SBERT (Reimers and Gurevych, 2019). It scores each sentence based on its cosine similarity with the average embedding of the example summaries (query text) and computes a summary using top-k sentences in the document.

PEGASUS is a state-of-the-art abstractive summarization model (Zhang et al., 2020) based on transformers (Vaswani et al., 2017). We use the Pegasus model pre-trained on the CNN-DailyMail dataset.

BERTSUMEXT is a state-of-the-art extractive summarization model (Liu and Lapata, 2019). We use the publicly released model pre-trained on the CNN-DailyMail dataset.

SUDOCU (Fariha et al., 2020) is an example-driven summarization approach that models extractive summarization as an integer linear program.

Metric	Example-Driven (EX)					Query-Based (QB)			
	KEYWORD	SBERT	BERTSUMEXT	PEGASUS	SUDOCU	KEYWORD	SBERT	BERTSUMEXT	PEGASUS
ROUGE-1	30.6	53.2	31.6	23.9	33.2	30.4	41.1	21.7	18.2
ROUGE-2	7.3	36.9	21.1	14.5	15.7	9.6	20.8	10.3	7.7
ROUGE-L	16.7	41.0	23.3	18.2	20.6	16.7	27.1	15.8	13.5

Table 2: ROUGE F_1 scores for baseline techniques averaged across ten random example/test summary splits.

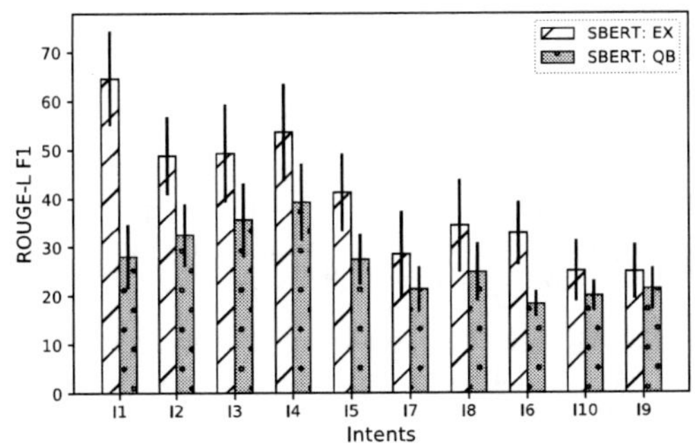

Figure 3: ROUGE-L F_1 for SBERT-EX and SBERT-QB for each intent. From left to right, intents are ordered in increasing order of their subjectiveness score shown in Table 1. The Pearson's correlation between the subjectiveness score and the F_1 score for SBERT-EX and SBERT-QB is -0.97 and -0.77 respectively.

4.2 Results

Table 2 shows the performance of each baseline averaged over all user-intent pairs. As expected, example-driven versions of each baseline consistently outperform their query-based counterparts with SBERT-EX being the top-performing method. This confirms that when users are willing to expend the effort to provide examples, example-driven approaches are superior to query-based ones.

Figure 3 shows the average SBERT ROUGE-L F1-score for each intent in example-driven (EX) and query-based (QB) settings where SBERT-EX consistently outperforms SBERT-QB. As we go from intents with low subjectiveness scores to intents with high subjectiveness scores, the performance of SBERT decreases in both settings. This shows that the task of subjective summarization becomes more challenging with an increase in subjectiveness of the intents.

5 Conclusions

In this paper, we present SUBSUME, the first dataset for evaluation of subjective summarization systems, and evaluate existing baselines on the dataset. The results presented in this paper show that even the best-performing approaches leave significant room for improvement for subjective document summarization, encouraging further research. In future, we plan to investigate transfer-learning and few-shot learning approaches that naturally fit the task of subjective summarization by example. Another direction of future work is to investigate how our data-collection method can be extended to other domains beyond the domain of Wikipedia documents of US states.

6 Ethical Considerations

We obtained Institutional Review Board (IRB) approval for collecting data as it involved human annotators. All workers on MTurk were provided terms and conditions (as approved by IRB) and they could attempt the task only after agreeing to the terms and conditions. A screening test involved answering a few questions in order to filter users based on their English proficiency as the task involved understanding the intent/query and summarizing documents, both of which were in English. In our initial pilots without the screening test, we found that we received noisy datapoints perhaps due to the corresponding worker's limited proficiency in English. More details on the screening task are present in Appendix C. The post-task survey where we requested demographics of the user was completely optional and in no manner affected acceptance or rejection of the task completed by the user. In our initial pilot, we found that most workers could finish the task within an hour. Thus, we decided to pay each worker $6 per HIT, which is typical for an hour-long task. While we collected summaries for Wikipedia pages of the USA states, we believe that our intents and queries could be used to summarize Wikipedia pages of other countries and provinces or states in other countries. We discuss reasons for choosing Wikipedia pages of the states in the USA in Section 3 in more detail.

Acknowledgements

We thank Kanchi Masalia for her help with pilot dataset collection efforts. We would also like to thank anonymous reviewers for their helpful comments and suggestions. This work was supported by the NSF under grants IIS-1453543, IIS-1943971, and CCF-1763423, and a Microsoft Research Dissertation Grant. Any opinions, findings and conclusions or recommendations expressed in this material are those of the authors and do not necessarily reflect those of the sponsor.

References

Wei-Fan Chen, Shahbaz Syed, Benno Stein, Matthias Hagen, and Martin Potthast. 2020. Abstractive snippet generation. In *Proceedings of The Web Conference 2020*, pages 1309–1319.

Hal Daumé III and Daniel Marcu. 2006. Bayesian query-focused summarization. In *Proceedings of the 21st International Conference on Computational Linguistics and 44th Annual Meeting of the Association for Computational Linguistics*, pages 305–312.

Ian Drosos, Titus Barik, Philip J. Guo, Robert DeLine, and Sumit Gulwani. 2020. Wrex: A unified programming-by-example interaction for synthesizing readable code for data scientists. In *CHI '20: CHI Conference on Human Factors in Computing Systems, Honolulu, HI, USA, April 25-30, 2020*, pages 1–12.

DUC. 2000-2007. DUC. `https://duc.nist.gov/data.html`.

Alexander Fabbri, Irene Li, Tianwei She, Suyi Li, and Dragomir Radev. 2019. Multi-news: A large-scale multi-document summarization dataset and abstractive hierarchical model. In *Proceedings of the 57th Annual Meeting of the Association for Computational Linguistics*, pages 1074–1084.

Anna Fariha, Matteo Brucato, Peter J. Haas, and Alexandra Meliou. 2020. Sudocu: Summarizing documents by example. *Proc. VLDB Endow.*, 13(12):2861–2864.

Anna Fariha and Alexandra Meliou. 2019. Example-driven query intent discovery: Abductive reasoning using semantic similarity. *Proc. VLDB Endow.*, 12(11):1262–1275.

FlashFill. FlashFill. `https://www.microsoft.com/en-us/research/project/flash-fill-excel-feature-office-2013/`.

Lea Frermann and Alexandre Klementiev. 2019. Inducing document structure for aspect-based summarization. In *Proceedings of the 57th Annual Meeting of the Association for Computational Linguistics*, pages 6263–6273.

Emma Frid, Celso Gomes, and Zeyu Jin. 2020. Music creation by example. In *CHI '20: CHI Conference on Human Factors in Computing Systems, Honolulu, HI, USA, April 25-30, 2020*, pages 1–13.

Sumit Gulwani. 2016. Programming by examples - and its applications in data wrangling. In *Dependable Software Systems Engineering*, pages 137–158.

Kai Hong, John M Conroy, Benoit Favre, Alex Kulesza, Hui Lin, and Ani Nenkova. 2014. A repository of state of the art and competitive baseline summaries for generic news summarization. In *LREC*, pages 1608–1616. Citeseer.

Jeevana Priya Inala and Rishabh Singh. 2017. Webrelate: integrating web data with spreadsheets using examples. *Proceedings of the ACM on Programming Languages*, 2(POPL):1–28.

Dileep Kini and Sumit Gulwani. 2015. Flashnormalize: Programming by examples for text normalization. In *Proceedings of the Twenty-Fourth International Joint Conference on Artificial Intelligence, IJCAI 2015, Buenos Aires, Argentina, July 25-31, 2015*, pages 776–783.

Vu Le and Sumit Gulwani. 2014. Flashextract: a framework for data extraction by examples. In *ACM SIGPLAN Conference on Programming Language Design and Implementation, PLDI '14, Edinburgh, United Kingdom - June 09 - 11, 2014*, pages 542–553.

Guy Lev, Michal Shmueli-Scheuer, Jonathan Herzig, Achiya Jerbi, and David Konopnicki. 2019. Talksumm: A dataset and scalable annotation method for scientific paper summarization based on conference talks. In *Proceedings of the 57th Conference of the Association for Computational Linguistics*, pages 2125–2131.

Yanran Li and Sujian Li. 2014. Query-focused multi-document summarization: Combining a topic model with graph-based semi-supervised learning. In *Proceedings of COLING 2014, the 25th International Conference on Computational Linguistics: Technical Papers*, pages 1197–1207.

Chin-Yew Lin. 2004. ROUGE: A package for automatic evaluation of summaries. In *Text Summarization Branches Out*, pages 74–81. Association for Computational Linguistics.

Yang Liu and Mirella Lapata. 2019. Text summarization with pretrained encoders. In *Proceedings of the 2019 Conference on Empirical Methods in Natural Language Processing and the 9th International Joint Conference on Natural Language Processing (EMNLP-IJCNLP)*, pages 3730–3740.

Edward Loper and Steven Bird. 2002. Nltk: The natural language toolkit. In *In Proceedings of the ACL Workshop on Effective Tools and Methodologies for Teaching Natural Language Processing and Computational Linguistics. Philadelphia: Association for Computational Linguistics*.

Ramesh Nallapati, Bowen Zhou, Cicero dos Santos, Caglar Gulcehree, and Bing Xiang. 2016. Abstractive text summarization using sequence-to-sequence RNNs and beyond. In *Proceedings of The 20th SIGNLL Conference on Computational Natural Language Learning*, pages 280–290.

Shashi Narayan, Shay B. Cohen, and Mirella Lapata. 2018. Don't give me the details, just the summary! topic-aware convolutional neural networks for extreme summarization. In *Proceedings of the 2018 Conference on Empirical Methods in Natural Language Processing*, pages 1797–1807.

Martin F Porter. 1980. An algorithm for suffix stripping. *Program.*

Nils Reimers and Iryna Gurevych. 2019. Sentence-BERT: Sentence embeddings using Siamese BERT-networks. In *Proceedings of the 2019 Conference on Empirical Methods in Natural Language Processing and the 9th International Joint Conference on Natural Language Processing (EMNLP-IJCNLP)*, pages 3982–3992.

Alexander M. Rush, Sumit Chopra, and Jason Weston. 2015. A neural attention model for abstractive sentence summarization. In *Proceedings of the 2015 Conference on Empirical Methods in Natural Language Processing*, pages 379–389.

Ashish Vaswani, Noam Shazeer, Niki Parmar, Jakob Uszkoreit, Llion Jones, Aidan N Gomez, Ł ukasz Kaiser, and Illia Polosukhin. 2017. Attention is all you need. In *Advances in Neural Information Processing Systems.*

Suzan Verberne, Emiel Krahmer, Sander Wubben, and Antal van den Bosch. 2020. Query-based summarization of discussion threads. *Natural Language Engineering*, 26(1):3–29.

Michael Völske, Martin Potthast, Shahbaz Syed, and Benno Stein. 2017. TL;DR: Mining Reddit to learn automatic summarization. In *Proceedings of the Workshop on New Frontiers in Summarization*, pages 59–63.

Thomas Wolf, Lysandre Debut, Victor Sanh, Julien Chaumond, Clement Delangue, Anthony Moi, Pierric Cistac, Tim Rault, Rémi Louf, Morgan Funtowicz, Joe Davison, Sam Shleifer, Patrick von Platen, Clara Ma, Yacine Jernite, Julien Plu, Canwen Xu, Teven Le Scao, Sylvain Gugger, Mariama Drame, Quentin Lhoest, and Alexander M. Rush. 2020. Transformers: State-of-the-art natural language processing. In *Proceedings of the 2020 Conference on Empirical Methods in Natural Language Processing: System Demonstrations*, pages 38–45.

Michihiro Yasunaga, Jungo Kasai, Rui Zhang, Alexander R Fabbri, Irene Li, Dan Friedman, and Dragomir R Radev. 2019. Scisummnet: A large annotated corpus and content-impact models for scientific paper summarization with citation networks. In *Proceedings of the AAAI Conference on Artificial Intelligence*, volume 33, pages 7386–7393.

Kuat Yessenov, Shubham Tulsiani, Aditya Krishna Menon, Robert C. Miller, Sumit Gulwani, Butler W. Lampson, and Adam Kalai. 2013. A colorful approach to text processing by example. In *The 26th Annual ACM Symposium on User Interface Software and Technology, UIST'13, St. Andrews, United Kingdom, October 8-11, 2013*, pages 495–504.

Jingqing Zhang, Yao Zhao, Mohammad Saleh, and Peter Liu. 2020. Pegasus: Pre-training with extracted gap-sentences for abstractive summarization. In *International Conference on Machine Learning*, pages 11328–11339. PMLR.

Appendix

A Implementation details

For all baselines, we pre-processed the text within the documents by removing all stop-words and converting all characters to lower case; except for SBERT, which does not require stop-words to be removed. For these experiments, we set the value of $k = 10$ for the Keyword-based and SBERT-embeddings-based methods. Additionally, for the Keyword-based approach, we set the keyword coverage threshold t_k to the average keyword-coverage score of all the sentences in the document. Lastly, the number of latent topics extracted by LDA for SUDOCU was limited to 10. For evaluation, we use F_1 scores of the ROUGE-1, ROUGE-2, and ROUGE-L metrics (Lin, 2004) for all the baselines using rouge-score package [1] with Porter stemming (Porter, 1980) turned on.

We implement the following unsupervised baselines, which summarize a new test document based on either the query text (QB) or the example summaries of other documents (EX).

KEYWORD first extracts keywords from the example summaries or query text using Gensim's keywords_extractor method. Each sentence in the test document is then given a *keyword-coverage* score based on the number of keywords it contains. Sentences that cover at least t_k (a threshold) extracted keywords are considered candidate sentences for the summary. Lastly, the TF-IDF scores of the candidate sentences are calculated and the summary is constructed using the top-k sentences; ranked based on their TF-IDF scores.

SBERT embeds example summaries or query text and sentences in test documents using

[1] `https://pypi.org/project/rouge-score/`

SBERT (Reimers and Gurevych, 2019). It scores each sentence based on its cosine similarity with the average embedding of the example summaries or the query text and computes a summary using top-k high-scoring sentences in the document.

PEGASUS is a state-of-the-art abstractive summarization language model (Zhang et al., 2020). PEGASUS follows the standard Transformer-based encoder-decoder construction popular for abstractive summarization. In this work, we use the HuggingFace API (Wolf et al., 2020) to access a Pegasus model fine-tuned on the CNN-DailyMail dataset released by the authors. In the extractive setting, we use the example summaries or the query text with the pre-trained PEGASUS model as follows. First, the example summaries (or query text) are used to first filter out unimportant sentences before the document is given the PEGASUS to be summarized. This is done by first finding the average SBERT embedding of the example summaries (or query-text). Then, each sentence from the target document is ranked based on their cosine similarity to the average example summary (or query-text) embedding. Finally, the top-$2k$ sentences are used as input for PEGASUS. In the query-driven setting, this same process is performed, but instead of using the example summaries to filter out unimportant sentences, the query itself is used.

BERTSUMEXT is a state-of-the-art extractive summarization model (Liu and Lapata, 2019). BERTSUMEXT introduces a novel, BERT-based document level encoder, which is used as input to several inter-sentence Transformer layers which learn document-level features to guide sentence extraction. In this work we rely on the publicly released models pre-trained on the CNN-DailyMail dataset from the authors of the original work. We use the same pre-filtering approach as used in PEGASUS baseline to use the example summaries or the query text in the summary generation process.

SUDOCU (Fariha et al., 2020) is an example-driven summarization approach that models extractive summarization as an integer linear program.

B HIT Description

Figure 4 shows the instruction page of the data-collection interface and Figure 5 shows the interface where the workers construct the summaries. Below we outline the process the workers go through to complete a HIT.

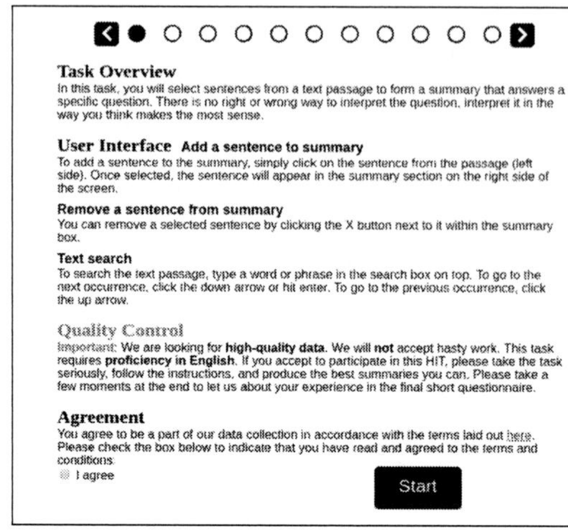

Figure 4: Snapshot of the page with instructions for users on the data collection interface.

1. If a worker has not previously taken our screening test they are prompted to do so, otherwise they can proceed to the task. More information about the screening protocol is in Appendix C,
2. The worker is brought to an instruction page that gives them an overview of the task, instructions on how to use the interface, and our expectations for summaries, and our methods for quality control. We also provide the terms for the study and the worker has to agree to the terms by checking a checkbox before proceeding with the task.
3. After the worker has agreed to the terms and continued to the next page, the summary construction interface is shown for the first document (Figure 5). The intent is shown at the top of the page with the document text directly below it. The worker can search for keywords in the text using the search bar above the document. They can add sentences to the summary by clicking on them and remove them by clicking the “X" button next to the sentence in the summary box (to the right of the document).
4. Once the worker has added the appropriate number of sentences to the summary, they can continue to the next page. We allowed a maximum of 20 sentences in a summary. This process is repeated for eight documents and the user constructs eight summaries in total.
5. On completion of the previous steps, a “summary overview” page (Figure 7) is loaded where the worker can read the summaries for all eight states. If necessary, from this page, they can

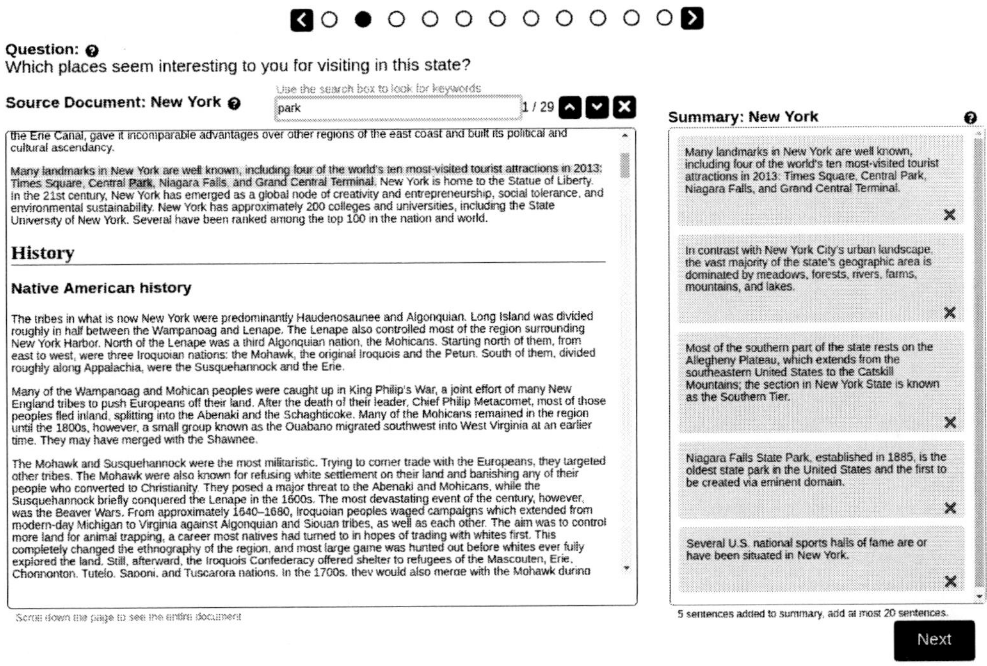

Figure 5: Interface to construct summary used to collect data from workers on Amazon Mechanical Turk.

go back to the individual document pages to modify their summaries.

6. After the worker is satisfied with all the summaries, they submit them, and the task ends.
7. On completion of the task of summary construction, the worker is requested to complete a post-task survey, where they are asked a few questions about their interpretation of intents and strategies they followed to construct the summaries, along with optional questions to collect their demographic information.

C Worker Screening Protocol

During initial pilots, we observed that a large proportion of summaries were of poor quality, generally containing sentences added at random from throughout the document with a majority of sentences having little or no relevance to the intent. To avoid poor-quality summaries, we included a screening test using MTurk's qualification system, and got significantly higher-quality summaries. The screening test consisted of five multiple-choice questions that tested written English skills and knowledge of relevant topics. The first three questions were inspired by the Cambridge English online evaluation test. We created the last two questions manually. Our priority was to make sure workers had a good grasp of written English, as well as to check if they had knowledge of potentially relevant topics such as fiscal policy. A screenshot of the screening test is shown in Figure 6.

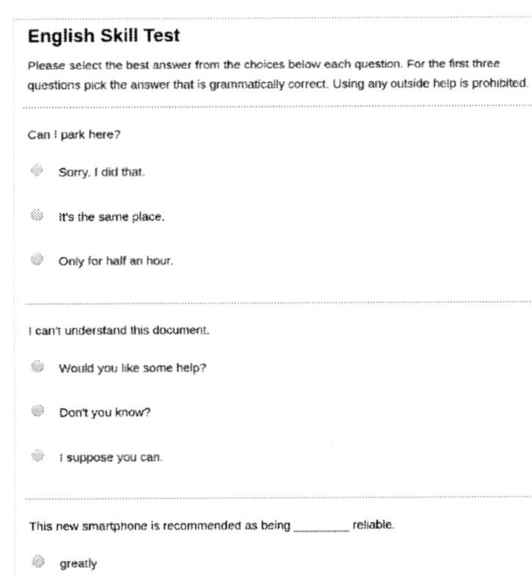

Figure 6: Screenshot of the (partial) screening test workers had to pass before participating in the HITs.

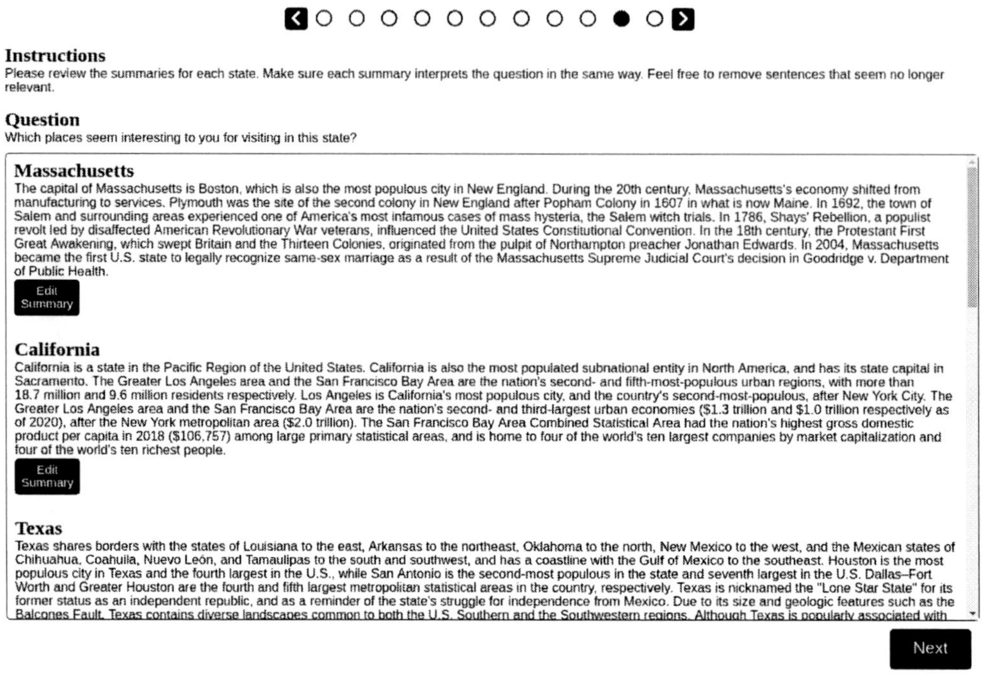

Figure 7: Screenshot of the summary overview page.

D Quality Control

To ensure high-quality summaries, we used a heuristic scoring method to filter out potential poor-quality summaries. Our scoring method is based on the similarity of the distributions of indices of the selected sentences that form the summaries across different documents within a HIT. The intuition is that if someone picks sentences randomly from the documents, then the standard deviation of the indices of the selected sentence are similar across states. This is because if someone picks sentences at random, then it would have a lower standard deviation than when they pick relevant sentences, which are often in various parts of different pages. This scoring works better for mostly objective intents as the sentences related to objective intents are usually more concentrated.

E Worker Demographics

Out of the 103 workers, 47 reported themselves as 'male', 38 as 'female', 16 did not report their gender, and 2 reported 'other'. 36 out of 103 workers are within the age group '30-45', 25 were '16-30', 22 were '45+' years old, and 20 did not report age group. 68 of the workers are US-resident, 13 live outside the U.S., and 22 did not report residency. Finally, 70 out of 103 workers reported very strong English proficiency, while others reported a varying level of English proficiency.

F Example Summaries

A data point, containing one of the 8 summaries within a HIT result, is shown in Figure 8. We omit other information such as time-stamps indicating when each sentence was selected etc for brevity. Figure 9 shows two significantly different summaries of the state of Delaware for the same intent, constructed by two different workers.

Intent: Which places seem interesting to you for visiting in this state?

Summary of Colorado: The northwestern corner of Colorado [...] contains part of the noted Dinosaur National Monument, which not only is a paleontological area, but is also a scenic area of rocky hills, canyons, arid desert, and streambeds [...] There are also a number of established film festivals in Colorado, including Aspen Shortsfest, Boulder International Film Festival, Castle Rock Film Festival [...] The state's diverse geography and majestic mountains attract millions of tourists every year [...] Colorado is home to 4 national parks, 8 national monuments, 2 national recreation areas, 2 national historic sites, 3 national historic trails [...].

Interpretation: Things I would like to do includes nature spots I would like for outdoor recreation, cities for touring and special events.

Strategy: I looked for the capitol, any other interesting cities, nature, sports, cultural experiences and special events native to the state.

Keywords: tourism, national park, Denver, Mesa

Figure 8: A datapoint from SUBSUME. For brevity, we leave out demographics, document-view-percentage, and timestamp information.

Intent: What are some of the most interesting things about this state?

Summary 1: Delaware: [...] The state was named after the Delaware River, which in turn derived its name from Thomas West, 3rd Baron De La Warr (1577–1618) who was the ruling governor of the Colony of Virginia at the time Europeans first explored the river [...] A 2012 Gallup poll found that Delaware's proportion of lesbian, gay, bisexual, and transgender adults stood at 3.4 percent of the population [...] Gambling provides significant revenue to the state. For instance, the casino at Delaware Park Racetrack provided more than $100 million to the state in 2010 [...] Delaware has several museums, wildlife refuges, parks, houses, lighthouses, and other historic places.

Summary 2: Delaware: On December 7, 1787, Delaware became the first state to ratify the Constitution of the United States, and has since been known as The First State. Since the turn of the 20th century, Delaware is also a de facto onshore corporate haven [...] The only real engagement on Delaware soil was the Battle of Cooch's Bridge, fought on September 3, 1777, at Cooch's Bridge in New Castle County, although there was a minor Loyalist rebellion in 1778. According to a 2013 study by Phoenix Marketing International, Delaware had the ninth-largest number of millionaires per capita in the United States, with a ratio of 6.2 percent [...] Unlike many states, Delaware's educational system is centralized in a state Superintendent of Education, with local school boards retaining control over taxation and some curriculum decisions [...] Several ships have been named USS Delaware in honor of this state.

Figure 9: Two example summaries for the Wikipedia page of the state of Delaware for the same intent that demonstrate the range of valid summaries for subjective intents.

TLDR9+: A Large Scale Resource for Extreme Summarization of Social Media Posts

Sajad Sotudeh [1*], **Hanieh Deilamsalehy**[2], **Franck Dernoncourt**[2], and **Nazli Goharian**[1]

[1]IRLab, Georgetown University
{sajad,nazli}@ir.cs.georgetown.edu
[2]Adobe Research
{deilamsa,franck.dernoncourt}@adobe.com

Abstract

Recent models in developing summarization systems consist of millions of parameters and the model performance is highly dependent on the abundance of training data. While most existing summarization corpora contain data in the order of thousands to one million, generation of large-scale summarization datasets in order of couple of millions is yet to be explored. Practically, more data is better at generalizing the training patterns to unseen data. In this paper, we introduce TLDR9+ —a large-scale summarization dataset— containing over 9 million training instances extracted from Reddit discussion forum (`https://github.com/sajastu/reddit_collector`). This dataset is specifically gathered to perform *extreme* summarization (i.e., generating one-sentence summary in high compression and abstraction) and is more than twice larger than the previously proposed dataset. We go one step further and with the help of human annotations, we distill a more fine-grained dataset by sampling **H**igh-**Q**uality instances from TLDR9+ and call it TLDRHQ dataset. We further pinpoint different state-of-the-art summarization models on our proposed datasets.

> We go to school together, we have three lessons a week together. She normally sits at the front and I sit at the back, but recently the person I sit next to has been struggling with mental health and hasn't been in, so I moved and sit next to her most lessons. We also do this engineering scheme together, so we have maybe half an hour a week with two other people working on that. For a while now we 've texted each other a few times a week with pictures of our cats, since we both love them. Outside of that, we don't really hang out at all. I see a lot of theatre, and about a week ago she said she wanted to come see something with me. So I agree, I love showing people theatre. When we find our seats, mine has a pole in the way so I can't see a section of the stage unless I lean away from her, but her view is perfect. About half an hour in, she leans on my shoulder. Halfway through act 2 she starts hugging my arm, while still leaning on my shoulder. She was kind of cuddling all day, we went to an arcade earlier as well. She doesn't seem like the cuddling type of friend, and I'm very worried she has a crush on me. I don't want to ruin a friendship, I don't like her back. Should I just ignore it until she asks me? What if she thinks that was a date?

> **TL;DR** I took my friend to see a show, she leant on my shoulder the whole time. I 'm not into her but I think she has a crush on me?

Figure 1: An example Reddit post with TLDR summary. As seen, the TLDR summary is extremely short, and highly abstractive.

1 Introduction

Text summarization is defined as generating a concise sequence of text as summary, given relatively a longer document as source. A high-quality summary conveys the most important points of its associated source. The task is generally performed in two ways: 1) extractive in which salient sentences are identified and concatenated to form the final summary (Nallapati et al., 2017; Dong et al., 2018; Sotudeh et al., 2021a; Narayan et al., 2020; Cho et al., 2020); and 2) abstractive that produces a paraphrasing of the main contents of the given text. (See et al., 2017; Gehrmann et al., 2018; MacAvaney et al., 2019; Zhang et al., 2019; Sotudeh et al., 2020a; Lewis et al., 2020; Lebanoff et al., 2020) and is considered more challenging as the model needs to deal with novel words generation beyond sentence extraction.

Over the past few years, different neural models including RNN (Hochreiter and Schmidhuber, 1997) and Transformer-based (Vaswani et al., 2017) networks have been proposed to facilitate the summarization task. While promising, the performance of such models is bound to the abundance of training data due to the massive model complexity (Ying, 2019). Lack of sufficient training data worsens the model's ability to generalize patterns in training data to unseen data (Althnian et al., 2021). In addition, overfitting will be likely inevitable as the model is forced to learn from a limited set of data; hence, hindering the generalization. This justifies the necessity of large-scale corpora for training large and complex models.

Prevalence of social media platforms has provided communities with an opportunity to ex-

*Work done during the internship at Adobe Research.

Proceedings of the Third Workshop on New Frontiers in Summarization, pages 142–151
November 10, 2021.

Dataset	Domain	# instances
Non-social media		
SciTLDR	Scientific	3.2K
XSUM	News	227K
Social media		
Reddit TIFU	Social Media	120K
Webis-TLDR-17	Social Media	4M
TLDRHQ (ours)	Social Media	**1.7M**
TLDR9+ (ours)	Social Media	**9.2M**

Table 1: Overview of *extreme* summarization datasets across different social and non-social domains with number of instances.

change different types of data while interacting with each other. *Reddit* [1] is one of such popular platforms where users post their content of interest in a variety of domains. TLDR, acronym for "Too Long; Didn't Read", is a common practice that aims at removing unnecessary information from the lengthy post, and presenting its gist information in a few words. Figure 1 shows a sample of Reddit post with its TLDR, which aims at abstracting post with extreme compression. Abundance of posts that contain such TLDRs during the recent years has given rise to generation of data collections that can be utilized for training deep neural networks; hence, addressing the challenge of large-scale datasets' scarcity. Despite the possibility of acquiring large-scale datasets from social media platforms, training deep neural networks on such datasets is yet challenging. This might be due to the specific writing style of social media content such as *informal* language and massive *noise* within such content (Sotudeh et al., 2020b).

Table 1 shows some of the existing summarization datasets in social and non-social media domains. These datasets are specifically proposed for *extreme summarization* task, where the aim is to produce one to two summary sentences in extreme compression and high abstraction. In this paper, we introduce our dataset, TLDR9+ with over 9 millions instances which is more than twice larger than the previous dataset (Völske et al., 2017). We further sample high-quality instances in virtue of human annotations from TLDR9+ to construct TLDRHQ yielding 1.7 million instances in the hope of providing firm grounds for future work. Owing to extremely short length of TLDR summaries (less that 40 words), our datasets are rather suitable for *extreme summarization* task, than for longer ones.

In this research, we aim at harvesting instances that include TLDRs written by the Reddit users spanning the period of 2005-2021. Our early attempt at gathering such instances yields over 9 millions instances with TLDRs as the initial set (i.e., TLDR9+). Since social media posts are inherently noisy, we consider applying a heuristic method to cut out low-quality instances from the initial set, which ultimately results in 1.7 million high-quality instance. For deciding such heuristic, we employ human annotators to help obtaining a more fine-grained dataset (i.e., TLDRHQ). Furthermore, we establish various state-of-the-art extractive and abstractive summarization models on our proposed datasets. Finally, we carry out an analysis over the results on both datasets to shed lights on future direction. We believe that our datasets can be utilized to pave the path for future research. Our miner code and data are made publicly available at `https://github.com/sajastu/reddit_collector`, along with the licensing details included.

2 Related work

Over the past few years, summarization community has witnessed variety of summarization datasets in different domains (See et al., 2017; Cohan et al., 2018; Kornilova and Eidelman, 2019; Grusky et al., 2018; Sotudeh et al., 2021b). While these collections have provided a fair basis to perform different neural text summarization models, the necessity of introducing large-scale collections, in magnitude of over 4 millions, has not been much explored.

Among the first attempts on this track, Rush et al. (2015) gathered the English Gigaword corpus (Graff et al., 2003) which contains around 4 millions article-headline pairs for the task of news headline generation. Researchers have noted that *lead bias* is the common phenomenon in most news datasets, where early parts of the article generally include the most important information (Kedzie et al., 2018; Zhu et al., 2019; Grenander et al., 2019). To alleviate the lead bias for training summarization models, there have been recent efforts to propose summarization datasets, where the lead bias phenomenon is mitigated and summaries are sampled from diverse source regions. Amongst those, Sharma et al. (2019) proposed BIGPATENT, consisting 1.3 million patent documents, collected from Google Patents Public Datasets, with human-

[1] `https://www.reddit.com/`

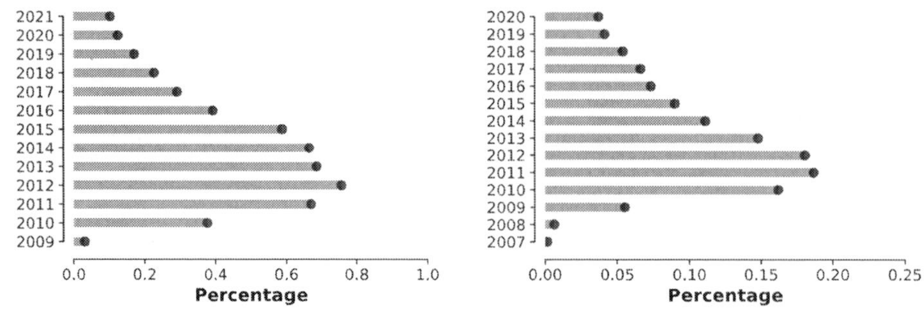

(a) submission-TLDR

(m) comment-TLDR

Figure 2: The proportion of TLDRs over entire posts (submissions and comments) submitted per year (Figures (c) and (d)). At the time of writing this paper, submissions dumps are partly uploaded for 2021 (until 2021-06), while there is no comments dumps uploaded for 2021.

written abstractive summaries. Kim et al. (2019) proposed *Reddit TIFU* in which the abstractive gold summaries are sampled from diverse regions of the source document, rather than lead regions.

Our proposed datasets are more suited for the task of *extreme summarization* (Narayan et al., 2018; Cachola et al., 2020), where the task is to create a short one-sentence summary. To this end, Narayan et al. (2018) proposed *XSUM* dataset which is a real-word dataset compiling online articles from the British Broadcasting Corportation (BBC). TLDR generation task is also a new form of extreme summarization. Kim et al. (2019) collected *Reddit-TIFU* dataset, consisting of 120K posts from the online discussions from Reddit. Recent efforts have mined around 4 millions Reddit posts along with their TLDR summaries (Völske et al., 2017) which resulted in Webis-TLDR-17 dataset. While our work is similar to theirs, our collected dataset is more than twice larger than the one previously proposed.

3 The *Reddit* Collection

3.1 Data Collection

Reddit is a social news aggregation, and discussion website platform that has been officially launched since June 2005. It supports some features specific to social platforms such as web content rating though up-voting, and discussion topics via subreddits. The user-created content can be of any domain such as News, Politics, Science, Sport and etc. Users can post or comment on a specific topic which falls into a specific subreddit. Within subreddits, users submit their post as *submission*, and others can react through commenting under the posted submission. Each submission and comment has a *text body/selftext* which reflects the users' information exchange regarding a specific topic. The existence of social platforms such as Reddit has provided the research community with an opportunity to experiment with resources that use *informal* language, rather than those in news, scientific or legal documents which use formal language.

TLDR—Too Long; Didn't Read— is a common practice in Reddit that often appears at the end of long reddit posts. It is denoted as an extremely short summary that urges users to read shorter version of a longer text when they do not have time to read the entire posts. Figure 2 shows the ratio of posts containing such TLDR summaries over the entire submitted posts (and comments) across different years. It is observable that although we see an ascending trend since 2005, the number of TLDRs remains fixed (see Section 3.4) while the number of posts increases drastically.

Pushshift [2] is a social media data repository platform that has been recently made available to NLP researchers (Baumgartner et al., 2020). It contains recent and historical dumps of Reddit posts that are updated in real-time. In order to create the TLDR dataset, we downloaded the whole data dumps (submissions and comments) which covers the period of 2005-2021, and extracted instances that contain TLDRs within the posted source text. This mining process resulted in TLDR9+ dataset, that contains over 9 millions instances. To acquire a more fine-grained dataset, with the help of human annotations, we obtained TLDRHQ dataset, con-

[2] `https://files.pushshift.io/`

sisting of 1.7 millions high-quality instances. The datasets' construction details are discussed in what follows.

3.2 Datasets Construction: TLDR9+ and TLDRHQ

TLDR9+. After downloading Reddit data dumps, we extract posts in which a mention of TLDR-style keywords is found. To find TLDR-style keywords within a given text, we declare a regular expression that matches words starting with "TL" and ending with "DR", with permission of having up to three characters in-between as also done by Völske et al. (2017). This stage yields the **TLDR9+** dataset as the *full* corpus. At the next filtering stage, we utilize a heuristic method along with human supervision to narrow down to a more fine-grained dataset that contain high-quality instances.

TLDRHQ. A few studies have noted that user-generated content in social media platforms is noisy (Liu and Inkpen, 2015) in terms of having spams, bad grammar, and spelling errors. To filter out such noisy instances from the TLDR9+ dataset, we use a heuristic method to drop low-quality instances while retaining high-quality ones. To be more specific, given a post-TLDR pair, we firstly identify the highest score source sentence in terms of ROUGE-2 and ROUGE-L mean scores (i.e., *oracle* sentence). The choice of oracle sentence lies in the fact that we postulate to extract a sentence from the longer post that has the highest similarity with the TLDR summary as the gold standard. We then decide to either drop or retain the instance if the score surpasses a pre-defined *threshold*. We experiment with different thresholds of 0.15, 0.17, 0.20, 0.22 and 0.25, and choose one considering the annotations done by human annotators. The details of human annotation process is discussed in what follows.

3.3 Human Annotation

As mentioned earlier, we first define 5 fixed thresholds including 0.15, 0.17, 0.20, 0.22, and 0.25 to create 5 data subsets from TLDR9+ dataset. Specifically, we take TLDR9+ as the initial seed, from which 5 subsets is created as follows. To gather instances for each of the pre-defined thresholds, we check if the oracle sentence's score in the given instance surpasses the experimented threshold. If it does so, we add it to the subset, otherwise it is dropped. We then randomly sample 20 cases from each of these subsets with their oracle sentence and TLDR summaries, yielding 100 cases for annotation in total. We have four human annotators from our NLP group either confirm (labeling with 1) or reject (labeling with 0) if the oracle sentence *validates* the TLDR summary. By definition, the sentence *validates* the TLDR summary if at least one fragment can be found within the sentence that semantically occurs in TLDR summary.

We further provide the instances' text (i.e., source) as the "Context" for the oracle sentence, and ask the annotators to confirm or reject if the context also validates the TLDR summary. Context is specifically important for the cases where the oracle sentence does not validate the TLDR summary. In fact, by providing context, we aspire to verify if an ideal summarizer is able to generate the TLDR using the context when the oracle sentence is not much informative. For tie cases [3], we employ a fifth annotator to make the final decision.

Threshold	score w/o context	score w/ context
0.15	0.65	0.90
0.17	0.90	**1.0**
0.20	0.85	0.95
0.22	**1.0**	**1.0**
0.25	0.75	0.90

Table 2: Average decision scores given by the annotators for each threshold.

Table 2 presents the average *decision score* assigned to the samples on each threshold. The decision score for a given sample is defined as the annotators' average confidence at giving label 1 to that specific sample. If the average confidence score surpasses 0.50, we assign 1 and if it is below 0.50, the sample is annotated with 0. Otherwise, the fifth annotator decides the label. As shown, threshold 0.22 attains the full score in the presence and absence of the context. Overall, this shows that most of the annotators believe the TLDR can be distilled considering both oracle sentence and the entire source.

Figure 3 shows pair-wise inter-rater S score agreement (Bennet et al., 1954) throughout the annotation process on threshold 0.22, denoting that annotators have mostly slight or fair agreement in labeling process. Specifically, when the context is not provided (i.e., merely with consideration of oracle sentence), raters (2, 4), (2, 3), and (1, 3) have

[3] Suppose a case where two annotators confirm (label 1), while the other two reject (label 0).

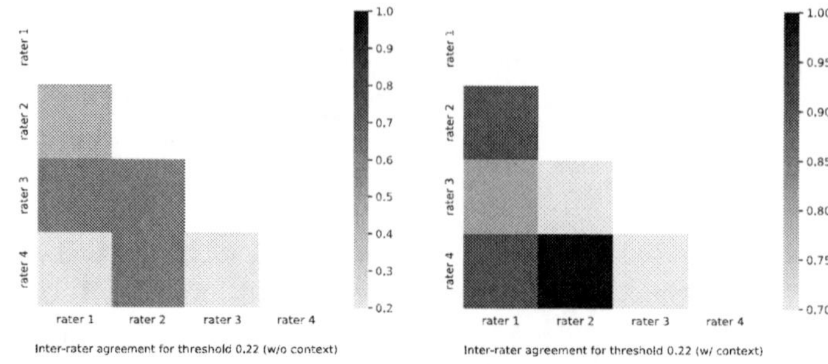

(a) Annotation with the oracle sentence (b) Annotation with context

Figure 3: S score inter-rater agreement for annotation without context (left), and annotation with context (right)

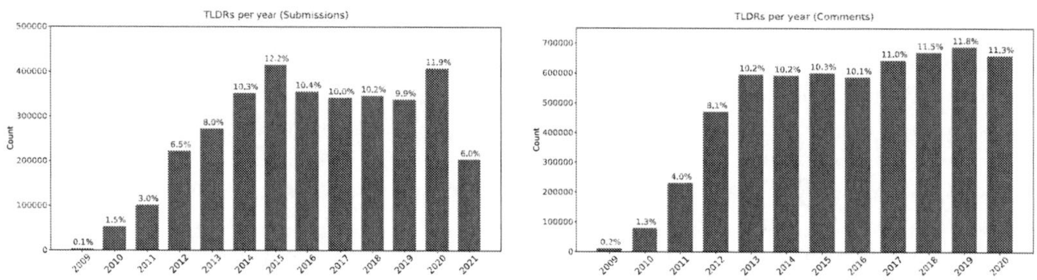

(a) submission-TLDR (b) comment-TLDR

Figure 4: The proportion of instances containing TLDR in TLDR9+ dataset. As seen, the number of TLDRs is increasing each year. At the time of conducting this research, the submission data dumps are partially uploaded for 2021 (until 2021-06), while there is no comments uploaded for 2021 in the Pushshift repository.

quite a high rate of agreement. On the other hand, most pairs of annotators including (1, 2), (1, 4), and (2, 4) achieve a high agreement rate when the context is given. As the given decision scores —either only with oracle sentence or provided context— sum up to 1.0, and considering moderately high agreement rate between the annotators, we decide to sample our TLDRHQ dataset from the instances in that was in threshold 0.22's subset. This leads us to choose human-decided threshold 0.22 as our ground to sample **H**igh-**Q**uality TLDRs for constructing TLDRHQ dataset.

3.4 Dataset Analysis

In this section, we give statistics, along with analyses on the proposed datasets.

Table 3 shows general statistics of datasets in terms of post and TLDR length. As shown, the compression rate [4] is 8.7 and 12.5 in TLDR9+, and TLDRHQ datasets, respectively. This shows that authors generally tend to write much shorter TLDRs that highly shortens the post's text, which is expected due to the nature of TLDR summaries.

Dataset	# instances	post (words/sent.)	TLDR (words/sent.)	Compression ratio
TLDR9+	9,227,437	310.3/14.0	35.6/2.3	8.7
TLDRHQ	1,671,099	332.0/15.7	27.0/1.8	12.5

Table 3: Average words length and number of sentences per instance along with the compression ratio in our proposed datasets.

Figure 4 demonstrates the number of TLDR pairs in TLDR9+ across different years. As observed, 83.65% of these TLDRs occur after 2013 which shows the popularity of this writing style among the Reddit users. We also see a similar trend for years after 2013, each of which constitutes a fixed amount (10%-12%) of the dataset. Table 4 demonstrates the detailed information including data size, sentence length and vocabulary statistics of TLDRHQ dataset.

As mentioned earlier, we define the oracle sentence to be the one within the longer post that has the highest overlap with TLDR summary in terms of ROUGE-2 and ROUGE-L mean scores. The oracle sentence's relative position in post's text along

[4]Compression rate = $\frac{\text{Avg post length}}{\text{Avg TLDR length}}$

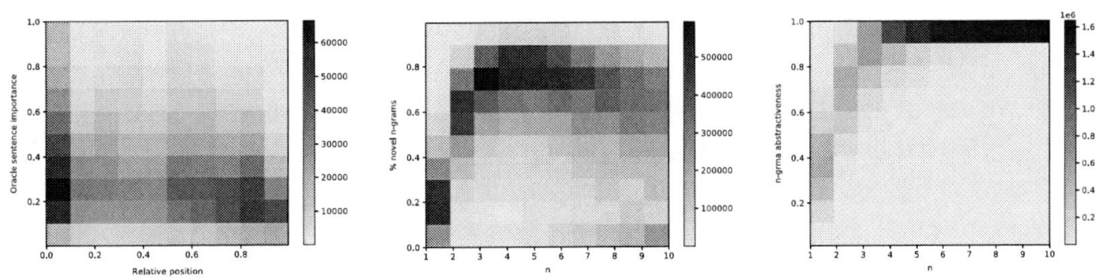

(a) (b) (c)

Figure 5: Heatmaps of TLDRHQ showing (a) the oracle sentence's importance to its relative position; (b) percentage of novel n-grams; and (c) n-gram abstractiveness. The heat extent shows the number of the instances within the specific bin.

Dataset Size	1,671,099 posts
Train Set Size	1,590,132 posts
Mean Sentence Length	21.1 tokens
Min Sentence Length	1 token
Max Sentence Length	4,370 tokens
Total Vocabulary Size	1,582,436
Occurring 10+ Times	226,754
Train Vocabulary Size	1,138,415
Validation Vocabulary Size	248,148
Test Vocabulary Size	249,079
Train/Test Vocabulary Overlap	72.5%

Table 4: Detailed statistics of TLDRHQ dataset

with its importance is shown in Figure 5 (a). We define the oracle importance score as follows:

$$\text{oracle importance} = \frac{\max \mathrm{RG}_{2+\mathrm{L}}(s_i)}{\sum\limits_{s_i \in D} \mathrm{RG}_{2+\mathrm{L}}}$$

where D is the set of all sentences within the post, and s_i denotes the ith sentence. $\mathrm{RG}_{2+\mathrm{L}}(.)$ is a function that takes in a post's sentence, and outputs the mean of its ROUGE-2 and ROUGE-L score with respect to TLDR summary. Intuitively, the oracle importance score can be framed as the attention score over the oracle sentences when the scoring function is ROUGE. Observing Figure 5, while more of the oracle sentences occur in early parts of the post's text (< 0.10) with importance score of less than 0.30, it appears that the oracle sentences are spread out across the post's text overall. This observation is substantial, justifying the usability of this dataset for extractive summarization task.

To analyze the abstraction level of TLDRHQ dataset, we plot the percentage of novel n-grams within the TLDR summary (See et al., 2017) in Figure 5 (b), as well as the TLDR's n-gram abstractiveness (Gehrmann et al., 2019) in Figure 5 (c) over the all instances in TLDRHQ dataset. As indicated, there are quite a large proportion of novel n-gram words appeared in the TLDR summary as the heat extent is mostly concentrated in the upper half of the y-axis. These plots show the promising capability and challenges of this dataset to be used for abstractive summarization models.

4 Experimental Setup

4.1 Baselines

We benchmark several extractive and abstractive summarization baselines over our two proposed datasets.

BERTSUMEXT. (Liu and Lapata, 2019) BertSumExt model is the extractive variant of BERTSUM which is the BERT Model fine-tuned on text summarization task. In this regard, BERT `[CLS]` tokens are appended to the start of each input sentence, and their associated representations are used to predict if the sentence should be included in the final summary or not.

BERTSUMABS. (Lewis et al., 2020) BERTSUMABS is the abstractive model of BERTSUM, where a Transformers-based decoder is added to the BERT Encoder.

BART. (Lewis et al., 2020) BART is a regressive autoencoder model that is pre-trained by first corrupting the text with an arbitrary noising function, and secondly, trying to reconstruct the original input text. BART is particularly effective when fine-tuned on text generation tasks such as summarization. As BART has both encoder and decoder pre-trained, it can be perceived as an extension to general BERT models in which only encoder is pre-trained.

Model	TLDR9+			TLDRHQ		
	RG-1(%)	RG-2(%)	RG-L(%)	RG-1(%)	RG-2(%)	RG-L(%)
BERTSUMEXT (Liu and Lapata, 2019)	20.94	4.98	14.48	28.40	11.35	21.38
BERTSUMABS (Liu and Lapata, 2019)	23.05	9.48	18.07	28.96	12.08	22.08
BART (Lewis et al., 2020)	23.59	9.69	18.62	32.44	14.85	27.39
ORACLE-EXT	30.26	9.74	20.60	45.29	25.47	36.86

Table 5: ROUGE (F1) results of the state-of-the-art summarization models on the test sets of the proposed TLDR summarization datasets (TLDR9+, and TLDRHQ).

4.2 Dataset

We randomly split our datasets to construct training, validation, and test sets. Specifically, for TLDR9+, we use 99-0.5-0.5 split which results in 9,139,935 (train), 43,753 (validation), and 43,749 (test) instances. To split TLDRHQ, we use 95-2.5-2.5 division yielding 1,590,132 (train), 40,481 (validation), and 40,486 (test) pairs.

4.3 Training and Hyper-parameters

To train the summarization models, we utilize HuggingFace's Transformers (Wolf et al., 2020) for BART, and the open implementation [5] of BERTSUMEXT, BERTSUMABS. We use warm-up steps of 32K, and 20K for BART and BERTSUM variants, respectively. The AdamW optimizer (Loshchilov and Hutter, 2019) is used with learning rate of $3e-5$, beta parameter of 0.98, and weight decay of 0.01 for BART model. For BERTSUM variants, we use the default Adam (Kingma and Ba, 2015) optimizer with learning rates of $2e-3$ for the encoder, and $1e-2$ for the decoder as suggested by the main paper (Liu and Lapata, 2019). For all models, we use cross-entropy loss function. We train the models on 8 Nvidia Tesla V100 GPUs for 5 epochs with early stopping of the training when the validation loss does not decrease for 3 consecutive validation steps. The validation step is done every 25K training steps. To visualize and keep track of the learning process, we use Weight and Biases (Biewald, 2020) toolkit.

5 Experimental Results

Table 5 presents the performance of the state-of-the-art summarization models on our proposed datasets in terms of ROUGE-1, ROUGE-2, and ROUGE-L scores. As indicated, BART outperforms all other models across all ROUGE variants in both datasets. This is expected as BART's both encoder and decoder have been pre-trained on a large amount of unlabelled data, unlike BERTSUM variants that only have pre-trained encoders.

Comparing abstractive models with BERTSUMEXT, we observe relatively large performance gap. This might be due to the fact that TLDRs in both TLDR9+ and TLDRHQ datasets are rather abstractive than extractive as also shown in Section 3.4. Yet with the existence of such a huge gap, the ORACLE-EXT (i.e., upper bound of an extractive summarizer) scores prove that more developed extractive summarizers can perform out-of-the-box and mitigate this gap. The performance gap on TLDR9+ brings various challenges to develop summarization models that better fit on the larger dataset that include noisy data (Kumar et al., 2020). This noise might be handled via methods such as noise-aware training models (Namysl et al., 2020), while enabling the models to benefit from the large-scale TLDR9+ dataset. We leave this part for future work. It has to be mentioned that automatic evaluation of summarization continues to be an issue and while this dataset does not solve that, instead can be used with any evaluation metric as they evolve.

6 Analysis

To gain insights into the qualities of summarization model, we analyze the outputs generated by the models. The diagrams demonstrating n-gram abstractiveness and percentage of novel n-grams, generated by BART and BERTSUMABS, are plotted in Figure 6. As observed, BART model appears to have a similar trend to the ground truth TLDRs. On the other hand, BERTSUMABS model has increasing n-gram abstractiveness, and novel n-gram percentage with increasing n. It is also interesting that after 6-gram, BERTSUMEXT model reaches a

[5] https://github.com/nlpyang/PreSumm

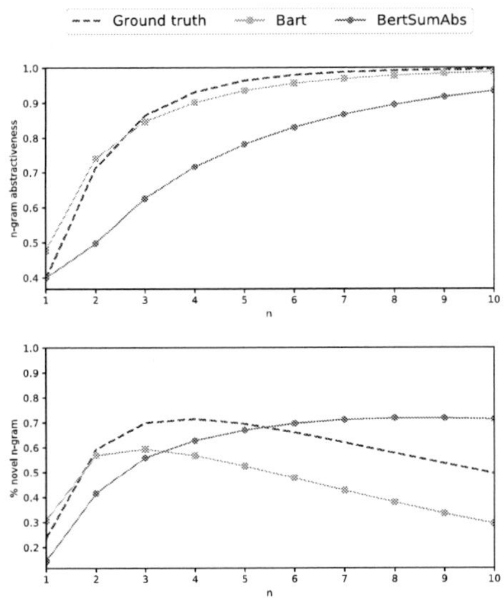

Figure 6: The n-gram abstractiveness and percentage of novel n-gram metrics across different n-grams on TLDRHQ's test set. As seen, BART generates more abstractive summaries than BERTSUMABS as it mitigates the gap between BERTSUMABS and ground truth summary.

Let me start this off by saying I'm not sure if this is the right spot to ask , and matching is not really my forte. I have my nostril pierced , as well as my septum. I got them done earlier this year and I've been playing around with different jewelry .all my jewelry has been white gold / silver... until now (edit - I originally had a silver hoop in my nostril and it was constantly irritated so I read up on it and found that silver is not good for piercings so I only use 14k white gold currently). I purchased a 14k solid rose gold nose hoop (20g). I'm curious if it would look weird wearing a rose gold nose hoop with a white gold seamless septum ring (16g) ?? or any white gold septum jewelry? I don't want to look like a fool who can't match her facial jewelry!

BertSumExt. I purchased a 14k solid rose gold nose hoop (20g).

BertSumAbs. would it look weird wearing a rose gold nose hoop with a white gold seamless septum ring (16g) ?? or any white gold septum jewelry ? I don't want to look like a fool who can't match her facial jewelry .

BART. would it look weird to wear a rose gold nosering with a white gold hoop septum ring?

Ground truth. would it look weird to wear a rose gold hoop in my nostril with a white gold hoop in my septum?

Figure 7: A sample from TLDRHQ test set along with the model generated summaries. Underlined text in source shows the important regions of the source for generating TLDR summary.

plateau when generating novel n-grams, but we a drop after 3-grams for BART and the ground truth TLDRs. This shows that from 1-gram to 3-gram, there are increasing number of novel words appeared in the ground-truth and BART, but after that, they both tend to copy n-grams rather than generating those.

To understand the limitation and qualities of current state-of-the-art summarization models, we conduct a qualitative analysis on several samples from TLDRHQ dataset, of which one is shown in Figure 7. Analyzing this sample, we observe that BART generated a better summary in terms of faithfulness to the ground truth TLDR. On the other hand, while BERTSUMABS could identify the important region of the source document, it has produced a longer TLDR with additional information that is present in the source, but not in the ground truth summary. BERTSUMEXT model could have identified a source sentence which is partly in connection with the ground truth TLDR, but it leaves out the most important sentence as the oracle to be extracted. Considering the upper performance of extractive summarizers (i.e., ORACLE-EXT score in Table 5), we believe that there is a large room for improvement on this dataset. Investigations of more advanced models remains for future work.

7 Conclusion

In this paper, we proposed two large-scale summarization datasets called TLDR9+, and TLDRHQ. The TLDR9+ dataset contains over 9 millions Reddit post-TLDR instances. To distill a more fine-grained dataset out of TLDR9+, we sample high-quality instances with the help of human annotations to construct TLDRHQ. Our analyses over TLDR9+ and TLDRHQ datasets show its usability for performing both extractive and abstractive summarization tasks. We further establish extractive and abstractive baseline results using state-of-the-art summarization models on both datasets. We hope our datasets can pave the path for future studies on this direction.

Acknowledgements

We warmly thank the anonymous reviewers as well as Tracy King for their helpful feedback and suggestions.

References

A. Althnian, D. AlSaeed, Heyam H. Al-Baity, Amani K. Samha, Alanoud Bin Dris, Najla Alzakari, A. A. Elwafa, and H. Kurdi. 2021. Impact of dataset size on classification performance: An empirical evaluation in the medical domain. *Applied Sciences*, 11:796.

Jason Baumgartner, Savvas Zannettou, Brian Keegan, Megan Squire, and J. Blackburn. 2020. The pushshift reddit dataset. In *ICWSM*.

E. M. Bennet, R. Alpert, and A. C. Goldstein. 1954. Communications Through Limited-Response Questioning*. *Public Opinion Quarterly*, 18(3):303–308.

Lukas Biewald. 2020. Experiment tracking with weights and biases. Software available from wandb.com.

Isabel Cachola, Kyle Lo, Arman Cohan, and Daniel S. Weld. 2020. Tldr: Extreme summarization of scientific documents. In *FINDINGS*.

Sangwoo Cho, Kaiqiang Song, Chen Li, Dong Yu, H. Foroosh, and Fei Liu. 2020. Better highlighting: Creating sub-sentence summary highlights. In *EMNLP*.

Arman Cohan, Franck Dernoncourt, Doo Soon Kim, Trung Bui, Seokhwan Kim, W. Chang, and Nazli Goharian. 2018. A discourse-aware attention model for abstractive summarization of long documents. In *NAACL-HLT*.

Yue Dong, Yikang Shen, E. Crawford, H. V. Hoof, and J. Cheung. 2018. Banditsum: Extractive summarization as a contextual bandit. In *EMNLP*.

Sebastian Gehrmann, Y. Deng, and Alexander M. Rush. 2018. Bottom-up abstractive summarization. *EMNLP*.

Sebastian Gehrmann, Zachary M. Ziegler, and Alexander M. Rush. 2019. Generating abstractive summaries with finetuned language models. In *INLG*.

David Graff, Junbo Kong, Ke Chen, and Kazuaki Maeda. 2003. English gigaword. *Linguistic Data Consortium, Philadelphia*, 4(1):34.

Matt Grenander, Yue Dong, J. C. K. Cheung, and Annie Louis. 2019. Countering the effects of lead bias in news summarization via multi-stage training and auxiliary losses. In *EMNLP*.

Max Grusky, M. Naaman, and Yoav Artzi. 2018. Newsroom: A dataset of 1.3 million summaries with diverse extractive strategies. In *NAACL*.

S. Hochreiter and J. Schmidhuber. 1997. Long short-term memory. *Neural Computation*, 9:1735–1780.

Chris Kedzie, K. McKeown, and Hal Daumé. 2018. Content selection in deep learning models of summarization. In *EMNLP*.

Byeongchang Kim, Hyunwoo Kim, and Gunhee Kim. 2019. Abstractive summarization of reddit posts with multi-level memory networks. In *NAACL*.

Diederik P. Kingma and Jimmy Ba. 2015. Adam: A method for stochastic optimization. *CoRR*, abs/1412.6980.

A. Kornilova and Vladimir Eidelman. 2019. Billsum: A corpus for automatic summarization of us legislation. *ArXiv*, abs/1910.00523.

Ankit Kumar, Piyush Makhija, and Anuj Gupta. 2020. Noisy text data: Achilles' heel of bert. In *WNUT*.

Logan Lebanoff, Franck Dernoncourt, Doo Soon Kim, Lidan Wang, W. Chang, and Fei Liu. 2020. Learning to fuse sentences with transformers for summarization. In *EMNLP*.

M. Lewis, Yinhan Liu, Naman Goyal, Marjan Ghazvininejad, A. Mohamed, Omer Levy, V. Stoyanov, and Luke Zettlemoyer. 2020. Bart: Denoising sequence-to-sequence pre-training for natural language generation, translation, and comprehension. *ACL*.

Ji Liu and D. Inkpen. 2015. Estimating user location in social media with stacked denoising auto-encoders. In *VS@HLT-NAACL*.

Yang Liu and Mirella Lapata. 2019. Text summarization with pretrained encoders. In *EMNLP/IJCNLP*.

I. Loshchilov and F. Hutter. 2019. Decoupled weight decay regularization. In *ICLR*.

Sean MacAvaney, Sajad Sotudeh, Arman Cohan, Nazli Goharian, Ish A. Talati, and Ross W. Filice. 2019. Ontology-aware clinical abstractive summarization. *Proceedings of the 42nd International ACM SIGIR Conference on Research and Development in Information Retrieval*.

Ramesh Nallapati, Feifei Zhai, and Bowen Zhou. 2017. Summarunner: A recurrent neural network based sequence model for extractive summarization of documents. In *AAAI*.

Marcin Namysl, Sven Behnke, and J. Kohler. 2020. Nat: Noise-aware training for robust neural sequence labeling. In *ACL*.

Shashi Narayan, Shay B. Cohen, and Mirella Lapata. 2018. Don't give me the details, just the summary! topic-aware convolutional neural networks for extreme summarization. In *EMNLP*.

Shashi Narayan, Joshua Maynez, Jakub Adámek, Daniele Pighin, Blavz Bratanivc, and Ryan T. McDonald. 2020. Stepwise extractive summarization and planning with structured transformers. In *EMNLP*.

Alexander M. Rush, Harvard Seas, S. Chopra, and J. Weston. 2015. A neural attention model for sentence summarization.

A. See, Peter J. Liu, and Christopher D. Manning. 2017. Get to the point: Summarization with pointer-generator networks. In *ACL*.

Eva Sharma, Chen Li, and L. Wang. 2019. Bigpatent: A large-scale dataset for abstractive and coherent summarization. In *ACL*.

Sajad Sotudeh, Arman Cohan, and Nazli Goharian. 2021a. On generating extended summaries of long documents. *The AAAI-21 Workshop on Scientific Document Understanding (SDU)*.

Sajad Sotudeh, Arman Cohan, and Nazli Goharian. 2021b. On generating extended summaries of long documents. *SDU@AAAI*, abs/2012.14136.

Sajad Sotudeh, Nazli Goharian, and R. Filice. 2020a. Attend to medical ontologies: Content selection for clinical abstractive summarization. In *ACL*.

Sajad Sotudeh, Tong Xiang, Hao-Ren Yao, Sean MacAvaney, Eugene Yang, Nazli Goharian, and Ophir Frieder. 2020b. Guir at semeval-2020 task 12: Domain-tuned contextualized models for offensive language detection. *SemEval2020*.

Ashish Vaswani, Noam M. Shazeer, Niki Parmar, Jakob Uszkoreit, Llion Jones, Aidan N. Gomez, Lukasz Kaiser, and Illia Polosukhin. 2017. Attention is all you need. *ArXiv*, abs/1706.03762.

Michael Völske, Martin Potthast, Shahbaz Syed, and Benno Stein. 2017. Tl;dr: Mining reddit to learn automatic summarization. In *NFiS@EMNLP*.

Thomas Wolf, Lysandre Debut, Victor Sanh, Julien Chaumond, Clement Delangue, Anthony Moi, Pierric Cistac, Tim Rault, Rémi Louf, Morgan Funtowicz, Joe Davison, Sam Shleifer, Patrick von Platen, Clara Ma, Yacine Jernite, Julien Plu, Canwen Xu, Teven Le Scao, Sylvain Gugger, Mariama Drame, Quentin Lhoest, and Alexander M. Rush. 2020. Transformers: State-of-the-art natural language processing. In *Proceedings of the 2020 Conference on Empirical Methods in Natural Language Processing: System Demonstrations*, pages 38–45, Online. Association for Computational Linguistics.

Xue Ying. 2019. An overview of overfitting and its solutions. *Journal of Physics: Conference Series*, 1168:022022.

Jingqing Zhang, Yao Zhao, Mohammad Saleh, and Peter J. Liu. 2019. Pegasus: Pre-training with extracted gap-sentences for abstractive summarization. In *ICML*.

Chenguang Zhu, Ziyi Yang, R. Gmyr, Michael Zeng, and Xuedong Huang. 2019. Make lead bias in your favor: Zero-shot abstractive news summarization. *arXiv: Computation and Language*.

A New Dataset and Efficient Baselines for Document-level Text Simplification in German

Annette Rios Nicolas Spring Tannon Kew Marek Kostrzewa
Andreas Säuberli Mathias Müller Sarah Ebling
Department of Computational Linguistics, University of Zurich
{rios,spring,kew,mmueller,ebling}@cl.uzh.ch
{marek.kostrzewa,andreas.saeuberli}.uzh.ch

Abstract

The task of document-level text simplification is very similar to summarization with the additional difficulty of reducing complexity. We introduce a newly collected data set of German texts, collected from the Swiss news magazine *20 Minuten* ('20 Minutes') that consists of full articles paired with simplified summaries. Furthermore, we present experiments on ATS with the pretrained multilingual mBART and a modified version thereof that is more memory-friendly, using both our new data set and existing simplification corpora. Our modifications of mBART let us train at a lower memory cost without much loss in performance, in fact, the smaller mBART even improves over the standard model in a setting with multiple simplification levels.

1 Introduction

Text simplification is the process of reducing the complexity of a text to make it more easily understandable and improve its accessibility for a wider audience. Depending on the use case, target groups of simplified texts may include low-proficiency readers such as persons with intellectual disabilities, prelingually deaf persons, or non-native readers. Automatic text simplification (ATS) employs natural language processing methods for generating a simplified version of a given text in standard language.

In general, simplification often results in a reduction of content similar to summarization, but with additional syntactic and lexical changes. Considering only a compression ratio in terms of sentence length or word count can be somewhat misleading since the simplified documents often elaborate on concepts and split complex sentences into smaller units.

Research on text simplification for German is still sparse but has gained momentum in recent years due to a number of legal and political developments in German-speaking countries, such as the introduction of a set of regulations for accessible information technology (*Barrierefreie-Informationstechnik-Verordnung*, BITV 2.0) in Germany, the approval of rules for accessible information and communication (*Barrierefreie Information und Kommunikation*, BIK) in Austria, and the ratification of the United Nations Convention on the Rights of Persons with Disabilities (UN CRPD) in Germany, Austria, and Switzerland.

In this work, we report on two contributions regarding ATS for German:

1. We introduce a new data set of simplified news articles from the Swiss daily magazine *20 Minuten* ('20 Minutes'). The source side of the corpus contains the full, standard German news, whereas the target side consists of a shortened and simplified version that is meant to give readers an easy and fast-to-read overview.[1]

2. We apply an adapted version of the mBART model (Liu et al., 2020) to the task of document-level ATS. The model needs to learn to reduce the content of the original document to the most salient parts, just as in summarization tasks. However, on top of that, the model also needs to account for linguistic changes that correspond to the targeted simplification level.[2]

In addition to the new *20 Minuten* data set, we evaluate our adapted mBART model with pre-existing corpora for German ATS (see Section 3).

2 Related Work

Traditionally, ATS has relied on rule-based approaches in separate steps, e.g. lexical substitutions

[1] The data set is available from: https://github.com/ZurichNLP/20Minuten

[2] Code is available from: https://github.com/a-rios/longmbart

Proceedings of the Third Workshop on New Frontiers in Summarization, pages 152–161
November 10, 2021.

followed by syntactic modifications. In the case of lexical simplification (i.e. the identification of difficult words and the substitution with simpler synonyms), most modern approaches include features based on semantics, context, and language models (Glavaš and Štajner, 2015; Qiang et al., 2020). Syntactic simplification (the identification and simplification of difficult syntactic structures) is mostly done using manually written rules applied to a syntax tree (Siddharthan, 2006; Scarton et al., 2017). Such systems are still among the most successful for languages with little simplification data such as Basque (Aranzabe et al., 2012), Bulgarian (Lozanova et al., 2013), or French (Brouwers et al., 2014).

For languages with enough parallel data (i.e. mainly English), data-driven approaches that rely on machine learning have emerged, where ATS is most often framed as a monolingual machine translation task. Statistical machine translation has been applied to learn complex-simple phrase correspondences from parallel sentence-aligned corpora (Wubben et al., 2012), sometimes in conjunction with rule-based simplification (Narayan and Gardent, 2014) or via integration of syntactic information through syntax-based SMT (Xu et al., 2016a).

More recently, neural machine translation (NMT) has been used to train models to directly map complex to simple sentences. Supervised learning with recurrent or transformer architectures dominate current state-of-the-art research, some with additional simplification-specific adaptations such as lexical constraints, rule-based preprocessing, or parametrization mechanisms (Nisioi et al., 2017; Zhang and Lapata, 2017; Sulem et al., 2018; Mallinson and Lapata, 2019; Kriz et al., 2019; Martin et al., 2020a). Some unsupervised or semi-supervised neural models, which reduce the need for parallel data, have reached similar performances (Surya et al., 2019; Kumar et al., 2020; Zhao et al., 2020; Martin et al., 2020b). Finally, experiments with multi-task learning have shown promising results (Guo et al., 2018; Dmitrieva and Tiedemann, 2021), with the possibility of zero-shot translations for languages without any parallel data (Mallinson et al., 2020). These approaches represent the current state of the art, but are largely limited to English (Al-Thanyyan and Azmi, 2021) due to a lack of training data in other languages. Initial experiments with German are ongoing (Battisti et al., 2020).

When simplifying text, operations often occur across sentence borders, affecting the structure of a text as a whole. This complicates the use of sentence alignment and limits the effectiveness of sentence-level simplification models. Initial experiments exist that use document-level data to avoid these problems (Zhong et al., 2020; Dmitrieva and Tiedemann, 2021).

In this paper, we treat text simplification as a document-level task similar to summarization: the model needs to identify the most relevant information from the original text and generate a condensed version thereof. On top of that, the model should ideally learn to modify syntactic structures (e.g. split long sentences) and replace complex words (e.g. compound nouns) with simpler alternatives.

3 Data

We introduce a new data set collected from the Swiss news magazine *20 Minuten* that consists of full articles paired with shortened, simplified summaries that serve as a quick "tl;dr" for the reader. In contrast to other data used in our work, this data set does not distinguish different simplification levels. The corpus contains a total of 18,305 articles published since 2020. For each article we collect the title, the lead, the full news text, and the summary. We also keep track of paragraph formatting, even though this information is not used in the models presented in this paper.

Additionally, we use a combination of two existing corpora for German ATS that explicitly label the difficulty level of the target documents according to the Common European Framework of Reference for Languages (CEFR) (Council of Europe, 2009). For some documents, we have multiple levels of simplification available.[3] The levels available to us are A1, A2 and B1 (from most simplified to close to standard German). The three corpora we use for our experiments have the following characteristics:

APA is an extended version of the Austrian Press Agency corpus described in Säuberli et al. (2020). This data set contains news articles professionally simplified to levels A2 and B1.

[3]Note that our train/dev/test split is based on document IDs: if a document has multiple versions in different levels, we assign all of those to the same split, in order to avoid a scenario where we would train on a document de→A2 and then test on the same document with de→B1, as this would give the model an unfair advantage.

20m is a newly collected corpus from the Swiss news portal *20 Minuten*. Similar to the APA data, these are news articles paired with condensed, simplified summaries. The target side in this corpus does not distinguish between simplification levels.

capito is a corpus of documents from *capito*, the largest provider of human simplification services for German. This data set covers a wide range of topics and domains, from official information (e.g. what to do in case of a suspected covid infection) to local news, technical guidelines and instruction manuals. The *capito* documents are much more varied than the other data sets, both in content and length. The simplified target texts in this corpus cover levels A1, A2 and B1.

For both the APA and the 20m data set, the compression ratio is comparable to summaries, as the simplified documents are generally much shorter than the original text. For the *capito* data, this is not always the case, at least in terms of word count; the simplified texts often elaborate on concepts or processes, which leads to a similar word count between the standard and the simplified documents. However, regarding content, the simplified texts usually do condense the original information to the most salient facts. For this reason, we argue that even on this data set, the task is very similar to summarization.

Table 1 illustrates the size of the different data sets and compression ratios according to simplification levels. See Appendix A.2 for samples from all three data sets.

4 Model and Training

Initial experiments showed that fine-tuning the standard pretrained mBART model (Liu et al., 2020) from Huggingface (Wolf et al., 2020), performs relatively well with our data, however, training is very memory-intensive, requiring a 32GB GPU even with a small batch size. For this reason, we modify the original model to allow us to train on devices with less memory.[4] Our modifications are based on the code for BART with Longformer attention by the Allen Institute for AI (Beltagy et al., 2020).[5]

As in the BART model with Longformer attention, we swap the standard attention in the mBART encoder for Longformer's windowed attention.[6] This allows for increasing the maximum input positions and avoids having to truncate long source documents to a predefined length. We use a maximum input length of 4096 to cover most of the documents in our data. The new positional embeddings are initialized with a copy of the original pretrained embeddings of size 1024, as described in Beltagy et al. (2020). The decoder remains unchanged with a maximum sequence length of 1024.

Furthermore, we reduce the original mBART vocabulary from 250k to 20k, keeping only those subwords and their embeddings that are most relevant for German.[7] We apply the pretrained multilingual sentencepiece model to ~4.5 million German sentences[8] and use the most frequent 20k subwords to filter the original mBART vocabulary.

We then extend the special language tokens with tags for the different simplification levels (e.g. "de_A1"). These are initialized with the pretrained embedding for the German language tag ("de_DE") and updated during fine-tuning. And lastly, we add the option to train and translate mixed batches with multiple target language labels.

We train our models with early stopping according to rougeL on a held-out validation set. The models converge after training for 2 to 5 days, the exact configuration and hyperparameters can be found in Appendix A.1. All models are trained on a single V100 GPU with the same accumulated batch size (60), but note that the standard mBART can only fit a batch size of 1 on the GPU, whereas our modified version can fit 4 samples in a batch and thus needs fewer accumulation steps.

5 Results

The results in Table 2 for the CEFR-labeled APA+capito data clearly show that with higher simplification levels, the task becomes harder: scores for both the standard mBART and our modified

[4]All models in this paper are trained on 32GB V100 GPUs for comparability to the baseline standard mBART, but with our modifications, we can load and fine-tune mBART on smaller GPUs (tested on a single 12GB Titan X).

[5]https://github.com/allenai/longformer

[6]We use a more recent version of both pytorch lightning and huggingface libraries and therefore have to make some changes, not only to the Longformer code, but also to the mBART model in huggingface itself. All code will be released upon publication.

[7]The step of trimming the embedding matrix is the most effective in reducing the size of the model and allowing it to be fine-tuned on smaller devices.

[8]Parts of the Common Crawl corpus 2019, News Commentary v15, Europarl v10 (all available from `http://www.statmt.org/wmt20/translation-task.html`) and our own data, see Section 3.

	train			dev			test			compression ratio		
	capito	APA	20m	capito	APA	20m	capito	APA	20m	capito	APA	20m
A1	652	–	–	50	–	–	50	–	–	54%	–	–
A2	1708	2250	–	87	113	–	91	109	–	97%	23%	–
B1	1074	2302	–	56	144	–	65	135	–	98%	25%	–
simple	–	–	17905	–	–	200	–	–	200	–	–	11%

Table 1: Number of documents with compression ratio. APA and *capito* use simplification levels A2/B1 and A1/A2/B1, respectively. 20m does not distinguish between simplification levels (labeled as 'simple'). See Appendix A.2 for examples.

	APA+capito			20m
	A1	A2	B1	simple
		rougeL		
mBART	21.68	24.27	28.46	21.62
small mBART	26.05	26.22	29.40	19.96
		SARI		
mBART	30.85	32.42	32.88	33.29
small mBART	32.35	32.90	32.87	33.29
		BLEU		
mBART	6.31	8.91	13.15	7.47
small mBART	8.25	10.02	14.40	6.29

Table 2: Results of automatic simplification with fine-tuned standard mBART and our modified, smaller version with longformer attention (small mBART). Since standard mBART does not have labels for simplification levels, target language is set to 'de_DE' for fine-tuning and evaluation. Decoding for all models is done with beam size=6.

version ('small mBART') generally decrease with increasing distance to standard German.[9] The mBART modifications to reduce memory-usage come at a small loss in performance according to rougeL and BLEU on the 20m data set. However, this smaller model with the additional language level tags outperfoms standard mBART on the APA+capito data set. Overall, the 20m articles are harder to simplify, since the compression ratio is relatively high (11%, see Table 1).

6 Conclusions

In this paper, we have introduced a data set of simplified news articles from the Swiss magazine *20 Minuten*, aligned on document level. The task of document-level simplification resembles that of summarization, as models need to identify the salient parts and produce a condensed version of the original text. For simplification, models should also learn to simplify syntactic structures and lexical items.

Experiments based on fine-tuning the pretrained mBART model from huggingface show that the model can learn to produce not just condensed, but also simpler output. Our added modifications make mBART fine-tuning significantly more memory-friendly. Since the new 20m data set does not distinguish between simplification levels, we use an existing data set annotated with CEFR levels (Säuberli et al., 2020) to evaluate our models according to specific simplification levels. Results show that our modified mBART, while using considerably less memory, can simplify documents without much loss in performance on the 20m data and even improves over standard mBART on documents labeled with CEFR tags.

In future work, we will conduct ablation studies to measure the effect of our modifications individually, specifically, seeing whether using windowed attention to give the model access to the full source document instead of a clipped version is beneficial. Lastly, automatic evaluation with metrics such as rougeL, BLEU, and SARI do not provide sufficient insights. To get more accurate feedback and better understand issues specific to simplification, we plan to conduct an evaluation with professional translators.

[9] Apart from BLEU and rougeL, we evaluate with SARI (Xu et al., 2016b), a metric introduced specifically for ATS.

References

Suha S Al-Thanyyan and Aqil M Azmi. 2021. Automated text simplification: A survey. *ACM Computing Surveys (CSUR)*, 54(2):1–36.

Maria Jesús Aranzabe, Arantza Dıaz De Ilarraza, and Itziar Gonzalez-Dios. 2012. First approach to automatic text simplification in basque. In *Proceedings of the Natural Language Processing for Improving Textual Accessibility (NLP4ITA) workshop (LREC 2012)*, pages 1–8, Istanbul, Turkey.

Alessia Battisti, Dominik Pfütze, Andreas Säuberli, Marek Kostrzewa, and Sarah Ebling. 2020. A corpus for automatic readability assessment and text simplification of German. In *Proceedings of the 12th Language Resources and Evaluation Conference*, pages 3302–3311, Marseille, France. European Language Resources Association.

Iz Beltagy, Matthew E. Peters, and Arman Cohan. 2020. Longformer: The long-document transformer. *arXiv:2004.05150*.

Laetitia Brouwers, Delphine Bernhard, Anne-Laure Ligozat, and Thomas François. 2014. Syntactic sentence simplification for French. In *Proceedings of the 3rd Workshop on Predicting and Improving Text Readability for Target Reader Populations (PITR)*, pages 47–56, Gothenburg, Sweden. Association for Computational Linguistics.

Council of Europe. 2009. *Common European Framework of Reference for Languages: Learning, teaching, assessment*. Cambridge University Press, Cambridge.

Anna Dmitrieva and Jörg Tiedemann. 2021. A multitask learning approach to text simplification. *Recent Trends in Analysis of Images, Social Networks and Texts*, 1357:78.

Goran Glavaš and Sanja Štajner. 2015. Simplifying lexical simplification: Do we need simplified corpora? In *Proceedings of the 53rd Annual Meeting of the Association for Computational Linguistics and the 7th International Joint Conference on Natural Language Processing (Volume 2: Short Papers)*, pages 63–68, Beijing, China. Association for Computational Linguistics.

Han Guo, Ramakanth Pasunuru, and Mohit Bansal. 2018. Dynamic multi-level multi-task learning for sentence simplification. In *Proceedings of the 27th International Conference on Computational Linguistics*, pages 462–476, Santa Fe, New Mexico, USA. Association for Computational Linguistics.

Reno Kriz, João Sedoc, Marianna Apidianaki, Carolina Zheng, Gaurav Kumar, Eleni Miltsakaki, and Chris Callison-Burch. 2019. Complexity-weighted loss and diverse reranking for sentence simplification. In *Proceedings of the 2019 Conference of the North American Chapter of the Association for Computational Linguistics: Human Language Technologies, Volume 1 (Long and Short Papers)*, pages 3137–3147, Minneapolis, Minnesota. Association for Computational Linguistics.

Dhruv Kumar, Lili Mou, Lukasz Golab, and Olga Vechtomova. 2020. Iterative edit-based unsupervised sentence simplification. In *Proceedings of the 58th Annual Meeting of the Association for Computational Linguistics*, pages 7918–7928, Online. Association for Computational Linguistics.

Yinhan Liu, Jiatao Gu, Naman Goyal, Xian Li, Sergey Edunov, Marjan Ghazvininejad, Mike Lewis, and Luke Zettlemoyer. 2020. Multilingual denoising pre-training for neural machine translation. *Transactions of the Association for Computational Linguistics*, 8(0):726–742.

Slavina Lozanova, Ivelina Stoyanova, Svetlozara Leseva, Svetla Koeva, and Boian Savtchev. 2013. Text modification for Bulgarian Sign Language users. In *Proceedings of the Second Workshop on Predicting and Improving Text Readability for Target Reader Populations*, pages 39–48, Sofia, Bulgaria. Association for Computational Linguistics.

Jonathan Mallinson and Mirella Lapata. 2019. Controllable sentence simplification: Employing syntactic and lexical constraints. *arXiv preprint arXiv:1910.04387*.

Jonathan Mallinson, Rico Sennrich, and Mirella Lapata. 2020. Zero-shot crosslingual sentence simplification. In *Proceedings of the 2020 Conference on Empirical Methods in Natural Language Processing (EMNLP)*, pages 5109–5126, Online. Association for Computational Linguistics.

Louis Martin, Éric de la Clergerie, Benoît Sagot, and Antoine Bordes. 2020a. Controllable sentence simplification. In *Proceedings of the 12th Language Resources and Evaluation Conference*, pages 4689–4698, Marseille, France. European Language Resources Association.

Louis Martin, Angela Fan, Éric de la Clergerie, Antoine Bordes, and Benoît Sagot. 2020b. MUSS: Multilingual unsupervised sentence simplification by mining paraphrases. *arXiv preprint arXiv:2005.00352*.

Shashi Narayan and Claire Gardent. 2014. Hybrid simplification using deep semantics and machine translation. In *Proceedings of the 52nd Annual Meeting of the Association for Computational Linguistics (Volume 1: Long Papers)*, pages 435–445, Baltimore, Maryland. Association for Computational Linguistics.

Sergiu Nisioi, Sanja Štajner, Simone Paolo Ponzetto, and Liviu P. Dinu. 2017. Exploring neural text simplification models. In *Proceedings of the 55th Annual Meeting of the Association for Computational Linguistics (Volume 2: Short Papers)*, pages 85–91,

Vancouver, Canada. Association for Computational Linguistics.

Jipeng Qiang, Yun Li, Yi Zhu, Yunhao Yuan, and Xindong Wu. 2020. Lexical simplification with pretrained encoders. In *Proceedings of the Thirty-Fourth AAAI Conference on Artificial Intelligence*, volume 34, pages 8649–8656. Association for the Advancement of Artificial Intelligence.

Andreas Säuberli, Sarah Ebling, and Martin Volk. 2020. Benchmarking data-driven automatic text simplification for German. In *Proceedings of the 1st Workshop on Tools and Resources to Empower People with REAding DIfficulties (READI)*, pages 41–48, Marseille, France. European Language Resources Association.

Carolina Scarton, Alessio Palmero Aprosio, Sara Tonelli, Tamara Martín Wanton, and Lucia Specia. 2017. MUSST: A multilingual syntactic simplification tool. In *Proceedings of the IJCNLP 2017, System Demonstrations*, pages 25–28, Tapei, Taiwan. Association for Computational Linguistics.

Advaith Siddharthan. 2006. Syntactic simplification and text cohesion. *Research on Language and Computation*, 4(1):77–109.

Elior Sulem, Omri Abend, and Ari Rappoport. 2018. Simple and effective text simplification using semantic and neural methods. In *Proceedings of the 56th Annual Meeting of the Association for Computational Linguistics (Volume 1: Long Papers)*, pages 162–173, Melbourne, Australia. Association for Computational Linguistics.

Sai Surya, Abhijit Mishra, Anirban Laha, Parag Jain, and Karthik Sankaranarayanan. 2019. Unsupervised neural text simplification. In *Proceedings of the 57th Annual Meeting of the Association for Computational Linguistics*, pages 2058–2068, Florence, Italy. Association for Computational Linguistics.

Thomas Wolf, Lysandre Debut, Victor Sanh, Julien Chaumond, Clement Delangue, Anthony Moi, Pierric Cistac, Tim Rault, Rémi Louf, Morgan Funtowicz, Joe Davison, Sam Shleifer, Patrick von Platen, Clara Ma, Yacine Jernite, Julien Plu, Canwen Xu, Teven Le Scao, Sylvain Gugger, Mariama Drame, Quentin Lhoest, and Alexander M. Rush. 2020. Transformers: State-of-the-art natural language processing. In *Proceedings of the 2020 Conference on Empirical Methods in Natural Language Processing: System Demonstrations*, pages 38–45, Online. Association for Computational Linguistics.

Sander Wubben, Antal van den Bosch, and Emiel Krahmer. 2012. Sentence simplification by monolingual machine translation. In *Proceedings of the 50th Annual Meeting of the Association for Computational Linguistics (Volume 1: Long Papers)*, pages 1015–1024, Jeju Island, Korea. Association for Computational Linguistics.

Wei Xu, Courtney Napoles, Ellie Pavlick, Quanze Chen, and Chris Callison-Burch. 2016a. Optimizing statistical machine translation for text simplification. *Transactions of the Association for Computational Linguistics*, 4:401–415.

Wei Xu, Courtney Napoles, Ellie Pavlick, Quanze Chen, and Chris Callison-Burch. 2016b. Optimizing Statistical Machine Translation for Text Simplification. *Transactions of the Association for Computational Linguistics*, 4(401–415).

Xingxing Zhang and Mirella Lapata. 2017. Sentence simplification with deep reinforcement learning. In *Proceedings of the 2017 Conference on Empirical Methods in Natural Language Processing*, pages 584–594, Copenhagen, Denmark. Association for Computational Linguistics.

Xu Zhao, Zihao Wang, Hao Wu, and Yong Zhang. 2020. Semi-supervised bilingual lexicon induction with two-way interaction. In *Proceedings of the 2020 Conference on Empirical Methods in Natural Language Processing (EMNLP)*, pages 2973–2984, Online. Association for Computational Linguistics.

Yang Zhong, Chao Jiang, Wei Xu, and Junyi Jessy Li. 2020. Discourse level factors for sentence deletion in text simplification. In *Proceedings of the Thirty-Fourth AAAI Conference on Artificial Intelligence*, volume 34, pages 9709–9716. Association for the Advancement of Artificial Intelligence.

A Appendix

A.1 Model Configurations

	standard mBART	small mBART
max output length	1024	1024
max input length	**1024**	**4096**
batch size	**1**	**4**
gradient accumulation	**60**	**15**
gpus	1	1
seed	222	222
attention dropout	0.1	0.1
dropout	0.3	0.3
attention mode	–	**sliding chunks**
attention window size	–	**512**
label smoothing	0.2	0.2
learning rate	0.00003	0.00003
early stopping metric	rougeL	rougeL
patience	10	10
min delta	0.0005	0.0005
learning rate scheduler	ReduceOnPlateau	ReduceOnPlateau
lr reduce patience	8	8
lr reduce factor	0.5	0.5
vocabulary size	**250k**	**20k**

Table 3: Training configurations for standard mBART fine-tuning and modified version. Differences highlighted in bold.

A.2 Examples

Original (standard German)	English
Bestätigung über die Durchführung der Erstunterweisung Ich habe die Erstunterweisung gemäß § 14 ASchG für neue MitarbeiterInnen erhalten. Mit meiner Unterschrift auf diesem Blatt bestätige ich, dass ich die Information über: atempo und Arbeitssicherheit Gefahren durch Elektrizität Benützung von Leitern Unfälle und Erste Hilfe Wichtige Personen und Telefonnummern gelesen und verstanden habe.	Confirmation that the initial instruction has been carried out I have received the initial instruction in accordance with § 14 ASchG for new employees. With my signature on this sheet, I confirm that I have received and read information about: atempo and occupational safety dangers due to electricity use of ladders accidents and first aid important people and telephone numbers
A2 German	**English**
Bestätigung: Ich habe die wichtigen Informationen bekommen Sie müssen wichtige Informationen bekommen, wenn Sie in einer Firma anfangen. Wenn Sie unterschreiben, heißt das: Sie haben die wichtigen Informationen gelesen und verstanden. Sie haben wichtige Informationen zu diesen Themen bekommen: Wie arbeite ich sicher? Wie kann ich ein Feuer vermeiden? Was muss ich tun, wenn es brennt? Warum kann Strom gefährlich sein? Wie muss ich eine Leiter benutzen? Was muss ich tun, wenn sich jemand verletzt? Wer sind wichtige Personen bei atempo? Wo stehen wichtige Telefon-Nummern?	Confirmation: I have received the important information You should receive important information when you start in a company. Your signature means: you have read and understood the important information. You have received important information on these topics: How do I work safely? How can I avoid a fire? What should I do if there is a fire? Why can electricity be dangerous? How do I use a ladder? What should I do if someone is injured? Who are the important people at atempo? Where can I find the important phone numbers?
A1 German	**English**
Wichtige Informationen Sie sind neu bei atempo. Wir müssen Ihnen wichtige Informationen geben. Wie arbeite ich sicher? Es brennt. Warum ist Strom gefährlich? Wie muss ich eine Leiter verwenden? Eine Person hat sich weh getan. Wer sind wichtige Personen bei atempo? Wo stehen wichtige Telefon-Nummern? Haben Sie diese Informationen bekommen? Haben Sie diese Informationen verstanden? Dann unterschreiben Sie bitte diesen Zettel.	Important Information You are new at atempo. We have important information to give you. How do I work safely? There is a fire. Why is electricity dangerous? How do I use a ladder? Someone is injured. Who are the important people at atempo? Where can I find the important phone numbers? Did you receive this information? Did you understand this information? Then please sign this piece of paper.

Table 4: *capito* simplification example for levels A2 and A1 with elaborations. Document length for *capito* varies considerably, from documents with one sentence to documents with several thousand sentences.

Original (standard German)	English
"Lonely Planet" kürt Salzburg für 2020 zur besten Stadt Salzburg ist im kommenden Jahr für den Reisebuchverlag "Lonely Planet" die beste Stadt zum Bereisen. Im neuen "Lonely Planets Best in Travel 2020" führt die Mozartstadt das Ranking in der Kategorie der Städte nicht zuletzt wegen des 100-Jahr-Jubiläums der Festspiele an. Der Reiseführer "Best in Travel" kürt jedes Jahr zehn Top-Städte, -Länder und -Regionen. "Trommelwirbel, bitte", heißt es auf der Homepage des Verlages. "Der Herzensbrecher einer Alpenstadt besingt das Jubiläum in vollen Tönen." Salzburg führt das Ranking 2020 vor den Städten Washington DC, Kairo, dem irischen Galway und der Beethoven-Stadt Bonn an. In der Länderkategorie liegt Buthan voran, als Top-Region wurde die Seidenstraße in Zentralasien angegeben. Österreich kommt im Ranking 2020 kein zweites Mal vor.	"Lonely Planet" selects Salzburg as the best city to visit in 2020 Salzburg is the best city to travel to next year according to the travel book publisher "Lonely Planet". In the new "Lonely Planet's Best in Travel 2020", the city of Mozart leads the ranking in the category of cities, not least because of the 100th anniversary of the festival. The "Best in Travel" publication selects the top ten cities, countries and regions each year. "Drum roll, please," reads the publisher's homepage. "The heartbreaker of an Alpine city celebrates the anniversary in full tones." Salzburg leads the 2020 ranking ahead of Washington DC, Cairo, Galway, Ireland, and Bonn, the city of Beethoven. Buthan leads in the country category, with the Silk Road in Central Asia given as the top region. Austria does not appear a second time in the 2020 ranking.
B1 German	**English**
Reiseführer erklärt Salzburg zur besten Stadt der Welt Die österreichische Stadt Salzburg ist weltweit die beste Stadt zum Bereisen im kommenden Jahr. Das sagt die Rangliste des britischen Reiseführers "Lonely Planet". "Lonely Planet" erstellt jedes Jahr eine Rangliste der besten 10 Städte, Länder und Regionen auf der ganzen Welt. Für das Jahr 2020 liegt Salzburg auf Platz 1. Salzburg führt vor den Städten Washington in den USA, Kairo in Ägypten, Galway in Irland und Bonn in Deutschland. In der Rangliste der besten Länder zum Bereisen 2020 gewann das Land Buthan in Süd-Asien.	Travel guide declares Salzburg the best city in the world The Austrian city of Salzburg is the best city in the world to travel in the coming year. The ranking of the British travel guide "Lonely Planet" says so. "Lonely Planet" ranks the best 10 cities, countries and regions around the world each year. For the year 2020, Salzburg made it to first place. Salzburg leads, ahead of the following cities: Washington in the USA, Cairo in Egypt, Galway in Ireland and Bonn in Germany. In the ranking of the best countries to travel in 2020, the country of Buthan in South Asia won.
A2 German	**English**
Salzburg ist 2020 die beste Stadt zum Bereisen Die Stadt Salzburg ist im Jahr 2020 die beste Stadt zum Bereisen. Das sagt der Verlag von den Reise-Büchern namens Lonely Planet. Salzburg gewann vor den Städten Washington in den USA, Kairo in Ägypten und Galway in Irland. Der Verlag sucht jedes Jahr die besten 10 Städte, Länder und Regionen zum Bereisen.	Salzburg is the best city to travel in 2020 The city of Salzburg is the best city to travel in 2020. The publisher of travel books called Lonely Planet says so. Salzburg won ahead of the following cities: Washington in the USA, Cairo in Egypt and Galway in Ireland. Every year, the publisher looks for the best 10 cities, countries and regions to travel.

Table 5: APA example for levels A2 and B1. APA news articles are generally relatively short with up to $\sim$100 sentences.

Original (standard German)	English
Eine 58-jährige Frau war am Samstag, um 15.15 Uhr mit dem Auto auf der St. Gallerstrasse in Gossau unterwegs.	A 58-year-old woman was driving her car on St. Gallerstrasse in Gossau at 3:15 p.m. on Saturday.
Während der Fahrt bemerkte die Frau, dass sie ihr Handy auf dem Autodach vergessen hatte.	While driving, the woman noticed that she had forgotten her cell phone on the roof of the car.
Sie bremste ab.	She braked.
In diesem Moment fuhr ein 22-jähriger Töfffahrer hinter ihr.	At that moment, a 22-year-old motorcyclist was driving behind her.
Wie die Kantonspolizei St. Gallen mitteilt, war das Handy mittlerweile zu Boden gefallen und der Töfffahrer richtete seinen Blick auf den Gegenstand am Boden.	According to the cantonal police of St. Gallen, the cell phone had fallen to the ground and the motorcyclist turned his gaze to the object on the ground.
Dabei bemerkte der Mann nicht, dass das Auto vor ihm abbremst.	In doing so, the man did not notice that the car in front of him was slowing down.
Er prallte mit dem Töff in das Auto der 58-Jährigen.	He crashed his motorcycle into the car of the 58-year-old.
Dabei erlitt der Töfffahrer unbestimmte Verletzungen.	The driver of the motorcycle suffered unspecified injuries.
Mit einem Rettungswagen wurde er ins Spital gebracht.	He was taken to hospital in an ambulance.
Laut der Polizei entstand ein Sachschaden von mehr als 20"000 Franken.	According to the police, the damage to property amounted to more than 20,000 Swiss francs.
Simplified German	**English**
Eine Autofahrerin hat ihr Handy auf dem Dach vergessen.	A car driver forgot her cell phone on the roof.
Als sie das bemerkte, bremste sie während der Fahrt ab.	When she realized, she braked abruptly while driving.
Ein Töfffahrer hinter ihr war durch das heruntergefallene Handy abgelenkt und prallte darauf in das Auto.	A motorcyclist behind her got distracted by the dropped cell phone and crashed into the car.
Der 22-jährige Töfffahrer erlitt unbestimmte Verletzungen.	The 22-year-old motorcyclist suffered unspecified injuries.

Table 6: 20m example, language levels are not distinguished in this corpus.

Association for Computational Linguistics
209 N. Eighth Street
Stroudsburg, Pennsylvania 18360

CURRAN ASSOCIATES INC.
proceedings.com

ISBN 978-1-7138-9178-9